ILLUSTRATED SERIES™

MICROSOFT® OFFICE 365®
EXCEL® 2019

LYNN WERMERS

CENGAGE

Australia • Brazil • Mexico • Singapore • United Kingdom • United States

**Illustrated Series™ Microsoft® Office 365®
Excel® 2019 Comprehensive**

Lynn Wermers

SVP, GM Skills & Global Product Management:
  Jonathan Lau

Product Director: Lauren Murphy

Product Assistant: Veronica Moreno-Nestojko

Executive Director, Content Design: Marah
  Bellegarde

Director, Learning Design: Leigh Hefferon

Associate Learning Designer: Courtney Cozzy

Vice President, Marketing—Science, Technology,
  and Math: Jason R. Sakos

Senior Marketing Director: Michele McTighe

Marketing Manager: Timothy J. Cali

Director, Content Delivery: Patty Stephan

Content Manager: Grant Davis

Digital Delivery Lead: Laura Ruschman

Designer: Lizz Anderson

Text Designer: Joseph Lee, Black Fish Design

Cover Template Designer: Lisa Kuhn, Curio Press,
  LLC www.curiopress.com

Mac Users: If you're working through this product using a Mac, some of the steps may vary. Additional information for Mac users is included with the Data files for this product.

Disclaimer: This text is intended for instructional purposes only; data is fictional and does not belong to any real persons or companies.

Disclaimer: The material in this text was written using Microsoft Windows 10 and Office 365 Professional Plus and was Quality Assurance tested before the publication date. As Microsoft continually updates the Windows 10 operating system and Office 365, your software experience may vary slightly from what is presented in the printed text.

Windows, Access, Excel, and PowerPoint are registered trademarks of Microsoft Corporation. Microsoft and the Office logo are either registered trademarks or trademarks of Microsoft Corporation in the United States and/or other countries. This product is an independent publication and is neither affiliated with, nor authorized, sponsored, or approved by, Microsoft Corporation.

Some of the product names and company names used in this book have been used for identification purposes only and may be trademarks or registered trademarks of Microsoft Corporation in the United States and/or other countries.

For product information and technology assistance, contact us at
**Cengage Customer & Sales Support, 1-800-354-9706 or
support.cengage.com.**

For permission to use material from this text or product,
submit all requests online at **www.cengage.com/permissions.**

Library of Congress Control Number: 2019940993

Student Edition ISBN: 978-0-357-02570-3
Looseleaf available as part of a digital bundle

Cengage
20 Channel Center Street
Boston, MA 02210
USA

Cengage is a leading provider of customized learning solutions with employees residing in nearly 40 different countries and sales in more than 125 countries around the world. Find your local representative at
www.cengage.com.

Cengage products are represented in Canada by Nelson Education, Ltd.

To learn more about Cengage platforms and services, visit
www.cengage.com.

Notice to the Reader

Publisher does not warrant or guarantee any of the products described herein or perform any independent analysis in connection with any of the product information contained herein. Publisher does not assume, and expressly disclaims, any obligation to obtain and include information other than that provided to it by the manufacturer. The reader is expressly warned to consider and adopt all safety precautions that might be indicated by the activities described herein and to avoid all potential hazards. By following the instructions contained herein, the reader willingly assumes all risks in connection with such instructions. The publisher makes no representations or warranties of any kind, including but not limited to, the warranties of fitness for particular purpose or merchantability, nor are any such representations implied with respect to the material set forth herein, and the publisher takes no responsibility with respect to such material. The publisher shall not be liable for any special, consequential, or exemplary damages resulting, in whole or part, from the readers' use of, or reliance upon, this material.

Printed at CLDPC, USA, 04-20

Brief Contents

Contents

Getting to Know Microsoft Office Versions

Cengage is proud to bring you the next edition of Microsoft Office. This edition was designed to provide a robust learning experience that is not dependent upon a specific version of Office.

Microsoft supports several versions of Office:

- **Office 365:** A cloud-based subscription service that delivers Microsoft's most up-to-date, feature-rich, modern productivity tools direct to your device. There are variations of Office 365 for business, educational, and personal use. Office 365 offers extra online storage and cloud-connected features, as well as updates with the latest features, fixes, and security updates.

- **Office 2019:** Microsoft's "on-premises" version of the Office apps, available for both PCs and Macs, offered as a static, one-time purchase and outside of the subscription model.

- **Office Online:** A free, simplified version of Office web applications (Word, Excel, PowerPoint, and OneNote) that facilitates creating and editing files collaboratively.

Office 365 (the subscription model) and Office 2019 (the one-time purchase model) had only slight differences between them at the time this content was developed. Over time, Office 365's cloud interface will continuously update, offering new application features and functions, while Office 2019 will remain static. Therefore, your onscreen experience may differ from what you see in this product. For example, the more advanced features and functionalities covered in this product may not be available in Office Online or may have updated from what you see in Office 2019.

For more information on the differences between Office 365, Office 2019, and Office Online, please visit the Microsoft Support site.

Cengage is committed to providing high-quality learning solutions for you to gain the knowledge and skills that will empower you throughout your educational and professional careers.

Thank you for using our product, and we look forward to exploring the future of Microsoft Office with you!

Using SAM Projects and Textbook Projects

SAM and *MindTap* are interactive online platforms designed to transform students into Microsoft Office and Computer Concepts masters. Practice with simulated SAM Trainings and MindTap activities and actively apply the skills you learned live in Microsoft Word, Excel, PowerPoint, or Access. Become a more productive student and use these skills throughout your career.

If your instructor assigns SAM Projects:

1. Launch your SAM Project assignment from SAM or MindTap.
2. Click the links to download your **Instructions file**, **Start file**, and **Support files** (when available).
3. Open the Instructions file and follow the step-by-step instructions.
4. When you complete the project, upload your file to SAM or MindTap for immediate feedback.

To use SAM Textbook Projects:

1. Launch your SAM Project assignment from SAM or MindTap.
2. Click the links to download your **Start file** and **Support files** (when available).
3. Locate the module indicated in your book or eBook.
4. Read the module and complete the project.

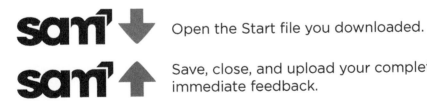

sam ⬇ Open the Start file you downloaded.

sam ⬆ Save, close, and upload your completed project to receive immediate feedback.

IMPORTANT: To receive full credit for your Textbook Project, you must complete the activity using the Start file you downloaded from SAM or MindTap.

Getting Started with Excel

CASE ▶ You have been hired as an assistant at JCL Talent, a company that provides recruitment services for employers and job seekers. You report to Dawn LaPointe, the director of technical careers. As Dawn's assistant, you create worksheets to analyze data from various company offices to help her make sound decisions on company expansion, investments, and new recruiting opportunities.

Module Objectives

After completing this module, you will be able to:

- Explore Excel
- Enter data
- Edit data
- Copy and move cell data
- Enter formulas and use AutoSum
- Copy formulas with relative cell references
- Copy formulas with absolute cell references
- Enter a formula with multiple operators
- Insert a function
- Switch worksheet views
- Choose print options

Files You Will Need

IL_EX_1-1.xlsx   IL_EX_1-4.xlsx
IL_EX_1-2.xlsx   IL_EX_1-5.xlsx
IL_EX_1-3.xlsx

Explore Excel

Microsoft Excel is an **electronic spreadsheet program**, a computer program used to perform calculations and analyze and present numeric data. An Excel file, a **workbook**, is a collection of related worksheets contained within a single file with the file extension xlsx. A workbook is made up of one or more worksheets. A **worksheet** contains a grid of columns and rows where you can enter and manipulate data, perform calculations with data, and analyze data. **CASE** *You decide to review the distribution of technical postings in JCL's North American offices, to learn more about where and when these types of jobs have been posted.*

STEPS

1. **sam↓** Click the Start button ⊞ on the Windows taskbar, type Excel, click Excel, click Open, navigate to the location where you store your Data Files, click IL_EX_1-1.xlsx, then click Open

2. **Click the** File tab, **click** Save As **on the navigation bar, click** Browse, **navigate to the location where you store your Data Files if necessary, type** IL_EX_1_Postings **in the File name box, then click** Save

   Using **FIGURE 1-1** as a guide, identify the following items:

   • The **Name box** is the box to the left of the formula bar that shows the cell reference or name of the active cell. "A1" appears in the Name box.

   • The **formula bar** is the area above the worksheet grid where you enter or edit data in the active cell.

   • The **worksheet window** is an area of the program window that displays part of the current worksheet, which can contain a total of 1,048,576 rows and 16,384 columns. The columns and rows intersect to form cells, where you can enter and manipulate text, numbers, formulas, or a combination of all three. Every cell has its own unique location or **cell address**, a cell's location, expressed by its column letter and row number such as A1.

   • The **cell pointer** is a dark rectangle that outlines the active cell in a worksheet. In the figure, the cell pointer outlines cell A1, so A1 is the active cell.

   • By default, a workbook file contains one worksheet named Sheet1—but you can have as many sheets as your computer's memory allows in a workbook. The New sheet button to the right of Sheet1 allows you to add worksheets to a workbook. **Sheet tab scrolling buttons** are triangles that let you navigate to additional sheet tabs when available; they're located to the left of the sheet tabs.

   • You can use the scroll bars to move around in a worksheet that is too large to fit on the screen at once.

   • The status bar provides a brief description of the active command or task in progress. The **mode indicator** on the left end of the status bar indicates the program's status, such as the Edit mode in Excel. You are in Edit mode any time you are entering or changing the contents of a cell. You can use the Zoom In and Zoom Out buttons in the status bar to increase or decrease the scale of the displayed worksheet.

   • You can use the **Tell me box** on the ribbon to find a command or access the Excel Help system.

   • The AutoSave button on the Quick Access Toolbar is on if you are working on a file saved on OneDrive. When AutoSave is on, your file will be automatically saved as you make changes.

3. **Click cell** B4

   Cell B4 becomes the active cell. To activate a different cell, you can click the cell or press the arrow keys on your keyboard to move to it.

4. **Click cell** B4, **drag** ⊹ **to cell** B11, **then release the mouse button**

   You selected a group of cells and they are highlighted, as shown in **FIGURE 1-2**. A series of two or more adjacent cells in a column, row, or rectangular group of cells, notated using the cell address of its upper-left and lower-right corners, such as B4:B11, is called a **range**; you select a range when you want to perform an action on a group of cells at once, such as moving them or formatting them.

FIGURE 1-1: Open workbook

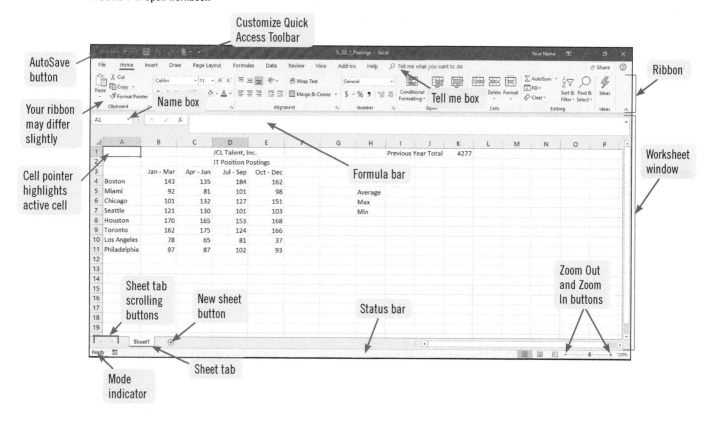

AutoSave button

Customize Quick Access Toolbar

Your ribbon may differ slightly

Name box

Tell me box

Ribbon

Cell pointer highlights active cell

Formula bar

Worksheet window

Sheet tab scrolling buttons

New sheet button

Status bar

Zoom Out and Zoom In buttons

Mode indicator

Sheet tab

FIGURE 1-2: Selected range

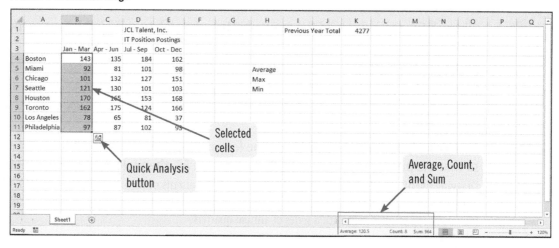

Selected cells

Quick Analysis button

Average, Count, and Sum

Navigating a worksheet

With over a million cells available in a worksheet, it is important to know how to move around in, or navigate, a worksheet. You can use the arrow keys on the keyboard ↑, ↓, →, or ← to move one cell at a time, or press PAGE UP or PAGE DOWN to move one screen at a time. To move one screen to the left, press ALT+PAGE UP; to move one screen to the right, press ALT+PAGE DOWN.

You can also use the mouse pointer to click the desired cell. If the desired cell is not visible in the worksheet window, use the scroll bars or use the Go To command by clicking the Find & Select button in the Editing group on the Home tab on the ribbon. To quickly jump to the first cell in a worksheet, press CTRL+HOME; to jump to the last cell, press CTRL+END.

Excel

Enter Data

Learning Outcomes
• Enter labels
• Enter values
• Copy data using the fill handle
• Enter a series of data with Auto Fill

To enter content in a cell, you can type in the formula bar or directly in the cell itself. **Labels** are descriptive text or other information that identifies data in rows, columns, or charts, not included in calculations, such as "2021 Sales" or "Expenses". **Values** are numbers, formulas, and functions used in calculations.

CASE ▶ *You want to enter and edit information in the Postings workbook.*

STEPS

QUICK TIP

If you change your mind and want to cancel an entry in the formula bar, click the Cancel button ☒ on the formula bar.

1. **Click cell F3, type** Total, **then click the** Enter button ✓ **on the formula bar**

   Clicking the Enter button accepts the entry without moving the cell pointer to a new location. The new text is left-aligned in the cell because labels are left-aligned by default. Excel recognizes an entry as a value if it is a number or it begins with one of these symbols: +, –, =, @, #, or $. When a cell contains both text and numbers, Excel recognizes it as a label.

2. **Click cell A12, type** Vancouver, **then press TAB**

   Pressing TAB accepts the entry and moves the active cell to the right, to cell B12.

3. **With B12 as the active cell, type 120, press TAB, type 130, press TAB, type 117, press TAB, type 130, then press TAB**

   The quarterly data is displayed for the Vancouver office, as shown in **FIGURE 1-3**. The numbers are right-aligned because values are right-aligned by default. You want to replace the monthly labels in row 3 with quarter labels.

4. **Click cell B3, then press DEL**

   You can delete each cell entry individually or delete a range of cells.

QUICK TIP

If you want to clear a cell's content, including its formatting, click the Clear button ◇ in the Editing group, then click Clear All.

5. ▶ **Click cell C3, press and hold the mouse button, drag ⊹ to cell E3, release the mouse button, then press DEL**

6. **Click cell B3, type** Quarter 1, **then click** ✓ **on the formula bar**

   You could continue to type quarter labels into columns C, D, and E, but it is easier to use Auto Fill to enter these labels. **Auto Fill** lets you drag a fill handle to copy a cell's contents or continue a selected series into adjacent cells.

QUICK TIP

You can insert a worksheet into a workbook by clicking the New sheet button ⊕.

7. ▶ **Click cell B3, position the pointer on the** lower-right corner of the cell **(the** fill handle**) so that the pointer changes to ✛, drag ✛ to cell E3, then release the mouse button**

   Dragging the fill handle across a range of cells copies the contents of the first cell into the other cells in the range or completes a data series. In this case, since Excel detected a data pattern in the selected cells, it filled the remaining selected cells with a series of annual quarters.

8. **Click the** Auto Fill Options button ▦

   Options for filling the selected range include Fill Series, which is selected, as shown in **FIGURE 1-4**. The other available options allow you to change to copying cells, fill the cells with formatting only, or fill the cells without formatting.

9. **Save your work**

FIGURE 1-3: Vancouver data entered

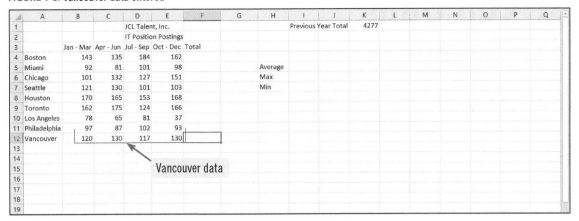

FIGURE 1-4: Auto Fill options

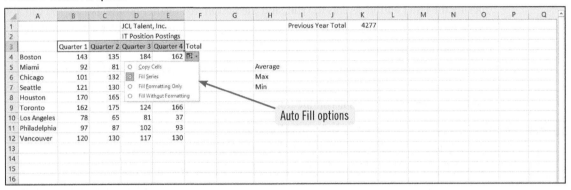

Inserting and deleting selected cells

As you add formulas to your workbook, you may need to insert or delete cells. To insert cells, click the Insert arrow in the Cells group on the Home tab, then click Insert Cells. The Insert dialog box opens, asking if you want to insert a cell and move the current active cell down or to the right of the new one. To delete one or more selected cells, click the Delete arrow in the Cells group, click Delete Cells, and in the Delete dialog box, indicate which way you want to move the adjacent cells. When using this option, be careful not to disturb row or column alignment that may be necessary to maintain the accuracy of cell references on the worksheet. You can also click the Insert button or Delete button in the Cells group to insert or delete a single cell. Excel automatically adjusts cell references within the formulas of any moved cells to reflect their new locations.

Using Auto Fill and Flash Fill

Auto Fill is an Excel feature that lets you drag a fill handle to copy a cell's contents or continue a series into adjacent cells. This can be used to enter the months of the year, days of the week, and custom lists of a series. Flash Fill, although similar to Auto Fill, isn't used to fill in a series of data. It is an Excel feature that looks for patterns in the data you enter and automatically fills or formats data in remaining cells based on those patterns. The filled data must be adjacent to the example data. Flash Fill often detects the pattern as you enter data and shows the new data in a light font. Pressing ENTER accepts the suggestion and enters the data. If Excel doesn't detect a pattern automatically, you can click the Flash Fill button in the Data Tools group on the Data tab to fill in the data.

Edit Data

Learning
Outcomes
• Edit cell entries in
  the formula bar
• Edit cell entries in
  the cell

You can change, or edit, the contents of an active cell at any time. To do so, double-click the cell, and then click in the formula bar or just start typing. Excel switches to Edit mode when you are making cell entries. Different pointers, shown in **TABLE 1-1**, guide you through the editing process. **CASE** *You noticed some errors on the worksheet and want to make corrections.*

STEPS

1. **Click cell B4, then click to the left of 4 in the formula bar**

   As soon as you click in the formula bar, a blinking vertical line called the **insertion point** appears on the formula bar at the location where new text will be inserted. See **FIGURE 1-5**.

2. **Press DEL, type 3, then click the Enter button ☑ on the formula bar**

   Clicking the Enter button accepts the edit, and the Boston first quarter posting is 133. You can also press ENTER to accept an edit. Pressing ENTER to accept an edit moves the cell pointer down one cell.

3. **Click cell B6, then press F2**

   Excel switches to Edit mode, and the insertion point blinks in the cell. Pressing F2 activates the cell for editing directly in the cell instead of the formula bar. Whether you edit in the cell or the formula bar is simply a matter of preference; the results on the worksheet are the same.

4. **Press BACKSPACE, type 9, then press ENTER**

   The value in the cell changes from 101 to 109, and cell B7 becomes the active cell.

5. **Click cell H6, then double-click the word Max in the formula bar**

   Double-clicking a word in a cell selects it. When you selected the word, the Mini toolbar automatically opened.

6. **Type Maximum, then press ENTER**

   When text is selected, typing deletes it and replaces it with the new text.

7. **Double-click cell H7, click to the right of n, type imum, then click ☑**

   Double-clicking a cell activates it for editing directly in the cell. Compare your screen to **FIGURE 1-6**.

8. **Save your work**

Recovering unsaved changes to a workbook file

You can use Excel's AutoRecover feature to automatically save (Autosave) your work as often as you want. This means that if you suddenly lose power or if Excel closes unexpectedly while you're working, you can recover all or some of the changes you made since you saved it last. (Of course, this is no substitute for regularly saving your work; it's just added insurance.) To customize the AutoRecover settings, click the File tab, click Options, then click Save. AutoRecover lets you decide how often and into which location it should Autosave files. When you restart Excel after losing power, you will see a new section, Recovered files, above the listing of recent files. You can click Show Recovered Files to access the saved and Autosaved versions of files that were open when Excel closed.

FIGURE 1-5: Worksheet in Edit mode

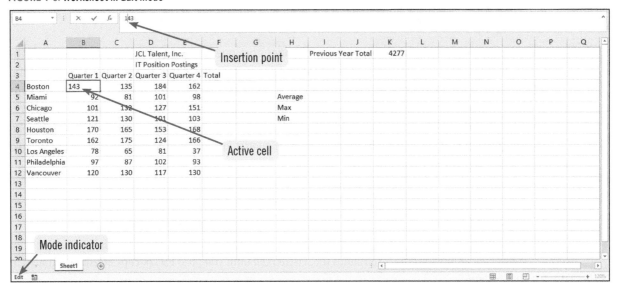

FIGURE 1-6: Edited worksheet

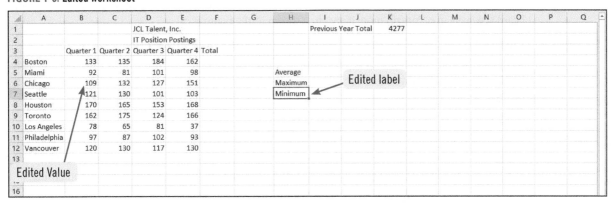

TABLE 1-1: Common pointers in Excel

name	pointer	use to	visible over the
Normal	⊕	Select a cell or range; indicates Ready mode	Active worksheet
Fill handle	+	Copy cell contents or series to adjacent cells	Lower-right corner of the active cell or range
I-beam	I	Edit cell contents in active cell or formula bar	Active cell in Edit mode or over the formula bar
Move	⤢	Change the location of the selected cell(s)	Perimeter of the active cell(s)
Copy	⤢⁺	Create a duplicate of the selected cell(s)	Perimeter of the active cell(s) when CTRL is pressed
Column resize	↔	Change the width of a column	Border between column heading indicators

Copy and Move Cell Data

Learning Outcomes
- Copy cell data to the Clipboard
- Paste a Clipboard entry
- Move a range

You can copy or move the contents in cells and ranges from one location to another using several methods, including the Cut, Copy, and Paste buttons on the Home tab on the ribbon, the fill handle of the active cell or range, or the drag-and-drop feature. When you copy cells, the original data remains in its original location; when you cut or move cells, the original data is deleted from its original location. You can copy and move cells or ranges within a worksheet or from one worksheet to another. **CASE** ▶ *You want to show totals and statistical information for each quarter in your worksheet, so you decide to copy and move selected cells to speed up your task.*

STEPS

QUICK TIP

To cut or copy selected cell contents, activate the cell, then select the characters within the cell that you want to cut or copy.

1. **Click cell F3, then click the Copy button 🗐 in the Clipboard group on the Home tab**

   The cell data is copied to the **Clipboard**, a temporary Windows storage area that holds the selections you copy or cut. A moving border surrounds the selected cell until you press ESC or copy an additional item to the Clipboard.

2. **Click the dialog box launcher 🔲 in the Clipboard group**

   The Office Clipboard opens in the Clipboard task pane, as shown in **FIGURE 1-7**. When you copy or cut an item, it is cut or copied both to the Clipboard provided by Windows and to the Office Clipboard. The Office Clipboard can hold up to 24 of the most recently cut or copied items from any Office program. Your Clipboard task pane may contain more items than shown in the figure.

QUICK TIP

You can have multiple items in the Clipboard resulting from multiple copy operations. You can paste these items individually or all the items at the same time by clicking the Paste All button.

3. **Click cell A13, then click the Paste button 🗐 in the Clipboard group**

   A copy of the contents of cell F3 is pasted into cell A13. Notice that the information you copied remains in the original cell F3; if you had cut instead of copied, the information would have been deleted from its original location once it was pasted. You can also paste an item by clicking it in the Office Clipboard.

4. **Click the Paste Options button 🗐 (Ctrl) ▾**

   The Paste Options open, as shown in **FIGURE 1-8**. These options allow you to determine what you want pasted and how you want the pasted data to appear on the worksheet. Review the three categories, Paste, Paste Values, and Other Paste Options. The current pasted data doesn't need any change in formatting.

5. **Press ESC twice, then click the Close button ✕ on the Clipboard task pane**

6. **Select the range H5:H7, point to any edge of the selected range until the pointer changes to 🔀, drag the range to cell A15, then release the mouse button**

   The move pointer displays an outline of the range you are dragging. When you release the mouse button, you "drop" the selection to the range A15:A17. When pasting an item from the Clipboard, you only need to specify the upper-left cell of the range where you want to paste the selection. If you press and hold CTRL while dragging and dropping, the information is copied instead of moved.

FIGURE 1-7: Copied data in Office Clipboard

Paste button

Copy button

Clipboard dialog box launcher

Item in Office Clipboard

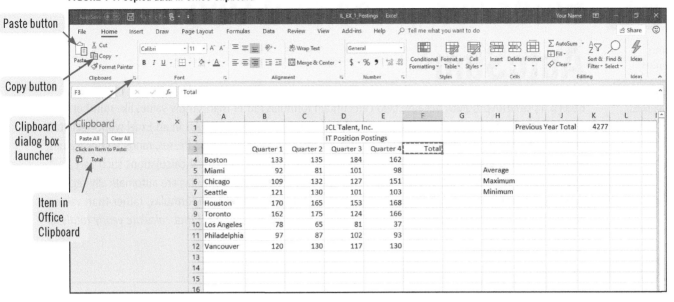

FIGURE 1-8: Paste options

Copied label

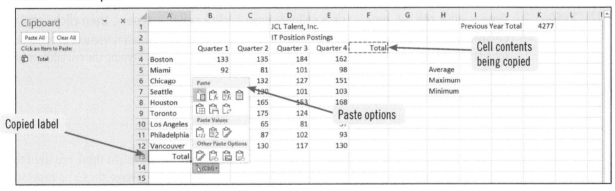

Using Paste Options and Paste Preview

You can selectively paste copied or cut formulas, values, or other data by using the Paste Options button that opens on the worksheet after you paste data or the Paste arrow in the Clipboard. The Paste Preview feature shows how the current selection will look when pasted. When you click the Paste Options button (or simply press [Ctrl] or the Paste arrow, a gallery of paste option icons opens, organized by category. The Paste category includes pasting formulas, pasting formulas and number formatting, pasting using the source formatting, pasting with no borders (to remove any borders around pasted cells), pasting with the source column widths, and pasting transposed data so that column data appears in rows and row data appears in columns. The Paste Values category includes pasting values only (without formatting), pasting values and number formatting, and pasting values with source formatting. The Other Paste Options category includes pasting formatting, links, pictures, and linked pictures. Clicking Paste Link in this category creates a link to the source data so that in the future, changes to the copied data update the pasted data. Clicking Picture in this category pastes the data as a picture where the picture tools can be used to format it, resize it, or move it.

Enter Formulas and Use AutoSum

Learning Outcomes
- Use cell references to create a formula
- Build formulas with the AutoSum button

Excel is a powerful program because cells can contain formulas rather than simply values like numbers and text. A **formula** is a mathematical statement that calculates a value. Formulas in an Excel worksheet start with the equal sign (=), also called the **formula prefix**, followed by cell addresses, range names, values, and **arithmetic operators**, which are symbols that perform mathematical calculations such as +, –, *, and /. See **TABLE 1-2** for a list of commonly used arithmetic operators. Formulas are automatically recalculated when worksheet data changes. For this reason, use cell references in formulas, rather than values, whenever possible. **CASE** ▸ *You want to create formulas in the worksheet that calculate yearly totals for each location.*

STEPS

1. **Click cell F4**

   This is the first cell where you want to insert a formula. To calculate the yearly total for the Boston location, you need to add the quarterly totals.

2. **Type =, click cell B4, type +, click cell C4, type +, click cell D4, type +, then click cell E4**

   Compare your formula bar to **FIGURE 1-9**. The blue, red, purple, and green cell references in cell F4 correspond to the color of the cells. When entering a formula, clicking cells rather typing the cell addresses helps avoid typing errors.

3. **Click the Enter button ☑ on the formula bar**

   The result of the formula =B4+C4+D4+E4, 614, appears in cell F4.

4. **Click cell B13**

   You want this cell to total first quarter positions for all the locations. You might think you need to create a formula that looks like this: =B4+B5+B6+B7+B8+B9+B10+B11+B12. However, there's an easier way to achieve this result.

5. **On the ribbon, click the AutoSum button Σ in the Editing group on the Home tab**

   The SUM function is inserted in the cell, and a suggested range appears in parentheses. A **function** is a predefined procedure that returns a value; it includes the **arguments** (the information necessary to calculate an answer) as well as cell references and other unique information. Clicking the AutoSum button sums the adjacent range (that is, the cells next to the active cell) above or to the left, although you can adjust the range if necessary by selecting a different range before accepting the cell entry. Using the SUM function is quicker than entering a formula, and using the range B4:B12 is more efficient than entering individual cell references.

6. **Click ☑ on the formula bar**

   Excel calculates the total contained in cells B4:B12 and displays the result, 1082, in cell B13. The cell actually contains the formula =SUM(B4:B12), but it displays the result. Compare your screen to **FIGURE 1-10**.

7. **Save your work**

FIGURE 1-9: Entering a formula

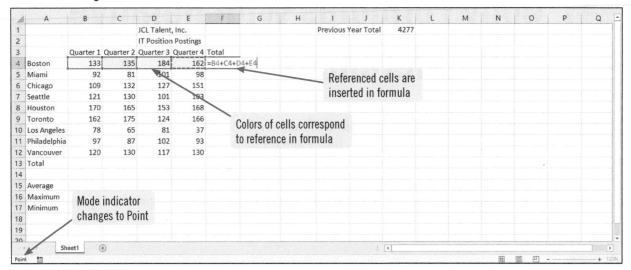

FIGURE 1-10: SUM function in a worksheet

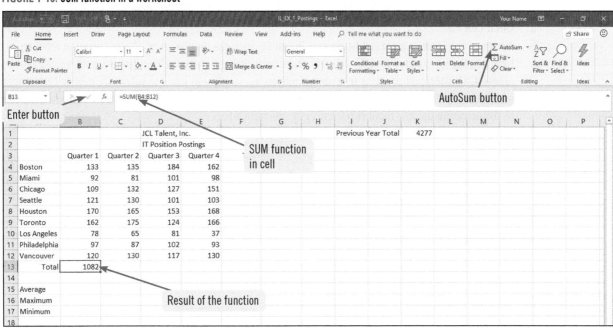

TABLE 1-2: Excel arithmetic operators

operator	purpose	example
+	Addition	=A5+A7
−	Subtraction or negation	=A5−10
*	Multiplication	=A5*A7
/	Division	=A5/A7
%	Percent	=35%
^ (caret)	Exponent	=6^2 (same as 6^2)

Learning
Outcomes
• Copy formulas
  with relative cell
  references
• Use the fill handle
  to copy formulas

Copy Formulas with Relative Cell References

As you work in Excel, you may want to reuse formulas by copying them. When you copy formulas, Excel automatically adjusts any cell addresses in the formula so they remain consistent relative to the formula's new location. For example, if you copy a formula containing a cell reference down a column, the row number in each copied formula increases by one. This type of cell reference in a formula is called a **relative cell reference**, because it changes to reflect the new formula's new location; it's the default type of addressing used in Excel worksheets. **CASE** ▶ *You want to reuse a formula you created, so you will copy it to other cells.*

STEPS

1. **Click cell F4, then drag the fill handle down to cell F12**

   The formula for calculating the total for all four quarters is copied into the range F5:F12.

2. **Click cell F5**

   A copy of the formula from cell F4 appears in cell F5, with the new result of 372, as shown in **FIGURE 1-11**. Notice in the formula bar that the cell references have changed so that cells in row 5 are referenced instead of row 4. This formula contains relative cell references, which tells Excel to substitute new cell references within the copied formulas as necessary. In this case, Excel adjusted the cell references in the formula in cell F5 by increasing the row number references by one from 4 to 5.

3. **Click cell F6**

   Because the location of this cell is two rows below the original formula, Excel adjusted the cell references in the copied formula by increasing the row number references by two from 4 to 6.

4. **Click cell B13, then drag the fill handle to the right to cell F13**

   A formula similar to the one in cell B13 now appears in the range C13:F13.

5. **Click cell C13**

   In copying the formula one cell to the right, the cell references in the formula bar are adjusted by increasing the column letter references by one from B to C. Compare your worksheet to **FIGURE 1-12**.

6. **Save your work**

FIGURE 1-11: Formula copied using the fill handle

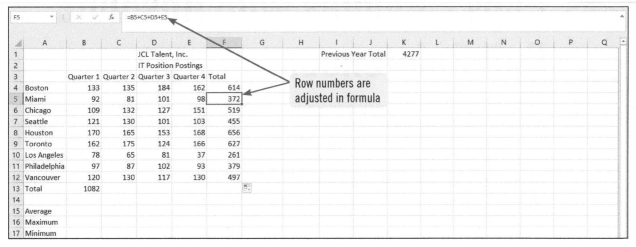

Row numbers are adjusted in formula

FIGURE 1-12: Formula column references changed

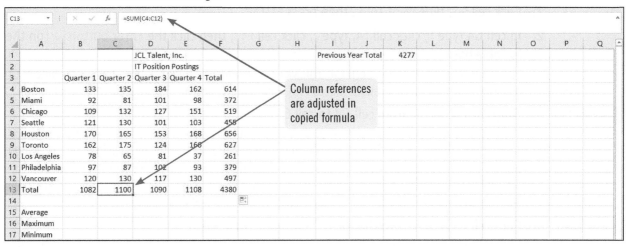

Column references are adjusted in copied formula

Inserting functions into formulas

You can insert a function on its own or as part of another formula. For example, you have used the SUM function on its own to add a range of cells—for example, =SUM(B5:B9). You could also use the SUM function within a formula that adds a range of cells and then multiplies the total by a decimal—for example, =SUM(B5:B9)*.5.

Excel

Learning
Outcomes
• Create an absolute
  cell reference
• Use the fill handle
  to copy absolute
  cell references

Copy Formulas with Absolute Cell References

When copying formulas, you might want one or more of the cell references in the formula to remain unchanged. For example, you might have a price in a specific cell that you want to use in all the copied formulas, regardless of their location. If you use relative cell referencing, the formula results would be incorrect, because the formula would reference a different cell every time you copy it. In this situation, you need to use an **absolute cell reference**, which refers to a specific cell and does not change when you copy the formula. Absolute cell references display a dollar sign ($) before the column letter and row number of the address (for example, $A$1). You can either type the dollar sign when typing the cell address in a formula, or you can select a cell address on the formula bar and then press F4, and the dollar signs are added automatically. When copying a formula, absolute cell references remain fixed in the copied formulas. **CASE** *You decide to calculate each location's percentage of the total postings.*

STEPS

1. **Click cell G3, type % of Total, then press ENTER**

2. **In cell G4 type =, click cell F4, type /, click cell F13, then click the Enter button ☑ on the formula bar**

   The result, 14.02%, appears in cell G4. This value represents the total positions for Boston (in cell F4) divided by the total for all locations (in cell F13). You want to calculate this percentage for each location.

QUICK TIP

Before you copy or move a formula, always check to see if you need to use an absolute cell reference.

3. **Drag the fill handle from cell G4 to cell G12**

   The resulting values in the range G5:G12 are the error messages #DIV/0!. Because you used relative cell addressing in the formula in cell G4, the copied formula adjusted so that the formula in cell G5 is =F5/F14; because there is no value in cell F14, the result is a division by 0 error. You need to use an absolute reference for cell F13 in the formula to keep the denominator from adjusting in a relative way as the formula is copied. That way, the denominator will always reference the total for all locations in cell F13.

QUICK TIP

When changing a cell reference to an absolute reference, make sure the reference is selected or the insertion point is to the left of the reference you want to change before pressing F4.

4. **Click cell G4, press F2 to change to Edit mode, then press F4**

   When you press F2, the range finder outlines the arguments of the equation in blue and red. The insertion point appears next to the F13 cell reference in cell G4. When you press F4, dollar signs are inserted in the F13 cell reference, making it an absolute reference. See **FIGURE 1-13**.

5. **Click ☑, then drag the fill handle from cell G4 to cell G12**

   Because the formula correctly contains an absolute cell reference, the correct percentage values appear for each location in cells G5:G12. Compare your worksheet to **FIGURE 1-14**.

6. **Save your work**

FIGURE 1-13: Absolute reference created in formula

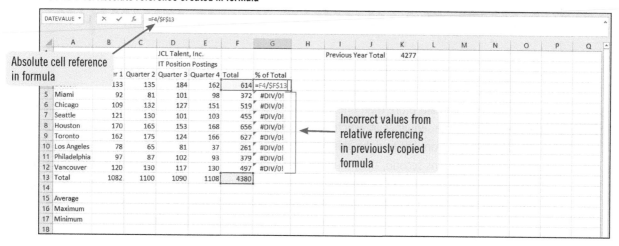

	A	B	C	D	E	F	G	H	I	J	K
DATEVALUE ▾	× ✓ ƒ×	=F4/$F$13									
1				JCL Talent, Inc.					Previous Year Total		4277
2				IT Position Postings							
3		r 1	Quarter 2	Quarter 3	Quarter 4	Total	% of Total				
4		133	135	184	162	614	=F4/$F$13				
5	Miami	92	81	101	98	372	#DIV/0!				
6	Chicago	109	132	127	151	519	#DIV/0!				
7	Seattle	121	130	101	103	455	#DIV/0!				
8	Houston	170	165	153	168	656	#DIV/0!				
9	Toronto	162	175	124	166	627	#DIV/0!				
10	Los Angeles	78	65	81	37	261	#DIV/0!				
11	Philadelphia	97	87	102	93	379	#DIV/0!				
12	Vancouver	120	130	117	130	497	#DIV/0!				
13	Total	1082	1100	1090	1108	4380					
14											
15	Average										
16	Maximum										
17	Minimum										
18											

Absolute cell reference in formula

Incorrect values from relative referencing in previously copied formula

FIGURE 1-14: Correct percentages calculated

	A	B	C	D	E	F	G	H	I	J	K
1				JCL Talent, Inc.					Previous Year Total		4277
2				IT Position Postings							
3		Quarter 1	Quarter 2	Quarter 3	Quarter 4	Total	% of Total				
4	Boston	133	135	184	162	614	14.02%				
5	Miami	92	81	101	98	372	8.49%				
6	Chicago	109	132	127	151	519	11.85%				
7	Seattle	121	130	101	103	455	10.39%				
8	Houston	170	165	153	168	656	14.98%				
9	Toronto	162	175	124	166	627	14.32%				
10	Los Angeles	78	65	81	37	261	5.96%				
11	Philadelphia	97	87	102	93	379	8.65%				
12	Vancouver	120	130	117	130	497	11.35%				
13	Total	1082	1100	1090	1108	4380					
14											
15	Average										
16	Maximum										
17	Minimum										
18											

Correct percentages

Using a mixed reference

Sometimes when you copy a formula, you want to change the row reference, but keep the column reference the same. This type of cell referencing, where one factor remains constant and the other one varies, is a **mixed reference**. For example, when copied, a formula containing the mixed reference C$14 would change the column letter relative to its new location, but not the row number.

In the mixed reference $C14, the column letter would not change, but the row number would be updated relative to its location. Like an absolute reference, a mixed reference can be created by pressing F4 with the cell reference selected. With each press of the F4 key, you cycle through all the possible combinations of relative, absolute, and mixed references (C14, $C$14, C$14, and $C14).

Excel

Enter a Formula with Multiple Operators

Learning
Outcomes
• Understand
the order of
operations
• Create a formula
with multiple
operators

Formulas often contain more than one arithmetic operator. In these formulas, Excel follows the **order of operations**, the sequence in which operators are applied in a mathematical calculation. Instead of calculating simply from left to right, this order calls for calculations in parentheses to be performed first, exponent calculations second, then multiplication and division, and finally addition and subtraction. If there are multiple occurrences of an operation, such as two multiplication operations, they are calculated from left to right. If your formula requires addition or subtraction to be calculated before multiplication or division, you can change the calculation order using parentheses around the addition or subtraction. For example, the formula to average the numbers 100, 200, and 300 is (100+200+300)/3 to make sure the numbers are totaled before the division operation. **TABLE 1-3** shows more examples of how calculations are performed in Excel. **CASE** *You need to analyze the percentage increase of this year's total for the North American locations from last year's total.*

STEPS

1. **Click cell J3, type This Year, then click the Enter button ✓ on the formula bar**
   You will enter this year's total using the calculation in cell F13.

2. **Click cell K3, type =, click cell F13, then click the Enter button ✓ on the formula bar**
   The value in cell F13 is copied to cell K3. You entered a cell reference rather than the value, so if any worksheet data is edited you won't have to reenter this total.

3. **Click cell J5, type % Increase, then click the Enter button ✓ on the formula bar**
   You want the formula to calculate the percentage increase of this year's total postings over last year. Percentage increase is calculated by subtracting the old value from the new value and dividing that difference by the old value, or (new − old)/old.

4. **Click cell K5, type =, type (, click cell K3, type -, click cell K1, then type)**
   In this first part of the formula, you are finding the difference in totals between this year and last year. You enclosed this calculation with parentheses so it will be performed before any other calculations, because calculations in parentheses are always calculated first. Compare your screen to **FIGURE 1-15**.

5. **Type /, click cell K1, then click the Enter button ✓ on the formula bar**
   The second part of this formula divides the difference in yearly totals by the total for the previous year to find the percentage of the growth. Because you enclosed the subtraction calculation in parentheses, it was calculated before the division calculation. The value in cell K5 is in decimal format. You want to display this value as a percentage with two decimal places.

6. **Click the Percent Style button % in the Number group on the Home tab, then click the Increase Decimal button ⬆ in the Number group twice**
   The percentage increase in cell K5 is 2.41%, as shown in **FIGURE 1-16**.

7. **Save your work**

FIGURE 1-15: Formula with parentheses

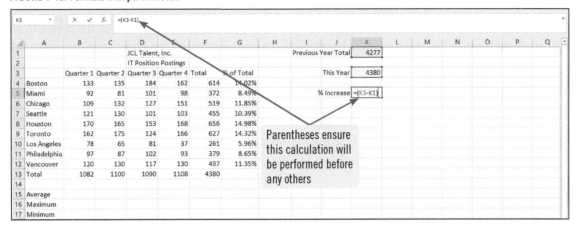

Parentheses ensure this calculation will be performed before any others

FIGURE 1-16: Formula with percentage increase

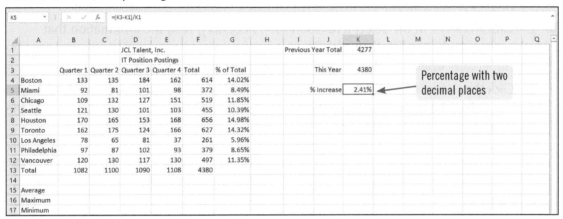

Percentage with two decimal places

TABLE 1-3: Calculation results in Excel formulas

formula	result
10+20+40/2	50
(10+20+40)/2	35
10+5*2	20
(10+5)*2	30
20–10/2	15
(20–10)/2	5

Insert a Function

You can insert functions in several ways. So far, you have used the AutoSum button on the ribbon to add the SUM function. To choose from all available functions you can use the Insert Function dialog box. This is especially valuable if you're not sure of the name of the function you need, because functions are organized into categories, such as Financial, Date & Time, and Statistical, and you are guided through the process. Other ways to insert a function include manually typing it in a cell and using the AutoSum arrow to insert commonly used functions. **CASE** ▶ *You need to calculate the average, maximum, and minimum location postings for the first quarter of the year and decide to use functions to do so.*

STEPS

1. **Click cell B15, then click the Insert Function button f_x on the formula bar**

   An equal sign (=) is inserted in the active cell, and the Insert Function dialog box opens, as shown in **FIGURE 1-17**. In this dialog box, you specify the function you want to use by clicking it in the Select a function list of recently used functions, clicking the Or select a category arrow to choose a desired function category, or typing the function name, or its description, in the Search for a function field.

2. **Click AVERAGE in the Select a function list if necessary, read the information that appears under the list, then click OK**

   The Function Arguments dialog box opens, as shown in **FIGURE 1-18**.

3. **Click the Collapse button ⬆ in the Number1 field of the Function Arguments dialog box, select the range B4:B12 on the worksheet, then click the Expand button ⬇ in the Function Arguments dialog box**

   Clicking the Collapse button minimizes the dialog box so that you can select cells on the worksheet. When you click the Expand button, the dialog box is restored. You can also begin dragging on the worksheet to automatically minimize the dialog box; after you select the desired range, the dialog box is restored.

4. **Click OK**

   The Function Arguments dialog box closes, and the calculated value is displayed in cell B15. The average postings per location for Quarter 1 is 120.222.

5. **Click cell B16, type =, then type m**

   Because you are manually typing this function, you must manually type the opening equal sign (=). Once you type an equal sign in a cell, each letter you type acts as a trigger to activate the Excel **Formula Auto-Complete**, a feature that automatically suggests text, numbers, or dates to insert based on previous entries. Because you entered the letter *m*, this feature suggests a list of function names beginning with "M."

6. **Double-click MAX in the list, select the range B4:B12, then click the Enter button ✓ on the formula bar**

   The result, 170, appears in cell B16. When you completed the entry, the closing parenthesis was automatically added to the formula.

7. **Click cell B17, type =, type m, double-click MIN in the list of function names, select the range B4:B12, then press ENTER**

   The result, 78, appears in cell B17.

8. **Select the range B15:B17, drag the fill handle to the range C15:E17, then save your work**

   The average, maximum, and minimum values for all the quarters appear in the selected range, as shown in **FIGURE 1-19**.

FIGURE 1-17: Insert Function dialog box

Search for a function field

Your list of recently used functions may differ

Or select a category list arrow

Description of selected function

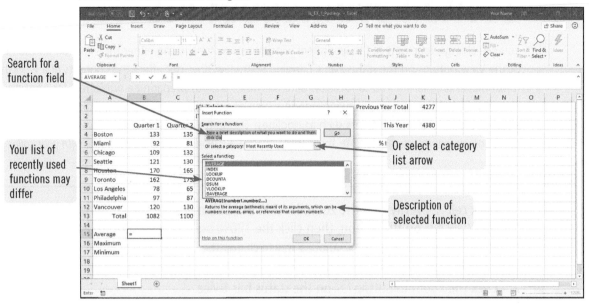

FIGURE 1-18: Function Arguments dialog box

Insert Function button

Argument

Drag title bar of dialog box to move it if necessary

Collapse button

Description of function and arguments

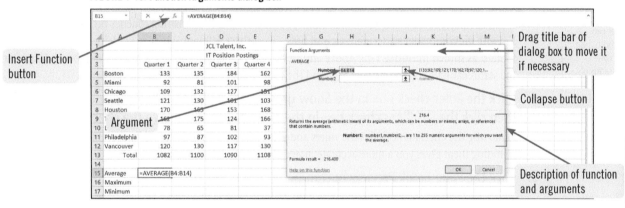

FIGURE 1-19: Completed AVERAGE, MAX, and MIN functions

	A	B	C	D	E	F	G	H	I	J	K	L	M	N	O	P
1				JCL Talent, Inc.					Previous Year Total		4277					
2				IT Position Postings												
3		Quarter 1	Quarter 2	Quarter 3	Quarter 4	Total	% of Total		This Year		4380					
4	Boston	133	135	184	162	614	14.02%									
5	Miami	92	81	101	98	372	8.49%		% Increase		2.41%					
6	Chicago	109	132	127	151	519	11.85%									
7	Seattle	121	130	101	103	455	10.39%									
8	Houston	170	165	153	168	656	14.98%									
9	Toronto	162	175	124	166	627	14.32%									
10	Los Angeles	78	65	81	37	261	5.96%									
11	Philadelphia	97	87	102	93	379	8.65%									
12	Vancouver	120	130	117	130	497	11.35%									
13	Total	1082	1100	1090	1108	4380										
14																
15	Average	120.222	122.222	121.111	123.111											
16	Maximum	170	175	184	168											
17	Minimum	78	65	81	37											
18																

Excel

Switch Worksheet Views

Learning Outcomes
• Change worksheet views
• Zoom a worksheet
• Adjust page breaks in a worksheet

You can change your view of the worksheet window at any time, using either the View tab on the ribbon or the View buttons on the status bar. Changing your view does not affect the contents of a worksheet; it just makes it easier for you to focus on different tasks, such as preparing a worksheet for printing. The View tab includes a variety of viewing options, such as View buttons, zoom controls, and the ability to show or hide worksheet elements such as gridlines. The status bar offers fewer View options but can be more convenient to use. **CASE** ▶ *You want to review your worksheet before sharing it with your colleagues.*

STEPS

1. **Click cell A1, verify that the zoom level in the Zoom area of the status bar is 120%, click the View tab on the ribbon, then click the 100% button in the Zoom group**
    The worksheet zooms to 100%. Another way to change the zoom level is to use the Zoom slider on the status bar.

2. **Click the Zoom in button ⊞ on the status bar twice**
    The worksheet zooms in 10% at a time, to 120%.

3. **Click the Page Layout button in the Workbook Views group on the View tab**
    The view switches from the default view, Normal, to Page Layout view. **Normal view** shows the worksheet without including certain features like headers and footers; it's ideal for creating and editing a worksheet but may not be detailed enough when you want to put the finishing touches on a document. **Page Layout view** provides an accurate view of how a worksheet will look when printed, including headers and footers, as shown in FIGURE 1-20. Above and to the left of the page are rulers. A page number indicator on the status bar tells you the current page and the total number of pages in this worksheet.

4. **Click the Ruler check box in the Show group on the View tab to remove the checkmark, then click the Gridlines check box in the Show group to remove the checkmark**
    Removing the checkmarks hides the rulers and gridlines. By default, gridlines in a worksheet do not print, so hiding them gives you a more accurate image of your final document.

5. **Click the Page Break Preview button ▦ on the status bar**
    Your view changes to Page Break Preview, which displays a reduced view of each page of your worksheet, along with page break indicators that you can drag to include more or less information on a page.

6. **Drag the pointer ↕ from the bottom page break indicator to the bottom of row 20, as shown in FIGURE 1-21**
    When you're working on a large worksheet with multiple pages, sometimes you need to adjust where pages break; in this worksheet, however, the information all fits comfortably on one page.

7. **Click the Page Layout button in the Workbook Views group, click the Ruler box in the Show group, then click the Gridlines box in the Show group**
    Adding checkmarks to the check boxes displays the rulers and gridlines. You can show or hide View tab items in any view.

8. **Click the Normal button in the Workbook Views group, then save your work**

FIGURE 1-20: Page Layout view

Turns ruler on/off

If header is added, it appears here

Workbook Views group

Turns gridlines on/off

Vertical ruler

Horizontal ruler

Add header

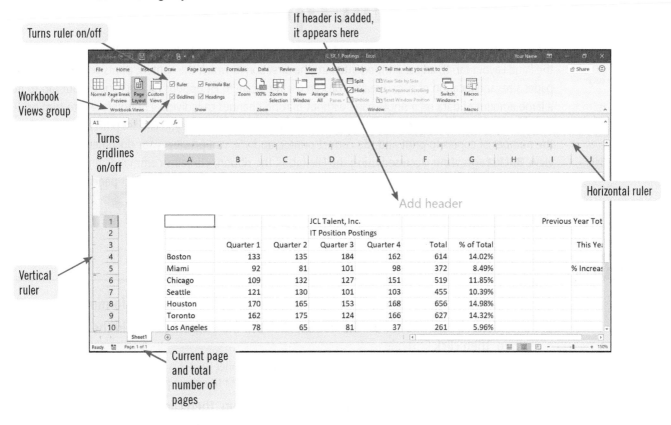

	Quarter 1	Quarter 2	Quarter 3	Quarter 4	Total	% of Total		Previous Year Tot
Boston	133	135	184	162	614	14.02%		This Yea
Miami	92	81	101	98	372	8.49%		% Increas
Chicago	109	132	127	151	519	11.85%		
Seattle	121	130	101	103	455	10.39%		
Houston	170	165	153	168	656	14.98%		
Toronto	162	175	124	166	627	14.32%		
Los Angeles	78	65	81	37	261	5.96%		

Current page and total number of pages

FIGURE 1-21: Page Break Preview

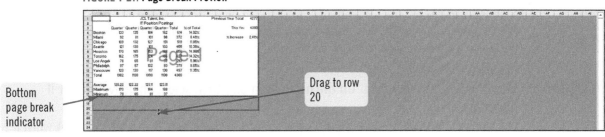

Drag to row 20

Bottom page break indicator

Choose Print Options

Before printing a document, you may want to make final adjustments to the output. You can use tools on the Page Layout tab to adjust print orientation (the direction in which the content prints across the page), paper size, and location of page breaks. You can use the Scale to Fit options on the Page Layout tab to fit a large amount of data on a single page without making changes to individual margins, and to turn gridlines and column/row headings on and off. When you are ready to print, you can set print options such as the number of copies to print and the correct printer, and you can preview your document in Backstage view. **Backstage view**, accessed using the File tab of the ribbon, contains commands that allow you to manage files and options for the program such as print settings. You can also adjust page layout settings in Backstage view and immediately see the results in the document preview. **CASE** *You are ready to prepare your worksheet for printing.*

STEPS

1. **Click cell A20, type your name, then click the Enter button ✓ on the formula bar**

2. **Click the Page Layout tab on the ribbon, click the Orientation button in the Page Setup group, then click Portrait**

   The orientation changes to **portrait**, so the printed page is taller than it is wide. You can see from the vertical dotted line, indicating a page break, that all columns don't fit on one page in this orientation.

3. **Click the Orientation button in the Page Setup group, then click Landscape**

   The paper orientation returns to **landscape**, so the printed page is wider than it is tall. Now all the content fits on one page.

4. **Click the Gridlines Print box in the Sheet Options group on the Page Layout tab, then save your work**

   Printing gridlines makes the data easier to read, but the gridlines will not print unless the Gridlines Print box is selected. You can also print row numbers and column letters by clicking the Headings Print box. If you don't want to print gridlines or headings, make sure these boxes are not selected.

5. **Click the File tab, click Print on the navigation bar, then select an active printer if necessary**

   The Print tab in Backstage view displays a preview of your worksheet exactly as it will look when it is printed. To the left of the preview, you can also change a number of document settings and print options. Compare your screen to **FIGURE 1-22**. You can print from this view by clicking Print, or you can return to the worksheet without printing by clicking the Back button ⊙.

6. **Click the Page Setup link in the Settings list, click the Margins tab in the Page Setup dialog box, click the Horizontally check box in the Center on page section, click the Vertically check box in the Center on page section, then compare your screen to FIGURE 1-23**

   The printed worksheet will be centered on the page.

7. **Click OK, then click Print**

   One copy of the worksheet prints.

8. **sam ↑ Save your workbook, submit your work to your instructor as directed, click File, click Close, then click the Close button ✕ on the title bar**

FIGURE 1-22: Worksheet in Backstage view

Click to return to worksheet

Click to change number of copies

Print button

Active printer; yours will be different

Click arrows or enter values to specify which pages to print

Click to zoom in or out on the page

Click to select scaling options

Click to change paper size

Click to print entire workbook or selection

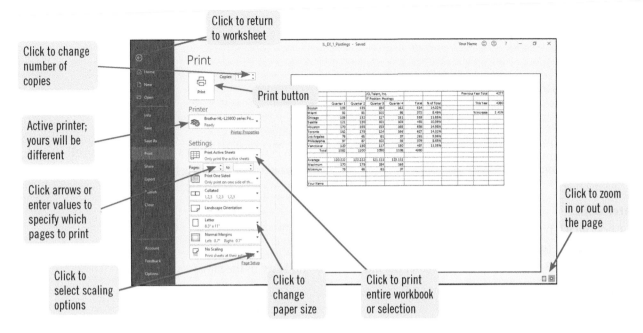

FIGURE 1-23: Page Setup dialog box

Margins tab

Click to center on printed page

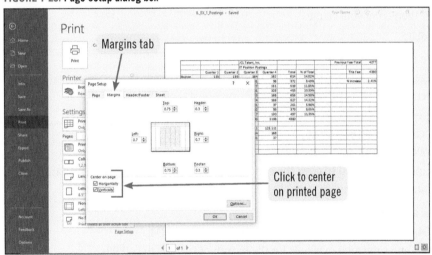

Setting a print area

If you want to print a selected worksheet area repeatedly, it's best to define a **print area**, so that the Quick Print feature prints only that portion of the worksheet area. To define a print area, select the range you want to print on the worksheet, click the Page Layout tab on the ribbon, click the Print Area button in the Page Setup group, then click Set Print Area. A print area can consist of one contiguous range of cells, or multiple ranges in different parts of a worksheet. To clear a print area, click the Page Layout tab on the ribbon, click the Print Area button in the Page Setup group, then click Clear Print Area.

Scaling to fit

If you have a large amount of data that you want to fit to a single sheet of paper, you can control how much of your work to print on a single sheet by clicking the No Scaling arrow in the Settings list in the Print screen in Backstage view, then clicking Fit Sheet on One Page, Fit All Columns on One Page, or Fit all Rows on One Page. Another method for fitting worksheet content onto one page is to click the Page Layout tab on the ribbon, then change the Width and Height settings in the Scale to Fit group to 1 page each. You can also click the Page Setup link in the Print screen in Backstage view, click the Page tab if necessary in the Page Setup dialog box, click the Fit to option button, then enter 1 in the page(s) wide by and tall fields.

Excel

Practice

Skills Review

1. **Explore Excel.**
   a. Start Excel.
   b. Open IL_EX_1-2.xlsx from the location where you store your Data Files, then save it as **IL_EX_1_Travel**.
   c. Locate the Name box, formula bar, worksheet window, cell pointer, sheet tab scrolling buttons, mode indicator, and Tell me box.

2. **Enter data.**
   a. Click cell B3, type **Jan**, then confirm the entry.
   b. Click cell D7, type **202497**, then conform the entry.
   c. Activate cell B3, then use Auto Fill to enter the months **Feb** and **Mar** in the range C3:D3.
   d. Save your changes to the file.

3. **Edit data.**
   a. Use F2 to correct the spelling of Maimi in cell A6 (the correct spelling is Miami).
   b. Click cell C7, then use the formula bar to change the value to **188270**.
   c. Click cell A17, then enter your name.
   d. Save your changes.

4. **Copy and move cell data.**
   a. Select the range G4:G6.
   b. Copy the selection to the Clipboard.
   c. Open the Clipboard task pane, then paste the selection to cell A10.
   d. Delete the labels in the range G4:G6.
   e. Close the Clipboard task pane, then activate cell A8.
   f. Use the drag-and-drop method to copy the contents of cell A8 to cell E3. (*Hint*: Press and hold CTRL while dragging.)
   g. Save your work.

5. **Enter formulas and use AutoSum.**
   a. Activate cell E4, then enter a formula that adds cells B4, C4, and D4.
   b. Use AutoSum to enter the total expenses for the month of January in cell B8.
   c. Save your changes.

6. **Copy formulas with relative cell references.**
   a. Activate cell E4, then use the fill handle to copy the formula in cell E4 to the range E5:E7.
   b. Activate cell B8, then use the fill handle to copy the formula in cell B8 to the range C8:E8.
   c. Save your work.

7. **Copy formulas with absolute cell references.**
   a. Enter **% of Total** in cell F3.
   b. In cell F4, create a formula that divides the value in cell E4 by the value in cell E8 using an absolute reference to cell E8.
   c. Use the fill handle to copy the formula in cell F4 to the range F5:F7.
   d. Save your work.

Skills Review (continued)

8. Enter a formula with multiple operators.

  a. Enter a formula in cell B10 that calculates the average travel expenses for the month of January. Use a formula that contains cell references and not a function. (*Hint*: The formula is =(B4+B5+B6+B7)/4.)

  b. Review the use of the parentheses in the formula.

  c. Save your work.

9. Insert a function.

  a. Use the Insert Function button to create a formula in cell B11 that calculates the maximum travel expense for January.

  b. In cell B12, enter a function to calculate the minimum travel expenses for January.

  c. Select the range B10:B12, then use the fill handle to copy the functions into the range C10:D12.

  d. Save your work.

10. Switch worksheet views.

  a. Click the View tab on the ribbon, then switch to Page Layout view.

  b. Verify that the Ruler and Gridlines check boxes contain checkmarks.

  c. Switch to Page Break view and adjust the page break so it comes at the bottom of row 20.

  d. Switch to Normal View, use a button in the Zoom group of the View tab to zoom the worksheet to 100%, then use the Zoom buttons in the Status bar to zoom the worksheet back to 120%.

  e. Save your changes.

11. Choose print options.

  a. Use the Page Layout tab to change the orientation to Portrait.

  b. Turn on gridlines for printing using a check box in the Sheet Options group of the Page Layout tab.

  c. Preview the worksheet in Backstage view, then use the Page Setup dialog box to center the worksheet vertically and horizontally on the page. (*Hint*: The commands are located on the Margins tab.) Compare your screen to **FIGURE 1-24**.

  d. Save your changes, submit your work to your instructor as directed, close the workbook, then exit Excel.

FIGURE 1-24

	Jan	Feb	Mar	Total	% of Total
Reed & Allen Legal Services					
Travel Expenses					
New York	220,125	187,012	240,185	647,322	24.26%
Los Angeles	289,134	302,184	219,750	811,068	30.39%
Miami	157,368	207,305	257,217	621,890	23.30%
Chicago	197,516	188,270	202,497	588,283	22.04%
Total	864,143	884,771	919,649	2,668,563	
Average	216,036	221,193	229,912		
Maximum	289,134	302,184	257,217		
Minimum	157,368	187,012	202,497		
Your Name					

Independent Challenge 1

The CFO at Riverwalk Medical Clinic has hired you to help him analyze departmental insurance reimbursements. He also would like to see what quarterly revenues would look like with a 20% increase in quarterly reimbursements. You've been given a worksheet for this project that contains some but not all of the data.

  a. Open IL_EX_1-3.xlsx from the location where you store your Data Files, then save it as **IL_EX_1_Reimbursements**.

  b. Enter the data shown in **TABLE 1-4** in the range E4:E11.

  c. Type your name in cell A17.

  d. Move the label in cell F2 to cell A15.

Excel

Independent Challenge 1 (continued)

e. Use the Clipboard to copy and paste the label in cell F3 to cell A12.

f. Use the formula bar to correct the spelling error in the label in cell A6. (*Hint*: The correct spelling is Immunology.)

g. Edit cell A8 to correct the spelling error in the label. (*Hint*: The correct spelling is Ophthalmology.)

h. Type **Quarter 1** in cell B3, then use Auto Fill to enter Quarter 2, Quarter 3, and Quarter 4 in the range C3:E3.

i. Create a formula in cell F4 that uses cell references and totals the quarterly reimbursements for the Cardiology department.

j. Use the fill handle to copy the formula in cell F4 to the range F5:F11.

k. Using AutoSum, create a formula in cell B12 that totals the first quarter reimbursements for all the departments.

l. Copy the formula in cell B12 to the range C12:E12.

m. Enter a formula in cell B14 to calculate a 20% increase in the first quarter reimbursement total in cell B12. (*Hint:* You need to add B12 to B12 multiplied by .20. Use parentheses if necessary to follow the order of operations.)

n. Enter a function, using the help of AutoComplete, in cell B15 that calculates the average first quarter reimbursement amount for the departments.

o. Copy the formulas in the range B14:B15 to the range C14:E15.

p. Switch to Page Break view and adjust the page break to the bottom of row 18.

q. Switch to Normal View, then zoom the worksheet to 120%.

r. Turn on gridlines for printing.

s. Change the page orientation to landscape.

t. Preview the worksheet in Backstage view, then use the Page Setup dialog box to center the worksheet horizontally and vertically on the page. Compare your screen to FIGURE 1-25.

u. Submit your work to your instructor as directed.

v. Close the workbook, then exit Excel.

TABLE 1-4

cell address	value
E4	67247.90
E5	45581.20
E6	43000.60
E7	48539.20
E8	38125.00
E9	28909.50
E10	39216.90
E11	71189.10

FIGURE 1-25

	Riverwalk Medical Clinic				
	Insurance Reimbursements				
	Quarter 1	Quarter 2	Quarter 3	Quarter 4	Total
Cardiology	61,762.00	61,738.20	72,076.60	67,247.90	262,824.70
Dermatology	36,109.90	40,214.60	44,374.00	45,581.20	166,279.70
Immunology	43,877.60	44,719.80	46,702.10	43,000.60	178,300.10
Neurology	41,321.00	45,897.40	46,790.60	48,539.20	182,548.20
Ophthalmology	51,827.70	30,045.20	36,611.20	38,125.00	156,609.10
Orthopedics	15,682.50	26,103.00	27,650.20	28,909.50	98,345.20
Pediatrics	33,715.00	36,561.40	83,403.50	39,216.90	192,896.80
Psychology	72,950.60	66,427.60	73,403.60	71,189.10	283,970.90
Total	357,246.30	351,707.20	431,011.80	381,809.40	
20% increase	428,695.56	422,048.64	517,214.16	458,171.28	
Average	44,655.79	43,963.40	53,876.48	47,726.18	
Your Name					

1 of 1

Independent Challenge 2

As the assistant to the Dean of STEM (science, technology, engineering, and mathematics) at West Shore Community College, it is your responsibility to review the budgets for the departments in the division and help with a budget forecast for the upcoming academic year. You've decided to use Excel formulas and functions to help with this analysis.

a. Open IL_EX_1-4.xlsx from the location where you store your Data Files, then save it as **IL_EX_1_Budgets**.

b. Move the labels in the range A6:A11 to the range A5:A10.

c. Enter **Total** in cell A11, then use AutoSum to calculate the total 2020 expenses for all departments in cell B11.

d. Enter **Average** in cell A12, then use the AutoSum arrow to enter a function in cell B12 that calculates the average 2020 expenses for all departments. (*Hint*: make sure you include only the department data.)

e. Use the fill handle to copy the formulas in the range B11:B12 to the range C11:C12.

f. Using cell references, enter a formula in cell D5 that calculates the 2022 Budget for the engineering department, using the increase shown in cell F2 over the 2021 expenses in cell C5. Use absolute cell references where necessary. (*Hint*: Multiply the percentage in cell F2 by the 2021 expenses in cell C5, then add that amount to the 2021 expenses in cell C5.)

g. Use the fill handle to copy the formula in cell D5 to the range D6:D10.

h. Use the fill handle to copy the formulas in the range C11:C12 to the range D11:D12.

i. Enter a formula in cell F5 that calculates the percentage increase in total expenses from 2020 to 2021. (*Hint*: The 2020 total is in cell B11 and the 2021 total is in cell C11.)

j. Change the page orientation to landscape, then turn on gridlines for printing.

k. Enter your name in cell A14.

l. Preview the worksheet in Backstage view. Compare your screen to FIGURE 1-26.

m. Save your work, then submit the worksheet to your instructor as directed.

n. Close the workbook and exit Excel.

FIGURE 1-26

West Shore Community College					2022 Budget Increase	
STEM Division					2.15%	
Departmental Budgets						
Department	2020 Expenses	2021 Expenses	2022 Budget		% Increase in Expenses 2020 to 2021	
Engineering	$50,124.17	$52,457.65	$53,585.49		6.01%	
Computer Science	$45,287.23	$55,214.98	$56,402.10			
Biology	$36,784.98	$36,799.88	$37,591.08			
Chemistry	$58,214.78	$59,847.47	$61,134.19			
Physics	$61,002.27	$62,178.78	$63,515.62			
Math	$37,512.32	$39,781.33	$40,636.63			
Total	$288,925.75	$306,280.09	$312,865.11			
Average	$48,154.29	$51,046.68	$52,144.19			
Your Name						

Visual Workshop

Open IL_EX_1-5.xlsx from the location where you store your Data Files, then save it as **IL_EX_1_Royalties**. Complete the worksheet shown in FIGURE 1-27 using the skills you learned in this module. Use functions to calculate the values in B8:B11 and C11. The values in column C are calculated by multiplying the gross revenues in column B by the percentage in cell E2. Adjust your zoom level as necessary to match the figure. Enter your name in cell A14. Submit your work to your instructor as directed.

FIGURE 1-27

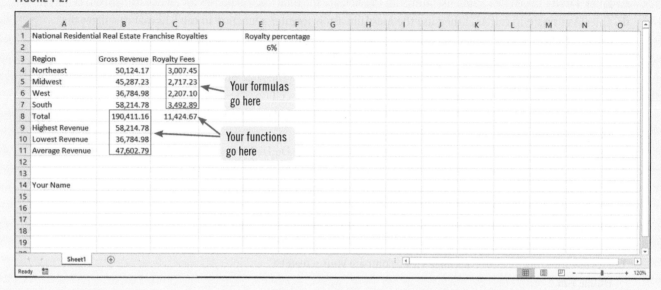

Formatting a Worksheet

CASE ▶ Cheri McNeil, the manager of the Boston office at JCL Talent, has gathered data from all JCL recruiters on technology position postings for the first quarter of the year. Cheri has created a worksheet listing this information, and she asks you to format the worksheet to make it easier to read and understand.

Module Objectives

After completing this module, you will be able to:

- Format values
- Change font and font size
- Change font styles and alignment
- Adjust column width
- Insert and delete rows and columns

- Apply colors, borders, and documentation
- Apply conditional formatting
- Rename and move a worksheet
- Check spelling

Files You Will Need

IL_EX_2-1.xlsx IL_EX_2-4.xlsx
IL_EX_2-2.xlsx IL_EX_2-5.xlsx
IL_EX_2-3.xlsx

Format Values

**Learning
Outcomes**
• Format a number
• Format a date
• Increase/decrease
  decimals

When you **format** a cell, you enhance the appearance of information by changing its font, size, color, or alignment. Formatting changes only the appearance of a value or label; it does not alter the actual data in any way. To format a cell or range, first you select it, then you apply the formatting using the ribbon, Mini toolbar, or a keyboard shortcut. You can apply formatting before or after you enter data in a cell or range.
CASE ▸ *Cheri has provided you with a worksheet that details technology postings, and you're ready to improve its appearance. You start by formatting some cells to better reflect the type of information they contain, such as currency, percentages, and dates.*

STEPS

1. **sam ↓ Start Excel, open IL_EX_2-1.xlsx from the location where you store your Data Files, then save it as IL_EX_2_Tech**

   This worksheet is difficult to interpret because all the information is crowded and looks the same. In some columns, such as D, the contents appear cut off because there is too much data to fit given the current column width. You decide not to widen the columns yet, because the other changes you plan to make might affect column width and row height.

2. **Select the range G3:G15, then click the Accounting Number Format button $ in the Number group on the Home tab**

   A **number format** is applied to values to express numeric concepts, such as currency, date, and percentage. The default Accounting number format adds dollar signs and two decimal places to the expense data, as shown in **FIGURE 2-1**.

3. **Select the range H3:H15, then click the Comma Style button 9 in the Number group**

   The values in column H display the Comma Style format, which does not include a dollar sign but can be useful for some types of accounting data.

4. **Click cell M1, click the Number Format arrow, click Percentage, then click the Increase Decimal button 🔆 in the Number group**

   The revenue rate is now formatted with a percent sign (%) and three decimal places. The Number Format arrow lets you choose from popular number formats and shows an example of what the selected cell or cells would look like (when multiple cells are selected, the example is based on the first cell in the range). Each time you click the Increase Decimal button, you add one decimal place; clicking the button twice would add two decimal places.

5. **Click the Decrease Decimal button 🔅 in the Number group three times**

   All three decimal places are removed from the revenue rate value.

6. **Select the range C3:C15, then click the launcher 🔲 in the Number group**

   The Format Cells dialog box opens with the Date category already selected on the Number tab.

7. **Click the 14-Mar format in the Type list box, as shown in FIGURE 2-2, then click OK**

   The dates in column C appear in the 14-Mar format.

8. **Select the range I3:J15, right-click the range, click Format Cells on the shortcut menu, in the Category list click Currency, in the Decimal places box type 2 if necessary, then click OK**

   This number format looks similar to the Accounting format but aligns currency symbols and decimal points slightly differently. Compare your worksheet to **FIGURE 2-3**.

9. **Select the range G3:I15, click the Decrease Decimal button 🔅 in the Number group twice, press CTRL+HOME, then save your work**

   The cell values in this range now use a custom format that doesn't display decimal places. This format is applied to all cells in the range, including the cells in column H that display the $ symbol.

FIGURE 2-1: Accounting number format applied to range

Number Format list arrow

Accounting Number Format button

Increase Decimal button

Decrease Decimal button

Cells formatted with Accounting number format

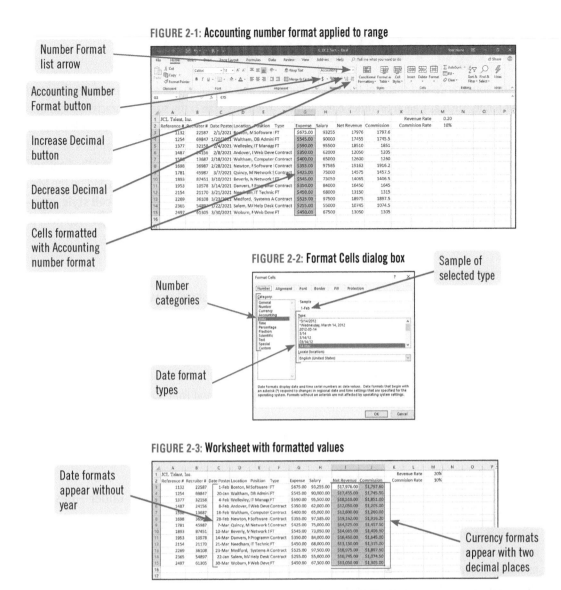

FIGURE 2-2: Format Cells dialog box

Number categories

Date format types

Sample of selected type

FIGURE 2-3: Worksheet with formatted values

Date formats appear without year

Currency formats appear with two decimal places

Working with online pictures, other images, and symbols

You can illustrate your worksheets using online pictures and other images. To add a picture to a worksheet, click the Online Pictures button in the Illustrations group on the Insert tab. The Online Pictures dialog box opens. Here you can search for online pictures from the Bing search engine or OneDrive, as shown in FIGURE 2-4. To search, type one or more keywords in the search box, then press ENTER. When you double-click an image in the Search Results window, the image is inserted at the location of the active cell. Clicking an image selects it and adds resizing handles. To resize an image proportionally, drag any corner sizing handle. If you drag an edge sizing handle, the image will be resized nonproportionally. You can add alternative text to an image by right-clicking it, clicking Edit Alt Text on the shortcut menu, then entering the text in the Alt Text pane. To move an image, point inside the image until the pointer changes to ✛, then drag it to a new location. To delete a picture, select it, then press DEL. To work with an image it must be selected. You

FIGURE 2-4: Results of Online Picture search

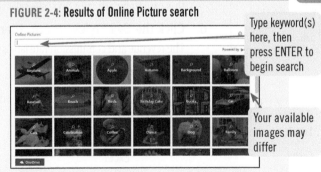

Type keyword(s) here, then press ENTER to begin search

Your available images may differ

can select an image, or any object, by clicking it. To work with multiple images at once, hold CTRL while clicking each image. You can insert a symbol in a worksheet by clicking the Insert tab, clicking the Symbols button in the Symbols group, clicking Symbol, clicking a symbol from the Symbols tab in the Symbol dialog box, clicking Insert, then clicking Close to close the Symbol dialog box.

Excel

Change Font and Font Size

Learning
Outcomes
• Change a font
• Change a font size

A **font** is the appearance and shape of the letters, numbers, and special characters and is usually designed with a font name, such as Calibri or Times New Roman. The **font size** is the size of characters, measured in units called points. A **point** is a unit of measure used for font size and row height; one point is equal to $\frac{1}{72}$ of an inch. The default font and font size in Excel is 11-point Calibri. TABLE 2-1 shows examples of several fonts in different font sizes. You can change the font and font size of any cell or range using the Font and Font Size arrows. The Font and Font Size arrows are located on the Home tab on the ribbon and on the Mini toolbar, which opens when you right-click a cell or range. To save time, you can also use a **cell style**, a pre-designed combination of font, font size, and font color that you can apply to a cell. **CASE** *You want to change the font and font size of the labels and the worksheet title, so this information stands out.*

STEPS

1. **Click the Font arrow in the Font group on the Home tab, scroll down in the Font list to see an alphabetical listing of the fonts available on your computer, then click Calibri, as shown in FIGURE 2-5**

   The font in cell A1 changes to Calibri to match the rest of the worksheet.

2. **Click the Font Size arrow in the Font group, then click 20**

   The worksheet title is formatted in 20-point Calibri, and the Font and Font Size boxes on the Home tab display the new font and font size information.

3. **Click the Cell Styles button in the Styles group, then click Heading 1 under Titles and Headings**

   The title is formatted in the Heading 1 cell style.

4. **Select the range A2:J2, click the Cell Styles button, then click Heading 2 under Titles and Headings**

   Notice that some of the column labels are now too wide to appear fully in the column. Excel does not automatically adjust column widths to accommodate cell formatting; these column widths must be adjusted manually. You'll learn to do this in a later lesson.

5. **Click cell L1, hold SHIFT, then click cell L2**

   Holding SHIFT while clicking a cell selects that cell and any cells between it and the cell first selected. In this case there are only two cells selected.

6. **Click the Cell Styles button, then click Heading 4 under Titles and Headings**

   The revenue and commission rate labels are now formatted consistently. Compare your worksheet to FIGURE 2-6.

7. **Save your work**

TABLE 2-1: Examples of fonts and font sizes

font name	12 point	24 point
Calibri	Excel	Excel
Playbill	Excel	Excel
Comic Sans MS	Excel	Excel
Times New Roman	Excel	Excel

FIGURE 2-5: Font list

Font list arrow

Active cell displays preview of selected formatting change

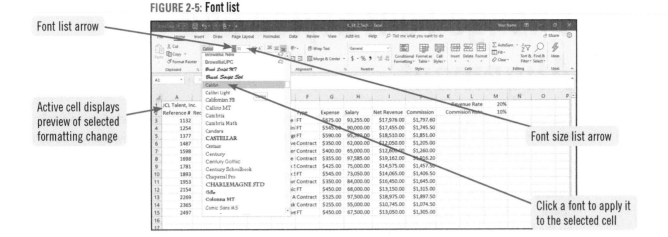

Font size list arrow

Click a font to apply it to the selected cell

FIGURE 2-6: Worksheet with formatted headings and column labels

Title formatted in Heading 1 cell style

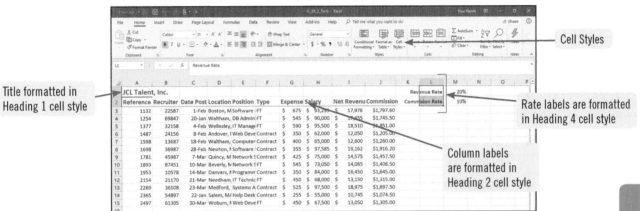

Cell Styles

Rate labels are formatted in Heading 4 cell style

Column labels are formatted in Heading 2 cell style

Working with cell styles

You can modify any style in the Cell Styles gallery. In the Cell Styles gallery, right-click the cell style that you want to modify, on the shortcut menu shown in **FIGURE 2-7**, click Modify, select the style options from the Style Includes list in the Style dialog box, click the Format button to choose new customized formatting, then click OK twice. To create a new cell style, click New Cell Style at the bottom of the Cell Styles gallery, enter a name in the Style name box, select style options from the Style Includes list, click the Format button to choose customized formatting for your style, then click OK twice. You can merge styles from a different workbook by opening the workbook that contains the cell styles that you want to copy, clicking Merge Styles at the bottom of the Cell Styles gallery, clicking the workbook

FIGURE 2-7: Shortcut menu in Cell Styles gallery

in the Merge styles from list, then clicking OK. If styles in the workbooks have the same name, you will be asked if you want to merge those styles.

Excel

Change Font Styles and Alignment

Font styles are formats that indicate how characters are emphasized, such as bold, underline, and italic. You have seen font styles applied with cell styles, and you can also apply them individually. You can change the **alignment**, the placement of cell contents in relation to a cell's edges, such as left or centered, of labels and values in cells. See TABLE 2-2 for a description of common font style and alignment buttons that are available on the Home tab. Once you have formatted a cell the way you want it, you can "paint" or copy the cell's formats to other cells by using the Format Painter button in the Clipboard group on the Home tab. This is similar to using copy and paste, but instead of copying cell contents, it copies only the cell's formatting. **CASE** *You want to further enhance the worksheet's appearance by adding bold and underline formatting and centering some of the labels.*

STEPS

1. **Select the range A3:A15, then click the** Bold button B **in the Font group on the Home tab**
   The reference numbers in column A appear in bold.

2. **Click the** Italic button I **in the Font group**
   The reference numbers now appear in boldface and italic type. Notice that the Bold and Italic buttons in the Font group are selected.

3. **Click the** Italic button I **to deselect it**
   The italic font style is removed from the reference numbers but the bold font style remains.

4. **Click the** Center button ≡ **in the Alignment group**
   The reference numbers are centered within their cells.

5. **Click the** Format Painter button 🖌 **in the Clipboard group, then select the range B3:B15**
   The formatting in column A is copied to the recruiter number data in column B. To paint the formats to more than one selection, double-click the Format Painter button to keep it activated until you turn it off. You can turn off the Format Painter by pressing ESC or by clicking 🖌.

6. **Click cell A1, select the range A1:J1, then click the** Merge & Center button 🖽 **in the Alignment group**
   The Merge & Center button creates one cell out of the ten cells across the row, then centers the text in that newly created, merged cell. The title "JCL Talent, Inc." is centered across the 10 columns you selected. To split a merged cell into its original components, select the merged cell, then click the Merge & Center button 🖽 to deselect it. Occasionally, you may find that you want cell contents to wrap within a cell. You can do this by selecting the cells containing the text you want to wrap, then clicking the Wrap Text button 🔤 in the Alignment group on the Home tab on the ribbon.

7. **Compare your screen to** FIGURE 2-8, **then save your work**

FIGURE 2-8: Worksheet with font styles and alignment applied

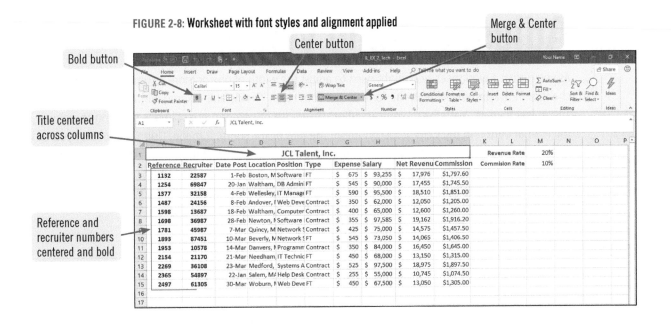

Bold button

Center button

Merge & Center button

Title centered across columns

Reference and recruiter numbers centered and bold

TABLE 2-2: Common font style and alignment buttons

button	description
B	Bolds cell content
I	Italicizes cell content
U	Underlines cell content
	Centers content across columns; also merges two or more selected, adjacent cells into one cell; also unmerges previously merged cells
	Aligns content at the left edge of the cell
	Centers content horizontally within the cell
	Aligns content at the right edge of the cell
ab	Wraps long text into multiple lines to fit within a column
	Aligns content at the top of a cell
	Aligns content at the bottom of a cell
	Aligns content in the middle of a cell

Rotating and indenting cell entries

In addition to applying fonts and font styles, you can rotate or indent data within a cell. To rotate text within a cell, click the Home tab, select the cells you want to modify, then click the dialog box launcher in the Alignment group to open the Alignment tab of the Format Cells dialog box. Click a position in the Orientation box or type a number in the Degrees box to rotate text from its default horizontal orientation, then click OK. You can indent cell contents by clicking the Increase Indent button in the Alignment group, which moves cell contents to the right one space, or the Decrease Indent button, which moves cell contents to the left one space.

Adjust Column Width

Learning
Outcomes
• Change a column
  width by dragging
• Resize a column
  with AutoFit
• Change the
  width of multiple
  columns

As you format a worksheet, you might need to adjust the width of one or more columns to accommodate changes in the amount of text, the font size, or font style. The default column width is 8.43 characters, a little less than 1". With Excel, you can adjust the width of one or more columns by using the mouse, the Format button in the Cells group on the Home tab, or the shortcut menu. Using the mouse, you can drag or double-click the right edge of a column heading. The Format button and shortcut menu include commands for making more precise width adjustments. TABLE 2-3 describes common column formatting commands. **CASE** *You have noticed that some of the labels in columns A through L don't fit in the cells. You want to adjust the widths of the columns so that the labels appear in their entirety.*

STEPS

QUICK TIP

If "#######"
appears after you
adjust a column of
values, the column
is too narrow to dis-
play the values com-
pletely; increase the
column width until
the values appear.

1. **Position the pointer on the line between the column C and column D headings until it changes to ↔**

   See FIGURE 2-9. A **column heading** is a box that appears above each worksheet column and identifies it by a letter. You positioned the mouse pointer here because in order to adjust column width using the mouse, you need to position the pointer on the right edge of the column heading for the column you want to adjust.

2. **Click and drag ↔ to the right until the column fully displays the column label Date Posted (approximately 12.71 characters or 94 pixels)**

   As you change the column width, a ScreenTip opens listing the column width.

3. **Position the pointer on the line between columns D and E until it changes to ↔, then double-click**

   Column D automatically widens to fit the widest entry. Double-clicking the right edge of a column heading activates **AutoFit**. This feature adjusts column width or row height to accommodate its widest or tallest entry.

QUICK TIP

You can paste copied
cell data with the
same column width
by clicking Keep
Source Column
Widths in the Paste
menu.

4. **Use AutoFit to resize columns E, F, G, H, and L**

5. **Position the pointer in the column heading area for column I until it changes to ↓, then drag to select columns I and J**

6. **Click the Format button in the Cells group, then click Column Width**

   The Column Width dialog box opens. Column width measurement is based on the number of characters that will fit in the column when formatted in the Normal font and font size (in this case, 11-point Calibri).

QUICK TIP

If an entire column
rather than a column
cell is selected, you
can change the
width of the column
by right-clicking the
selection, then click-
ing Column Width
on the shortcut
menu.

7. **Type 14 in the Column width box, then click OK**

   The widths of columns I and J change to reflect the new setting. See FIGURE 2-10.

8. **Click cell A1, then save your work**

FIGURE 2-9: Preparing to change the column width

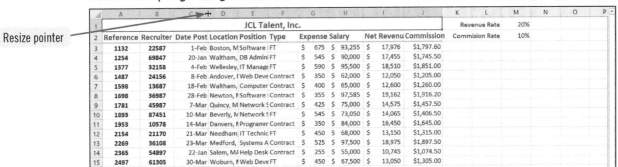

Resize pointer

FIGURE 2-10: Worksheet with column widths adjusted

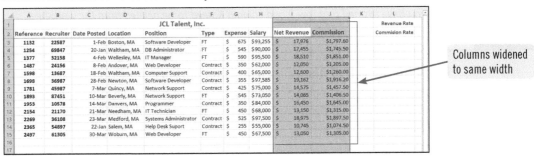

Columns widened
to same width

TABLE 2-3: Common column formatting commands

command	description	available using
Column Width	Sets the width to a specific number of characters	Format button; shortcut menu
AutoFit Column Width	Fits to the widest entry in a column	Format button; mouse
Hide & Unhide	Hides or displays selected column(s)	Format button; shortcut menu
Default Width	Resets column to worksheet's default column width	Format button

Changing row height

Changing row height is as easy as changing column width. Row height is calculated in points, the same unit of measure used for fonts. The row height must exceed the size of the font you are using. Normally, you don't need to adjust row height manually, because row heights adjust automatically to accommodate font size changes. If you format something in a row to be a larger point size, Excel adjusts the row to fit the largest point size in the row. However, you have just as many options for changing row height as you do column width. Using the mouse, you can place the ✛ pointer on the line dividing a row heading from the heading below it, and then drag to the desired height; double-clicking the line AutoFits the row height where necessary. You can also select one or more rows, then use the Row Height command on the shortcut menu, or click the Format button on the Home tab, then click the Row Height or AutoFit Row Height command.

Insert and Delete Rows and Columns

Learning Outcomes
• Use the Insert dialog box
• Use column and row heading buttons to insert and delete

As you modify a worksheet, you might find it necessary to insert or delete rows and columns to keep your worksheet current. For example, you might need to insert rows to accommodate new inventory products or remove a column of yearly totals that are no longer necessary. When you insert a new row, the row is inserted above the cell pointer and the contents of the worksheet shift down from the newly inserted row. When you insert a new column, the column is inserted to the left of the cell pointer and the contents of the worksheet shift to the right of the new column. To insert multiple rows, select the same number of row headings as you want to insert before using the Insert command. **CASE** *You want to improve the overall appearance of the worksheet by inserting a row between the company name and the column labels. Also, you have learned that row 9 and column K need to be deleted from the worksheet.*

STEPS

1. **Right-click cell F2, then click Insert on the shortcut menu**

   The Insert dialog box opens. See **FIGURE 2-11**. You can choose to insert a single cell and shift the cells in the active column to the right, insert a single cell and shift the cells in the active row down, or insert an entire column or a row.

2. **Click the Entire row option button, then click OK**

   A blank row appears between the company name and the column labels, visually separating the worksheet data, and the Insert Options button ☑ opens next to cell F3.

3. **Click the Insert Options button ☑, then review your choices**

   This menu lets you format the inserted row in Format Same As Above (the default setting, already selected), Format Same As Below, or Clear Formatting.

4. **Click ☑ to close the menu without making changes, then click the row 9 heading**

   All of row 9 is selected, as shown in **FIGURE 2-12**.

5. **Click the Delete button in the Cells group; do not click the Delete arrow**

   Excel deletes row 9, and all rows below it shift up one row. You must use the Delete button or the Delete command on the shortcut menu to delete a row or column; pressing DEL on the keyboard removes only the *contents* of a selected row or column.

6. **Click the column K heading**

   The column is empty and isn't necessary in this worksheet.

7. **Click the Delete button in the Cells group**

   Excel deletes column K. The remaining columns to the right shift left one column.

8. **Save your work**

FIGURE 2-11: Insert dialog box

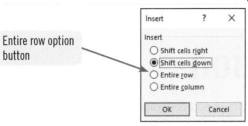

Entire row option button

FIGURE 2-12: Worksheet with row 9 selected

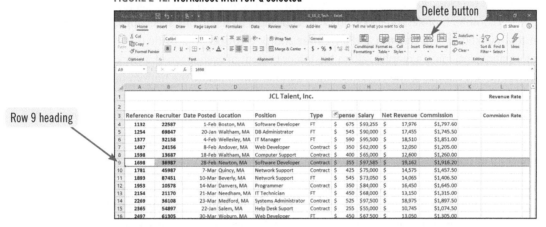

Delete button

Row 9 heading

Hiding and unhiding columns and rows

When you don't want data in a column or row to be visible, but you don't want to delete it, you can hide the column or row. To hide a selected column, click the Format button in the Cells group on the Home tab, point to Hide & Unhide, then click Hide Columns. A hidden column is indicated by a dark green vertical line in its original position. This green line is removed when you click elsewhere on the worksheet, but a thin double line remains between the column heading to remind you that one or more columns are hidden. You can display a hidden column by selecting the column headings on either side of the hidden column, clicking the Format button in the Cells group, pointing to Hide & Unhide, then clicking Unhide Columns. (To hide or unhide one or more rows, substitute Hide Rows and Unhide Rows for the Hide Columns and Unhide Columns instructions.)

Create and apply a template

A **template** is a predesigned, preformatted Office file that contains default text formats, themes, placeholder text, headers and footers, and graphics that you can replace with your own information for hundreds of purposes, including budgets, flyers, and resumes. Template files have a file extension of .xltx. You can create your own template to provide a model for creating a new workbook by saving a workbook with this extension. To use a template, you apply it, which means you create a workbook based on the template. A workbook based on a template has the same content, formulas, and formatting defined in the template, but is saved in the standard workbook format, .xlsx. The template file itself remains unchanged. To save a file as a template, click the File tab, click Save As, click This PC if necessary, click More options, click the Save as type arrow, click Excel Template in the list of file types, as shown

FIGURE 2-13: Save menu file types

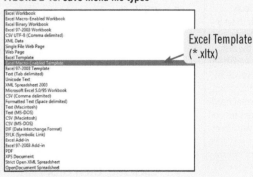

Excel Template (*.xltx)

in **FIGURE 2-13**, type a name for the new template in the File name box (the default save location is the Custom Office Templates folder), then click Save.

Apply Colors, Borders, and Documentation

Learning
Outcomes
• Change text and
  fill color
• Apply a border to
  a cell
• Add a header
  and footer to a
  worksheet

You have seen how you can use cell styles to add predesigned formatting, including colors and borders to a worksheet. If a cell style doesn't capture the formatting you need for a worksheet, you can add this formatting individually. Color options are based on the worksheet theme. A **theme** is a predefined, coordinated set of colors, fonts, graphical effects, and other formats that can be applied to a spreadsheet to give it a consistent, professional look. In Excel, applying a theme to one sheet applies it to all other sheets in that workbook. You can also add a **header** and/or a **footer** to provide useful text, date and other information, including a graphic, along the top or bottom of every page of a worksheet. A header prints above the top margin of the worksheet, and a footer prints below the bottom margin. **CASE** *You want to add a border and color to the reference numbers on the worksheet to make them stand out from the other information. You also want to add information about the worksheet in a header and footer.*

STEPS

QUICK TIP
Themes can be
changed by clicking
the Page Layout tab,
clicking the Themes
button, and select-
ing a Theme from
the Themes gallery.

1. **Select the range A4:A15, click the Fill Color arrow ⬙ ⌄ in the Font group, then click the Blue-Gray, Text 2, Lighter 80% color (second row, fourth column from the left)**
   The color is applied to the background (or fill) of this range. When you change fill or font color, the color on the Fill Color or Font Color button changes to the last color you selected.

2. **Click the Borders arrow ⊞ ⌄ in the Font group, review the Borders menu, as shown in FIGURE 2-14, then click Right Border**
   You can use the options at the bottom of the Borders menu to draw a border or to change a border line color or style.

3. **Click the Font Color arrow A ⌄ in the Font group, then click the Blue-Gray, Text 2 color (first row, fourth column from the left)**
   The new color is applied to the labels in the selected range. This color will make the first column reference numbers stand out.

QUICK TIP
You can use the set-
tings in the Options
group on the Header
& Footer Tools
Design tab to set a
different header or
footer for the first
page of a worksheet.
You can also use an
option in this group
to set different head-
ers or footers for odd
and even worksheet
pages.

4. **Click the Insert tab, click the Text button, then click the Header & Footer button**
   The header is divided into three sections, as shown in FIGURE 2-15, where you can enter or edit text. The Header & Footer Tools Design tab includes elements and options for customizing the header or footer.

5. **Click the Sheet Name button in the Header & Footer Elements group on the Header & Footer Tools Design tab**
   The & [Tab] code is added, which will display the current sheet name in this location. Using codes instead of manually typing the information ensures this information is always up to date.

6. **Click the Go to Footer button in the Navigation group, enter your name in the center footer section, click any cell on the worksheet, click the Normal button ▦ in the status bar, then press CTRL+HOME**
   The header and footer are only visible in Page Layout view and Print Preview.

7. **Click File, then click Print**
   Your header and footer will provide useful information to others viewing the worksheet.

8. **Click the Back button ⊖ to return to your worksheet, then save your work**

FIGURE 2-14: Borders menu

Borders menu

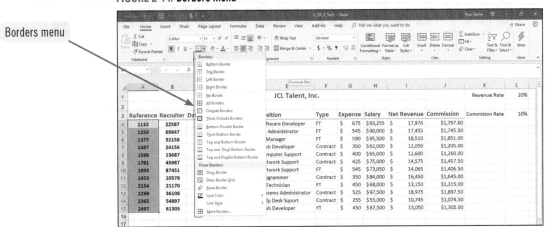

FIGURE 2-15: Header & Footer Tools Design tab

Go To Footer button

Options for header

Three sections
of header

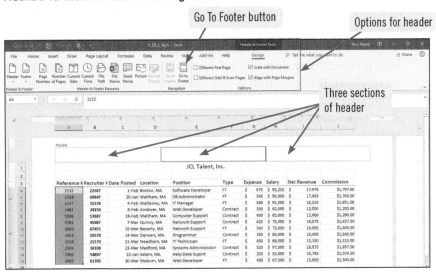

Checking worksheet accessibility

Part of successfully formatting your worksheets includes checking to see if any format presents accessibility problems. **Accessibility** is the quality of removing barriers that may prevent individuals with disabilities from interacting with data or an app. You can check for accessibility issues by clicking File, clicking the Check for Issues arrow in the Info window, then clicking Check Accessibility. The Accessibility Checker pane opens and displays an Inspection Results Warnings listing is displayed, as shown in **FIGURE 2-16**. You can click the warnings to see additional information below the Warnings list and directions on how to fix the issue.

FIGURE 2-16: Accessibility Checker pane

Warnings

Excel

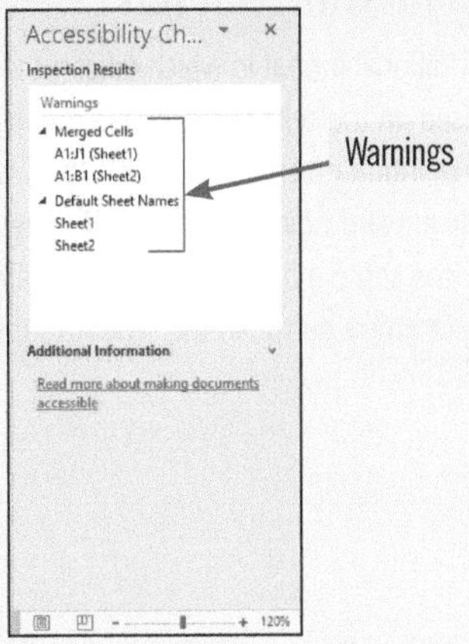

Apply Conditional Formatting

Learning
Outcomes
• Create a Data Bars rule
• Create a Highlight Cells rule

So far, you've used formatting to change the appearance of different types of data, but you can also use **conditional formatting**, special formatting that is applied if values meet specified criteria. **CASE** *Cheri is concerned about hiring expenses exceeding the yearly budget. You decide to use conditional formatting to highlight certain trends and patterns in the data so that it's easy to compare net revenue and spot the highest expenses.*

STEPS

1. **Select the range I4:I15, click the** Conditional Formatting button **in the Styles group on the Home tab, point to** Data Bars, **then click** Blue Data Bar **under Gradient Fill (first row, first column)**

   Data bars are colored horizontal bars that visually illustrate differences between values in a range of cells.

2. **Select the range G4:G15, click the** Quick Analysis button ▣ **that opens next to the selection, then click the** Greater Than button **on the Formatting tab**

   The Greater Than dialog box opens, displaying an input box you can use to define the condition and a default format (Light Red Fill with Dark Red Text) selected for cells that meet that condition. You can define the condition using the input box and assigning the formatting you want to use for cells that meet that condition. The Quick Analysis tool offers a powerful but limited number of options. To set more conditions, you can click the Highlight Cells Rules option on the Conditional Formatting menu instead. For example, you can create a rule for values that are between two amounts. Values used in input boxes for a condition can be constants, formulas, cell references, or dates.

3. **Type** 500 **in the Format cells that are GREATER THAN box, click the** with list arrow, **click** Light Red Fill, **compare your settings to** FIGURE 2-17, **then click** OK

   All cells with values greater than $500 in column G appear with a light red fill.

4. **Click cell** G4, **type** 499, **then press** ENTER

   Because of the rule you created, the appearance of cell G4 changes because the new value no longer meets the condition you set. Compare your results to FIGURE 2-18.

5. **Press** CTRL+HOME, **then save your work**

Formatting data with icon sets

Icon sets are a conditional format in which different icons are displayed in a cell based on the cell's value. In one group of cells, for example, upward-pointing green arrows might represent the highest values, while downward-pointing red arrows represent the lower values. To add an icon set to a data range, select a data range, click the Conditional Formatting button in the Styles group, point to Icon Sets, then click an icon set. You can customize the values that are used as thresholds for color scales and icon sets by clicking the Conditional Formatting button in the Styles group, clicking Manage Rules, clicking the rule in the Conditional Formatting Rules Manager dialog box, clicking Edit Rule, entering new values, clicking OK, clicking Apply, then clicking OK to close the dialog box.

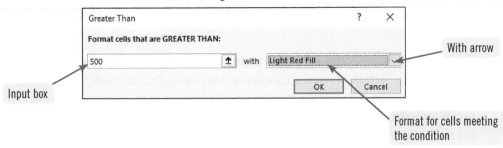

FIGURE 2-17: Greater Than dialog box

Input box

With arrow

Format for cells meeting the condition

FIGURE 2-18: Worksheet with conditional formatting

	A	B	C	D	E	F	G	H	I	J	K	L
1					JCL Talent, Inc.						Revenue Rate	20%
2												
3	Reference	Recruiter	Date Posted	Location	Position	Type	Expense	Salary	Net Revenue	Commission	Commision Rate	10%
4	1132	22587	1-Feb	Boston, MA	Software Developer	FT	$ 499	$93,255	$ 18,152	$1,815.20		
5	1254	69847	20-Jan	Waltham, MA	DB Administrator	FT	$ 545	$90,000	$ 17,455	$1,745.50		
6	1377	32158	4-Feb	Wellesley, MA	IT Manager	FT	$ 590	$95,500	$ 18,510	$1,851.00		
7	1487	24156	8-Feb	Andover, MA	Web Developer	Contract	$ 350	$62,000	$ 12,050	$1,205.00		
8	1598	13687	18-Feb	Waltham, MA	Computer Support	Contract	$ 400	$65,000	$ 12,600	$1,260.00		
9	1781	45987	7-Mar	Quincy, MA	Network Support	Contract	$ 425	$75,000	$ 14,575	$1,457.50		
10	1893	87451	10-Mar	Beverly, MA	Network Support	FT	$ 545	$73,050	$ 14,065	$1,406.50		
11	1953	10578	14-Mar	Danvers, MA	Programmer	Contract	$ 350	$84,000	$ 16,450	$1,645.00		
12	2154	21170	21-Mar	Needham, MA	IT Technician	FT	$ 450	$68,000	$ 13,150	$1,315.00		
13	2269	36108	23-Mar	Medford, MA	Systems Administrator	Contract	$ 525	$97,500	$ 18,975	$1,897.50		
14	2365	54897	22-Jan	Salem, MA	Help Desk Suport	Contract	$ 255	$55,000	$ 10,745	$1,074.50		
15	2497	61305	30-Mar	Woburn, MA	Web Developer	FT	$ 450	$67,500	$ 13,050	$1,305.00		
16												

Managing conditional formatting rules

If you create a conditional formatting rule and then want to change a condition, you don't need to create a new rule; instead, you can edit the rule using the Rules Manager. Click the Conditional Formatting button in the Styles group, then click Manage Rules. The Conditional Formatting Rules Manager dialog box opens, as shown in FIGURE 2-19, listing any rules you have set. Use the Show Formatting rules for arrow to see rules for other parts of a worksheet or for other sheets in the workbook. Select the rule you want to edit, click Edit Rule, then modify the settings in the Edit the Rule Description area in the Edit Formatting Rule dialog box. To change the formatting for a rule, click the Format button in the Edit the Rule Description area, select the formatting styles you want the cells to have, then click OK three times to close the Format Cells dialog box, the Edit Formatting Rule dialog box, and the Conditional Formatting Rules Manager dialog box. To delete a rule, select the

FIGURE 2-19: Conditional Formatting Rules Manager dialog box

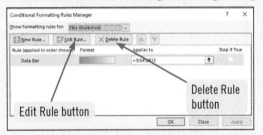

Edit Rule button

Delete Rule button

rule in the Conditional Formatting Rules Manager dialog box, then click the Delete Rule button. You can quickly clear conditional formatting rules by clicking the Conditional Formatting button in the Styles group, pointing to Clear Rules, then clicking Clear Rules from Selected Cells or Clear Rules from Entire Worksheet.

Rename and Move a Worksheet

Learning Outcomes
- Rename a sheet
- Apply color to a sheet tab
- Reorder sheets in a workbook

By default, an Excel workbook initially contains one worksheet named Sheet1, although you can add sheets anytime. Each sheet name appears on a sheet tab at the bottom of the worksheet. To move from sheet to sheet, you can click any sheet tab at the bottom of the worksheet window. The **sheet tab scrolling buttons** let you navigate to additional sheet tabs when available; they are located to the left of the sheet tabs and are useful when a workbook contains too many sheet tabs to display at once. To make a workbook more accessible, you can rename worksheets with descriptive names. Worksheets are easier to identify if you add color to the tabs. You can also organize worksheets in a logical order. **CASE** *In the current worksheet, Sheet1 contains detailed information about technical job postings in the Boston office. Sheet2 contains commission information, and Sheet3 contains no data. You want to rename these sheets to reflect their contents. You also want to add color to a sheet tab to easily distinguish one from the other and change their order.*

STEPS

1. **Click the Sheet2 sheet tab**

   Sheet2 becomes active, appearing in front of the Sheet1 tab; this worksheet contains the commission information. See **FIGURE 2-20**.

2. **Click the Sheet1 tab**

   Sheet1, which contains the detailed job posting data, becomes active again.

QUICK TIP

If a workbook contains more sheet tabs than are visible, you can navigate between sheets by using the tab scrolling buttons to the left of the sheet tabs: the Previous Worksheet button ◀ and the Next Worksheet button ▶.

3. **Double-click the Sheet2 tab, type Commission, then press ENTER**

   The new name for Sheet2 automatically replaces the default name on the tab. Worksheet names can have up to 31 characters, including spaces and punctuation.

4. **Right-click the Commission tab, point to Tab Color on the shortcut menu, then click the Blue, Accent 5, Darker 25% color (fifth row, second column from the right), as shown in FIGURE 2-21**

5. **Right-click the Sheet1 tab, click Rename on the shortcut menu, type Boston Tech, then press ENTER**

   Notice that the color of the Commission tab changes depending on whether it is the active tab; when the Boston Tech tab is active, the color of the Commission tab changes to the blue tab color you selected. You decide to rearrange the order of the sheets so that the Commissions tab is to the right of the Sheet3 tab.

6. **Click the Commissions tab, hold down the mouse button, drag it to the right of the Sheet3 tab, as shown in FIGURE 2-22, then release the mouse button**

   As you drag, the pointer changes to ▯⃔, the sheet relocation pointer, and a small black triangle just above the tabs shows the position where the moved sheet will be when you release the mouse button. The last sheet in the workbook is now the Commission sheet. See **FIGURE 2-23**. You can move multiple sheets by pressing and holding SHIFT while clicking the sheets you want to move, then dragging the sheets to their new location.

QUICK TIP

To insert a worksheet, click the New sheet button ⊕ to the right of the sheet tabs.

7. **Right-click the Sheet3 tab, click Delete on the shortcut menu, press CTRL+HOME, then save your work**

   The sheet is deleted.

FIGURE 2-20: Sheet tabs in workbook

Sheet2 tab

Sheet1 tab

Sheet3 tab

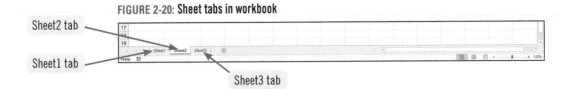

FIGURE 2-21: Tab Color palette

Blue, Accent 5,
Darker 25%

Sheet2
renamed

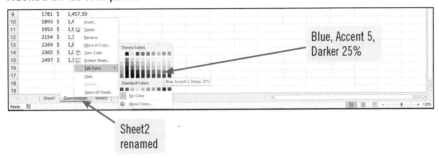

FIGURE 2-22: Moving the Commission sheet

Sheet relocation
pointer

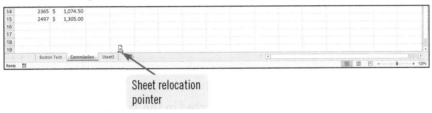

FIGURE 2-23: Reordered sheets

Commission sheet
is the last sheet

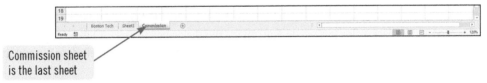

Copying, adding, and deleting worksheets

There are times when you may want to copy a worksheet. For example, a workbook might contain a sheet with Quarter 1 expenses, and you want to use that sheet as the basis for a sheet containing Quarter 2 expenses. To copy a sheet within the same workbook, press and hold CTRL, drag the sheet tab to the desired tab location, release the mouse button, then release CTRL. A duplicate sheet appears with the same name as the copied sheet followed by "(2)" indicating that it is a copy. You can then rename the sheet to a more meaningful name. To copy a sheet to a different workbook, both the source and destination workbooks must be open. Select the sheet to copy or move, right-click the sheet tab, click Move or Copy in the shortcut menu, then

complete the information in the Move or Copy dialog box. Be sure to click the Create a copy check box if you want to copy rather than move the worksheet. Carefully check your calculation results whenever you move or copy a worksheet. You can add multiple worksheets quickly by pressing and holding SHIFT, clicking the number of existing worksheet tabs that correspond with the number of sheets you want to add, clicking the Insert arrow in the Cells group on the Home tab, then clicking Insert Sheet. You can delete multiple worksheets from a workbook by clicking the Home tab on the ribbon, pressing and holding SHIFT, clicking the sheet tabs of the worksheets you want to delete, clicking the Delete arrow in the Cells group, then clicking Delete Sheet.

Check Spelling

Excel includes a spell checker to help you ensure that the words in your worksheet are spelled correctly. The spell checker scans your worksheet, displays words it doesn't find in its built-in dictionary, and suggests replacements when they are available. To check all the sheets in a multiple-sheet workbook, you need to display each sheet individually and run the spell checker for each one. Because the built-in dictionary cannot possibly include all the words that anyone needs, you can add words to the dictionary, such as your company name, an acronym, or an unusual technical term. Once you add a word or term, the spell checker no longer considers that word misspelled. Any words you've added to the dictionary using Word, Access, or PowerPoint are also available in Excel. **CASE** ▸ *Before you share this workbook with Cheri, you want to check the spelling.*

STEPS

1. **Click the Boston Tech sheet tab, click the Review tab on the ribbon, then click the Spelling button in the Proofing group**

   The Spelling: English (United States) dialog box opens, as shown in **FIGURE 2-24**, with "Commision" selected as the first misspelled word on the worksheet, and with "Commission" selected in the Suggestions list as a possible replacement. For any word, you have the option to Ignore this case of the flagged word, Ignore All cases of the flagged word, Change the word to the selected suggestion, Change All instances of the flagged word to the selected suggestion, or Add to Dictionary to add the flagged word to the dictionary.

2. **Click Change**

   Next, the spell checker finds the word "Suport" and suggests "Support" as an alternative.

3. **Verify that the word "Support" is selected in the Suggestions list, then click Change**

   When no more incorrect words are found, Excel displays a message indicating that the spell check is complete.

4. **Click OK**

5. **Click the Home tab, click Find & Select in the Editing group, then click Replace**

   The Find and Replace dialog box opens. You can use this dialog box to replace a word or phrase. It might be a misspelling of a proper name that the spell checker didn't recognize as misspelled, or it could simply be a term that you want to change throughout the worksheet.

6. **Type Contract in the Find what text box, press TAB, then type Temp in the Replace with text box**

   Compare your dialog box to **FIGURE 2-25**.

7. **Click Replace All, click OK to close the Microsoft Excel dialog box, then click Close to close the Find and Replace dialog box**

   Excel made six replacements, changing each instance of "Contract" on the worksheet to "Temp."

8. **Click the File tab, click Print on the navigation bar, click the Custom Scaling setting in the Settings section on the Print tab, then click Fit Sheet on One Page**

9. **sam ↑ Click the Back button ⬅ to return to your worksheet, save your work, submit it to your instructor as directed, close the workbook, then close Excel**

   The completed worksheet is shown in **FIGURE 2-26**.

Translating text

You can translate text in a worksheet by clicking the Review tab, clicking the Translate button in the Language group, then, if necessary, clicking Turn on when asked if you want to use intelligent services. The Translator pane opens and allows you to select the From language and the To language from menus of world languages. The translated text appears in the To language box.

FIGURE 2-24: Spelling: English (United States) dialog box

FIGURE 2-24: Spelling: English (United States) dialog box

Misspelled word

Click to ignore all occurrences of misspelled word

Suggested replacements for misspelled word

Click to add word to dictionary

FIGURE 2-25: Find and Replace dialog box

FIGURE 2-26: Completed worksheet

JCL Talent, Inc.

Revenue Rate 20%

Commission Rate 10%

Reference #	Recruiter #	Date Posted	Location	Position	Type	Expense	Salary	Net Revenue	Commission
1132	22587	1-Feb	Boston, MA	Software Developer	FT	$ 499	$ 93,255	$ 18,152	$1,815.20
1254	69847	20-Jan	Waltham, MA	DB Administrator	FT	$ 545	$ 90,000	$ 17,455	$1,745.50
1377	32158	4-Feb	Wellesley, MA	IT Manager	FT	$ 590	$ 95,500	$ 18,510	$1,851.00
1487	24156	8-Feb	Andover, MA	Web Developer	Temp	$ 350	$ 62,000	$ 12,050	$1,205.00
1598	13687	18-Feb	Waltham, MA	Computer Support	Temp	$ 400	$ 65,000	$ 12,600	$1,260.00
1781	45987	7-Mar	Quincy, MA	Network Support	Temp	$ 425	$ 75,000	$ 14,575	$1,457.50
1893	87451	10-Mar	Beverly, MA	Network Support	FT	$ 545	$ 73,050	$ 14,065	$1,406.50
1953	10578	14-Mar	Danvers, MA	Programmer	Temp	$ 350	$ 84,000	$ 16,450	$1,645.00
2154	21170	21-Mar	Needham, MA	IT Technician	FT	$ 450	$ 68,000	$ 13,150	$1,315.00
2269	36108	23-Mar	Medford, MA	Systems Administrator	Temp	$ 525	$ 97,500	$ 18,975	$1,897.50
2365	54897	22-Jan	Salem, MA	Help Desk Support	Temp	$ 255	$ 55,000	$ 10,745	$1,074.50
2497	61305	30-Mar	Woburn, MA	Web Developer	FT	$ 450	$ 67,500	$ 13,050	$1,305.00

Using Find & Select features

You can navigate to a specific place in a workbook by clicking the Find & Select button in the Editing group on the Home tab, clicking Go To, typing a cell address, then clicking OK. Clicking the Find & Select button also allows you to quickly go to comments, formulas, constants, data validation, and conditional formatting in a worksheet. You can use the Go to Special dialog box to navigate to cells with special elements such as different types of formulas or objects. Some Go to Special commands also appear on the Find & Select menu. Using this menu, you can also change the mouse pointer shape to the Select Objects pointer so you can quickly select drawing objects when necessary. To return to the standard Excel pointer, press ESC.

Practice

Skills Review

1. Format values.

    a. Start Excel, open IL_EX_2-2.xlsx from the location where you store your Data Files, then save it as **IL_EX_2_Investments**.

    b. Format the range B3:B7 using the Accounting number format.

    c. Change the format of the date in cell B9 so it appears as 18-Jun.

    d. Increase the number of decimals in cell D1 to 1, using a button in the Number group on the Home tab.

    e. Save your work.

2. Change font and font size.

    a. Select the range A3:A7.

    b. Change the font of the selection to Calibri.

    c. Increase the font size of the selection to 11 point.

    d. Increase the font size of the label in cell A1 to 11 point.

    e. Save your changes.

3. Change font styles and alignment.

    a. Apply the Heading 2 cell style to cell A1.

    b. Use the Merge & Center button to center the label in cell A1 over columns A and B.

    c. Apply the italic and bold font formats to the label in cell C1.

    d. Use the Format Painter to copy the format in cell C1 to the label in cell A9.

    e. Change the alignment of cell B2 to Align Right using a button in the Alignment group on the Home tab.

    f. Save your changes.

4. Adjust column width.

    a. Resize column C to a width of 21.00 characters.

    b. Use the AutoFit feature to automatically resize both columns A and B at the same time.

    c. Change the text in cell B2 to **Total Managed Assets**.

    d. Adjust the width of column B to display all of the content in cell B2.

    e. Save your changes.

5. Insert and delete rows and columns.

    a. Use the Insert dialog box to insert a new row between rows 1 and 2.

    b. Use a column heading button to insert a new column between columns B and C.

    c. Type **Fee** in cell C3 and center the label in the cell.

    d. Create a formula in cell C4 that calculates the fee for the Boston office by multiplying the total managed assets in cell B4 by the annual fee percentage in cell E1. (*Hint*: Make sure you use the correct type of cell references in the formula.)

    e. Copy the formula in cell C4 to the range C5:C8.

    f. Use a row heading button to delete the Philadelphia row from the worksheet.

    g. Save your changes.

6. Apply colors, borders, and documentation.

    a. Add an outside border around the range A3:C7.

    b. Apply the Green, Accent 6, Lighter 80% fill color (second row, last column) to the range D1:E1.

    c. Change the color of the font in the range A9:B9 to Green, Accent 6, Darker 50% (last row, last column under Theme Colors).

    d. Add a header in the center section of the worksheet that contains the sheet name.

Skills Review (continued)

e. Enter your name in the center section of the worksheet footer.

f. Save your changes.

7. **Apply conditional formatting.**

a. Select the range C4:C7, then create a Highlight Cells rule that changes cell contents to green fill with dark green text if the value is greater than 50000.

b. Select the range B4:B7, then apply Gradient Fill green data bars. (*Hint*: Click Green Data Bar in the Gradient Fill section.)

c. Open the Conditional Formatting Rules Manager dialog box and view the conditional formatting rules for the worksheet. (*Hint*: Click Manage Rules on the Conditional Formatting menu, then click the Show formatting rules for arrow.)

d. Review the rules for the worksheet, making sure your rules are correct, then close the dialog box.

e. Save your changes.

8. **Rename and move a worksheet.**

a. Rename the Sheet1 tab to **Active Management** and rename the Sheet2 tab to **Passive Management**.

b. Add a sheet to the workbook, then name the new sheet **Total Fees**.

c. Change the Active Management tab color to Green, Accent 6, Darker 50%.

d. Change the Passive Management tab color to Blue, Accent 5, Darker 50%.

e. Reorder the sheets so that the Total Fees sheet comes before (to the left of) the Active Management sheet.

f. Delete the Total Fees sheet.

g. Activate the Active Management sheet, then save your work.

9. **Check spelling.**

a. Move the cell pointer to cell A1.

b. Use the Find & Select feature to replace the word "Boston" with **New York**.

c. Use the Spelling tool to check the spelling on the worksheet and correct any spelling errors, using suggestions as appropriate.

d. Save your changes, then compare your Active Management sheet to FIGURE 2-27.

e. Preview the Active Management sheet in Backstage view, submit your work to your instructor as directed, then close the workbook and close Excel.

FIGURE 2-27

	A	B	C	D	E	F
1	CGS Investments			*Annual Fee Percentage*	1.1%	
2						
3	Office	Total Managed Assets	Fee			
4	New York	$ 5,426,324.35	$ 59,689.57			
5	Los Angeles	$ 4,895,714.77	$ 53,852.86			
6	Cincinnati	$ 3,415,981.19	$ 37,575.79			
7	Indianapolis	$ 4,213,257.23	$ 46,345.83			
8						
9	*Report date:*	18-Jun				
10						

Independent Challenge 1

As an accountant for Riverwalk medical clinic, you have been asked to review the expenses for the emergency room. You've organized the data in an Excel workbook, and now you want to format the data to improve its readability and highlight trends in expenses.

a. Start Excel, open IL_EX_2-3.xlsx from the location where you store your Data Files, then save it as **IL_EX_2_Riverwalk**.

b. Format the values in the Total column in the Accounting number format with two decimal places.

c. Format the values in the % of Total column as Percent format with two decimal places.

d. Format the values in the Inv. Date column with the Date format 14-Mar.

Independent Challenge 1 (continued)

e. Apply bold formatting to the column labels and increase the font size of the labels to 12.

f. Italicize the inventory Type items in column A.

g. Change the font of the Sales Tax label in cell K1 to Calibri.

h. Apply the Title cell style to cell A1.

i. Delete column I, then delete row 13.

j. Merge and center the title in cell A1 over columns A1:I1.

k. Resize column widths as necessary, using AutoFit or by dragging, so that all columns are wide enough to display the data and labels.

l. Use the Format Painter to copy the date format in the Inv. Date column to the values in the Inv. Due column.

m. Change the fill color of the sales tax information in the range J1:K1 to the Light Turquoise, Background 2 color (first row, third column from the left).

n. Change the font color of the sales tax information in the range J1:K1 to the Dark Teal, Text 2 color (first row, fourth column from the left).

o. Add a bottom border to the column labels.

p. Use conditional formatting to apply blue gradient data bars to the Total column data. Do not include the total in cell H38 at the bottom of the column.

q. Add the 3 Arrows (Colored) (first set in the Directional group) icon set to the Quantity column to illustrate the relative differences between quantities. Do not include the total in cell E38 at the bottom of the column in this format.

r. Rename Sheet3 to **Budget** and rename Sheet1 to **Actual**. Change the color of the Budget sheet to Red in the Standard colors. Change the color of the Actual sheet to Purple in the Standard colors.

s. Move Sheet2 to the right of the Budget sheet.

t. Activate the Actual Sheet and spell check the worksheet. Correct any spelling errors.

u. Using Find and Select, replace all instances of Maxi on the worksheet with ACE.

v. Delete Sheet2, enter your name in the center section of the Actual worksheet header, enter the sheet name in the center section of the worksheet footer, then save the file.

w. Preview the Actual worksheet in Backstage view. Compare your worksheet to **FIGURE 2-28**.

x. Submit your work to your instructor as directed, close the workbook, then close Excel.

FIGURE 2-28

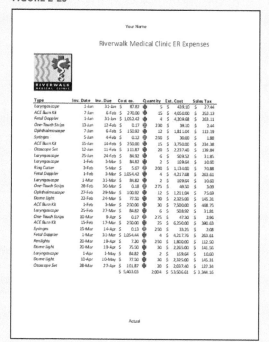

Formatting a Worksheet

Independent Challenge 2

You are assisting the head of business operations at First Financial Services. You have been asked to format a worksheet showing the first-quarter business services for the company's five branches. As part of this effort, you want to illustrate service trends among the branches.

a. Start Excel, open IL_EX_2-4.xlsx from the location where you store your Data Files, then save it as **IL_EX_2_FinancialServices**.

b. Enter a formula in cell B8 for the Main total, then copy the formula to the range C8:F8.

c. Enter a formula in cell G3 for the Credit card processing total, then copy the formula to the range G4:G8.

d. Apply the Title cell style to cell A1, apply the Heading 4 cell style to the column headings in row 2, and apply the Total cell style to the range A8:G8.

e. Merge and center the title in cell A1 across the range A1:G1.

f. Format the range B3:G8 using the Accounting number format. AutoFit the widths of all columns and format the range with no decimal places.

g. Format the date in cell B9 using the first 14-Mar-12 date format.

h. Rotate the label in cell A2 up by 45 degrees. Copy this rotated format to the other column headings.

i. Format the range A9:B9 with a Blue-Gray, Text 2, Lighter 80% (second row, fourth column from the left) fill.

j. Format the range A9:B9 with a Blue, Accent 1, Darker 50% (last row, fifth column from the left, under Theme Colors) font color.

k. Create a conditional format in the range G3:G8 so that entries less than 25,000,000 appear in light red fill with dark red text.

l. Create a conditional format in the range B8:F8 to add the 3 Stars Ratings icon set. Widen the columns as necessary to fully display the data and formatting.

m. Use the Spelling tool to check spelling in the sheet.

n. Rename Sheet1 to **First Quarter**. Copy the First Quarter sheet and rename the copied sheet **Second Quarter**. Move the Second Quarter sheet if necessary so it is to the right of the First Quarter sheet.

o. On the Second Quarter sheet, delete the data in the range B3:F7 and delete the date in cell B9.

p. Activate the First Quarter sheet. Compare your worksheet to FIGURE 2-29.

q. Enter your name in the center header section, change the worksheet orientation to landscape, then save your work.

r. Preview the worksheet, make any final changes you think are necessary, then submit your work to your instructor as directed.

s. Close the workbook, then close Excel.

FIGURE 2-29

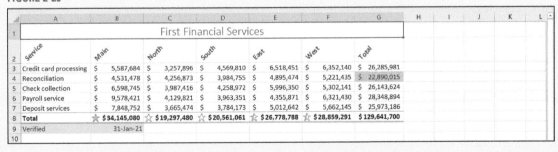

	A	B	C	D	E	F	G	H	I	J	K	L
1				First Financial Services								
2	Service	Main	North	South	East	West	Total					
3	Credit card processing	$ 5,587,684	$ 3,257,896	$ 4,569,810	$ 6,518,451	$ 6,352,140	$ 26,285,981					
4	Reconciliation	$ 4,531,478	$ 4,256,873	$ 3,984,755	$ 4,895,474	$ 5,221,435	$ 22,890,015					
5	Check collection	$ 6,598,745	$ 3,987,416	$ 4,258,972	$ 5,996,350	$ 5,302,141	$ 26,143,624					
6	Payroll service	$ 9,578,421	$ 4,129,821	$ 3,963,351	$ 4,355,871	$ 6,321,430	$ 28,348,894					
7	Deposit services	$ 7,848,752	$ 3,665,474	$ 3,784,173	$ 5,012,642	$ 5,662,145	$ 25,973,186					
8	Total	☆ $ 34,145,080	☆ $ 19,297,480	☆ $ 20,561,061	☆ $ 26,778,788	☆ $ 28,859,291	$ 129,641,700					
9	Verified	31-Jan-21										
10												

Visual Workshop

Open IL_EX_2-5.xlsx from the location where you store your Data Files, then save it as **IL_EX_2_EngineeringServices**. Use the skills you learned in this module to format the worksheet so it looks like the one shown in FIGURE 2-30. (Note that cell A1 is selected in the figure.) Use the blue gradient fill for the data bars in the Total column. Use the Title cell style for the company name in cell A1, the Heading 1 cell style for the column labels in row 2, and the Total cell style for the total values in the last row. The font color for the service packages listed in column A is Dark Blue in the standard colors. (*Hint:* A row has been deleted from the worksheet.) Enter your name in the upper-left section of the header, check the spelling on the worksheet, save your changes, then submit your work to your instructor as directed.

FIGURE 2-30

	A	B	C	D	E	F	G	H	I	J	K	L
1	TCR Engineering Services											
2	Service Packages	January	February	March	April	May	June	Total				
3	On site support	$ 758,840	$ 447,891	$ 332,171	$ 183,658	$ 396,556	$ 483,847	$ 2,602,963				
4	Outage Fulfillment	$ 410,123	$ 464,399	$ 708,911	$ 673,112	$ 673,259	$ 167,453	$ 3,097,257				
5	Data Center Services	$ 694,366	$ 462,919	$ 629,686	$ 533,313	$ 755,231	$ 518,836	$ 3,594,351				
6	Mining Services	$ 670,468	$ 648,633	$ 377,528	$ 145,195	$ 305,019	$ 577,551	$ 2,724,394				
7	Total	$ 2,533,797	$ 2,023,842	$ 2,048,296	$ 1,535,278	$ 2,130,065	$ 1,747,687	$ 12,018,965				
8												

Formatting a Worksheet

Analyzing Data Using Formulas

CASE Ellie Schwartz, the vice president of Finance at JCL, wants to know how North American revenues have performed compared to last year and relative to projected targets. She asks you to prepare a worksheet that summarizes and analyzes this revenue data.

Module Objectives

After completing this module, you will be able to:

- Enter a formula using the Quick Analysis tool
- Build a logical formula with the IF function
- Build a logical formula with the AND function
- Round a value with a function
- Build a statistical formula with the COUNTA function
- Enter a date function
- Work with equation tools
- Control worksheet calculations

Files You Will Need

IL_EX_3-1.xlsx   IL_EX_3-4.xlsx
IL_EX_3-2.xlsx   IL_EX_3-5.xlsx
IL_EX_3-3.xlsx

**Learning
Outcomes**
- Create a formula using the Quick Analysis tool
- Create a formula to find a percentage increase

Enter a Formula Using the Quick Analysis Tool

So far, you have used the AutoSum button on the ribbon to quickly add simple formulas that sum and average selected data. You can also add formulas using the Quick Analysis tool, which opens when you select a range of cells. This tool allows you to quickly format, chart, or analyze data by calculating sums, averages, and other selected totals. **CASE** ▶ *To help Ellie evaluate revenues at JCL, you want to calculate yearly revenue totals for each North American office and compare the yearly performance of each office to the previous year.*

STEPS

1. **sam** ↓ **Start Excel, open IL_EX_3-1.xlsx from the location where you store your Data Files, then save it as IL_EX_3_Revenue**

2. **Select the range B3:E12, click the Quick Analysis button** 🔲 **that appears below the selection, then click the Totals tab**
   The Totals tab in the Quick Analysis tool displays commonly used functions, as shown in **FIGURE 3-1**. This tab includes two Sum buttons, one that inserts the SUM function in a row beneath the selected range, and one that inserts the SUM function in the column to the right of the range.

   QUICK TIP
   Clicking the first AutoSum button enters totals in a row below a selected range.

3. **Click the Sum button displaying the gold column**
   The newly calculated totals display in the column to the right of the selected range, in cells F3:F12.

4. **Click cell H3, type =(, click cell F3, type -, click cell G3, then type)**
   This first part of the formula finds the difference in total revenue from the previous year to this year. You enclosed this operation in parentheses to make sure this difference is calculated first.

5. **Type /, then click cell G3**
   The second part of this formula divides the difference in revenue by the total revenue for the previous year, to calculate the increase or decrease.

6. **Click the Enter button** ✓ **on the formula bar**
   The result, .75405003, appears in cell H3. The column isn't wide enough to fully display this value but the number of decimal places will be adjusted in the next formatting step.

7. **Click the Percent Style button** 🔲 **in the Number group, then click the Increase Decimal button** 🔲 **in the Number group twice**
   The formatted percentage, 75.41%, appears in cell H3.

8. **Drag the fill handle from cell H3 to cell H12, then save your work**
   The percentage changes in annual revenue for each office appear in column H, as shown in **FIGURE 3-2**.

FIGURE 3-1: Quick Analysis tool

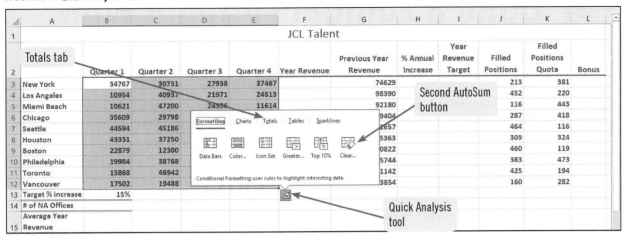

Totals tab

Second AutoSum button

Quick Analysis tool

	A	B	C	D	E	F	G	H	I	J	K	L
1						JCL Talent						
2		Quarter 1	Quarter 2	Quarter 3	Quarter 4	Year Revenue	Previous Year Revenue	% Annual Increase	Year Revenue Target	Filled Positions	Filled Positions Quota	Bonus
3	New York	34767	30731	27938	37467		74629			213	381	
4	Los Angeles	10954	40937	21971	24513		98390			452	220	
5	Miami Beach	10621	47200	24596	11614		92180			116	443	
6	Chicago	35609	29798				9404			287	418	
7	Seattle	44594	45186				1657			464	116	
8	Houston	43331	37250				5363			309	324	
9	Boston	22879	12300				0822			460	119	
10	Philadelphia	19984	38768				5744			383	473	
11	Toronto	15868	46942				1142			425	194	
12	Vancouver	17502	19488				3854			160	282	
13	Target % increase	15%										
14	# of NA Offices											
15	Average Year Revenue											

Formatting | Charts | Totals | Tables | Sparklines

Data Bars | Color... | Icon Set | Greater... | Top 10% | Clear...

Conditional Formatting uses rules to highlight interesting data.

FIGURE 3-2: Percentage changes

	A	B	C	D	E	F	G	H	I	J	K	L
1						JCL Talent						
2		Quarter 1	Quarter 2	Quarter 3	Quarter 4	Year Revenue	Previous Year Revenue	% Annual Increase	Year Revenue Target	Filled Positions	Filled Positions Quota	Bonus
3	New York	34767	30731	27938	37467	130903	74629	75.41%		213	381	
4	Los Angeles	10954	40937	21971	24513	98375	98390	-0.02%		452	220	
5	Miami Beach	10621	47200	24596	11614	94031	92180	2.01%		116	443	
6	Chicago	35609	29798	48737	44708	158852	119404	33.04%		287	418	
7	Seattle	44594	45186	46174	13921	149875	91657	63.52%		464	116	
8	Houston	43331	37250	19544	40013	140138	95363	46.95%		309	324	
9	Boston	22879	12300	16514	42119	93812	120822	-22.36%		460	119	
10	Philadelphia	19984	38768	11102	47482	117336	85744	36.84%		383	473	
11	Toronto	15868	46942	42394	16177	121381	91142	33.18%		425	194	
12	Vancouver	17502	19488	48411	36260	121661	113854	6.86%		160	282	
13	Target % increase	15%										
14	# of NA Offices											
15	Average Year Revenue											

% annual increases

Build a Logical Formula with the IF Function

Learning Outcomes
- Build a logical formula using the IF function
- Apply comparison operators in a logical test

You can build a formula in a worksheet using a **logical function** that returns a different value depending on whether the given condition is true or false. An **IF function** is a logical function that assigns a value to a cell based on a logical test. A **logical formula** makes calculations based on criteria that you create, called **stated conditions**. For example, you can build a formula to calculate bonuses based on a person's performance rating, where the stated condition is 5. If a person is rated a 5 on a scale of 1 to 5, he or she receives an additional 10% of his or her salary as a bonus; otherwise, there is no bonus. The IF function has three parts, including the **logical test**, which is the first part of the function. This test is a condition that can be answered with a true or false response. If the logical test is true, then the second part of the function is applied; if it is false, then the third part of the function is applied. When entering the logical test portion of an IF statement, you often use some combination of the comparison operators listed in TABLE 3-1.

CASE ▸ *Ellie asks you to calculate whether each office met or missed its revenue target for the year.*

STEPS

1. **Click cell I3, click the Formulas tab on the ribbon, click the Logical button in the Function Library group, then click IF**

   The Function Arguments dialog box opens, displaying three boxes for the three parts of a logical function: the Logical_test, which in this case tests if the annual increase is greater than or equal to the target increase; the Value_if_true box, which tells what to do if the test results are true; and the Value_if_false box, which tells what to do if the test results are false.

2. **With the insertion point in the Logical_test box click cell H3, type > =, click cell B13, press F4, then press TAB**

   The symbol (>) represents "greater than." B13 needs to be formatted as an absolute reference because it is a fixed value in a formula that will be copied into other cells. So far, the formula reads, "If the annual increase is greater than or equal to the target increase..."

3. **With the insertion point in the Value_if_true box type MET, then press TAB**

   This part of the function tells Excel to display the text MET if the annual increase equals or exceeds the target increase of 15%. Quotation marks are automatically added around the text you entered.

4. **Type MISSED in the Value_if_false box, then click OK**

   This part tells Excel to display the text MISSED if the results of the logical test are false—that is, if the increase does not equal or exceed the target. The function is complete, and the result, MET, appears in cell I3, as shown in FIGURE 3-3.

5. **Drag the fill handle to copy the formula in cell I3 into the range I4:I12**

   Compare your results with FIGURE 3-4. Most offices met their target increase but four offices did not.

6. **Save the workbook**

FIGURE 3-3: Worksheet with IF function

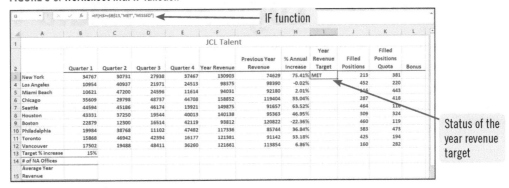

FIGURE 3-4: Worksheet showing yearly revenue status

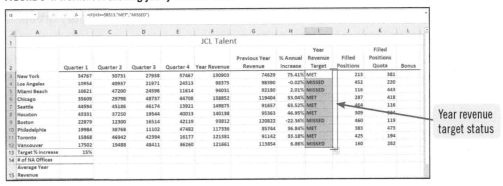

TABLE 3-1: Comparison operators

operator	meaning	operator	meaning
<	Less than	<=	Less than or equal to
>	Greater than	>=	Greater than or equal to
=	Equal to	<>	Not equal to

Nesting IF functions

You can nest IF functions to test several conditions in a formula. A nested IF function contains IF functions inside other IF functions to test these multiple conditions. To create a nested IF function, enter the second IF statement in the value_if_false argument of the first IF statement. For example, the nested statement =IF(H3<0%,"Warning",IF(H3<50%,"No Bonus","Bonus")) tests whether a warning should be issued based on the percentage increases for an office. Assuming the percentage increase of an office is in cell H3, the nested IF statement first checks to see if the increase was less than 0. If that first test is true, the text "Warning" will display. If the first test is false, a second test will be performed to check to see if the increase is less than 50%. If that second test is true (values are less than 50%), the text "No Bonus" will display. If that second test is false, the text "Bonus" will display.

Excel

Learning
Outcomes
• Build a logical
formula using the
AND function
• Apply logical tests

Build a Logical Formula with the AND Function

You can also build a logical function using the AND function. The AND function evaluates all of its arguments and returns, or displays, TRUE if every logical test in the formula is true. The AND function returns a value of FALSE if one or more of its logical tests is false. The AND function arguments can include text, numbers, or cell references. **CASE** *JCL awards bonuses to offices that meet targets for both annual revenue and filled positions. Now that you've determined which offices met their revenue goal, you need to see which offices are eligible for a bonus by meeting both this target and the filled positions target.*

STEPS

1. **Click cell L3, click the Logical button in the Function Library group, then click AND**

   The Function Arguments dialog box opens.

2. **With the insertion point in the Logical1 box, click cell J3, type >=, click cell K3, then press TAB**

   This part of the formula reads, "If the number of filled positions is greater than or equal to the filled positions quota…"

3. **With the insertion point in the Logical2 box, click cell I3, then type = "MET"**

   This part of the formula reads, "If the revenue goal was met…"

TROUBLE
If you get a formula error, check to be sure that you typed the quotation marks around MET.

4. **Click OK**

   The function is complete, and the result, FALSE, appears in cell L3, as shown in **FIGURE 3-5**, because both stated conditions were not met. Although the revenue target was met, the number of filled positions was not greater than or equal to the quota.

5. **Drag the fill handle to copy the formula in cell L3 into the range L4:L12**

   Compare your results with **FIGURE 3-6**.

QUICK TIP
You can place one function, such as an AND function, inside a formula containing another function, such as an IF function. For example, you could replace the formulas in cell I3 and L3 with one formula in L3 that reads =IF(AND(H3>=$B$13, J3>=K3), "TRUE", "FALSE").

6. **Enter your name in the center section of the footer, preview the worksheet, then save your work**

Using the OR and NOT logical functions

The OR logical function follows the same syntax as the AND function, but rather than returning TRUE if every argument is true, the OR function will return TRUE if any of its arguments are true. It will only return FALSE if all of its arguments are false. The NOT logical function reverses the value of its argument. For example, NOT(TRUE) reverses its argument of TRUE and returns FALSE. You might want to use this function in a worksheet to ensure that a cell is not equal to a particular value. See **TABLE 3-2** for examples of the AND, OR, and NOT functions.

FIGURE 3-5: Worksheet with AND function

FIGURE 3-5: Worksheet with AND function

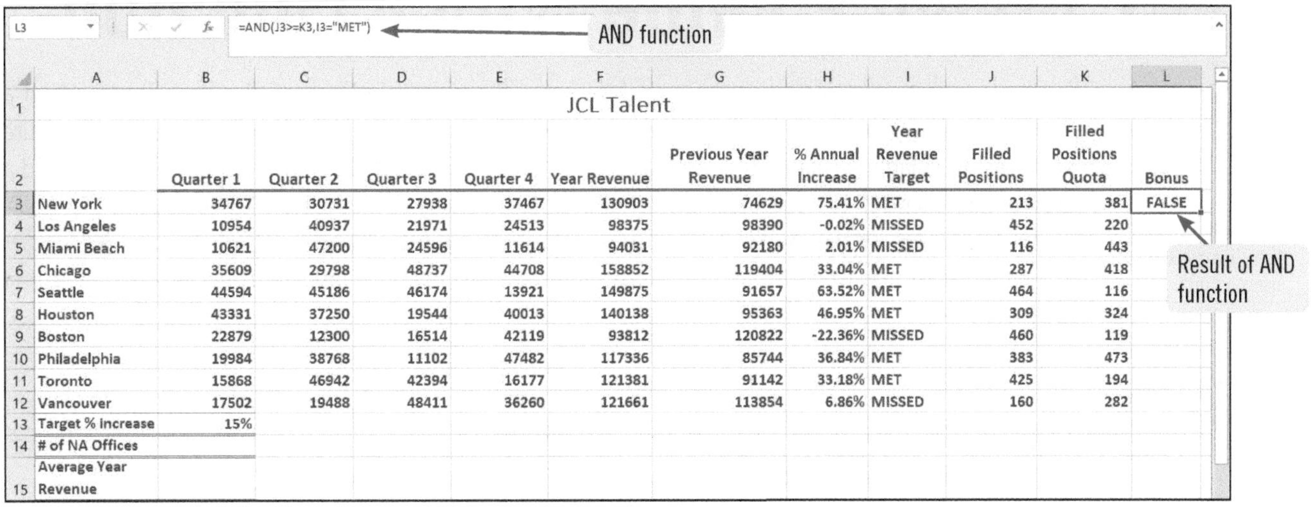

L3			f_x	=AND(J3>=K3,I3="MET")								AND function	

	A	B	C	D	E	F	G	H	I	J	K	L
1						JCL Talent						
2		Quarter 1	Quarter 2	Quarter 3	Quarter 4	Year Revenue	Previous Year Revenue	% Annual Increase	Year Revenue Target	Filled Positions	Filled Positions Quota	Bonus
3	New York	34767	30731	27938	37467	130903	74629	75.41%	MET	213	381	FALSE
4	Los Angeles	10954	40937	21971	24513	98375	98390	-0.02%	MISSED	452	220	
5	Miami Beach	10621	47200	24596	11614	94031	92180	2.01%	MISSED	116	443	
6	Chicago	35609	29798	48737	44708	158852	119404	33.04%	MET	287	418	
7	Seattle	44594	45186	46174	13921	149875	91657	63.52%	MET	464	116	
8	Houston	43331	37250	19544	40013	140138	95363	46.95%	MET	309	324	
9	Boston	22879	12300	16514	42119	93812	120822	-22.36%	MISSED	460	119	
10	Philadelphia	19984	38768	11102	47482	117336	85744	36.84%	MET	383	473	
11	Toronto	15868	46942	42394	16177	121381	91142	33.18%	MET	425	194	
12	Vancouver	17502	19488	48411	36260	121661	113854	6.86%	MISSED	160	282	
13	Target % increase	15%										
14	# of NA Offices											
15	Average Year Revenue											

Result of AND function

FIGURE 3-6: Worksheet with bonus status evaluated for all offices

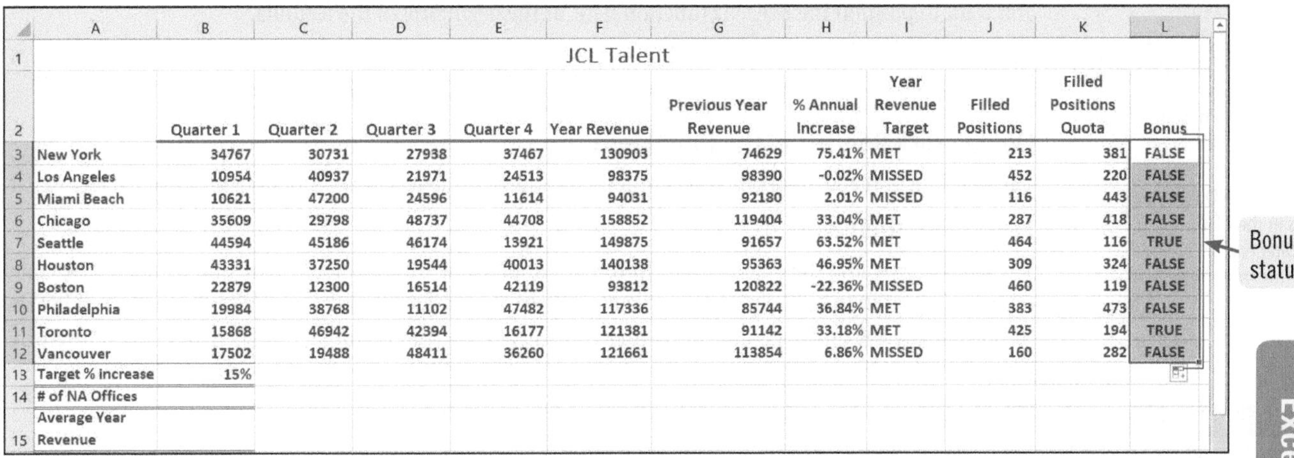

	A	B	C	D	E	F	G	H	I	J	K	L
1						JCL Talent						
2		Quarter 1	Quarter 2	Quarter 3	Quarter 4	Year Revenue	Previous Year Revenue	% Annual Increase	Year Revenue Target	Filled Positions	Filled Positions Quota	Bonus
3	New York	34767	30731	27938	37467	130903	74629	75.41%	MET	213	381	FALSE
4	Los Angeles	10954	40937	21971	24513	98375	98390	-0.02%	MISSED	452	220	FALSE
5	Miami Beach	10621	47200	24596	11614	94031	92180	2.01%	MISSED	116	443	FALSE
6	Chicago	35609	29798	48737	44708	158852	119404	33.04%	MET	287	418	FALSE
7	Seattle	44594	45186	46174	13921	149875	91657	63.52%	MET	464	116	TRUE
8	Houston	43331	37250	19544	40013	140138	95363	46.95%	MET	309	324	FALSE
9	Boston	22879	12300	16514	42119	93812	120822	-22.36%	MISSED	460	119	FALSE
10	Philadelphia	19984	38768	11102	47482	117336	85744	36.84%	MET	383	473	FALSE
11	Toronto	15868	46942	42394	16177	121381	91142	33.18%	MET	425	194	TRUE
12	Vancouver	17502	19488	48411	36260	121661	113854	6.86%	MISSED	160	282	FALSE
13	Target % increase	15%										
14	# of NA Offices											
15	Average Year Revenue											

Bonus status

TABLE 3-2: Examples of AND, OR, and NOT functions (cell A1=10, cell B1=20)

function	formula	result
AND	=AND(A1>5,B1>25)	FALSE
OR	=OR(A1>5,B1>25)	TRUE
NOT	=NOT(A1=0)	TRUE

Excel

Round a Value with a Function

You have used formatting to increase and decrease the decimal places of numbers displayed on a worksheet. In this case, only the formatting of these numbers changes. Their values, when used in future worksheet calculations, remain the same as they originally appeared on the worksheet. You can round a value or formula result to a specified number of decimal places by using the **ROUND function**; the resulting rounded value is then used instead of the original value in future worksheet calculations. **CASE** ▶

In your worksheet, you want to find the average yearly revenue and round that calculated value to the nearest integer.

STEPS

1. **Click cell B15, click the AutoSum arrow $\boxed{\Sigma \cdot}$, then click Average**

2. **Select the range F3:F12, then click the Enter button $\boxed{\checkmark}$ on the formula bar**

   The result, 122636.4, appears in cell B15.

3. **Click to the right of = in the formula bar**

   You want to position the ROUND function here, at the beginning of the formula.

4. **Type RO**

   Formula AutoComplete displays a list of functions beginning with RO beneath the formula bar.

5. **Double-click ROUND in the functions list**

   The new function and an opening parenthesis are added to the AVERAGE function, as shown in **FIGURE 3-7**.

6. **Press END, then type ,0)**

   The comma separates the arguments within the formula, and 0 indicates that you don't want any decimal places to appear in the calculated value. You may have also noticed that the parentheses at either end of the formula briefly became bold, indicating that you entered the correct number of open and closed parentheses so the formula is balanced.

7. **Click the Enter button $\boxed{\checkmark}$ on the formula bar**

8. **Compare your worksheet to FIGURE 3-8, then save your work**

FIGURE 3-7: ROUND function added to an existing function

ScreenTip indicates needed arguments

ROUND function and opening parenthesis inserted in formula

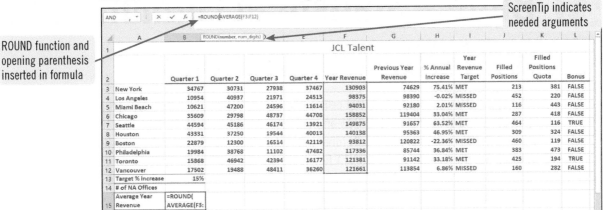

FIGURE 3-8: Rounded year average

Round function surrounds average formula

Calculated value with no decimals

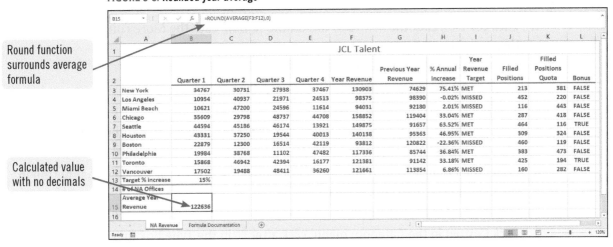

Using Excel rounding functions

You can use other rounding functions besides ROUND to fine-tune the rounding results you want to see. The **MROUND function** rounds a number to the nearest multiple of another number. The syntax is: MROUND(number, multiple). For example, MROUND(14,3) returns the value 15 because 15 is the nearest multiple of 3 to 14. The **ROUNDDOWN function** works like the ROUND function except that rather than rounding a number to the

next closest value, it always rounds down. The syntax is ROUNDDOWN(number, num_digits). For example, =ROUNDDOWN(15.778, 2) returns a value of 15.77 because this is the nearest two-digit number below 15.778. The **ROUNDUP function** works similarly but rounds a number up. The syntax is ROUNDUP(number, num_digits). For example, =ROUNDUP(15.778, 2) returns a value of 15.78.

Build a Statistical Formula with the COUNTA function

Learning Outcomes
- Insert a statistical function
- Build a function using the COUNTA function
- Create a number format

When you select a range, a count of cells in the range that are not blank appears in the status bar. For example, if you select the range A1:A5 and only cells A1, A4, and A5 contain data, the status bar displays "Count: 3." To count nonblank cells more precisely, or to incorporate these calculations in a worksheet, you can use the COUNT and COUNTA functions. The **COUNT function** tallies the number of cells in a range that contain numeric data, including numbers, dates, and formulas. The **COUNTA function** tallies how many cells in a specified range contain any entries (numbers, dates, or text). For example, the formula =COUNT(A1:A5) returns the number of cells in the range that contain numeric data, and the formula =COUNTA(A1:A5) returns the number of cells in the range that are not empty. **CASE** *In your worksheet, you want to calculate the number of offices in the North America region. You also want to format some worksheet values using a custom format, so that the data looks exactly the way you want.*

STEPS

1. **Click cell B14, click the** Formulas tab **on the ribbon, click the** More Functions button, **then point to** Statistical

   A gallery of statistical functions opens, as shown in FIGURE 3-9.

2. **Scroll down the list of functions if necessary, then click** COUNTA

   The Function Arguments dialog box opens.

3. **With the insertion point in the Value1 box select the range** A3:A12, **then click** OK

   The number of offices, 10, appears in cell B14.

4. **Select the range** H3:H12, **click the** Home tab **on the ribbon, click the** Format button **in the Cells group, then click** Format Cells

   Currently, the negative values in this range are difficult to distinguish from the positive values.

5. **Click** Custom **in the Category menu, click after % in the Type box, type** ;[Red](0.00%) **as shown in** FIGURE 3-10, **then click** OK

   The negative percentages in cells H4 and H9 now appear in red with parentheses.

6. **Select the range** B3:G12, **press and hold** CTRL, **then click cell** B15

   Holding CTRL allows you to select multiple ranges and cells.

7. **Click the** Accounting Number Format button $ **in the Number group, then click the** Decrease Decimal button **twice**

   Formatting these revenue figures makes them easier to read. Compare your worksheet to FIGURE 3-11.

Analyzing Data Using Formulas

FIGURE 3-9: Statistical functions

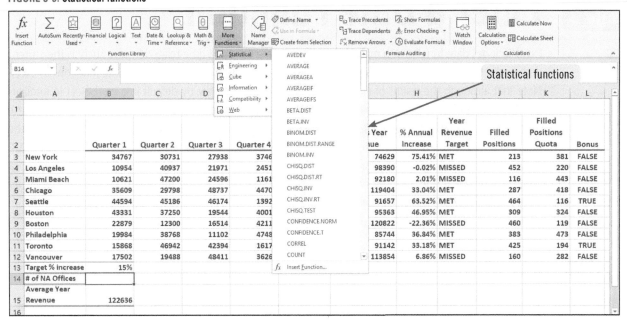

FIGURE 3-10: Custom number format

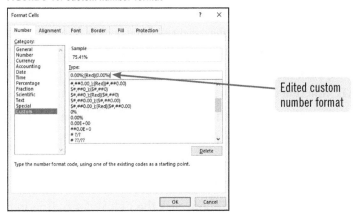

FIGURE 3-11: Formatted worksheet

	A	B	C	D	E	F	G	H	I	J	K	L
1						JCL Talent						
2		Quarter 1	Quarter 2	Quarter 3	Quarter 4	Year Revenue	Previous Year Revenue	% Annual Increase	Year Revenue Target	Filled Positions	Filled Positions Quota	Bonus
3	New York	$ 34,767	$ 30,731	$ 27,938	$ 37,467	$ 130,903	$ 74,629	75.41%	MET	213	381	FALSE
4	Los Angeles	$ 10,954	$ 40,937	$ 21,971	$ 24,513	$ 98,375	$ 98,390	(0.02%)	MISSED	452	220	FALSE
5	Miami Beach	$ 10,621	$ 47,200	$ 24,596	$ 11,614	$ 94,031	$ 92,180	2.01%	MISSED	116	443	FALSE
6	Chicago	$ 35,609	$ 29,798	$ 48,737	$ 44,708	$ 158,852	$ 119,404	33.04%	MET	287	418	FALSE
7	Seattle	$ 44,594	$ 45,186	$ 46,174	$ 13,921	$ 149,875	$ 91,657	63.52%	MET	464	116	TRUE
8	Houston	$ 43,331	$ 37,250	$ 19,544	$ 40,013	$ 140,138	$ 95,363	46.95%	MET	309	324	FALSE
9	Boston	$ 22,879	$ 12,300	$ 16,514	$ 42,119	$ 93,812	$ 120,822	(22.36%)	MISSED	460	119	FALSE
10	Philadelphia	$ 19,984	$ 38,768	$ 11,102	$ 47,482	$ 117,336	$ 85,744	36.84%	MET	383	473	FALSE
11	Toronto	$ 15,868	$ 46,942	$ 42,394	$ 16,177	$ 121,381	$ 91,142	33.18%	MET	425	194	TRUE
12	Vancouver	$ 17,502	$ 19,488	$ 48,411	$ 36,260	$ 121,661	$ 113,854	6.86%	MISSED	160	282	FALSE
13	Target % increase	15%										
14	# of NA Offices	10										
15	Average Year Revenue	$ 122,636										
16												

Excel

Enter a Date Function

Learning Outcomes
• Enter a date using the TODAY function
• Enter a date using the DATE function

Excel includes date functions to make it easy to calculate date and time related results, such as the current date or the time between events. See TABLE 3-3 for some of the available Date and Time functions in Excel. Note that although the results of all date and time functions appear by default in a worksheet in familiar-looking date and time formats, Excel actually stores them as sequential serial numbers and uses these numbers in calculations. January 1, 1900 is assigned serial number 1 and dates are represented as the number of days following that date. You can see the serial number of a date by using the **DATEVALUE function** or by applying the Number format to the cell. For example, to see the serial number of January 1, 2021 you would enter =DATEVALUE("1/1/2021"). The result would be the serial number 44197. **CASE** *To help document your work on this report, you decide to use a date function.*

STEPS

1. **Click cell A2, click the Formulas tab on the ribbon, then click the Date & Time button in the Function library**

   A list of date and time functions opens, as shown in FIGURE 3-12.

2. **Click TODAY, then click OK in the dialog box**

   The **TODAY function** displays the current date and updates each time a worksheet is opened. However, you want the workbook to show the date it was completed, rather than the date the workbook is opened.

3. **Press DEL, click the Date & Time button in the Function Library, then click DATE**

   The **DATE function** uses three arguments, year, month, and day, to enter a date.

4. **With the insertion point in the Year box type 2021, then press TAB**

5. **With the insertion point in the Month box type 2, then press TAB**

6. **Type 24 in the Day box, then click OK**

   The function is complete, and the result, 2/24/2021, appears in cell A2.

7. **Click the Home tab on the ribbon, click the Cell Styles button in the Styles group, then click 20% Accent1 in the Themed Cell Styles group**

   Compare your worksheet to FIGURE 3-13.

8. **Save the workbook**

FIGURE 3-12: Date & Time functions

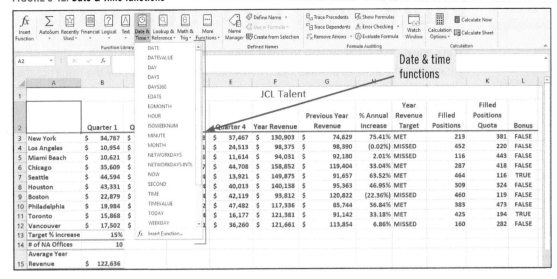

FIGURE 3-13: Formatted date

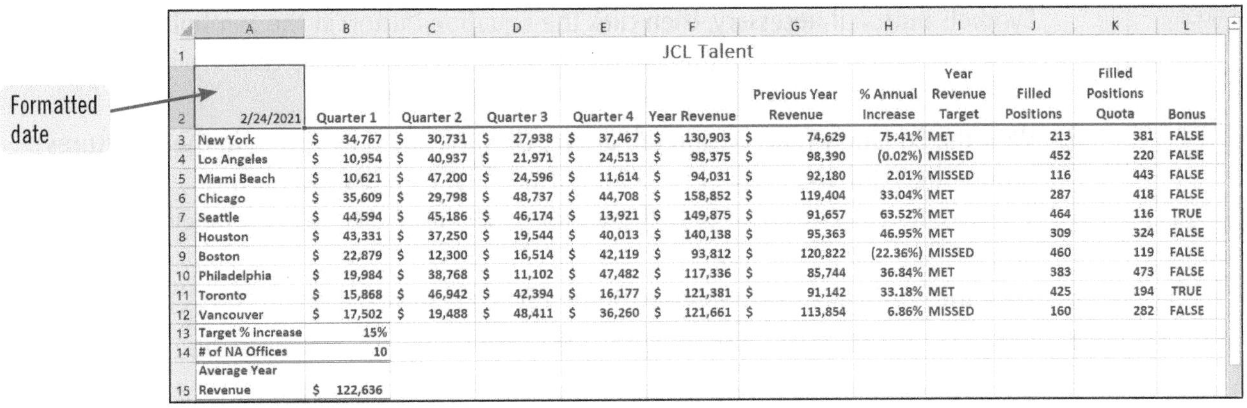

TABLE 3-3: Date and Time functions

function	calculates	example formula	example result
DAY	The day of the month using a date serial number	=DAY(44197)	1
NOW	The current date and time	=NOW()	1/1/2021 10:00
MONTH	The month number using a date serial number	=MONTH(44197)	1
TIME	A serial number in time format from hours, minutes, and seconds	=TIME(5,12,20)	0.216898
TIMEVALUE	A serial time in text format	=TIMEVALUE("5:15:24")	.219028
YEAR	The year portion of a date	=YEAR(44197)	2021
HOUR	The hour portion of a time	=HOUR("6:45:21 PM")	18
MINUTE	The minute portion of a time	=MINUTE("6:45:21 PM")	45
SECOND	The second portion of a time	=SECOND("6:45:21 PM")	21
WEEKDAY	The day of the week from a serial date (1 =Sunday, 2 = Monday...)	=WEEKDAY("6/21/2021")	2
WORKDAY	A serial number in date format after a certain number of working days	=WORKDAY(44198,5)	44204 (When formatted as a date: 1/8/2021)

Work with Equation Tools

Learning Outcomes
- Select an equation structure
- Enter an equation using the equation tools

Excel's equation tools allow you to insert many common equations, such as the area of a circle and the Pythagorean theorem, in a worksheet. The worksheet does not display the results of these expressions, it simply displays them with the correct syntax and structure. This can be helpful to illustrate the thinking behind a formula or to share mathematical information with others, such as algebraic formulas. You can also compose your own equations and formulas using structures such as fractions, exponents, radicals, and matrices along with many available mathematical symbols. **CASE** *Before sending the workbook to Ellie, you want to document the process you used to determine the revenue percentage increase. You have started this process on a separate worksheet in the workbook.*

STEPS

QUICK TIP

If your device is touch-enabled, you can click the Ink Equation button in the Tools group of the Equation Tools Design tab to write a math equation using your mouse, a stylus, or your fingertip.

1. **Click the** Formula Documentation sheet tab, **click the** Insert tab **on the ribbon, click the** Symbols button **if necessary, then click the** Equation button **in the Symbols group**

   The Equation Tools Design tab opens and the Drawing Tools Format tab becomes available. An equation placeholder that reads, "Type equation here," is added to the worksheet.

2. **With the Equation Tools Design tab active, click the** Fraction button **in the Structures group, then click the** Stacked Fraction button **(first row, first column)**

   The structure of a fraction is placed on the worksheet with a blank numerator and denominator, as shown in **FIGURE 3-14**.

3. **Click the** upper box **(the numerator), then type** (Year Revenue – Previous Year Revenue)

4. **Click the** lower box **(the denominator), then type** Previous Year Revenue

5. **Select the** equation **if necessary, place the** Move pointer ⬚ **on the edge of the equation, drag the** equation **so the upper left corner is in cell** A9, **then click cell** A1

6. **Compare your worksheet to** FIGURE 3-15, **then save your work**

FIGURE 3-14: Fraction structure added to worksheet

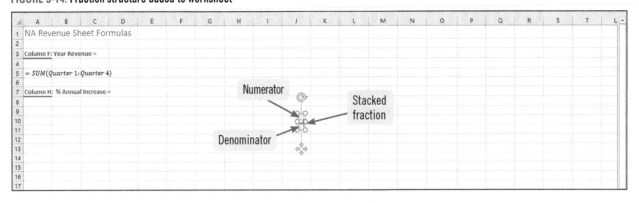

FIGURE 3-15: Completed equation

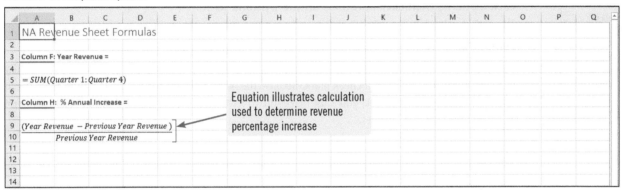

Using Draw tools

On a touch-enabled device you can use your mouse, a stylus, or even your finger to draw or write. If your device is touch-enabled, the Touch/Mouse Mode button appears on the Quick Access toolbar and the Draw tab automatically becomes available on the ribbon. You can add or remove the Touch/Mouse Mode button by clicking the Customize Quick Access Toolbar button ⯆, then clicking Touch/Mouse Mode. Touch mode adds space between the buttons on the ribbon, making them easier to access with your fingertip. You can manually turn on the Draw tab by clicking the File tab, clicking Options, clicking Customize Ribbon in the Excel Options dialog box, selecting the Draw box in the Main Tabs list, then clicking OK.

Clicking the Draw button in the Tools group of the Draw tab allows you to select a pen, pencil, or highlighter. If you click

the selected instrument you can change its thickness and color. As you work, you can correct drawing mistakes using the Eraser tool, also in the Tools group. Clicking the Ink to Shape button in the Convert group before beginning to draw converts your completed drawing to a geometric shape. The Ink to Shape feature works with pens and pencils but not highlighters. The Convert group includes an Ink to Math button that converts a handwritten mathematical expression to text. If you wish to see the steps followed in creating drawings on the worksheet, use the Ink Replay button in the Replay group to replay each step.

To modify an ink shape, you must select it, either by using the Lasso Select button in the Tools group to enclose it or by clicking the shape. Once a shape is selected, you can move, copy, rotate, and format it using the Drawing Tools Format tab.

Control Worksheet Calculations

Learning
Outcomes
• Control formula
  calculations
• Calculate work-
  sheet formulas

Whenever you change a value in a cell, Excel automatically recalculates all the formulas on the worksheet based on that cell. This automatic calculation is efficient unless you create a worksheet so large that the recalculation process slows down data entry and screen updating. Worksheets with many formulas, data tables, or functions may also recalculate slowly. In these cases, you might want to apply the **manual calculation** option to turn off automatic calculation of worksheet formulas, allowing you to selectively determine if and when you want Excel to perform calculations. When you turn on the manual calculation option, Excel stops automatically recalculating all open worksheets. **CASE** ▶ *Because you have added several formulas to the worksheet, you decide to review the formula settings in the workbook and see whether changing from automatic to manual calculation improves performance.*

STEPS

QUICK TIP
You can also change
the formula calcu-
lation to manual by
clicking the Formulas
tab, clicking the
Calculation Options
button in the Calcu-
lation group, then
clicking Manual.

1. **Click the NA Revenue sheet tab, click the File tab on the ribbon to open Backstage view, click Options, then click Formulas on the Options screen**

   The options related to formula calculation and error checking appear, as shown in FIGURE 3-16.

2. **Under Calculation options, click the Manual option button**

   When you select the Manual option, the Recalculate workbook before saving check box automatically becomes active and contains a check mark. Because the workbook will not recalculate until you save or close and reopen the workbook, you must make sure to recalculate your worksheet before you print it and after you finish making changes.

3. **Click OK**

   Ellie informs you that the first quarter revenue for the New York office is incorrect and needs updating.

4. **Click cell B3**

   Before proceeding, notice that in cell F3 the year revenue for the New York office is $130,903.

QUICK TIP
The Calculate Now
command calculates
the entire workbook,
not just the work-
sheet. You can also
manually recalculate
a workbook by
pressing F9. Pressing
SHIFT+F9 recalcu-
lates only the current
worksheet.

5. **Type 34305, then click the Enter button ✓ on the formula bar**

   Notice that the year revenue in cell F3 does not adjust to reflect the change in cell B3. The word "Calculate" appears in the status bar to indicate that a specific value on the worksheet did indeed change and remind-ing you that the worksheet must be recalculated.

6. **Click the Formulas tab, click the Calculate Sheet button in the Calculation group, click cell A1, then save the workbook**

   The year revenue in cell F3 is now $130,441. The other formulas on the worksheet affected by the value in cell B3 changed as well, as shown in FIGURE 3-17. Because this is a relatively small worksheet that recalcu-lates quickly, you decide that the manual calculation option is not necessary.

QUICK TIP
If your worksheet
contains a table,
such as a complex
payment schedule,
you may want to use
manual recalculation
just for the table.
To do so, click the
Automatic Except for
Data Tables option.

7. **Click the Calculation Options button in the Calculation group, then click Automatic**

   Now Excel will automatically recalculate the worksheet formulas any time you make changes.

8. **sam↑ Save your changes, activate cell A1, submit the workbook to your instructor as directed, close the workbook, then close Excel**

Analyzing Data Using Formulas

FIGURE 3-16: Excel formula options

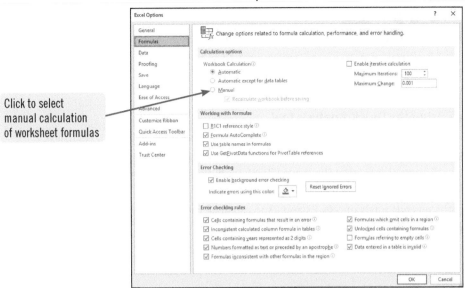

Click to select
manual calculation
of worksheet formulas

FIGURE 3-17: Worksheet with updated values

	A	B	C	D	E	F	G	H	I	J	K	L
1						JCL Talent						
2	2/24/2021	Quarter 1	Quarter 2	Quarter 3	Quarter 4	Year Revenue	Previous Year Revenue	% Annual Increase	Year Revenue Target	Filled Positions	Filled Positions Quota	Bonus
3	New York	$ 34,305	$ 30,731	$ 27,938	$ 37,467	$ 130,441	$ 74,629	74.79%	MET	213	381	FALSE
4	Los Angeles	$ 10,954	$ 40,937	$ 21,971	$ 24,513	$ 98,375	$ 98,390	(0.02%)	MISSED	452	220	FALSE
5	Miami Beach	$ 10,621	$ 47,200	$ 24,596	$ 11,614	$ 94,031	$ 92,180	2.01%	MISSED	116	443	FALSE
6	Chicago	$ 35,609	$ 29,798	$ 48,737	$ 44,708	$ 158,852	$ 119,404	33.04%	MET	287	418	FALSE
7	Seattle	$ 44,594	$ 45,186	$ 46,174	$ 13,921	$ 149,875	$ 91,657	63.52%	MET	464	116	TRUE
8	Houston	$ 43,331	$ 37,250	$ 19,544	$ 40,013	$ 140,138	$ 95,363	46.95%	MET	309	324	FALSE
9	Boston	$ 22,879	$ 12,300	$ 16,514	$ 42,119	$ 93,812	$ 120,822	(22.36%)	MISSED	460	119	FALSE
10	Philadelphia	$ 19,984	$ 38,768	$ 11,102	$ 47,482	$ 117,336	$ 85,744	36.84%	MET	383	473	FALSE
11	Toronto	$ 15,868	$ 46,942	$ 42,394	$ 16,177	$ 121,381	$ 91,142	33.18%	MET	425	194	TRUE
12	Vancouver	$ 17,502	$ 19,488	$ 48,411	$ 36,260	$ 121,661	$ 113,854	6.86%	MISSED	160	282	FALSE
13	Target % increase	15%										
14	# of NA Offices	10										
15	Average Year Revenue	$ 122,590										

Updated values

Showing and printing worksheet formulas

Sometimes you need to show or keep a record of all the formulas in a worksheet. You might want to do this to show exactly how you came up with a complex calculation, so you can explain it to others. To display formulas rather than results in a worksheet, first open the workbook. Click the Formulas tab on the ribbon, then click the Show Formulas button in the Formula Auditing group to select it. When the Show Formulas button is selected, formulas rather than resulting values are displayed on the worksheet, and any entered values appear without number formatting. You can print the worksheet to save a record of all the formulas. The Show Formulas button is a toggle: click it again to show the values, rather than the formulas, on the worksheet.

Excel

Practice

Skills Review

1. **Enter a formula using the Quick Analysis tool.**
   a. Start Excel, open IL_EX_3-2.xlsx from the location where you store your Data Files, then save it as **IL_EX_3_Labs**.
   b. On the First Quarter worksheet, select the range B3:D9, then use the Quick Analysis tool to enter the first quarter revenue totals in column E.
   c. In cell G3, use the revenue totals in cells E3 and F3 to calculate the percent increase in revenue from the previous quarter to the first quarter.
   d. Format the value in cell G3 using the percent style with two decimal places.
   e. Copy the formula in cell G3 into the range G4:G9.

2. **Build a logical formula with the IF function.**
   a. In cell H3, use the Function Arguments dialog box to enter the formula **=IF(G3>=$B$10,"Met","Missed")**.
   b. Copy the formula in cell H3 into the range H4:H9.
   c. Save your work.

3. **Build a logical formula with the AND function.**
   a. In cell J3, use the Function Arguments dialog box to enter the formula **=AND(H3="Met",I3>=4)**.
   b. Copy the formula in cell J3 into the range J4:J9.
   c. Enter your name in the center section of the footer for the First Quarter sheet.
   d. Save your work.

4. **Round a value with a function.**
   a. In cell B12, use the AutoSum list arrow to enter a function to average the first quarter revenue values in column E.
   b. Use Formula AutoComplete to edit this formula to include the ROUND function showing zero decimal places.
   c. Correct any errors in the formula.
   d. Save your work.

5. **Build a statistical formula with the COUNTA function.**
   a. In cell B11, use a statistical formula to calculate the number of lab locations in column A.
   b. Create a custom format for the percentages in column G so that the negative values appear in red with parentheses.
   c. Format the revenue values in the range B3:F9 and in cell B12 using the Accounting Number Format with no decimal places.
   d. Save your work.

6. **Enter a date function.**
   a. In cell D12, enter **Report Date**.
   b. In cell E12, use the TODAY function to enter today's date.
   c. Delete the TODAY function in cell E12, then use the DATE function to enter the date 4/3/2021.
   d. Use the Cell Style Rose, 20% - Accent 1 (the first row and first column in the Themed Cell Styles group) to format the range D12:E12.
   e. Activate cell A1, then save your work.

7. **Work with equation tools.**
   a. Activate the Formula Documentation sheet.
   b. Add a stacked fraction to the worksheet.
   c. Enter **(First Quarter Revenue – Previous Quarter Revenue)** as the numerator.
   d. Enter **Previous Quarter Revenue** as the denominator.

Skills Review (continued)

   e. Move the equation to place its upper left corner in cell A9.

   f. Activate cell A1, then save your work.

8. Control worksheet calculations.

   a. Activate the First Quarter sheet.

   b. Open the Formulas category of the Excel Options dialog box.

   c. Change the worksheet calculations to manual.

   d. Change the value in cell B3 to **72000**.

   e. Recalculate the worksheet manually.

   f. Change the worksheet calculation back to automatic using the Calculation Options button on the Formulas tab of the ribbon, then save the workbook.

   g. Preview the worksheet in Backstage view. Compare your screen to FIGURE 3-18.

   h. Save your changes, submit your work to your instructor as directed, close the workbook, then close Excel.

FIGURE 3-18

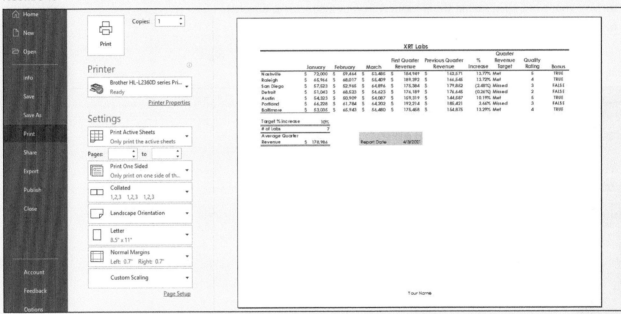

Independent Challenge 1

The manager at Riverwalk Medical Clinic has hired you to analyze patient accounts and insurance reimbursements for their Boston imaging facility. He would like you to flag overdue accounts and calculate the average procedure amount.

   a. Open IL_EX_3-3.xlsx from the location where you store your Data Files, then save it as **IL_EX_3_Accounts**.

   b. Use the DATE function to return the date 5/18/2021 in cell B3.

   c. Enter a formula in cell C5 that calculates the statement age by subtracting the statement date in cell B5 from the report date in cell B3. (*Hint:* The formula needs to use an absolute reference for the report date in cell B3 so this cell address doesn't change when copied.)

   d. Copy the formula in cell C5 to the range C6:C11.

Independent Challenge 1 (continued)

e. In cell F5, enter an IF function that calculates the patient responsibility. (*Hint*: The Logical_test should check to see if the procedure amount is greater than the insurance payment, the Value_if_true should calculate the procedure amount minus the insurance payment, and the Value_if_false should be 0.)

f. Copy the IF function in cell F5 to the range F6:F11.

g. In cell G5, enter an AND function to find accounts that are past due. Accounts are past due if a patient is responsible for a balance due and the statement age is over 30 days. (*Hint*: The Logical1 condition should check to see if the statement age is more than 30, and the Logical2 condition should check if the patient responsibility is greater than 0.)

h. Use the fill handle to copy the AND function in cell G5 into the range G6:G11.

i. In cell B13, enter a COUNTA function to calculate the number of accounts in column A.

j. Enter a function in cell B14 that averages the procedure amounts in column D.

k. Use Formula AutoComplete to enter a function to round the average in cell B14 to zero decimal places.

l. Enter your name in the center section of the footer.

m. Preview the worksheet in Backstage view. Compare your screen to FIGURE 3-19.

n. Save your work, then submit the worksheet to your instructor as directed.

o. Close the workbook and Excel.

FIGURE 3-19

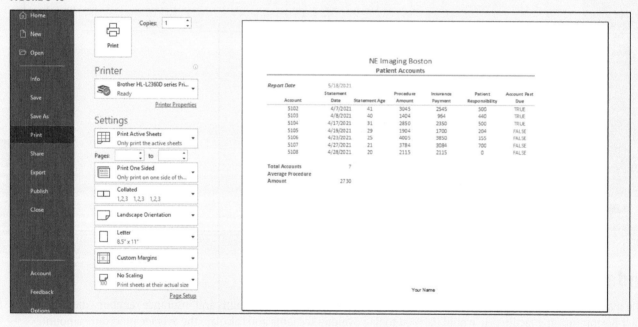

Independent Challenge 2

As the senior loan officer at North Shore Bank, one of your responsibilities is reviewing the quarterly loan portfolios for the four branches. This includes adding statistics including total loan amounts, average total loans, and the growth in loans issued at each branch. You are preparing a portfolio review for the 4th quarter, which you plan to issue on December 31.

a. Open IL_EX_3-4.xlsx from the location where you store your Data Files, then save it as **IL_EX_3_Loans**.

b. Use the TODAY function to enter today's date in cell B12. Verify today's date is displayed.

c. Delete the date in cell B12 and replace it with the date 12/31/2021 using the DATE function.

d. Use the Quick Analysis button to enter totals in the range F4:F7 and B8:E8. (*Hint*: You need to use two buttons on the Totals tab to accomplish this.)

e. Enter a formula in cell H4 to find the percentage increase for the total 4th quarter loans over the 3rd quarter total for the Main Street branch. Format the percentage increase using the percent style with two decimal places.

f. Copy the percentage increase formula in cell H4 to the range H5:H7.

g. In cell J4, enter an AND function to determine if the Main Street branch is eligible for a bonus. To be eligible, the 4th quarter percentage increase must be over 10% and the customer ratings must be higher than 85%.

h. Use the fill handle to copy the AND function in cell J4 into the range J5:J7.

i. Enter a function in cell B10 that averages the total 4th quarter loan amounts in column F, then round the average to zero decimal places.

j. In cell B11, enter a function to calculate the number of branches in column A.

k. Create a custom format for the percentages in column H so that the negative values appear in red with parentheses.

l. Format the loan values in the ranges B4:G7, B8:E8, and cell B10 using the Accounting Number Format with no decimals. Widen the columns as necessary to fully display all of the worksheet data.

m. Activate the Documentation tab and use a stacked fraction to document the 4th quarter % increase formula in cell A3.

n. Activate the 4th Quarter Report sheet. Switch to manual calculation for formulas. Change the personal loan amount for the Main Street branch in cell B4 to **1306500**. Calculate the worksheet formula manually. Turn on automatic calculation again.

o. Enter your name in the center footer section.

p. Preview the worksheet in Backstage view. Compare your screen to **FIGURE 3-20**.

q. Save your work, then submit the worksheet to your instructor as directed.

r. Close the workbook and Excel.

FIGURE 3-20

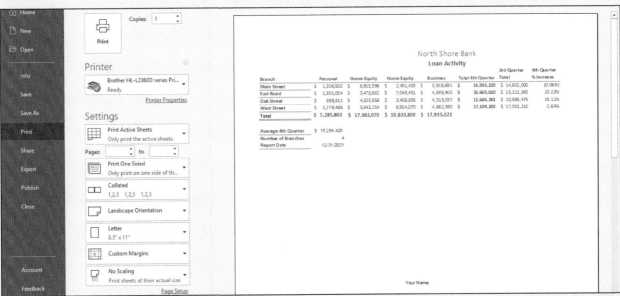

Visual Workshop

Open IL_EX_3-5.xlsx from the location where you store your Data Files, then save it as **IL_EX_3_Freight**. Use the skills you learned in this module to complete the worksheet so it looks like the one shown in FIGURE 3-21. To build the formulas in column G, calculate the percentage increase of the second quarter revenue over the first quarter revenue. (*Hint*: The percentage increases in column G must be calculated before calculating the average increase in cell B10.) To build the formulas in column I, a warning should be issued if the percentage increase is less than the average increase shown in cell B10 AND the on-time delivery is less than 75%. (*Hint*: Remember to use an absolute cell reference where necessary.) When you are finished, enter your name in the center footer section, then submit your work to your instructor as directed.

FIGURE 3-21

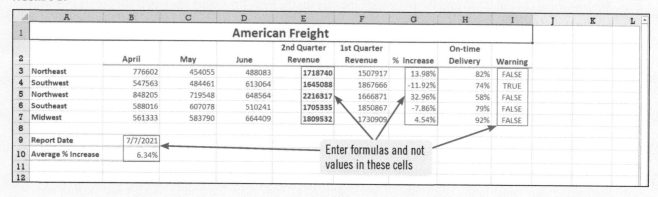

	A	B	C	D	E	F	G	H	I
1				American Freight					
2		April	May	June	2nd Quarter Revenue	1st Quarter Revenue	% Increase	On-time Delivery	Warning
3	Northeast	776602	454055	488083	1718740	1507917	13.98%	82%	FALSE
4	Southwest	547563	484461	613064	1645088	1867666	-11.92%	74%	TRUE
5	Northwest	848205	719548	648564	2216317	1666871	32.96%	58%	FALSE
6	Southeast	588016	607078	510241	1705335	1850867	-7.86%	79%	FALSE
7	Midwest	561333	583790	664409	1809532	1730909	4.54%	92%	FALSE
8									
9	Report Date	7/7/2021							
10	Average % Increase	6.34%							
11									
12									

Enter formulas and not values in these cells

Working with Charts

CASE ▶ At the upcoming annual meeting, Ellie Schwartz, the vice president of finance, wants to review expenses at JCL Talent's U.S. offices. She asks you to create charts showing the expense trends in these offices over the past four quarters.

Module Objectives

After completing this module, you will be able to:

- Plan a chart
- Create a chart
- Move and resize a chart
- Change the chart design
- Change the chart layout

- Format a chart
- Create a pie chart
- Summarize data with sparklines
- Identify data trends

Files You Will Need

IL_EX_4-1.xlsx   IL_EX_4-4.xlsx
IL_EX_4-2.xlsx   IL_EX_4-5.xlsx
IL_EX_4-3.xlsx

Plan a Chart

Learning
Outcomes
• Identify chart
  elements
• Explore common
  chart types

The process of creating a chart involves deciding which data to use and what type of chart best highlights the trends or patterns that are most important, such as steady increases over time or stellar performance by one sales rep compared to others in the same division. Understanding the parts of a chart makes it easier to evaluate specific elements to make sure the chart effectively illustrates your data. **CASE** ▸ *In preparation for creating the charts for Ellie's presentation, you review the purpose of the charts and decide how to organize the data.*

DETAILS

Use the following guidelines to plan the chart:

• **Determine the purpose of the chart, and identify the data relationships you want to graphically communicate**

  You want to create a chart that shows quarterly expenses for JCL U.S. offices. You also want to illustrate whether the quarterly expenses for each office increased or decreased from quarter to quarter.

• **Determine the results you want to see, and decide which chart type is most appropriate**

  Different chart types display data in distinctive ways. For example, a pie chart compares parts of a whole, whereas a line chart is best for showing trends over time. To choose the best chart type for your data, first decide how you want your data to be interpreted. **FIGURE 4-1** shows the available chart types in Excel, listed by category on the All Charts tab of the Insert Chart dialog box. **TABLE 4-1** describes several of these charts. Because you want to compare JCL expenses in multiple offices over a period of four quarters, you decide to use a column chart.

• **Identify the worksheet data you want the chart to illustrate**

  Sometimes you use all the data in a worksheet to create a chart, while at other times you may need to select a range within the sheet. The worksheet from which you are creating your chart contains expense data for each of the past four quarters and the totals for the past year. To create a column chart, you will need to use all the quarterly data except the quarterly totals.

• **Understand the elements of a chart**

  The chart shown in **FIGURE 4-2** contains basic elements of a chart. In the figure, JCL offices are on the category axis and expense dollar amounts are on the value axis. The **category axis**, also called the *x*-axis, is the horizontal axis in a chart, usually containing the names of data categories. The **value axis**, also called the vertical axis, contains numerical values. In a 2-dimensional chart, it is also known as the *y*-axis. (Three-dimensional charts contain a **z-axis**, for comparing data across both categories and values.) The area inside the horizontal and vertical axes that contains the graphical representation of the data series is the **plot area**. **Gridlines**, the horizontal and vertical lines, make a chart easier to read. Each individual piece of data plotted in a chart is a **data point**. In any chart, a **data marker** is a graphical representation of a data point, such as a bar or column. A set of values represented in a chart is a **data series**. In this chart, there are four data series: Quarter 1, Quarter 2, Quarter 3, and Quarter 4. Each is made up of columns of a different color. To differentiate each data series, information called a **legend** or a legend key identifies how the data is represented using colors and/or patterns.

FIGURE 4-1: **Insert Chart dialog box lists available charts by category**

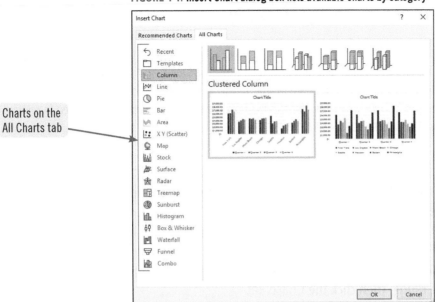

Charts on the
All Charts tab

FIGURE 4-2: **Chart elements**

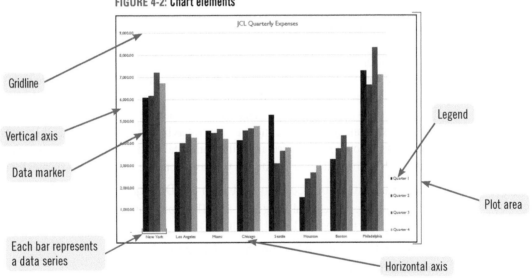

Gridline

Vertical axis

Data marker

Each bar represents
a data series

Legend

Plot area

Horizontal axis

TABLE 4-1: **Common chart types**

type	description
Column	A chart that displays data values as columns; column height represents its value
Line	A chart or visualization that displays data as separate lines across categories
Pie	A chart in the shape of a circle divided into slices like a pie, which shows data values as percentages of the whole
Bar	A column chart turned on its side so that the length of each bar is based on its value
Area	Shows how individual volume changes over time in relation to total volume
Line with Markers	Compares trends over time by showing data markers that represent worksheet data values

Create a Chart

Learning
Outcomes
• Create a chart
• Add a title to a
  chart

To create a chart in Excel, you first select the worksheet range or ranges containing the data you want to chart. Once you've selected a range, you can use the Quick Analysis tool or the Insert tab on the ribbon to create a chart based on the data in that range. **CASE** ▶ *Using the worksheet containing the quarterly expense data, you create a chart that shows how the expenses in each office varied in relation to each other, across all four quarters of the year.*

STEPS

1. **sam** ↓ **Start Excel, open IL_EX_4-1.xlsx from the location where you store your Data Files, then save it as IL_EX_4_USQuarterlyExpenses**

   You want the chart to include the quarterly office expenses values, as well as quarter and office labels, but not any totals.

2. **Select the range A4:E12, click the Quick Analysis button 📧 in the lower-right corner of the range, then click the Charts tab**

   The Charts tab on the Quick Analysis tool recommends commonly used chart types based on the range you have selected. It also includes a More Charts button for additional chart types.

QUICK TIP

You can change either the data source or the legend by clicking the Select Data button on the Chart Tools Design tab to open the Select Data Source dialog box. You can change the source data by editing the data range in the chart data range box. Clicking Add, Edit, or Remove under Legend Entries (Series) allows you to change the legend labels. When you finish making changes, click OK to close the dialog box.

3. **On the Charts tab, verify that Clustered Column is selected, as shown in FIGURE 4-3, then click Clustered Column**

   A clustered column chart is inserted in the center of the worksheet. **Clustered column charts** display data values in side-by-side columns. Two contextual Chart Tools tabs, Design and Format, become available on the ribbon. On the Design tab, which is currently active, you can quickly change the chart layout and chart style, and you can swap how the columns and rows of data in the worksheet are represented in the chart or select a different data range for the chart. In Normal view, three tools open to the right of the chart: the Chart Elements button ⊞ lets you add, remove, or change chart elements; the Chart Styles button 🖉 lets you set a style and color scheme; and the Chart Filters button ▽ lets you filter the results shown in a chart. Currently, the offices are charted along the horizontal *x*-axis, with the quarterly expense dollar amounts charted along the vertical *y*-axis. This lets you easily compare the quarterly expenses for each office.

4. **Click the Switch Row/Column button in the Data group on the Chart Tools Design tab**

   The quarters are now charted along the x-axis. The expense amounts per office are charted along the y-axis, as indicated by the updated legend. See FIGURE 4-4.

5. **Click the Undo button ↶ on the Quick Access Toolbar**

   The chart returns to its original data configuration.

6. **Click the Chart Title placeholder, type JCL Quarterly Expenses, click the Enter button ✓ then click anywhere in the chart to deselect the title**

   Adding a title helps identify the chart. The border around the chart, along with the **sizing handles**, the small circles at the corners and the edges, indicates that the chart is selected. See FIGURE 4-5. Your chart might be in a different location on the worksheet and may look slightly different; you will move and resize it in the next lesson. Any time a chart is selected, as it is now, a blue border surrounds the worksheet data range on which the chart is based, a purple border surrounds the cells containing the category axis labels, and a red border surrounds the cells containing the data series labels. This chart is known as an **embedded chart** because it is displayed as an object in the worksheet. Embedding a chart in the current sheet is the default selection when creating a chart, but you can also embed a chart on a different sheet in the workbook, or on a newly created chart sheet. A **chart sheet** is a separate sheet in a workbook that contains only a chart that is linked to the workbook data.

7. **Save your work**

FIGURE 4-3: Charts tab in Quick Analysis tool

Charts tab selected

Quick Analysis tool

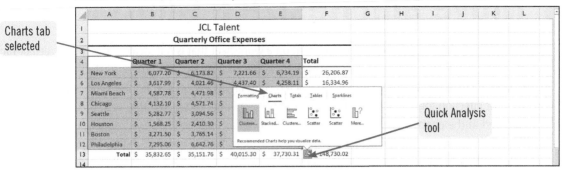

FIGURE 4-4: Clustered Column chart with different configuration of rows and columns

Undo button

Chart Tools tabs

Switch Row/Column button

Chart title placeholder

Click to change chart elements

Click to change style and color schemes

Click to filter results

Legend

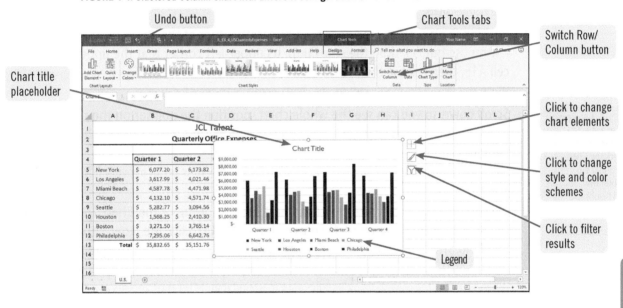

FIGURE 4-5: Chart with original configuration restored and title added

Column labels (data series labels)

Row labels (category axis labels)

Selected chart object

Legend

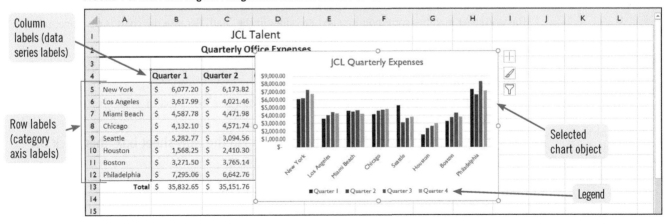

Move and Resize a Chart

Learning Outcomes
• Reposition a chart
• Resize a chart

A chart is an **object**, an independent element on a worksheet that is not located in a specific cell or range and can be moved and resized. You can select an object by clicking it; the object displays sizing handles to indicate it is selected. You can move a selected chart anywhere on a worksheet or to another worksheet without affecting formulas or data in the worksheet. Any data changed in the worksheet is automatically updated in the chart. You can resize a chart to improve its appearance by dragging its sizing handles. Dragging a corner sizing handle resizes the chart proportionally. Dragging a side, top, or bottom handle resizes it horizontally or vertically. **CASE** *You want the chart to be bigger and more noticeable.*

STEPS

1. **Make sure the chart is still selected, then position the pointer over the chart**

   The pointer shape ⁺⇧ indicates that you can move the chart.

2. **Position ⇧ on a blank area near the upper-left corner of the chart, press and hold the left mouse button, drag the chart until its upper-left corner is at the upper-left corner of cell A16, then release the mouse button**

   When you release the mouse button, the chart appears in the new location.

3. **Scroll down so you can see the whole chart, position the pointer on the right-middle sizing handle until it changes to ⬌, then drag the right border of the chart to the right edge of column G**

   The chart is widened. See **FIGURE 4-6**. You can also use the ↕ pointer on an upper or lower sizing handle to increase the chart size vertically.

4. **Click the Quick Layout button in the Chart Layouts group of the Chart Tools Design tab, click Layout 1 (in the upper-left corner of the palette), click the legend to select it, press and hold SHIFT, drag the legend down using ⁺⇧ to the bottom of the plot area, then release SHIFT**

   When you click the legend, sizing handles appear around it and "Legend" appears as a ScreenTip when the pointer hovers over the object. As you drag, a dotted outline of the legend border appears. Pressing and holding SHIFT holds the horizontal position of the legend as you move it vertically.

5. **Scroll up if necessary, click cell A7, type Miami, then click the Enter button ✓ on the formula bar**

   The axis label changes to reflect the updated cell contents, as shown in **FIGURE 4-7**. Changing any data in the worksheet modifies corresponding text or values in the chart. Because the chart is no longer selected, the Chart Tools tabs no longer appear on the ribbon.

6. **Click the chart to select it, click the Chart Tools Design tab, then click the Move Chart button in the Location group**

   The Move chart dialog box shows options to move a chart to a new sheet or as an object in an existing worksheet, as shown in **FIGURE 4-8**.

7. **Click the New sheet option button, type Column in the New sheet box, then click OK**

   The chart is placed on its own chart sheet, named Column.

FIGURE 4-6: **Moved and resized chart**

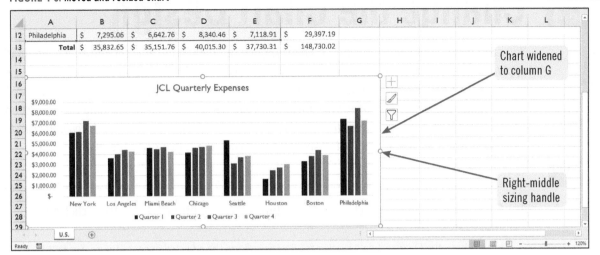

Chart widened to column G

Right-middle sizing handle

FIGURE 4-7: **Worksheet with modified legend and label**

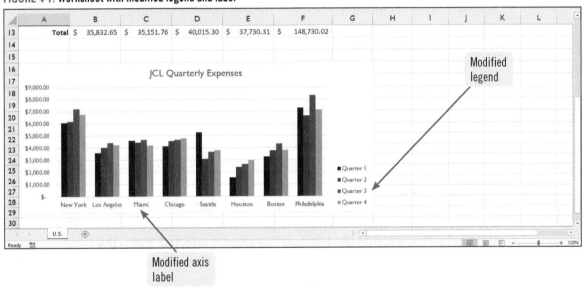

Modified legend

Modified axis label

FIGURE 4-8: **Move Chart dialog box**

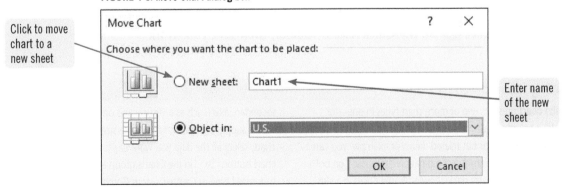

Click to move chart to a new sheet

Enter name of the new sheet

Change the Chart Design

Learning
Outcomes
• Modify chart data
• Change the chart
  type
• Apply a chart style

You can change the type of an existing chart, modify the data range and column/row configuration, apply a different chart style, and change the layout of objects within it. The layouts in the Chart Layouts group on the Chart Tools Design tab arrange multiple objects in a chart at once, such as its legend, title, and gridlines; choosing one of these layouts is a quick alternative to manually changing each object one at a time. **CASE** ➤ *You've discovered that the data for Boston's third quarter is incorrect. You also want to see if using different chart types and layouts helps make the trends and patterns easier to spot.*

STEPS

1. **Click the U.S. sheet tab, click cell D11, type 4775.20, press ENTER, then click the Column sheet tab**

   In the chart, the Quarter 3 data marker for Boston reflects the adjusted expense figure. See FIGURE 4-9.

2. **Select the chart, if necessary, by clicking a blank area within the chart border, click the Chart Tools Design tab on the ribbon, click the Quick Layout button in the Chart Layouts group, then click Layout 3**

   The legend moves to the bottom of the chart. You prefer the original layout.

3. **Click the Undo button ↶ ▾ on the Quick Access Toolbar, then click the Change Chart Type button in the Type group**

   The Change Chart Type dialog box opens, as shown in FIGURE 4-10. The left side of the dialog box lists available categories, and the right side shows the individual chart types. A pale gray border surrounds the currently selected chart type.

4. **Click Bar in the list of categories on the left, confirm that the first Clustered Bar chart type is selected on the right, then click OK**

   The column chart changes to a Clustered Bar chart. See FIGURE 4-11. You decide to see how the data looks in a 3-D column chart.

5. **Click the Change Chart Type button in the Type group, click Column on the left side of the Change Chart Type dialog box, click 3-D Clustered Column (fourth from the left in the top row), verify that the leftmost 3-D chart is selected, then click OK**

   A three-dimensional column chart appears. You notice that the three-dimensional column format gives you a sense of volume, but it is more crowded than the two-dimensional column format.

6. **Click the Change Chart Type button in the Type group, click Clustered Column (first from the left in the top row), then click OK**

7. **Click the Style 3 chart style in the Chart Styles group**

   The columns change to lighter shades of color. You prefer the previous chart style's color scheme.

8. **Click ↶ ▾ on the Quick Access Toolbar, then save your work**

Creating a combo chart

A **combo chart** presents two or more chart types in one—for example, a column chart with a line chart. Combo charts are useful when charting dissimilar but related data. For example, you can create a clustered column–line combination chart based on both home price and home size data, showing home prices in a clustered column chart and related home sizes in a line chart. Here, a secondary axis (such as a vertical axis on the right side of the chart) would supply the scale for the home sizes. To create a combo chart, select all the data you want to plot, click the Insert Combo chart button ▤ ▾ in the Charts group in the Insert tab, click a suggested type or Create Custom Combo Chart, supply additional series information if necessary, then click OK.

FIGURE 4-9: Chart with modified data

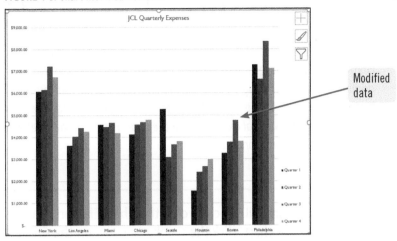

Modified data

FIGURE 4-10: Change Chart Type dialog box

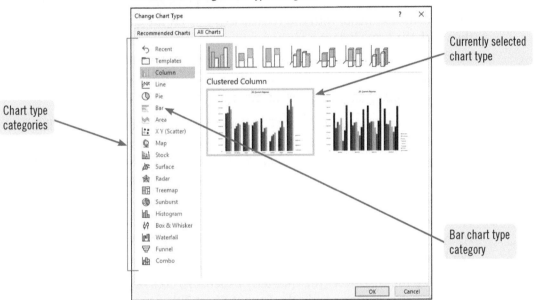

Currently selected chart type

Chart type categories

Bar chart type category

FIGURE 4-11: Column chart changed to bar chart

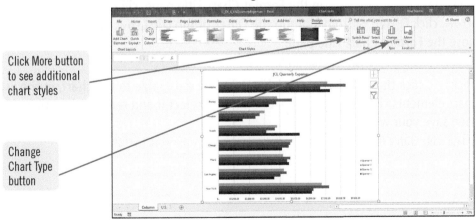

Click More button to see additional chart styles

Change Chart Type button

Excel

Change the Chart Layout

Learning
Outcomes
• Change the grid-
  lines display
• Add axis titles
• Add a data table

While the Chart Tools Design tab contains preconfigured chart layouts you can apply to a chart, the Chart Elements button makes it easy to add, remove, and modify individual chart objects such as a chart title, gridlines, or legend. Using options on this shortcut menu, you can also add a **data table**, a grid containing the chart data, to the chart. **CASE** ▸ *You want to change the layout of the chart by creating titles for the horizontal and vertical axes. Because the chart is on its own sheet, you also want to add a data table to provide more detailed information.*

STEPS

1. **With the chart still selected, click the Chart Elements button ⊞ in the upper-right corner of the chart, click the Gridlines arrow on the Chart Elements fly-out menu, click Primary Major Horizontal to deselect it, then click ⊞ to close the menu**
   The gridlines that extend across the chart's plot area are removed, as shown in FIGURE 4-12.

2. **Click ⊞, click the Axis Titles check box to add a checkmark, click ⊞ to close the Chart Elements fly-out menu, with the vertical axis title on the chart selected type Expenses, then click the Enter button ✓**
   Descriptive text on the category axis helps readers understand the chart.

3. **Click the horizontal axis title on the chart, type U.S. Offices, then click ✓**
   The horizontal axis labels are added, as shown in FIGURE 4-13.

4. **Right-click the horizontal axis labels ("New York," "Los Angeles," etc.), click Font on the shortcut menu, click the Latin text font arrow in the Font dialog box, scroll down the font list, click Times New Roman, select 9 in the Size box, type 12, then click OK**
   The font of the horizontal axis labels changes to Times New Roman, and the font size increases, making the labels easier to read.

5. **With the horizontal axis labels still selected, click the Home tab on the ribbon, click the Format Painter button in the Clipboard group, then click the area within the vertical axis labels**

6. **Right-click the chart title (JCL Quarterly Expenses), click Format Chart Title on the shortcut menu, click Border in the Format Chart Title pane to display the options if necessary, then click the Solid line option button in the pane**
   A solid border in the default blue color appears around the chart title.

7. **Click the Effects button ▢ in the Format Chart Title pane, click Shadow, click the Presets arrow, click Offset: Bottom Right in the Outer group (first row, first from the left), then close the Format Chart Title pane**
   A border with a drop shadow surrounds the title.

8. **Click ⊞, click the Data Table check box to add a data table to the chart, in the list of chart elements click the legend check box to deselect it and remove the original legend, then save your work**
   A data table with a legend shows the chart data. Compare your work to FIGURE 4-14.

FIGURE 4-12: Gridlines removed from chart

Chart Tools Design tab

Chart without gridlines

Chart Elements button

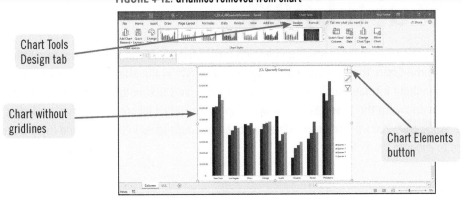

FIGURE 4-13: Axis titles added to chart

Vertical axis title

Horizontal axis labels

Vertical axis labels

Horizontal axis title

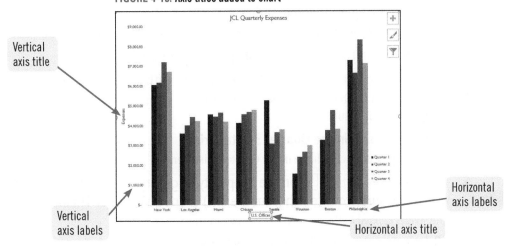

FIGURE 4-14: Enhanced chart

Border and shadow added to chart title

Data table with a legend

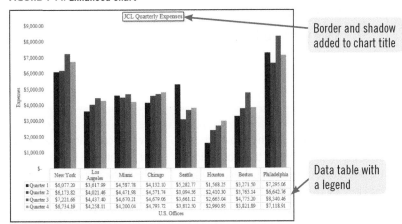

Working with chart axes

You can change both the number format and text formatting of a chart's axes. For example, you may want to change the starting and ending values of an axis. You can do this by right-clicking the axis, selecting Format Axis from the shortcut menu, clicking Axis Options in the Format Axis pane if necessary, then entering values in the Minimum and Maximum boxes. To change the number format of the values on an axis, scroll down in the Axis Options, click Number to display the options if necessary, then select from

the available number formats. In the Number area, you can also create a number format code by typing a code in the Format Code box and clicking Add. In addition to these axis options, you can work with axis text by clicking the Text Option button at the top of the pane, then clicking the Textbox button 🔠. The Text Box group includes options for changing the vertical alignment of the data labels on the axis and the text direction of axis data labels from horizontal to stacked or rotated.

Excel

Format a Chart

Learning Outcomes
- Change the fill of a data series
- Apply a style to a data series

Formatting a chart can make it easier to read and understand. You can make many formatting enhancements using the Chart Tools Format tab. Using a shape style in the Shape Styles group on this tab, you can apply multiple formats, such as an outline, fill color, and text color, all at once. You can use other buttons and arrows in the Shape Styles group to apply individual fill colors, outlines, and effects to chart objects. **CASE** ▶ *You want to use a different color for one data series in the chart and apply a shape style to another, to enhance the look of the chart.*

STEPS

QUICK TIP

You can remove a data series from a chart by selecting the data series, then pressing DEL.

1. **With the chart selected, click the Chart Tools Format tab on the ribbon, then click any column in the Quarter 4 data series**

   Handles appear on each column in the Quarter 4 data series, indicating that the entire series is selected.

2. **Click the Shape Fill button in the Shape Styles group**

3. **Click Plum, Accent 1, Lighter 90% (second row, fifth from the left)**

   All the columns for the series change to a light shade of plum, and the legend changes to match the new color, as shown in **FIGURE 4-15**.

QUICK TIP

You can add a texture fill by pointing to Texture in the Shape Fill menu and selecting a texture.

4. **Click any column in the Quarter 3 data series**

   Handles appear on each column in the Quarter 3 data series.

5. **Click the More button ⊽ on the Shape Styles gallery, then click the Subtle Effect – Pink, Accent 3 (fourth row, fourth from the left) shape style under Theme Styles**

   The style is applied to the data series, as shown in **FIGURE 4-16**.

QUICK TIP

You can change the colors used in a chart by clicking the Chart Tools Design tab, clicking the Change Colors button in the Chart Styles group, then clicking a color palette in the gallery.

6. **Click the Insert tab on the ribbon, click the Text button, click the Header & Footer button, click Custom Footer, type your name in the center section, click OK, then click OK again**

7. **Save your work**

Working with WordArt

You can insert WordArt into a worksheet or a chart. To insert WordArt in a worksheet, click the Insert tab on the ribbon, click the Text button in the Text group, click WordArt, then click a style in the gallery. You can change a WordArt style by clicking the WordArt to select it, clicking the WordArt Styles More button ⊽ on the Drawing Tools Format tab, then selecting a new WordArt style. You can change the fill color of the WordArt by clicking the Text Fill button in the WordArt Styles group and choosing a fill color, texture, gradient, or picture. You can change the outline of selected WordArt text by clicking the Text Outline button in the WordArt Styles group and choosing an outline color, weight, and/or dashes.

FIGURE 4-15: New shape fill applied to data series

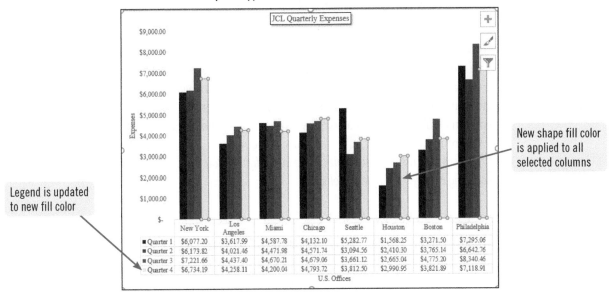

Legend is updated to new fill color

New shape fill color is applied to all selected columns

FIGURE 4-16: Style applied to data series

Shape style applied to selected columns

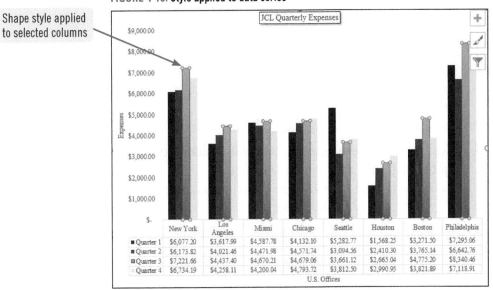

Aligning charts

If you have two or more embedded charts on a worksheet, you can line them up to make them easier to view. First, select the charts by clicking the first chart and holding CTRL, then click the other chart(s). With the charts selected, click the Drawing Tools Format tab, click the Align button in the Arrange group, then choose the alignment position for the charts. The chart shown in **FIGURE 4-17** uses the Align Top option.

FIGURE 4-17: Charts aligned at the top

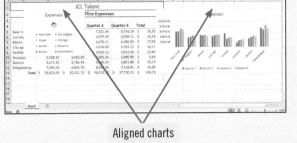

Aligned charts

Create a Pie Chart

Learning
Outcomes
• Create a pie chart
• Explode a pie
  chart slice

You can create multiple charts based on the same worksheet data, to illustrate different aspects of the data. For example, while a column chart may reveal top performers month by month, you may want to create a pie chart to compare overall performance for the year. Depending on the type of chart you create, you have additional options for calling attention to trends and patterns. With a pie chart, for example, you can emphasize one data point by **exploding**, or moving one slice, as if someone were taking a piece away from the pie. **CASE** ▶ *At an upcoming meeting, Ellie plans to discuss the total expenses and identify offices that need to economize more in the future. You want to create a pie chart she can use to compare spending between the different offices.*

STEPS

1. **Click the** U.S. sheet tab **to select it, select the range** A5:A12, **press and hold** CTRL, **select the range** F5:F12, **click the** Insert tab **on the ribbon if necessary, click the** Insert Pie or Doughnut Chart button 🌐▾ **in the Charts group, then click the first** 2-D Pie **in the chart gallery**

2. **Click the** Move Chart button **in the Location group, click the** New sheet option button, **type** Pie **in the New sheet box, then click** OK

   The chart is placed on a new worksheet named Pie.

3. **Select the** Chart Title placeholder, **click the** Chart Tools Format tab, **click the** WordArt Styles More button ▾, **click the** Fill: Pink, Accent Color 3; Sharp Bevel (second row, first from the right), **type** JCL Total Expenses, by Office, **then click the** Enter button ✔ **on the formula bar**

   The formatted WordArt title is added, as shown in **FIGURE 4-18**.

4. **Click the slice for the** Houston data point, **click it again so it is the only slice selected, right-click it, then click** Format Data Point

   You can use the Point Explosion slider to control the distance a pie slice moves away from the pie, or you can type a value in the Point Explosion box.

5. **Double-click** 0 **in the Point Explosion box, type** 10, **then click the** Close button ✖

   Compare your chart to **FIGURE 4-19**.

6. **Click the** Chart Elements button ⊞, **click the** Data Labels arrow ▸, **click** Outside End, **click** More Options, **in the Format Data Labels pane click the** Percentage check box **to add a checkmark, then click the** Values box **to deselect it**

   The data labels identify the pie slices by percentage.

7. **Click** ⊞, **point to** Data Labels, **click** ▸, **click** Data Callout, **click the** Legend check box **to deselect it, then click** ⊞

   The data is labeled using percentage callouts, as shown in **FIGURE 4-20**.

8. **Click the** Insert tab **on the ribbon, click the** Text button, **click the** Header & Footer button **in the Text group, click the** Custom Footer button, **enter your name in the center section, click** OK, **click** OK **again, then save your work**

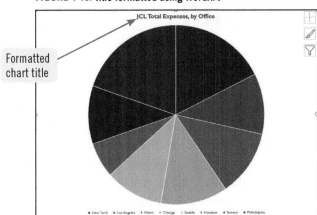

Formatted
chart title

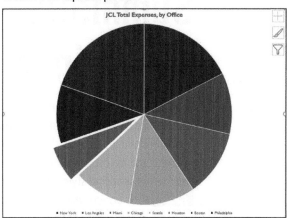

FIGURE 4-20: Pie chart with percentages

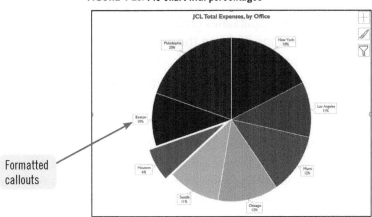

Formatted
callouts

Working with other chart types

Excel includes chart types that are useful for illustrating highly specific types of data. These include Waterfall, Histogram, Pareto, Box & Whisker, Treemap, Scatter, and Sunburst. A **treemap chart** is a hierarchy chart in which each category is placed within a rectangle and subcategories are nested as rectangles within those rectangles. A **sunburst chart** is also a hierarchy chart, but it groups categories within a series of concentric rings, with the upper levels of the hierarchy placed in the innermost rings. To insert one of these chart types, click the Insert tab, click the Insert Hierarchy Chart button in the Charts group, then click the chart type. **Waterfall charts** are used to track the addition and subtraction of values within a sum. To insert a Waterfall chart, click the Insert tab, click the Insert Waterfall, Funnel, Stock, Surface, or Radar Chart button in the Charts group, then click Waterfall. A **histogram chart** shows the distribution of data grouped in bins.

These charts look similar to column charts, but each column (or bin) represents a range of values. To insert a histogram chart, click the Insert tab on the ribbon, click the Insert Statistic Chart button in the Charts group, then click the Histogram chart button. You can edit the bins in a histogram chart by double-clicking the x-axis, clicking to expand the Axis Options group on the Format Axis pane, then choosing options under Bins.

A **scatter chart** displays the correlation between two numeric variables. It is a type of **XY scatter chart**, which shows the pattern or relationship between two or more sets of values. Scatter charts look similar to line charts but have two value axes. The data points on a scatter chart show the intersection of the horizontal and vertical axes values. To insert a scatter chart, select the data you want to chart, click the Insert tab, click the Insert Scatter (X,Y) or Bubble Chart button in the Charts group, then choose a scatter chart type.

Summarize Data with Sparklines

You can create a quick overview of your data by adding sparklines to the worksheet cells. A **sparkline** is a small, simple chart located within a worksheet cell that serves as a visual indicator of data trends. Sparklines usually appear close to the data they represent. Any changes that you make to a worksheet are reflected in the sparklines that represent the data. After you add sparklines to a worksheet, you can change the sparkline style and color, and you can format their high and low data points in special colors.

CASE ▶ *As a supplement to the charts, Ellie wants the U.S. worksheet to illustrate the expense trends for the year. You decide to add sparklines to tell a quick visual story within the worksheet cells.*

STEPS

1. **Click the U.S. sheet tab, click cell G5, click the Insert tab on the ribbon if necessary, click the Column button in the Sparklines group, verify that the insertion point is in the Data Range box, select the range B5:E5 on the worksheet, then click OK**
   Columns showing the expense trend for New York appear in cell G5.

2. **With cell G5 selected, drag the fill handle ✛ to fill the range G6:G12**
   The sparkline is copied, and column sparklines reflecting the data for each office are added, as shown in FIGURE 4-21.

3. **Click cell G5, then click the Line button in the Type group on the Sparkline Tools Design tab**
   When sparklines are copied they become a group, so all the sparklines in this group change to the Line sparkline type. When any sparkline type in a group is changed, the other sparklines in the group change to match the new type. You can ungroup and group sparklines using the Group and Ungroup buttons in the Group group.

4. **Click the Sparkline Color button in the Style group, then click Plum, Accent 1, Lighter 10% (last row, fifth color from the left)**

5. **Click the More button ⤓ in the Style group, then click Plum, Sparkline Style Accent 3, Darker 50% (third from the left in the first row)**
   The sparkline colors and styles are consistent with the colors on the worksheet.

6. **Click the Marker Color button in the Style group, point to High Point, select Plum Accent 2, Darker 50% (sixth from left, sixth row), click the Marker Color button in the Style group, point to Markers, select Blue-Gray, Accent 6 (last in Theme Colors), then click the Markers check box in the Show group to add a checkmark if necessary**
   Data markers indicate each quarter's expenses, with the highest quarter value in a different color.

7. **Click cell C5, type 6,742.13, click the Enter button ✓, then compare your screen to** FIGURE 4-22
   The sparklines update to reflect the new worksheet data.

8. **Click the Insert tab on the ribbon, click the Text button, click the Header & Footer button in the Text group, click the Go to Footer button in the Navigation group, enter your name in the center footer section, click any cell on the worksheet, click the Normal button ▦ on the status bar, then press CTRL+HOME**

9. **Save your changes**

FIGURE 4-21: Expense trend sparklines

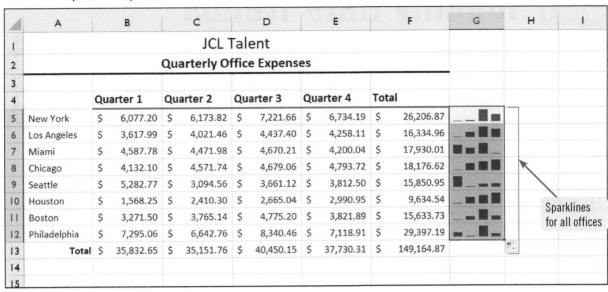

FIGURE 4-22: Formatted sparklines

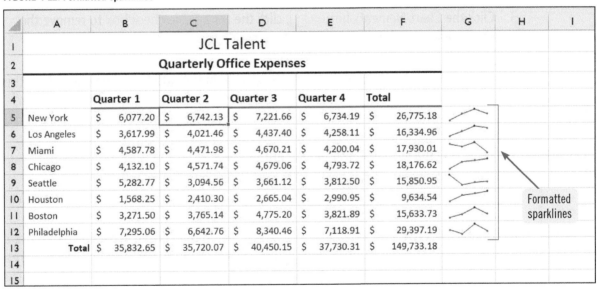

Excel
Module 4

Identify Data Trends

Learning Outcomes
- Compare chart data using trendlines
- Format a trendline
- Forecast future trends using trendlines

To emphasize trends and patterns that occur over a period of time, you can add one or more trendlines to a chart. A **trendline** is a series of data points on a line that shows data values representing the general direction of a data series. In some business situations, you can use trendlines to project future data based on past trends. CASE *As part of her presentation, Ellie wants to compare the New York and Houston expenses. You decide to use trendlines to highlight spending at these offices over the past year and project expenses for the next six months, if past trends continue.*

STEPS

1. **Right-click the Column sheet tab, click Move or Copy on the shortcut menu, click (move to end) in the Before sheet box, click the Create a copy check box to add a checkmark, then click OK**

   The new worksheet Column (2) is a copy of the Column sheet.

2. **Right-click the Column (2) sheet tab, click Rename on the shortcut menu, type Trends, click the Chart to select it, click the Chart Tools Design tab, then click the Switch Row/Column button in the Data group**

   The chart displays quarters, a time measure, on the x-axis.

3. **Click the Chart Elements button, click the Data Table check box to remove the checkmark, click the Legend arrow, then click Bottom**

   The data table is removed and a legend is added.

4. **Click Trendline, verify that New York is selected in the Add Trendline dialog box, then click OK**

   A linear trendline identifying the New York expense trend in the past year is added to the chart, along with an entry in the legend identifying the line.

QUICK TIP
To ensure that a chart element is not selected, simply click away from the element.

5. **Make sure the New York trendline is not selected, click if necessary, click the Trendline arrow, click Linear, click Houston in the Add Trendline dialog box, then click OK**

   The chart now has two trendlines, making it easy to compare the expense trends of the New York and Houston offices, as shown in FIGURE 4-23.

6. **Double-click the New York data series trendline, in the Format Trendline pane click the Trendline Options button if necessary, select 0.0 in the Forward box, type 1, press ENTER, click the Fill & Line button, select 1.5 in the Width box, type 2.5, then close the Format Trendline pane**

   Trendlines are often used to project future trends. The formatted New York trendline projects an additional quarter of future expenses trends for the office, assuming past trends continue.

7. **Double-click the Houston data series trendline, select 0.0 in the Forward box, type 1, press ENTER, click, select 1.5 in the Width box, type 2.5, then close the Format Trendline pane**

   The formatted Houston trendline also projects an additional quarter of future expenses, if past trends continue.

8. **sam Save your work, preview the Trends sheet, compare your chart to FIGURE 4-24, close the workbook, submit the workbook to your instructor, then close Excel**

FIGURE 4-23: Chart with two trendlines

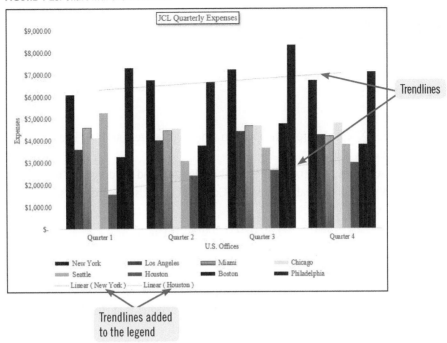

Trendlines

Trendlines added
to the legend

FIGURE 4-24: Expense chart with trendlines for New York and Houston data

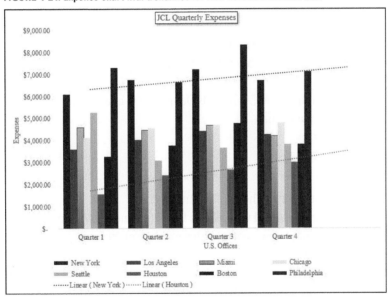

Choosing the right trendline options for your chart

When choosing a trendline, it is important to know which one is best for the information you want to communicate. If the data progression follows a straight line, using a linear trendline helps to emphasize that. If the pattern of a chart's data is linear but the data points don't follow a straight line, you can use a linear forecast trendline to chart a best-fit straight line. When data values increase or decrease in an arc shape, consider using an exponential or power trendline to illustrate this. A two-period moving average smooths out fluctuations in data by averaging the data points.

Practice

Skills Review

1. Create a chart.

   a. Start Excel, open IL_EX_4-2.xlsx from the location where you store your Data Files, then save it as **IL_EX_4_FoodServices**.

   b. In the worksheet, select the range containing all the sales data and headings. Do not include the totals.

   c. Use the Quick Analysis tool to create a Clustered Column chart. Use the first Clustered Column option, placing the months on the x-axis.

   d. Add the chart title **Brand Sales, by Month** above the chart.

   e. Save your work.

2. Move and resize a chart.

   a. Make sure the chart is still selected and close any open panes if necessary.

   b. Move the chart beneath the worksheet data so its upper-left corner is at the upper-left corner of cell A11.

   c. Widen the chart so it extends to the right edge of column H.

   d. Use the Quick Layout button in the Chart Layouts group on the Chart Tools Design tab to move the legend to the right of the charted data. (*Hint*: Use Layout 1.)

   e. Move the chart to a new worksheet that you name **Column**.

   f. Save your work.

3. Change the chart design.

   a. Activate the Q1 & Q2 sheet, then change the value in cell B4 to **80,000.00**. Activate the Column sheet and verify that the value for the Classic brand for January is $80,000.00.

   b. Select the chart if necessary.

   c. Use the Change Chart Type button on the Chart Tools Design tab to change the chart to a Clustered Bar chart, then change it back to a Clustered Column chart.

   d. Apply Chart Style 6 to the chart.

   e. Save your work.

4. Change the chart layout.

   a. Use the Chart Elements button to remove the gridlines in the chart.

   b. Change the font used in the horizontal and vertical axis labels to Times New Roman.

   c. Change the chart title's font to Times New Roman with a font size of 20 point.

   d. Insert **Sales** as the primary vertical axis title.

   e. Change the font size of the vertical axis title to 16 point and the font to Times New Roman.

   f. Add a solid line border to the chart title, using the default color and a (preset) shadow of Outer Offset: Bottom Right.

   g. Add a data table to the chart with a legend key.

   h. Save your work.

5. Format a chart.

   a. Use the Chart Tools Format tab to change the shape fill of the Classic data series to Olive Green, Accent 3, Darker 50% (last row of the theme colors, seventh from the left).

   b. Change the shape style of the Classic data series to Intense Effect – Blue, Accent 1 (sixth row, second from the left), then click the chart area to deselect the Classic data series.

   c. Save your work.

Skills Review (continued)

6. Create a pie chart.

  a. Switch to the Q1 & Q2 sheet, then select the range A4:A8 and H4:H8. (*Hint*: Holding CTRL allows you to select multiple nonadjacent ranges.)

  b. Create a 2-D pie chart and move the chart beneath the worksheet data so the upper-left corner is at the upper-left corner of cell A11.

  c. Add data callout labels and do not display the legend.

  d. Change the chart title to **Q1 & Q2 Sales** and format the title using the WordArt style Fill: Blue, Accent color 1, Shadow (second style in the first row).

  e. Explode the Artisan slice from the pie chart at **20%**.

  f. Enter your name in the center footer section of the worksheet, then save your work.

7. Summarize data with sparklines.

  a. Add a Line sparkline to cell I4 that represents the data in the range B4:G4.

  b. Copy the sparkline in cell I4 into the range I5:I8.

  c. Change the sparklines to columns.

  d. Apply the Sparkline style Blue Sparkline Style Dark #1 (fifth row, first column) to the group.

  e. Add high point markers with the color of Red, Accent 2 (first row, sixth from the left).

  f. Preview the worksheet and compare it to **FIGURE 4-25**.

  g. Save the workbook.

FIGURE 4-25

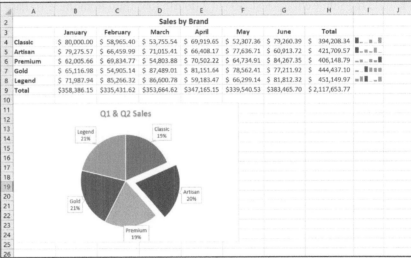

8. Identify data trends.

  a. Switch to the Column sheet.

  b. Add linear trendlines to the Premium and Gold data series.

  c. Set the forward option to 2 periods for both trendlines.

  d. Change the width of both trendlines to 3, then compare your screen to **FIGURE 4-26**.

  e. Add your name to the center footer section of the Column sheet, save the workbook, close the workbook, then submit the workbook to your instructor.

  f. Close Excel.

FIGURE 4-26

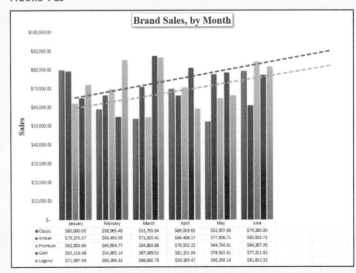

Independent Challenge 1

As an insurance manager for Riverwalk Medical Clinic, you have been asked to review the reimbursements for the clinic's departments. You will create a chart showing the insurance reimbursement over the past four quarters and predict future trends based on this history.

a. Start Excel, open IL_EX_4-3.xlsx from the location where you store your Data Files, then save it as **IL_EX_4_Reimbursements**.

b. Create a Clustered Column chart using the reimbursement amounts for the quarters and departments. (*Hint*: Do not include the totals.)

c. Switch the placement of the rows and columns, if necessary, to place the quarters on the x-axis.

d. Remove the chart gridlines.

e. Change the fill of the Psychology data series to Orange, Accent 6, Darker 50% (last row, last column of the Theme colors).

f. Add the Subtle effect – Red, Accent 2 (fourth row, third from the left) shape style to the Psychology data series.

g. Move the chart so the upper-left corner is at the upper-left corner of cell G2.

h. Change the fourth-quarter psychology reimbursement amount in cell E10 to **$60,254.20**.

i. Add the chart title **Reimbursements** and format the title with a solid line blue border from the Standard Colors.

j. Move the bottom chart border to the top of row 20, add a data table, then remove the chart legend.

k. Add trendlines to the cardiology and orthopedics department data forecasting 2 periods ahead.

l. Change the chart to a line chart, apply the Style 12 Chart Style to the chart, then compare your worksheet to FIGURE 4-27.

m. Enter your name in the center section of the worksheet footer, then save your work.

n. Submit your work to your instructor as directed.

o. Close the workbook, then close Excel.

FIGURE 4-27

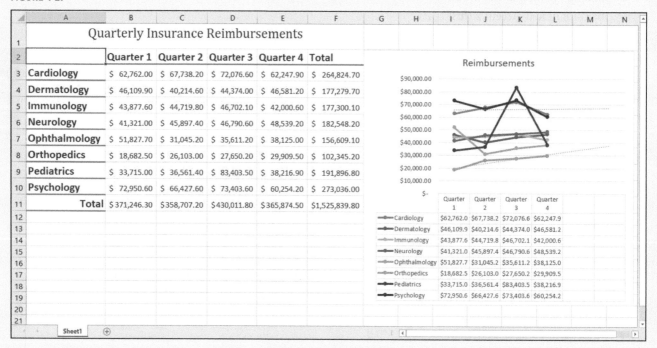

Independent Challenge 2

One of your responsibilities as the director of enrollment at Oceanview College is to present enrollment data to the executive staff at the end of the academic year. Your assistant has organized the college's enrollment data by division in a worksheet. You will review the data and create charts to visually represent the enrollment for the year.

a. Start Excel, open IL_EX_4-4.xlsx from the location where you store your Data Files, then save it as **IL_EX_4_Enrollments**.

b. Create a 3-D Clustered Column chart in the worksheet showing the enrollment data for all four terms. (*Hint:* The divisions, such as STEM, Business, and so forth, should appear on the x-axis.)

c. Add the chart title **Enrollment, by Division**, then format the title with the WordArt style of Fill: Blue, Accent color 1; Shadow (first row, second from left).

d. Move the chart so its upper-left corner is at the upper-left corner of cell H3.

e. On the worksheet, type **Average** in cell F3, then enter a formula in cell F4 to calculate the average STEM enrollment for the year.

f. Copy the average formula in cell F4 to the range F5:F9.

g. Add the average data from column F to the chart. (*Hint:* Use the Select Data button on the Chart Tools Design tab to select the new chart data, including the average data.)

h. Change the chart type to Combo Clustered Column - Line chart (first option of combo charts) with the average data series charted as a line. (*Hint:* After selecting the chart type in the Change Chart Type dialog box, scroll down to make sure the Fall, Spring, Summer, and Intersession series are charted as clustered columns and the Average data series is charted as a line. You may need to change the Intersession chart type. Do not use the secondary axis options.)

i. Add data labels to the Average data series only. (*Hint:* Select the Average data series on the chart before adding data labels.)

j. Save your work, then compare your worksheet to FIGURE 4-28.

k. Enter your name in the center footer section of the chart sheet, then preview the worksheet.

l. Submit your work to your instructor as directed, close the workbook, then close Excel.

FIGURE 4-28

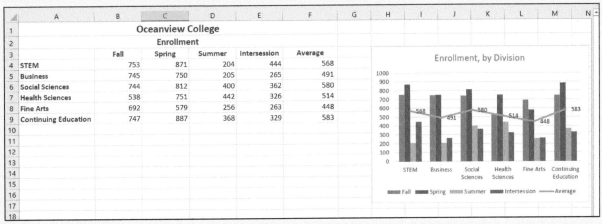

Visual Workshop

Open IL_EX_4-5.xlsx from the location where you store your Data Files, then save it as **IL_EX_4_Insurance**. Create, modify, and position the two charts, as shown in **FIGURE 4-29**. (*Hint*: Use the CTRL key as needed to select nonadjacent ranges.) You will need to make formatting, layout, and design changes once you create the charts. (*Hints*: The WordArt used in the pie chart title is Fill: Orange, Accent color 4: Soft Bevel. The WordArt used in the column chart title is Fill: Turquoise, Accent color 1: Shadow. The Life data point in the pie chart is exploded 30 degrees.) Enter your name in the center section of the footer, then save and preview the worksheet. Submit your work to your instructor as directed, then close the workbook and close Excel.

FIGURE 4-29

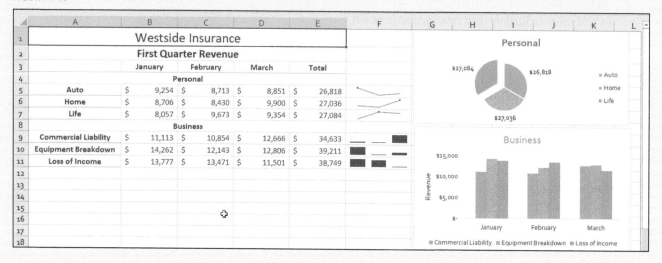

Working with Tables

CASE ▶ JCL uses tables to analyze placement data using placement dates, divisions, and commissions. The manager of the Boston office, Cheri McNeil, asks you to help her build and manage a table of information about the office's placements for the year. You will create the table, add information, organize it so it is easy to view, and perform calculations that help Cheri understand how the Boston office performed.

Module Objectives

After completing this module, you will be able to:

- Create and format a table
- Add and delete table data
- Sort table data
- Use formulas in a table
- Filter a table
- Look up values in a table
- Summarize table data
- Validate table data

Files You Will Need

IL_EX_5-1.xlsx   IL_EX_5-4.xlsx

IL_EX_5-2.xlsx   IL_EX_5-5.xlsx

IL_EX_5-3.xlsx

Create and Format a Table

Learning
Outcomes
• Create a table
• Format a table

You can analyze and manipulate data in a table structure to take advantage of Excel tools and features designed specifically for tables. An Excel **table** is an organized collection of rows and columns of similarly structured data on a worksheet. Tables offer a convenient way to understand and manage large amounts of information. A table is organized into rows of data called **records**, each of which represents a complete set of field values for a specific person, place, object, event, or idea. A **field** is a column containing a specific property for each record, such as a person's last name or street address. Each field has a field name, which is a column label, such as "Address," that describes its contents. The **header row** is the first row of the table, and it contains the field names. After you create a table you can add preset formatting combinations of fill color, borders, type style, and type color by applying a table style. **CASE** *You begin building the placement table by creating it using worksheet data and applying a table style.*

STEPS

1. **sam⁺** Start Excel, open IL_EX_5-1.xlsx from the location where you store your Data Files, then save it as IL_EX_5_BostonPlacements

2. With cell A1 selected, click the Insert tab on the ribbon, click the Table button in the Tables group, in the Create Table dialog box verify that the range $A$1:$H$65 appears in the Where is the data for your table? box and the My table has headers check box contains a checkmark, as shown in FIGURE 5-1, then click OK

   The data range is now defined as a table and is selected. **Filter list arrows**, which let you display portions of your data, appear next to each field name in the table. When you create a table, Excel automatically applies a table style. The default table style has a dark blue header row and alternating light and dark blue data rows. The Table Tools Design tab appears, and the Table Styles group displays a gallery of table formatting options.

3. Click the Table Styles More button ▼ on the Table Tools Design tab, scroll and view all of the table styles, then move the pointer over several styles without clicking

   The Table Styles gallery on the Table Tools Design tab contains three style categories—Light, Medium, and Dark—each of which includes numerous designs. The designs use the current workbook theme colors so the table coordinates with your existing workbook content. If you select a different workbook theme and color scheme in the Themes group on the Page Layout tab, the Table Styles gallery uses those colors.

4. Click the Green, Table Style Light 14 table style (the first style in the third row under Light), then click cell A1

5. Position the pointer in the column heading area for column A until it changes to ↓, drag to select columns A and B, press CTRL, then drag ↓ to select the column headings for columns F, G, and H

6. Click the Home tab on the ribbon, click the Format button in the Cells group, click Column Width, in the Column Width dialog box type 15.57 in the Column width box, then click OK

7. Position the pointer in the column D heading area until it changes to ↓, drag to select columns D and E, click the Format button in the Cells group, click Column Width, in the Column Width dialog box type 9.43 in the Column width box, then click OK

8. Click cell A1, compare your table to FIGURE 5-2, then save your work

FIGURE 5-1: **Create Table dialog box**

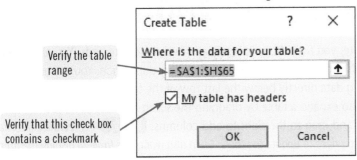

Verify the table range

Verify that this check box contains a checkmark

FIGURE 5-2: **Formatted table**

	A	B	C	D	E	F	G	H	I	J	K
1	Account #	Employer ID	Division	Posting Date	Filled Date	Position Type	Commission	Preferred Employer			
2	6686	69661	Finance & Accounting	10/13/21	11/10/21	Full-time	$16,171	Yes			
3	6488	49734	Creative	4/5/21	4/14/21	Consultant	$9,546	No			
4	5499	88302	Office Support	12/22/21	12/29/21	Full-time	$10,098	Yes			
5	4438	51467	Technical	3/26/21	5/3/21	Full-time	$15,751	Yes			
6	7569	30405	Creative	2/3/21	3/13/21	Full-time	$13,764	No			Division Info
7	7803	99768	Technical	2/24/21	3/29/21	Consultant	$8,547	No			Division
8	7701	26988	Office Support	8/14/21	9/13/21	Consultant	$5,324	Yes			Technica
9	2886	30993	Office Support	1/15/21	2/16/21	Consultant	$7,984	Yes			
10	9017	82305	Finance & Accounting	7/8/21	8/7/21	Full-time	$20,724	Yes			Total Con
11	4507	22043	Finance & Accounting	10/14/21	11/23/21	Consultant	$5,693	No			
12	5801	64998	Creative	2/8/21	3/12/21	Consultant	$2,478	No			Number of Pl
13	4890	37262	Creative	5/1/21	6/1/21	Consultant	$824	No			
14	3117	93040	Technical	4/26/21	5/17/21	Full-time	$18,434	Yes			
15	3100	85601	Office Support	8/2/21	8/24/21	Full-time	$14,277	Yes			
16	4302	74521	Technical	7/2/21	8/9/21	Full-time	$16,976	No			
17	6488	49734	Creative	4/5/21	4/14/21	Consultant	$9,546	No			
18	1262	26610	Office Support	4/16/21	5/5/21	Consultant	$6,321	No			

Changing table style options

You can change a table's appearance by using the check boxes in the Table Style Options group on the Table Tools Design tab, as shown in **FIGURE 5-3**. You can use the checkboxes to turn on or turn off the following options: Header Row, which displays or hides the header row; Total Row, which calculates totals for each column; Banded Rows, which applies or removes **banding**, a type of fill formatting in alternating rows or columns; and First Column and Last Column, which applies or removes special formatting in the first and last columns. You can display or hide the filter arrows on a table using the Filter Button check box; removing the checkmark removes the arrows.

You can also create your own table style by clicking the Table Styles More button, then clicking New Table Style at the bottom of the Table Styles Gallery. In the New Table Style dialog box, enter a name for the style in the Name box, click an item in the Table Element list, then click Format to format the selected element. You can also set a custom style as the default style for your tables by adding a checkmark to the Set as default table style for this document check box. You can remove a table style from the currently selected table by clicking Clear at the bottom of the Table Styles gallery.

FIGURE 5-3: **Table Style Options group**

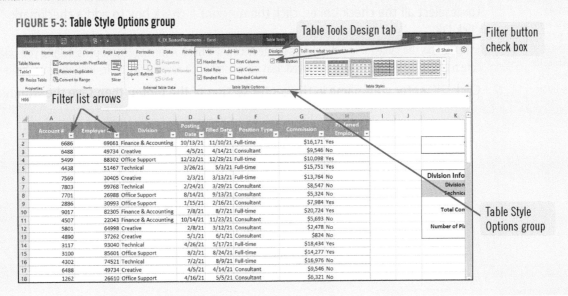

Table Tools Design tab

Filter button check box

Filter list arrows

Table Style Options group

Add and Delete Table Data

Learning
Outcomes
• Add a row to a
  table
• Delete a table row
• Add a column to
  a table
• Remove duplicate
  data from a table

To keep a table up to date, you need to periodically add and remove records. You also need to check a table for duplicate records so that you can remove unnecessary duplication. You can add records and columns to a table by typing data directly below the last row of the table or directly to the right of the last table column. You can also expand a table by dragging the sizing handle in a table's lower-right corner; drag down to add rows and drag to the right to add columns. **CASE** *A recruiter informs you of an additional placement, so you need to update the table. Cheri also wants the table to display the number of days a placement was posted before it was filled.*

STEPS

QUICK TIP
You can insert rows in a specific location by clicking the inside left edge of the cell in column A below where you want to add a row, clicking the Insert arrow in the Cells group, then clicking Insert Table Rows Above.

1. **Scroll down to the last table row, click cell** A66, **enter the data shown below, then press [Enter]**

Account #	Employer ID	Division	Posting Date	Filled Date	Position Type	Commission	Preferred Employer
9408	32231	Creative	12/13/2021	12/23/2021	Consultant	$8,125	Yes

As you scroll down, notice that the table headers are visible at the top of the table as long as the active cell is inside the table. The new placement is now part of the table.

2. **Click cell** I1, **type** Days Posted, **press ENTER, then resize the width of column I to 10.00**
The new field becomes part of the table, and the header formatting extends to the new field name, as shown in **FIGURE 5-4**. The table range is now A1:I66.

3. **Click the** inside left edge of cell A3 **to select the table row, click the** Delete arrow **in the Cells group, then click** Delete Table Rows
The placement in row 3 is deleted, and the placement in row 4 moves up to row 3. You can also delete a table row or a column by right-clicking the row or column, then clicking Delete.

4. **Click the** Table Tools Design tab **on the ribbon, then click the** Remove Duplicates button **in the Tools group**
The table is selected, and the Remove Duplicates dialog box opens, as shown in **FIGURE 5-5**.

QUICK TIP
You can remove duplicate rows from a worksheet by clicking the Data tab, then clicking the Remove Duplicates button in the Data Tools group.

5. **Make sure the** My data has headers check box **contains a checkmark, click** Unselect All **to deselect all the check boxes, click the** Account # check box **to add a checkmark, then click** OK
Excel checks the table for any duplicates in the Account # field. A message box opens, telling you one duplicate record has been found and removed, leaving a total of 64 rows in the table, including the header row.

6. **Click OK, enter your name in the center section of the footer, then save the workbook**

Working with Tables

FIGURE 5-4: New table column

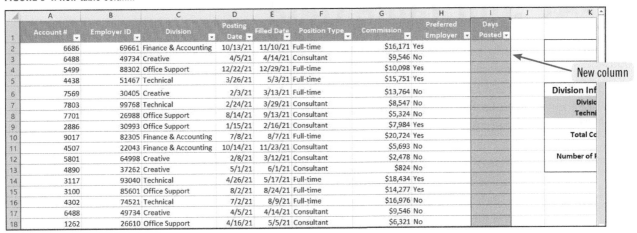

FIGURE 5-5: Remove Duplicates dialog box

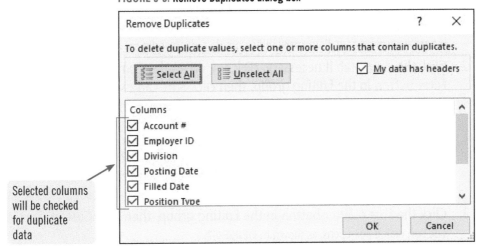

Selecting table elements

When working with tables you often need to select rows, columns, and even the entire table. Clicking to the right of a row number, inside column A, selects the table row. You can select a table column by clicking the top edge of the column. Be careful not to click a column letter or row number, however, because this selects the entire worksheet row or column. You can select the entire table by clicking the upper-left corner of the top-left table cell. When selecting a column or a table, the first click selects only the data in the column or table. If you click a second time, you add the headers to the selection.

Sort Table Data

Usually, you add table records in the order in which you receive information, rather than in alphabetical or numerical order, so new records commonly appear at the bottom of the table. You can change the order of records, or **sort** them, which organizes data in ascending or descending order, based on criteria such as date. Because the data is structured as a table, Excel changes the order of the records while keeping the data in each record, or row, together. You can sort a table in ascending or descending order on a field using the filter list arrows next to the field name, or using the Sort & Filter button on the ribbon. In **ascending order**, the lowest value (the beginning of the alphabet or the earliest date) appears at the top of the table, because data is sorted from lowest to highest, earliest to more recent, or alphabetically from A to Z; in a field containing labels and numbers, numbers appear first in the sorted list. In **descending order**, the highest value (the end of the alphabet or the latest date) appears at the top of the table because data is sorted from highest to lowest, most recent to earliest, or from Z to A; in a field containing labels and numbers, labels appear first. TABLE 5-1 provides examples of ascending and descending sorts. **CASE** ▶ *Cheri wants the table sorted by the date the placement was filled, with placements that were filled the earliest at the top of the table.*

STEPS

1. **Click the** Filled Date filter list arrow, **then click** Sort Oldest to Newest

   Excel rearranges the records in ascending order by filled date, as shown in **FIGURE 5-6**. The Filled Date filter list arrow displays a small up arrow indicating that an ascending sort in this field has been applied.

2. **Click the** Home tab **if necessary, click any** cell **in the Commission column, click the** Sort & Filter button **in the Editing group, then click** Sort Largest to Smallest

   Excel sorts the table, placing records with higher commissions at the top. The Commission filter list arrow now displays a small down arrow, indicating the descending sort order. You can also rearrange table data using a **multilevel sort**, which reorders records using more than one column or field at a time; each field is considered a different level, based on its importance in the sort. In a two-level sort, for instance, the records are sorted by the first field, and then within each grouping created by that first sort they are sorted by the second field.

3. **Click the** Sort & Filter button **in the Editing group, then click** Custom Sort

   The Sort dialog box opens, as shown in **FIGURE 5-7**.

4. **Click the** Sort by arrow, **click** Division, **click the** Order arrow, **click** A to Z, **click** Add Level, **click the** Then by arrow, **click** Commission, **click the second** Order arrow, **click** Smallest to Largest **if necessary, then click** OK

   As shown in **FIGURE 5-8**, the table is sorted alphabetically in ascending order (A–Z) by Division and, within each division grouping, in ascending order by the Commission (smallest amount to largest).

5. **Save the workbook**

TABLE 5-1: Sort order options and examples

option	alphabetic	numeric	date	alphanumeric
Ascending	A, B, C	7, 8, 9	1/1, 2/1, 3/1	12A, 99B, DX8, QT7
Descending	C, B, A	9, 8, 7	3/1, 2/1, 1/1	QT7, DX8, 99B, 12A

FIGURE 5-6: Table sorted by filled date

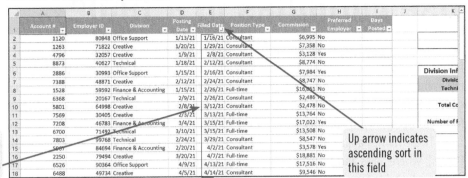

Records are sorted by filled date in ascending order

Up arrow indicates ascending sort in this field

FIGURE 5-7: Sort dialog box

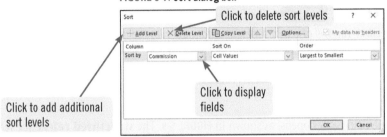

Click to delete sort levels

Click to add additional sort levels

Click to display fields

FIGURE 5-8: Table sorted using two levels

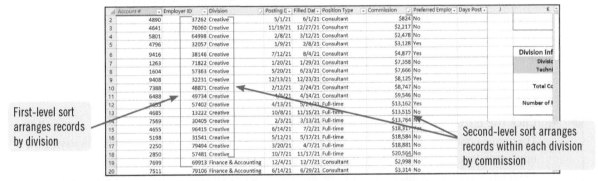

First-level sort arranges records by division

Second-level sort arranges records within each division by commission

Sorting conditional formatted data

You can emphasize top-ranked or bottom-ranked values in a field or column by applying conditional formatting to the sorted data. To highlight the top or bottom values in a field, select the field data, click the Conditional Formatting button in the Styles group on the Home tab, point to Top/Bottom Rules, click a rule, if necessary modify the percentage or number of cells you want to format, select the desired formatting, then click OK. You can also format your worksheet or table data using color scales based on the cell values. A **color scale** is a formatting scheme that uses a color set or shades of color to convey relative values of data. For example, you could use red fill to indicate cells that have higher values and green fill to signify lower values. To add a color scale, select a data range, click the Home tab, click the Conditional Formatting button in the Styles group, then point to Color Scales. On the submenu, you can select preformatted color sets or click More Rules to create your own color sets. If conditional formats have been applied to a table or worksheet data, you can sort the table using conditional formatting to arrange the rows. For example, if cells are conditionally formatted with color, you can use the Sort dialog box to sort a field on Cell Color, using the color with the order of On Top or On Bottom in the Sort dialog box.

Specifying a custom sort order

You can identify a custom sort order in the Sort dialog box if the standard alphabetic and numeric sort orders do not meet your needs. For example, you might want to sort records by days of the week (Sun, Mon, Tues, Wed, etc.); an alphabetic sort would not sort these items properly. In the Sort dialog box, first specify the field you want to sort on, click the Order arrow, then click Custom List. In the Custom Lists dialog box that opens, click an item under Custom lists, view the list entries, then click OK. To build your own custom list, click NEW LIST, click Add, type the desired list under List entries, then click OK.

Excel

Use Formulas in a Table

The Excel table calculation features help you summarize table data so you can see important patterns and trends. After you enter a single formula into a table cell, the **calculated column** feature automatically fills in the remaining cells in the column with formula results, using the formula you entered. The column continues to fill with the formula results as you enter rows in the table. This makes it easy to update your formulas because you only need to edit the formula once, and the change fills in to the other column cells. These names adjust as you add or delete table fields. An example of a table reference is =[Sales]–[Costs], where Sales and Costs are field names in the table. You can also add a **table total row** to the bottom of a table for calculations on the table data. Clicking a cell in this row displays an arrow you can click to open a list of functions that can be used for the column calculation. The table total row adapts to any changes in the table size. **CASE** ▶ *Cheri asks you to calculate the number of days each placement was posted before being filled. You will also add summary information to the end of the table.*

STEPS

1. **Click cell I2, then type =[**
   A list of the table field names opens, as shown in FIGURE 5-9. The **structured reference** feature allows table formulas to refer to table columns by names that are automatically generated when the table is created. You can choose a field name by clicking it and pressing TAB or by double-clicking it.

2. **Click [Filled Date], press TAB, then type]**
   Excel begins the formula, placing [Filled Date] in the cell, in blue, and framing the Filled Date data in a blue border.

3. **Type -[, double-click [Posting Date], then type]**
   Excel places [Posting Date] in the cell in red and outlines the Posting Date data in a red border.

4. **Click the Enter button ✓ on the Formula Bar**
   The formula result, 31, is displayed in cell I2. The table column also fills with the formula, displaying the number of days each placement was posted before being filled. The AutoCorrect Options button provides an option to turn off calculated columns. Because the calculated columns option saves time, you decide to leave the feature on.

5. **Click the Table Tools Design tab on the ribbon, then click the Total Row check box in the Table Style Options group to add a checkmark**
   A total row appears at the bottom of the table, and the sum of the number of days posted, 1367, is displayed in cell I65.

6. **Click cell I65, click the cell list arrow on the right side of the cell, click Average, click the Home tab on the ribbon, then click the Decrease Decimal button 🔢 in the Number group five times**

7. **Click cell G65 (in the Commission column), click the cell list arrow, then click Sum**
   The total row shows the average of days a placement was posted and the total amount of commissions earned by the office this year.

8. **Click cell A65, press DELETE, click cell F65 (in the Position Type column), type Total Commissions, click ✓, click cell H65, type Average Days, click ✓, widen column F to fully display the label in cell F65, compare your total row to FIGURE 5-10, then save your work**

FIGURE 5-9: Table field names

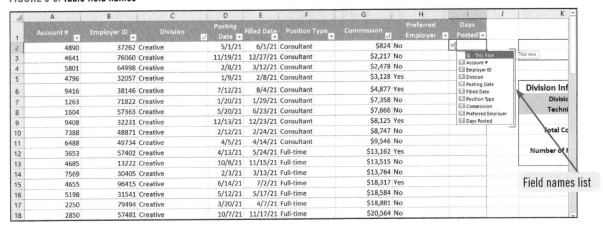

FIGURE 5-10: Table with total row

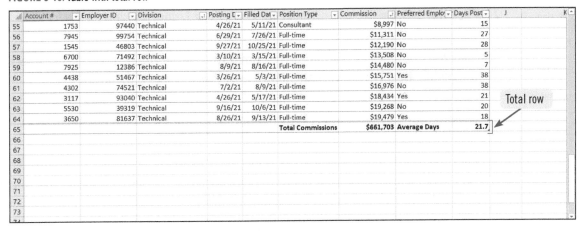

Filter a Table

In addition to sorting records, you can **filter** them, specifying a set of restrictions to only display specific records. You can filter quickly by using the **AutoFilter** feature to click a column's filter list arrow and then sort on or view selected values. **CASE** *Cheri asks you to display only the creative division's records. She also asks for information about the most lucrative placements, and placements that were posted in the second quarter.*

STEPS

1. **Click the** Division filter list arrow, **in the list of divisions for the field click** Select All **to clear the checkmarks, click** Creative, **then click** OK

   Only those records containing "Creative" in the Division field appear, as shown in **FIGURE 5-11**. The row numbers for the matching records change to blue, and the list arrow for the filtered field displays a filter icon 🔽. Both indicate that there is a filter in effect and that some of the records are temporarily hidden.

2. **Click the** Division list arrow, **then click** Clear Filter From "Division"

   You have cleared the Division filter, and all the records reappear.

3. **Click the** Commission filter list arrow, **point to** Number Filters, **click** Top 10, **select** 10 **in the middle box, type** 5, **click the** Items arrow, **click** Percent, **then click** OK

   Excel displays the records for the top five percent in the Commission field, as shown in **FIGURE 5-12**.

4. **Click the** Sort & Filter button **in the Editing group on the Home tab, then click** Clear

   You have cleared the filter and all the records reappear.

5. **Click the** Filled Date filter list arrow, **point to** Date Filters, **then click** Custom Filter

   The Custom AutoFilter dialog box allows you to create more detailed filters by entering your criteria in the text boxes. Your criteria can contain comparison operators such as greater than or less than. You can also use **logical conditions** such as And to display records that meet both a criterion in a field *and* another criterion in that same field, and you can use Or to display records that meet either criterion in a field.

6. **Click the** left text box arrow **on the first line, click** is after or equal to, **type** 4/1/2021 **in the right text box on the first line, verify that the** And option button **is selected, click the** left text box arrow **on the second line, click** is before or equal to, **type** 6/30/2021 **in the right text box on the second line, then click** OK

   Only the placements filled in the second quarter, after 4/1/2021 and before 6/30/2021, appear in the worksheet, as shown in **FIGURE 5-13**.

7. **Click the** Filled Date filter list arrow, **then click** Clear Filter From "Filled Date"

   You have cleared the filter and all the records reappear.

8. **Save the workbook**

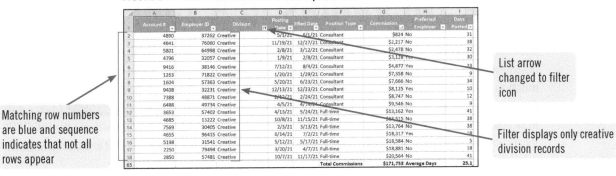

FIGURE 5-11: Table filtered to show Creative placements

	Account #	Employer ID	Division	Posting Date	Filled Date	Position Type	Commission	Preferred Employer	Days Posted
2	4890	37262	Creative	5/1/21	6/1/21	Consultant	$824	No	31
3	4641	76060	Creative	11/19/21	12/27/21	Consultant	$2,217	No	38
4	5801	64998	Creative	2/8/21	3/12/21	Consultant	$2,478	No	32
5	4796	32057	Creative	1/9/21	2/8/21	Consultant	$3,128	Yes	30
6	9416	38146	Creative	7/12/21	8/4/21	Consultant	$4,877	Yes	23
7	1263	71822	Creative	1/20/21	1/29/21	Consultant	$7,358	No	9
8	1604	57363	Creative	5/20/21	6/23/21	Consultant	$7,666	No	34
9	9408	32231	Creative	12/13/21	12/23/21	Consultant	$8,125	Yes	10
10	7388	48871	Creative	2/12/21	2/24/21	Consultant	$8,747	No	12
11	6488	49734	Creative	4/5/21	4/14/21	Consultant	$9,546	No	9
12	3653	57402	Creative	4/13/21	5/24/21	Full-time	$13,162	No	41
13	4685	13222	Creative	10/8/21	11/15/21	Full-time	$13,515	No	38
14	7569	30405	Creative	2/3/21	3/13/21	Full-time	$13,764	No	38
15	4655	96415	Creative	6/14/21	7/2/21	Full-time	$18,317	Yes	18
16	5198	31541	Creative	5/12/21	5/17/21	Full-time	$18,584	No	5
17	2250	79494	Creative	3/20/21	4/7/21	Full-time	$18,881	No	18
18	2850	57481	Creative	10/7/21	11/17/21	Full-time	$20,564	No	41
65						Total Commissions	$171,753	Average Days	25.1

Matching row numbers are blue and sequence indicates that not all rows appear

List arrow changed to filter icon

Filter displays only creative division records

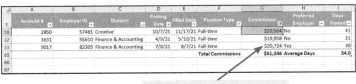

FIGURE 5-12: Table filtered with top 5% of commissions

	Account #	Employer ID	Division	Posting Date	Filled Date	Position Type	Commission	Preferred Employer	Days Posted
18	2850	57481	Creative	10/7/21	11/17/21	Full-time	$20,564	No	41
32	3631	55610	Finance & Accounting	4/9/21	5/10/21	Full-time	$19,958	No	31
33	9017	82305	Finance & Accounting	7/8/21	8/7/21	Full-time	$20,724	Yes	30
65						Total Commissions	$61,246	Average Days	34.0
66									
67									

Only records containing the top 5% in commissions appear

FIGURE 5-13: Results of custom filter

	Account #	Employer ID	Division	Posting Date	Filled Date	Position Type	Commission	Preferred Employer	Days Posted
2	4890	37262	Creative	5/1/21	6/1/21	Consultant	$824	No	31
8	1604	57363	Creative	5/20/21	6/23/21	Consultant	$7,666	No	34
11	6488	49734	Creative	4/5/21	4/14/21	Consultant	$9,546	No	9
12	3653	57402	Creative	4/13/21	5/24/21	Full-time	$13,162	Yes	41
16	5198	31541	Creative	5/12/21	5/17/21	Full-time	$18,584	No	5
17	2250	79494	Creative	3/20/21	4/7/21	Full-time	$18,881	No	18
18	7511	79106	Finance & Accounting	6/14/21	6/29/21	Consultant	$3,314	No	15
21	6967	84694	Finance & Accounting	2/20/21	4/2/21	Consultant	$3,578	Yes	41
27	1803	89294	Finance & Accounting	6/3/21	6/21/21	Full-time	$14,398	Yes	18
31	8806	76870	Finance & Accounting	4/22/21	5/18/21	Full-time	$19,035	No	26
32	3631	55610	Finance & Accounting	4/9/21	5/10/21	Full-time	$19,958	No	31
36	1949	55639	Office Support	4/5/21	5/3/21	Consultant	$5,447	No	28
39	1262	26610	Office Support	4/16/21	5/5/21	Consultant	$6,321	No	19
46	6526	90364	Office Support	4/9/21	4/13/21	Full-time	$17,516	No	4
50	3700	64735	Technical	5/19/21	6/3/21	Consultant	$5,968	Yes	15
52	2511	12281	Technical	4/1/21	4/17/21	Consultant	$7,642	No	16
55	1753	97440	Technical	4/26/21	5/11/21	Consultant	$8,997	No	15
60	4438	51467	Technical	3/26/21	5/3/21	Full-time	$15,751	Yes	38
62	3117	93040	Technical	4/26/21	5/17/21	Full-time	$18,434	Yes	21
65						Total Commissions	$215,022	Average Days	22.4

Placement dates are between 4/1 and 6/30

Using an advanced filter

When you want to see table data that meets a detailed set of conditions, you can use the Advanced Filter feature. This feature lets you specify data that you want to display from the table using And and Or conditions. Rather than entering the criteria in a dialog box, you enter the criteria in a criteria range on your worksheet. A **criteria range** is a location separate from the table that you use to list specific search specifications. This range is usually a copy of the column labels with at least one additional row beneath the labels that contains the criteria you want to match. Placing all criteria in the same row specifies an **And condition**, which searches only for records where all the entered criteria are matched. Placing criteria in different rows specifies an **Or condition**, which searches for records where at least one entered criterion is matched. To apply an advanced filter, add the criteria range to the worksheet, click any cell in the table, click the Data tab, click the Advanced button in the Sort & Filter group, in the Advanced Filter dialog box verify the table range in the List range box, click the Criteria range text box, select your criteria range on the worksheet, then click OK. The default setting under Action is to filter the table in its current location ("in-place") rather than copy it to another location. You can move the filtered table data to a different area of the worksheet or to a new worksheet. FIGURE 5-14 shows a worksheet with the And criteria range located in the range $A$67:$I$68 and the filtered results of consultant positions with commissions greater than $7,000.

FIGURE 5-14: Results of advanced filter

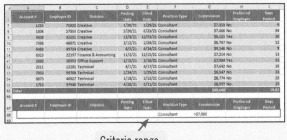

Criteria range

Excel

Look Up Values in a Table

Learning Outcomes
- Use table references in a VLOOKUP formula
- Find table information using VLOOKUP

The Excel VLOOKUP function helps you locate specific values in a table. VLOOKUP searches vertically (V) down the far-left column of a table, then reads across the row to find the value in the column you specify, much as you might look up a number in a name and address list: You read down the column to locate a person's name, then read across the row to find the phone number you want. **CASE** ▶ *Cheri wants to be able to find a division responsible for a placement by entering the account #. You will use the VLOOKUP function to accomplish this task. You begin by viewing the table name so you can refer to it in a lookup function.*

STEPS

1. **Click the** Formulas tab **on the ribbon, then click the** Name Manager button **in the Defined Names group**

   The table name appears in the Name Manager dialog box, as shown in **FIGURE 5-15**. The Excel structured reference feature automatically created the table name of Table1 when the table was created.

2. **Click** Close, **click cell** L2, **enter** 2850, **click cell** L3, **click the** Lookup & Reference button **in the Function Library group, then click** VLOOKUP

   The Function Arguments dialog box opens, with boxes for each of the VLOOKUP arguments.

3. **With the insertion point in the** Lookup_value text box **click cell** L2, **click the** Table_array text box, **then type** Table1

   Because the value you want to find is in cell L2, L2 is the Lookup_value. The table you want to search, Table1, is the Table_array.

QUICK TIP
If you want to find only the closest match for a value, enter TRUE in the Range_lookup text box. However, this can give misleading results if you are looking for an exact match. If you use FALSE and Excel can't find the value, you see an error message.

4. **Click the** Col_index_num text box, **type** 3, **click the** Range_lookup text box, **then enter** FALSE

   The column containing the information that you want to find and display in cell L3 is the third column from the left in the table range, so the Col_index_num is 3. Because you want to find an exact match for the value in cell L2, the Range_lookup argument is FALSE. Your completed Function Arguments dialog box should match **FIGURE 5-16**.

5. **Click** OK

   Excel searches down the far-left column of the table until it finds an account # that matches the one in cell L2. It then looks in column 3 of the table range and finds the division for that record, Creative, and displays it in cell L3.

6. **Click cell** L2, **type** 6234, **then click the** Enter button ☑ **on the formula bar**

   The VLOOKUP function returns the value of Technical in cell L3. You can use this function to determine the division for other account numbers.

7. **Press** CTRL+HOME, **then save the workbook**

FIGURE 5-15: **Named ranges in the workbook**

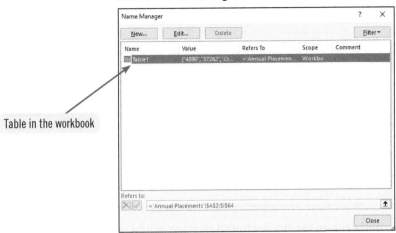

Table in the workbook

FIGURE 5-16: **Completed Function Arguments dialog box for VLOOKUP**

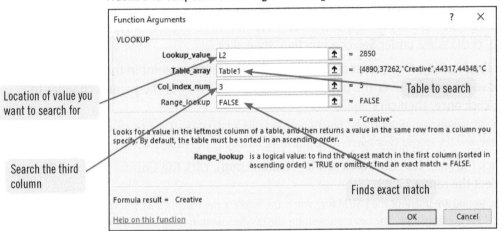

Location of value you want to search for

Search the third column

Table to search

Finds exact match

Using other LOOKUP functions

When your data is arranged horizontally in rows instead of vertically in columns, use the HLOOKUP (Horizontal Lookup) function. HLOOKUP searches horizontally across the upper row of a table until it finds the matching value, then looks down the number of rows you specify. The arguments are identical to those for the VLOOKUP function, except that instead of a Col_index_number, HLOOKUP uses a Row_index_number, which indicates the location of the row you want to search. When you want to know the position of an item in a range, you can use the MATCH function. The MATCH function uses the syntax: MATCH (lookup_value,lookup_array,match_ type) where the lookup_value is the value you want to match in the lookup_array range. The match_type can be 0 for an exact match, 1 for matching the largest value that is less than or equal to the lookup_value, or –1 for matching the smallest value that is greater than or equal to the lookup_value. The INDEX function is often used with the MATCH function, using the position obtained from the MATCH function and returning a value from a table or range. The syntax for the Index function is: INDEX(range,

row_num, column_num). For example, =INDEX(A1:D7, 3, 4) returns the value in the cell located at the intersection of the third row and fourth column in the range A1:D7. The MATCH function can be used to find the row for an INDEX function. For example:

=INDEX(A1:B5,MATCH(3250,E1:E4),2)

Here, the match function searches the database E1:E4 and finds the position of the value 3250. This position becomes the row value for the index function while 2 is the column position in the database A1:B5. The Transpose function is a LOOKUP function that can be used to rearrange a range of cells, which is also called an array. For example, a vertical range of cells will be arranged horizontally or vice versa. The Transpose array function is entered using the syntax =TRANSPOSE(range array). The LOOKUP function is used to locate information in a table. The syntax for the LOOKUP formula is LOOKUP(lookup_value, array). The lookup_value is the value that will be used in the search; the array is the range of cells that will be searched for the lookup_value.

Summarize Table Data

Learning Outcomes
- Select a database for a database function
- Summarize table data using a database function

An Excel table acts as a simple type of database, and you can use database functions to summarize table data in a variety of ways. When working with a sales activity table, for example, you can use Excel to count the number of client contacts by sales representative or to total the amount sold to specific accounts by month. **TABLE 5-2** lists commonly used database functions for summarizing table data. **CASE** ▶ *Cheri is reviewing the yearly performance of each division. She needs your help in analyzing the total number of placements and commissions for each division.*

STEPS

1. **Review the criteria range for the Technical division in the range K7:K8**

   The criteria range in K7:K8 tells Excel to summarize records with the entry "Technical" in the Division column.

2. **Click cell K11, click the Formulas tab on the ribbon, click the Insert Function button in the Function Library group, in the Search for a function text box type database, click Go, click DSUM under Select a function, then click OK**

   TROUBLE

   Because the DSUM formula uses the column headings to locate and sum the table data, you need to include the header row in the database range.

3. ▶ **In the Function Arguments dialog box, with the insertion point in the Database text box move the pointer over the upper-left corner of cell A1 until the pointer changes to ⬦, click once, then click again**

   The first argument of the DSUM function is the table, or database. The first click selects the table's data range, and the second click selects the entire table, including the header row.

   QUICK TIP

   You can move the Function Arguments dialog box if it overlaps a cell or range that you need to click. You can also click the Collapse Dialog Box button ⬆, select the cell or range, then click the Expand Dialog Box button ⬇ to return to the Function Arguments dialog box.

4. ▶ **Click the Field text box, click cell G1 (Commission), click the Criteria text box, then select the range K7:K8**

   The second argument of the DSUM function is the label for the column that you want to sum. You want to total the commissions. The last argument for the DSUM function is the criteria that will be used to determine which values to total. Your completed Function Arguments dialog box should match **FIGURE 5-17**.

5. **Click OK, click the Home tab on the ribbon, click the Accounting Number Format button $ in the Number group, then click the Decrease Decimal button twice**

   The result in cell K11 is $200,255. Excel totaled the information in the Commission column for those records that meet the criterion of Division equals Technical.

6. **Click cell K13, click the Insert Function button 𝑓ₓ on the formula bar, in the Search for a function text box type database, click Go, then double-click DCOUNTA in the Select a function list**

   The DCOUNT and the DCOUNTA functions can help you determine the number of records meeting specified criteria in a database field. DCOUNTA counts the number of nonblank cells.

   TROUBLE

   As an alternative to clicking to select a table, you can type the database argument, Table1[#All], in the Database text box.

7. ▶ **With the insertion point in the Database text box move the pointer over the upper-left corner of cell A1 until it changes to ⬦, click once, click again to include the header row, click the Field text box, click cell C1, click the Criteria text box and select the range K7:K8, then click OK**

   The result in cell K13 is 18, and it indicates that the technical division had 18 placements over the past year.

8. **Click cell K8, type Office Support, click the Enter button ✓ on the formula bar, then save your work**

   The formulas in cells K11 and K13 are updated to reflect the new criteria. **FIGURE 5-18** shows that the office support division had 13 placements and commissions of $112,230 over the past year.

FIGURE 5-17: Completed Function Arguments dialog box for DSUM

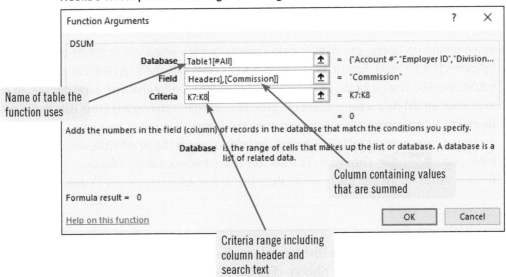

Name of table the function uses

Column containing values that are summed

Criteria range including column header and search text

FIGURE 5-18: Result generated by database functions

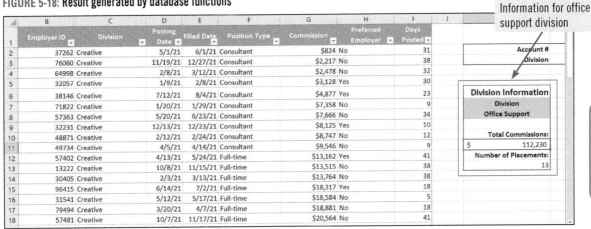

Information for office support division

TABLE 5-2: Common database functions

function	result
DGET	Extracts a single record from a table that matches criteria you specify
DSUM	Totals numbers in a given table column that match criteria you specify
DAVERAGE	Averages numbers in a given table column that match criteria you specify
DCOUNT	Counts the cells that contain numbers in a given table column that match criteria you specify
DCOUNTA	Counts the cells that contain nonblank data in a given table column that match criteria you specify

Excel

Validate Table Data

When setting up tables, you want to help ensure accuracy when you or others enter data. The Data Validation feature allows you to do this by specifying what data users can enter in a range of cells. Once you've specified what data the program should consider valid for that cell, Excel displays an error message when invalid data is entered and can prevent users from entering any other data that it considers to be invalid. When printing tables, you may have more rows than can fit on a page. In that case, you can define the first row of the table (containing the field names) as the **print title**, which prints at the top of every page. **CASE** *Cheri wants to make sure that information in the Division column is entered consistently in the future. She asks you to restrict the entries in that column to the office's divisions.*

STEPS

1. **Click the** top edge **of the Division column header to select the table data in this column, click the** Data tab **on the ribbon, click the** Data Validation button [icon] **in the Data Tools group, on the Settings tab of the Data Validation dialog box click the** Allow arrow, **click** List, **click the** Source box, **type** Creative, Finance & Accounting, Office Support, Technical, **verify that the** In-cell dropdown check box **contains a checkmark, then click** OK

2. **Click the** Home tab **on the ribbon, click any** cell **in the last table row, click the** Insert arrow **in the Cells group, click** Insert Table Row Below, **click the** Division cell **in this row, then click its** list arrow

   A list of valid list entries opens, based on the values entered in the Data Validation dialog box, as shown in **FIGURE 5-19**.

3. **Click the** list arrow **to close the list, type** Medical, **press** ENTER, **click** Cancel **in the warning dialog box, click the** list arrow, **then click** Creative

   The cell accepts the valid entry.

4. **Click the** Delete arrow **in the Cells group, click** Delete Table Rows, **click the** File tab **on the ribbon, click** Print, **in the Preview window click** No Scaling **under Settings, then click** Fit All Columns on One Page

   Below the table you see 1 of 2, which indicates you are viewing page 1 of a 2-page document.

5. **Click the** Next Page button [icon] **in the Preview area**

   The rows continue onto page 2, though you cannot see the field names.

6. **Return to the worksheet, click the** Page Layout tab **on the ribbon, click the** Print Titles button **in the Page Setup group, click inside the** Rows to repeat at top text box **under Print titles, in the worksheet scroll up to row** 1 **if necessary, click any** cell **in row 1 on the table, click the** Print Preview button **in the Page Setup dialog box, then click** [icon] **in the preview window to view the second page**

   A print title that repeats row 1 shows the field names at the top of each printed page.

7. **Return to the worksheet, click the** Insert tab, **click the** Text button, **click the** Header & Footer button, **click the** left header section text box **if necessary, type** 2021 Boston Office Placements, **click any** cell **on the worksheet, click the** Normal button [icon] **in the status bar, then press** CTRL+HOME

8. **sam↑ Save the table, preview it, close the workbook, close Excel, then submit the workbook to your instructor**

   Compare your printed table with **FIGURE 5-20**.

FIGURE 5-19: **Entering data in restricted cells**

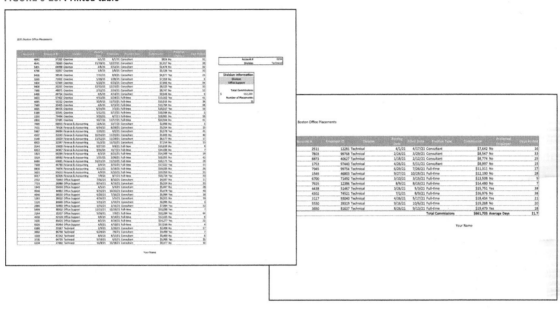

FIGURE 5-20: **Printed table**

Restricting cell values and data length

In addition to providing an in-cell dropdown list for data entry, you can use data validation to restrict the values that are entered into cells. For example, you might want to restrict cells in a selected range to values less than a certain number, date, or time. To do so, click the Data tab, click the Data Validation button 🗔 ▾ in the Data Tools group, on the Settings tab click the Allow arrow, select Whole number, Decimal, Date, or Time, click the Data arrow, select less than, then in the bottom text box, enter the maximum value. You can also limit the length of data entered into cells by choosing Text length in the Allow list, clicking the Data arrow and selecting less than, then entering the maximum length in the Maximum text box.

Adding input messages and error alerts

You can customize the way data validation works by adding input messages and setting alert styles. To do so, click the Input Message tab in the Data Validation dialog box, enter a message title and message, then click OK. To set an alert style, which controls how a user can proceed when entering invalid data, click the Error Alert tab, then click the Style arrow. The Information style displays your message with the information icon but allows the user to proceed with data entry. The Warning style displays your information with the warning icon and gives the user the option to proceed with data entry or not. The Stop style, which you used in this lesson, is the default; it displays your message and only lets the user retry or cancel data entry for that cell.

Practice

Skills Review

1. **Create and format a table.**
   a. Start Excel, open IL_EX_5-2.xlsx from the location where you store your Data Files, then save it as **IL_EX_5_Scientific**.
   b. Using the data in the range A1:I17, create a table.
   c. Apply a table style of Red, Table Style Light 14.
   d. Enter your name in the center section of the worksheet footer, enter **EOR Scientific Consulting** in the center section of the header, then activate cell A1.
   e. Save the workbook.

2. **Add and delete table data.**
   a. Insert a worksheet row below the table, then add a new record at the bottom of the table for Carlos Hurdo. Carlos's employee number is 2442. He was hired on 4/2/2021 to work in the Chicago office with a monthly salary of $5120.
   b. Add a column to the table by entering the label **Annual Compensation** in cell J1. Widen the column as necessary to fully display the label on two lines.
   c. Delete the record for Hank Gole in row 6.
   d. Remove duplicate data in the table by checking for matching employee numbers.
   e. Save the file.

3. **Sort table data.**
   a. Sort the table by Monthly Salary in descending (largest to smallest) order.
   b. Sort the table again by Last Name in ascending (A to Z) order.
   c. Perform a custom, multilevel sort by sorting the table first by Office in A to Z order, and then by Hire Date in Oldest to Newest order.
   d. Review the results of the multilevel sort to make sure the records are sorted first by Office and then by Hire Date.
   e. Save the file.

4. **Use formulas in a table.**
   a. In cell J2, enter a formula, using structured references, to calculate an employee's annual compensation by totaling the annual salary, annual bonus, and annual benefits columns.
   b. Check the table to make sure that the formula from cell J2 filled into the cells in column J, and that the annual compensation is calculated for the cells in the column.
   c. Add a total row to display the total annual compensation for all employees.
   d. Change the function in the total row to display the average annual compensation. Change the label in cell A17 from Total to **Average**.
   e. Save your work.

5. **Filter a table.**
   a. Filter the table to list only records for employees in the Dallas branch.
   b. Clear the filter.
   c. Use AutoFilter to list only the three employees with the highest annual compensation. (*Hint:* Find the top three items.)
   d. Redisplay all the records.
   e. Create a Custom AutoFilter showing employees hired in 2020. (*Hint:* Use the criteria after or equal to 1/1/2020 and before or equal to 12/31/2020.)
   f. Redisplay all the records and save your work.

Skills Review (continued)

6. Look up values in a table.

a. Open the Name Manager using a button on the Formulas bar, view named tables in the workbook, then close the Name Manager.

b. Enter the employee number **1322** in cell B22.

c. In cell C22, use the VLOOKUP function and enter **B22** as the Lookup_value, **Table1** as the Table_array, **10** as the Col_index_num, and **FALSE** as the Range_lookup; observe the compensation displayed for that employee number, then check it against the table to make sure it is correct.

d. Replace the existing Employee Number in cell B22 with **1080** and view the annual compensation for that employee.

e. Format cell C22 with the Accounting format with the $ symbol and no decimal places.

f. Save the workbook.

7. Summarize table data.

a. In cell F22, use the DAVERAGE function to find the average benefits for the Dallas office. (*Hint:* Click the upper-left corner of cell A1 twice to select the table and its header row as the Database, select cell I1 for the Field, and select the range E21:E22 for the Criteria.)

b. Verify that the average Dallas benefit amount is 13938.

c. Test the function further by entering the text **Chicago** in cell E22. When the criterion is entered, verify that the average Chicago benefit amount is 11534.04.

d. Format cell F22 in the Accounting format with the $ symbol and no decimal places.

e. Save the workbook.

8. Validate table data.

a. Select the table data in column E and set a validation criterion specifying that you want to allow a list of valid options.

b. Enter a list of valid options that restricts the entries to **LA**, **Chicago**, and **Dallas**. Remember to use a comma between each item in the list.

c. Confirm that the options will appear in an in-cell dropdown list, then close the dialog box.

d. Add a row to the bottom of the table. Select cell E17, open the dropdown list, then click Chicago.

e. Complete the new record by adding an Employee Number of **1119**, a First Name of **Cate**, a Last Name of **Smith**, a Hire Date of **10/1/2021**, and a monthly salary of **$5000**. Compare your screen to FIGURE 5-21.

f. Add column A as a print title that repeats at the left of each printed page.

g. Save the worksheet, then preview the worksheet to verify that the employee number column appears on both pages.

h. Submit your workbook to your instructor. Close the workbook, then close Excel.

FIGURE 5-21

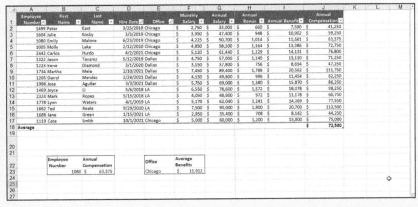

Independent Challenge 1

As the assistant to the clinic director at Riverwalk Medical Clinic, you have been asked to organize the billing information for the physical therapy department. Using data in an Excel worksheet, you will create a table and analyze the procedure data to help with the January billing.

a. Start Excel, open IL_EX_5-3.xlsx from the location where you store your Data Files, then save it as **IL_EX_5_RiverwalkPT**.

b. Using the data in the range A1:G64, create a table and format the table with the table style Blue-Gray, Table Style Medium 7. Widen the columns as necessary to fully display the field names.

c. Remove the banding of the table rows. (*Hint:* Use the Table Style Options group on the Table Tools Design tab.)

d. Add the record shown below to the end of the table:

Procedure Code	Procedure	Date	Amount Billed	Payment	Provider	Patient ID
601Q	Therap Proc 2	1/15/2021	$65	$30	Rubin	1189

e. Delete the record in row 8 for procedure code 251D.

f. Remove any duplicate records by checking for matching procedure codes.

g. Add a new column to the table by entering a field named **Balance** in cell H1. Calculate the balance for each procedure using structured references to subtract the payment from the amount billed. Format the balance amounts in column H in Accounting format with the $ symbol and no decimal places.

h. Sort the table by Balance in ascending order.

i. Use a custom sort to sort the table first by the procedure in descending order, and then within each procedure by the provider in ascending order.

j. Filter the table to show only Martin's procedures, then copy the filtered records to the Martin Procedures worksheet. Do not copy the field names. Clear the filter from the table on the January Procedures worksheet.

k. Filter the table to show only records where the amount billed is greater than or equal to $80 and less than or equal to $200. Copy the filtered records to the >= 80 <=200 worksheet. Do not copy the field names. Remove the filter from the table on the January Procedures worksheet.

l. On the January Procedures worksheet, enter **467B** in cell J2. Enter a VLOOKUP function in cell J4 to retrieve the procedure based on the procedure code entered in cell J2. Make sure you have an exact match with the procedure code. Test the function by changing the procedure code in cell J2 to **331E**.

m. Use the database function DSUM in cell J10 to total the amount billed for Rubin using the criteria in J7:J8. Format cell J10 in the Accounting format with the $ symbol and no decimal places.

n. Using the criteria in J7:J8, enter a database function in cell J12 to count the number of procedures performed by Rubin. (*Hint:* Use the DCOUNTA function.)

o. Use the Data Validation dialog box to add an in-cell dropdown list to the cells in the provider column that restricts entries to Axel, Martin, and Rubin. Check the list by clicking any cell in column F. Compare your table to FIGURE 5-22.

p. Add print titles to repeat the first row at the top of each printed page, enter your name in the center section of the worksheet footer, enter **January Procedures** in the center section of the header, then activate cell A1.

q. Save the workbook, preview it, then submit the workbook to your instructor.

r. Close the workbook, then close Excel.

Independent Challenge 1 (continued)

FIGURE 5-22

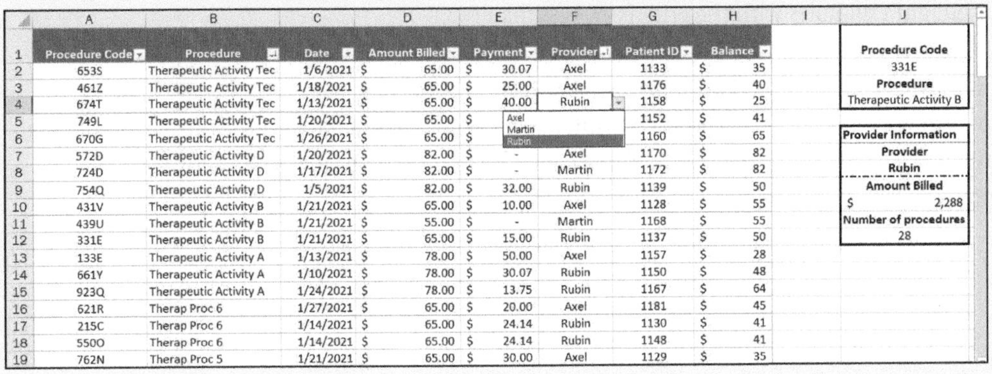

	Procedure Code	Procedure	Date	Amount Billed	Payment	Provider	Patient ID	Balance
2	653S	Therapeutic Activity Tec	1/6/2021	$ 65.00	$ 30.07	Axel	1133	$ 35
3	461Z	Therapeutic Activity Tec	1/18/2021	$ 65.00	$ 25.00	Axel	1176	$ 40
4	674T	Therapeutic Activity Tec	1/13/2021	$ 65.00	$ 40.00	Rubin	1158	$ 25
5	749L	Therapeutic Activity Tec	1/20/2021	$ 65.00	$	Axel	1152	$ 41
6	670G	Therapeutic Activity Tec	1/26/2021	$ 65.00	$	Martin Rubin	1160	$ 65
7	572D	Therapeutic Activity D	1/20/2021	$ 82.00	$ -	Axel	1170	$ 82
8	724D	Therapeutic Activity D	1/17/2021	$ 82.00	$ -	Martin	1172	$ 82
9	754Q	Therapeutic Activity D	1/5/2021	$ 82.00	$ 32.00	Rubin	1139	$ 50
10	431V	Therapeutic Activity B	1/21/2021	$ 65.00	$ 10.00	Axel	1128	$ 55
11	439U	Therapeutic Activity B	1/21/2021	$ 55.00	$ -	Martin	1168	$ 55
12	331E	Therapeutic Activity B	1/21/2021	$ 65.00	$ 15.00	Rubin	1137	$ 50
13	133E	Therapeutic Activity A	1/13/2021	$ 78.00	$ 50.00	Axel	1157	$ 28
14	661Y	Therapeutic Activity A	1/10/2021	$ 78.00	$ 30.07	Rubin	1150	$ 48
15	923Q	Therapeutic Activity A	1/24/2021	$ 78.00	$ 13.75	Rubin	1167	$ 64
16	621R	Therap Proc 6	1/27/2021	$ 65.00	$ 20.00	Axel	1181	$ 45
17	215C	Therap Proc 6	1/14/2021	$ 65.00	$ 24.14	Rubin	1130	$ 41
18	550O	Therap Proc 6	1/14/2021	$ 65.00	$ 24.14	Rubin	1148	$ 41
19	762N	Therap Proc 5	1/21/2021	$ 65.00	$ 30.00	Axel	1129	$ 35

Procedure Code
331E
Procedure
Therapeutic Activity B

Provider Information
Provider
Rubin
Amount Billed
$ 2,288
Number of procedures
28

Independent Challenge 2

As the director of development at a small, private independent college, you are responsible for managing alumni donations. The past two years' donation information is organized in a worksheet. You will analyze this information using table features.

a. Start Excel, open IL_EX_5-4.xlsx from the location where you store your Data Files, then save it as **IL_EX_5_Donations.**

b. Using the data in the range A1:E92, create a table and format the table with the table style Blue, Table Style Light 9. Widen the columns, as necessary, to fully display the field names.

c. Delete the record in row 5 for donor #18574. Check the table for duplicates, using the Donor # field, and check to see if there are any duplicate records.

d. Add a field named **% Increase** in cell F1. Widen the columns as necessary to display all field names.

e. Enter a table formula in cell F2 that calculates the percent increase in the donation amount from 2019 to 2020. Check that the formula was filled into the other column cells. Format the values in column F in the Percent Style format with two decimal places.(*Hint:* A % increase is calculated by subtracting the old value from the new value and then dividing that difference by the old value. Remember to use parentheses when calculating the difference between the old and new values.)

f. Use a custom filter for the Class field to find donations from the classes of years 2010 - 2020. Copy the results, including the field names, and paste them on a new sheet named 2010 - 2020 Classes. Widen the columns as necessary to fully display all of the worksheet data. Return to the 2019 - 2020 Donations sheet and remove the filter from the Class field.

g. Use the Data Validation dialog box to create an in-cell dropdown list that restricts entries in the School column to Business, Arts & Sciences, Engineering, and Health Sciences.

h. Use the Error Alert tab of the Data Validation dialog box to set the alert style to the Warning style with the error message "Data is not valid." Do not include the period after *valid*. Use the Input Message tab to add an input message of "Select the school." Do not include the period after *school*.

i. Add a new row at the end of the table and test the validation in the table with a valid entry. Use the new row to add a record for Donor # 10050, a graduate in the class of 1998 from the Engineering school, who donated $50 in 2019 and $100 in 2020.

j. Test the data validation by entering **Graduate** in cell B92. Verify the correct error message is displayed, then click Cancel to keep the existing valid data.

k. Add a total row to the table to display the total donations for 2019 and 2020. Delete any other total amounts in the row.

Excel

Independent Challenge 2 (continued)

l. Apply conditional formatting to the % Increase column to show the values less than 0% in Light Red Fill with Dark Red Text. (*Hint:* Use Highlight Cell Rules with the criteria of Less than 0%.)

m. Sort the records on the % Increase column, to display the Light Red Fill color cells at the top of the column. (*Hint:* Use a custom sort to sort by cell color with fill on top.)

n. Add print titles to repeat the first row at the top of each printed page, enter your name in the center section of the worksheet footer, enter **2019 - 2020 Donations** in the center section of the header, then activate **cell A1**.

o. Save the workbook, preview it, then compare your table to **FIGURE 5-23**.

p. Submit the workbook to your instructor, close the workbook, then close Excel.

FIGURE 5-23

2019 - 2020 Donations

Donor #	School	Class	2019 Donation	2020 Donation	% Increase
16430	Business	2018	$ 100	$ 50	-50.00%
24006	Health Sciences	2009	$ 75	$ 50	-33.33%
16532	Arts & Sciences	1996	$ 75	$ -	-100.00%
16695	Health Sciences	1943	$ 50	$ 25	-50.00%
12527	Health Sciences	1956	$ 100	$ -	-100.00%
13087	Arts & Sciences	1982	$ 100	$ 75	-25.00%
10479	Health Sciences	2013	$ 500	$ 300	-40.00%
18928	Business	2015	$ 100	$ 50	-50.00%
21897	Health Sciences	2004	$ 150	$ 75	-50.00%
18568	Business	1986	$ 500	$ 400	-20.00%
11637	Health Sciences	1985	$ 75	$ -	-100.00%
20374	Business	1995	$ 250	$ 150	-40.00%
15941	Business	1992	$ 1,000	$ 1,000	0.00%
17773	Arts & Sciences	2005	$ 250	$ 300	20.00%
13021	Engineering	1980	$ 100	$ 100	0.00%
20724	Business	2014	$ 400	$ 400	0.00%
20738	Arts & Sciences	2016	$ 400	$ 500	25.00%
11964	Arts & Sciences	1992	$ 25	$ 50	100.00%
18111	Business	1967	$ 75	$ 75	0.00%
24664	Arts & Sciences	2007	$ 100	$ 125	25.00%
12654	Health Sciences	1960	$ 500	$ 500	0.00%
24955	Engineering	2002	$ 250	$ 250	0.00%
16935	Business	1952	$ 100	$ 150	50.00%
20839	Engineering	2004	$ 400	$ 500	25.00%
14684	Engineering	2019	$ 100	$ 100	0.00%
17780	Arts & Sciences	1996	$ 50	$ 50	0.00%
21402	Health Sciences	2000	$ 50	$ 75	50.00%
15524	Health Sciences	1974	$ 50	$ 70	40.00%
17273	Health Sciences	1994	$ 150	$ 150	0.00%
22950	Arts & Sciences	2014	$ 75	$ 100	33.33%
14973	Business	1987	$ 1,000	$ 1,000	0.00%
16288	Health Sciences	2012	$ 400	$ 500	25.00%
16542	Health Sciences	1980	$ 500	$ 500	0.00%
21453	Arts & Sciences	2009	$ 150	$ 175	16.67%
19805	Business	1978	$ 200	$ 200	0.00%
17187	Engineering	1972	$ 400	$ 500	25.00%
24967	Engineering	1960	$ 1,000	$ 1,000	0.00%
23481	Arts & Sciences	2015	$ 200	$ 300	50.00%
15649	Arts & Sciences	1992	$ 75	$ 75	0.00%
22666	Arts & Sciences	2014	$ 25	$ 100	300.00%
18883	Engineering	1958	$ 150	$ 150	0.00%
21874	Arts & Sciences	2017	$ 100	$ 150	50.00%
11214	Arts & Sciences	1956	$ 150	$ 150	0.00%
11969	Business	1967	$ 1,000	$ 1,000	0.00%
22068	Business	1966	$ 250	$ 300	20.00%
23023	Health Sciences	1972	$ 400	$ 400	0.00%

Your Name

2019 - 2020 Donations

Donor #	School	Class	2019 Donation	2020 Donation	% Increase
14197	Engineering	1970	$ 75	$ 75	0.00%
21814	Arts & Sciences	1967	$ 200	$ 250	25.00%
18781	Health Sciences	1993	$ 400	$ 400	0.00%
15108	Health Sciences	2004	$ 100	$ 150	50.00%
12632	Business	1973	$ 500	$ 500	0.00%
19024	Business	1987	$ 400	$ 400	0.00%
22482	Arts & Sciences	1963	$ 50	$ 100	100.00%
12911	Arts & Sciences	1982	$ 500	$ 500	0.00%
13995	Health Sciences	2001	$ 1,000	$ 1,000	0.00%
16444	Engineering	1949	$ 1,000	$ 1,000	0.00%
22687	Engineering	2016	$ 1,000	$ 1,000	0.00%
24719	Engineering	2000	$ 1,000	$ 1,000	0.00%
12695	Business	1995	$ 500	$ 500	0.00%
10244	Engineering	2003	$ 200	$ 300	50.00%
10458	Engineering	1960	$ 400	$ 400	0.00%
23019	Health Sciences	1950	$ 150	$ 150	0.00%
22097	Business	1997	$ 1,000	$ 1,000	0.00%
12690	Engineering	1978	$ 150	$ 150	0.00%
17937	Engineering	1980	$ 1,000	$ 1,000	0.00%
16814	Business	2018	$ 75	$ 75	0.00%
24957	Business	1946	$ 100	$ 150	50.00%
15412	Health Sciences	2012	$ 50	$ 50	0.00%
12143	Health Sciences	1971	$ 75	$ 75	0.00%
23096	Arts & Sciences	1998	$ 200	$ 300	50.00%
10960	Arts & Sciences	2002	$ 250	$ 250	0.00%
11523	Health Sciences	2009	$ 500	$ 500	0.00%
23173	Arts & Sciences	2005	$ 150	$ 175	16.67%
16115	Engineering	1958	$ 500	$ 500	0.00%
15517	Engineering	2015	$ 400	$ 400	0.00%
13361	Business	1965	$ 250	$ 250	0.00%
17961	Engineering	2017	$ 400	$ 400	0.00%
24933	Engineering	1962	$ 500	$ 500	0.00%
12955	Engineering	1959	$ 150	$ 200	33.33%
24505	Business	1976	$ 400	$ 400	0.00%
22697	Arts & Sciences	2006	$ 400	$ 400	0.00%
18046	Health Sciences	2018	$ 100	$ 100	0.00%
10086	Arts & Sciences	2001	$ 500	$ 500	0.00%
17286	Business	2003	$ 150	$ 200	33.33%
15682	Arts & Sciences	1963	$ 150	$ 150	0.00%
16069	Arts & Sciences	2001	$ 1,000	$ 1,000	0.00%
13250	Engineering	2017	$ 100	$ 150	50.00%
17722	Engineering	1952	$ 25	$ 25	0.00%
20492	Engineering	1971	$ 75	$ 75	0.00%
13451	Business	2015	$ 25	$ 75	200.00%
10050	Engineering	1998	$ 50	$ 100	100.00%
Total			**$ 28,350**	**$ 29,045**	

Your Name

Visual Workshop

Open IL_EX_5-5.xlsx from the location where you store your Data Files, then save it as **IL_EX_4_Billings**. Create a table with the default table style. Sort, summarize, add a column, build a table formula, and add data validation so that your screen matches the table shown in FIGURE 5-24. Enter your name in the center section of the worksheet footer. Save the workbook, preview the table, close the workbook, submit the workbook to your instructor, then close Excel.

FIGURE 5-24

	Account #	Attorney	Office	Service	Referral	Billed	Paid	Balance				Attorney Billings	
	1008	Castro	Austin	Real Estate	Friend/Family	$ 1,200	$ 1,000	200				Attorney	
	1272	Castro	Austin	Real Estate	Other	$ 300	$ 200	100				Castro	
	1659	Castro	Austin	Real Estate	Chamber of Commerce	$ 1,200	$ -	1200				Billed	$ 2,950
	1663	Castro	Austin	Small Business	Friend/Family	$ 250	$ 100	150					
	1762	Rousseau	Dallas	Bankruptcy	Friend/Family	$ 4,500	$ 4,500	0				Referral Billings	
	1498	Tavarez	Dallas	Bankruptcy	Chamber of Commerce	$ 300	$ 100	200				Referral	
	1085	Rousseau	Dallas	Bankruptcy	Online Search	$ 500	$ 400	100				Chamber of Commerce	
	1992	Rousseau	Dallas	Civil Litigation	Social Media	$ 500	$ -	500				Billed	$ 7,800
	1214	Rousseau	Dallas	Civil Litigation	Social Media	$ 3,000	$ 1,000	2000					
	1153	Rousseau	Dallas	Civil Litigation	Online Search	$ 500	$ 500	0					
	1696	Tavarez	Dallas	Real Estate	Other	$ 500	$ 100	400					
	1512	Tavarez	Dallas	Real Estate	Other	$ 2,050	$ -	2050					
	1035	Rousseau	Dallas	Real Estate	Online Search	$ 1,500	$ 500	1000					
	1559	Rousseau	Dallas	Small Business	Online Search	$ 1,500	$ 1,500	0					
	1266	Tavarez	Dallas	Small Business	Chamber of Commerce	$ 300	$ 300	0					
	1063	Tavarez	Dallas	Small Business	Other	$ 500	$ -	500					
	1484	Lewis	Houston	Bankruptcy	Friend/Family	$ 2,050	$ 2,000	50					
	1742	Lewis	Houston	Bankruptcy	Social Media	$ 500	$ 500	0					
	1134	Lewis	Houston	Civil Litigation	Chamber of Commerce	$ 4,500	$ 1,000	3500					
	1300	Lewis	Houston	Estate Planning	Online Search	$ 3,000	$ 3,000	0					
	1167	Lewis	Houston	Small Business	Chamber of Commerce	$ 1,500	$ 500	1000					

Friend/Family
Online Search
Chamber of Commerce
Social Media
Other

Managing Workbook Data

CASE ► Ellie Schwartz, the vice president of finance at JCL, asks for your help in analyzing yearly sales revenues from the North America and worldwide offices. When the analysis is complete, she will distribute the workbook for office managers to review.

Module Objectives

After completing this module, you will be able to:

- View and arrange worksheets
- Protect worksheets and workbooks
- Save custom views of a worksheet
- Prepare a workbook for distribution

- Insert hyperlinks
- Save a workbook for distribution
- Group worksheet data
- Group worksheets

Files You Will Need

IL_EX_6-1.xlsx

Support_EX_6-2.xlsx

IL_EX_6-3.xlsx

IL_EX_6-4.xlsx

Support_EX_6-5.xlsx

IL_EX_6-6.xlsx

IL_EX_6-7.xlsx

Support_EX_6-8.xlsx

View and Arrange Worksheets

As you work with workbooks made up of multiple worksheets, you might need to compare data in the various sheets. To do this, you can view each worksheet in its own workbook window, called an **instance**, and display the windows in an arrangement that makes it easy to compare data. When you work with worksheets in separate windows, you are working with different views of the same workbook; the data itself remains in one file. **CASE** *Ellie asks you to compare the monthly revenue totals for the worldwide and North America locations. Because the revenue totals are on different worksheets, you want to arrange the worksheets side by side in separate instances.*

STEPS

1. **sam↓ Start Excel, open** IL_EX_6-1.xlsx **from the location where you store your Data Files, then save it as** IL_EX_6_Revenue

2. **With the Worldwide sheet active, click the** View tab **on the ribbon, then click the** New Window button **in the Window group**

   There are now two instances of the Revenue workbook open, each in their own workbook window.

3. **Point to the** Excel icon **on the taskbar**

   Two window thumbnails open, IL_EX_6_Revenue - 1 - Saved and IL_EX_6_Revenue - 2 - Saved.

4. **In the current instance, click the** North America sheet tab, **click the** View tab **on the ribbon, click the** Switch Windows button **in the Window group, then click** 1 IL_EX_6_Revenue - 1

   The IL_EX_6_Revenue - 1 instance moves to the front. The Worldwide sheet is active in this instance, and the North America sheet is active in the IL_EX_6_Revenue - 2 instance.

5. **Click the** Arrange All button **in the Window group**

   The Arrange Windows dialog box, shown in **FIGURE 6-1**, lets you choose how to display the instances. You want to view the workbooks next to each other.

6. **Click the** Vertical option button, **then click** OK

   The windows are arranged next to each other, as shown in **FIGURE 6-2**. The second instance of the workbook opens at a zoom of 100%, not the 120% zoom of the first instance. You can activate a workbook by clicking one of its cells.

7. **Scroll horizontally to view the data in the** IL_EX_6_Revenue - 1 **workbook, click anywhere in the** IL_EX_6_Revenue – 2 **workbook, scroll horizontally and view the data, then click the** Hide Window button ☐ **in the Window group**

   When you hide the second instance, only the IL_EX_6_Revenue - 1 workbook is visible.

8. **In the** IL_EX_6_Revenue – 1 **window, click the** Unhide Window button ☐ **in the Window group, then with the** IL_EX_6_Revenue – 2 **worksheet selected in the Unhide dialog box click** OK

9. **Click the** Close button ☒ **in the title bar of the** IL_EX_6_Revenue – 2 **instance, then maximize the** IL_EX_6_Revenue.xlsx **workbook**

   Closing the IL_EX_6_Revenue – 2 instance leaves only the first instance open. Its name in the title bar returns to IL_EX_6_Revenue. When closing an instance of a workbook, it is important to use the Close button and not the Close command on the File menu, which closes the workbook.

FIGURE 6-1: Arrange Windows dialog box

FIGURE 6-1: Arrange Windows dialog box

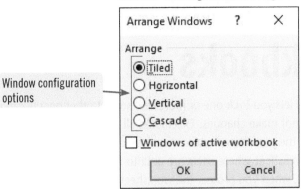

Window configuration options

FIGURE 6-2: Window instances displayed vertically

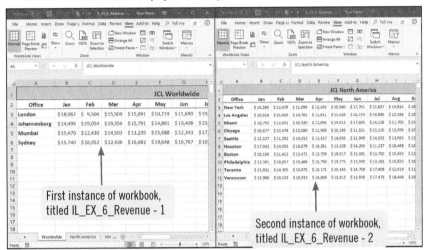

First instance of workbook, titled IL_EX_6_Revenue - 1

Second instance of workbook, titled IL_EX_6_Revenue - 2

Splitting the worksheet into multiple panes

Excel lets you split the worksheet area into vertical and/or horizontal **panes**, or sections of columns and rows. You can then click inside any one pane and scroll to locate information while the other panes remain in place, as shown in **FIGURE 6-3**. To split a worksheet area into multiple panes, click a cell below and to the right of where you want the split to appear, click the View tab on the ribbon, then click the Split button in the Window group. You can also split a worksheet into only two panes by selecting the row or column below or to the right of where you want the split to appear, clicking the View tab on the ribbon, then clicking Split in the Window group. To remove a split, click the View tab, then click Split in the Window group.

FIGURE 6-3: Worksheet split into four panes

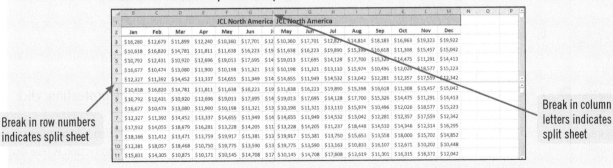

Break in row numbers indicates split sheet

Break in column letters indicates split sheet

Excel

Protect Worksheets and Workbooks

Learning Outcomes
• Protect a worksheet
• Create a data entry area on a worksheet by unlocking cells
• Protect a workbook

To protect information, Excel lets you **lock** one or more cells so that other people can view the values and formulas in those cells, but not make changes. Excel locks all cells by default, but this locking does not take effect until you activate the protection feature. A common worksheet protection strategy is to create an unlocked portion of a worksheet where users are able to enter and change data, sometimes called the **data entry area**. Then, when you protect the worksheet, the unlocked areas can still be changed.
CASE ▸ *Because the worldwide revenue figures for January through March have been finalized, Ellie asks you to protect that worksheet area. That way, users cannot change the figures for those months.*

STEPS

1. **On the Worldwide sheet, select the range E3:M6, click the Home tab on the ribbon, click the Format button in the Cells group, then point to Lock Cell on the menu**
   The lock icon for the Lock Cell option displays a gray box covering a lock, which indicates the cells are currently locked, as shown in **FIGURE 6-4**, so clicking will unlock them.

2. **Click Lock Cell to unlock the cells, click the Review tab on the ribbon, then click the Protect Sheet button in the Protect group**
   The Protect Sheet dialog box opens, as shown in **FIGURE 6-5**. The default options protect the worksheet while allowing users to select locked or unlocked cells only. You can enter a password in the Password to unprotect sheet box.

3. **Verify that Protect worksheet and contents of locked cells is checked, that the password text box is blank, and that the Select locked cells and Select unlocked cells check boxes contain checkmarks, then click OK**

4. **Click cell B3, type 1 to confirm that locked cells cannot be changed, click OK, click cell F3, type 1, notice that Excel lets you begin the entry, press ESC to cancel the entry, then save your work**
   When you try to change a locked cell on a protected worksheet, a dialog box, shown in **FIGURE 6-6**, reminds you of the protected cell's status and provides instructions to unprotect the worksheet.

5. **Click the Protect Workbook button in the Protect group, in the Protect Structure and Windows dialog box make sure the Structure check box contains a checkmark, verify that the password text box is blank, then click OK**
   The workbook's structure is protected from changes. If you wanted to provide additional protection to the workbook you could use a password.

6. **Right-click the Worldwide sheet tab**
   The Insert, Delete, Rename, Move or Copy, Tab Color, Hide, and Unhide options on the shortcut menu are not available because the structure is protected.

7. **Click the Protect Workbook button in the Protect group to turn off the protection, click the Unprotect Sheet button, then save your changes**
   The Protect Workbook button is a toggle, which means it's like an on/off switch. When it is highlighted, the workbook is protected. Clicking it again removes the highlighting, indicating the protection is removed from the workbook.

FIGURE 6-4: Lock Cell option

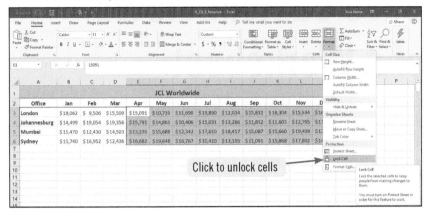

Click to unlock cells

FIGURE 6-5: Protect Sheet dialog box

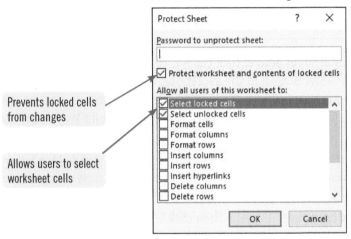

Prevents locked cells from changes

Allows users to select worksheet cells

FIGURE 6-6: Reminder of protected worksheet status

Microsoft Excel

⚠ The cell or chart you're trying to change is on a protected sheet. To make a change, unprotect the sheet. You might be requested to enter a password.

OK

Creating edit ranges

You can allow users to edit certain ranges on a worksheet by selecting the range, clicking the Review tab on the ribbon, clicking the Allow Edit Ranges button in the Protect group, clicking

New in the Allow User to Edit Ranges dialog box, entering an optional title for the range and a password to edit it, confirming the password, clicking Protect Sheet, then clicking OK.

Freezing rows and columns

A **pane** is a section of columns and/or rows that you can **freeze**, or set so that they remain visible as you scroll through your worksheet. To freeze panes, click the first cell in the area you want to scroll, click the View tab on the ribbon, click the Freeze Panes button in the Window group, then click Freeze Panes. Excel freezes the columns to the left and the rows above the selected cell, as shown in **FIGURE 6-7**. You can also select Freeze Top Row or Freeze First Column to freeze the top row or left

worksheet column. To unfreeze panes, click the View tab, click Freeze panes, then click Unfreeze Panes.

FIGURE 6-7: Worksheet with top two rows and left column frozen

Break in column letters and row numbers indicates first column and first two rows are frozen

Save Custom Views
of a Worksheet

A **view** is a set of display and/or print settings that you can name and save, and then access at a later time. By using the Custom Views feature, you can create several different views of a worksheet without having to create separate sheets. For example, if you often hide columns in a worksheet, you can create two views, one that displays all the columns and another with the columns hidden. You set the worksheet display first, then name the view. Then you can open the view whenever you want, using the name.

CASE ▶ *Because Ellie wants to generate a revenue report from the final revenue data for January through March, she asks you to create a custom view that shows only the first-quarter revenue data.*

STEPS

1. **With the Worldwide sheet active, click cell A1, click the View tab on the ribbon, then click the Custom Views button in the Workbook Views group**

   The Custom Views dialog box opens, as shown in **FIGURE 6-8**. Any previously defined views for the active worksheet appear in the Views box. No views are currently defined for the Worldwide worksheet.

2. **Click Add**

   The Add View dialog box opens. Here, you enter a name for the view and decide whether to include print settings and/or hidden rows, columns, and filter settings. By default, these settings will be included in the new view.

3. **In the Name box type Year Revenue, then click OK**

   You have created a view called Year Revenue that displays all the worksheet columns.

4. **Select columns E through M, right-click the selected area, then click Hide on the shortcut menu**

   The April through December columns are hidden.

5. **Click cell A1, click the Custom Views button in the Workbook Views group, click Add, in the Name box type First Quarter, then click OK**

6. **Click the Custom Views button in the Workbook Views group, click Year Revenue in the Views list, then click Show**

   The Year Revenue custom view displays all the months' revenue data.

7. **Click the Custom Views button in the Workbook Views group, then with First Quarter in the Custom Views dialog box selected, click Show**

   Only the January through March revenue figures appear on the screen, as shown in **FIGURE 6-9**.

8. **Click the Custom Views button, click Year Revenue, click Show, then save your work**

FIGURE 6-8: **Custom Views dialog box**

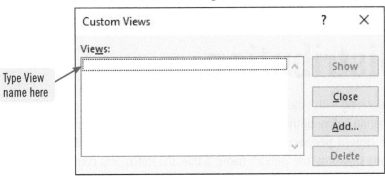

FIGURE 6-9: **First Quarter view**

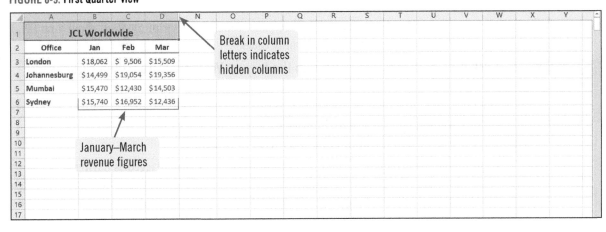

Using Page Break Preview

The vertical and horizontal dashed lines in the Normal view of worksheets represent page breaks. Excel automatically inserts a page break when your worksheet data doesn't fit on one page. These page breaks are **dynamic**, which means they adjust automatically when workbook content changes, such as when rows and columns are added, deleted, or resized. Everything to the left of the first vertical dashed line and above the first horizontal dashed line is printed on the first page. You can manually add or remove page breaks by clicking the Page Layout tab on the ribbon, clicking the Breaks button in the Page Setup group, then clicking Insert Page Break, Remove Page Break, or Reset All Page Breaks. Clicking Insert Page Break adds a page break above and to the left of a selected cell, and clicking Remove Page Break removes page breaks above and to the left of a cell. Reset All Page Breaks resets page breaks back to the default setting. You can also view and change page breaks manually by clicking the View tab on the ribbon, then clicking the Page Break Preview button in the Workbook Views group, or by clicking the Page Break Preview button on the status bar. You can drag the blue page break lines to the desired location. Some cells may temporarily display ##### while you are in Page Break Preview. If you drag a page break to the right to include more data on a page, Excel shrinks the type to fit the data on that page. To exit Page Break Preview, click the Normal button in the Workbook Views group.

Prepare a Workbook for Distribution

Learning Outcomes
- Add keywords to a worksheet
- Review a file using the Inspect Document feature
- Protect a workbook by using Mark as Final status

If you are collaborating with others and want to share a workbook with them, you might want to remove sensitive information before distributing the file. On the other hand, you might want to add details about a file, called **document properties**, to the file to help others identify, understand, and locate it. Properties might include keywords, the author's name, a title, the status, and comments. **Keywords**, also called **tags**, are terms you add to the file's properties that users can use when searching to help them locate your workbook. Properties are also called **metadata**, descriptive information that is used by Microsoft Windows in document searches. In addition, to ensure that others do not make unauthorized changes to your workbook, you can mark a file as final. This makes it a read-only file, which discourages others from making changes to it. **CASE** *Ellie wants you to protect the workbook and prepare it for distribution.*

STEPS

1. **Click the** File tab **on the ribbon**

   Backstage view opens and displays the Info pane, which displays information about your file. It also includes tools you can use to check for security issues.

   TROUBLE
   If asked to save your file before proceeding, click Yes.

2. **Click the** Check for Issues button **in the Inspect Workbook area, then click** Inspect Document

   The Document Inspector dialog box opens, as shown in **FIGURE 6-10**. It lists items that Excel can check in the file. All the options are selected by default.

3. **Click** Inspect, **then scroll to view the inspection results**

   Areas containing data have a red "!" in front of them. If areas are flagged as having data that you can remove from this dialog box, you can click the Remove All button. Some data cannot be removed from this dialog box; for example, hidden names are created by Excel and can't be deleted without running a special program.

   QUICK TIP
   You can view and edit a file's summary information by clicking the File tab on the ribbon and reviewing the information on the right side of the info place. The keywords are labeled as Tags. You can edit the Title, Tags, and Categories in this area.

4. **Click** Close, **click the** Properties list arrow **on the right side of the Info pane, then click** Advanced Properties

   The file's Properties dialog box opens with the Summary tab active, as shown in **FIGURE 6-11**. This tab allows you to enter identifying, and searchable, information for the file.

5. **In the Title text box type** Revenue, **in the Keywords text box type** Worldwide North America Revenue, **then in the Comments text box type** The first-quarter figures are final., **then click** OK

6. **Click the** Protect Workbook button **on the right side of the Info pane, click** Mark as Final, **click** OK, **then click** OK **again**

   The workbook is marked as final and "Read-Only" appears in the title bar indicating the workbook is saved as a read-only file. A yellow bar also appears below the tabs indicating the workbook is marked as final. The yellow bar also includes an Edit Anyway button.

   QUICK TIP
   You can also remove read-only status by clicking Mark as Final in the Protect Workbook menu to toggle the setting off.

7. **Click cell** B3, **type** 1 **to confirm that the cell cannot be changed, click the** Edit Anyway button **above the formula bar, then save the workbook**

   By clicking Edit Anyway, you removed the read-only status, making the workbook editable again. Marking a workbook as final is not a strong form of workbook protection because a workbook recipient can remove this Final status.

FIGURE 6-10: Document Inspector dialog box

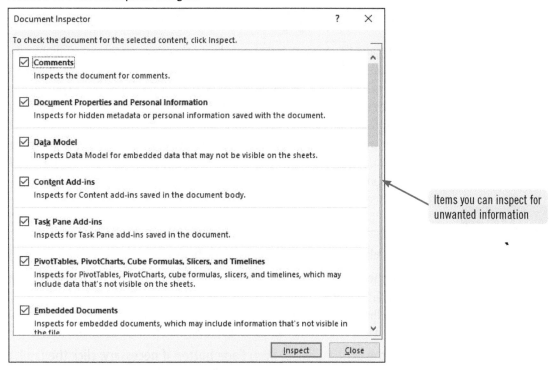

Items you can inspect for unwanted information

FIGURE 6-11: File's Properties dialog box

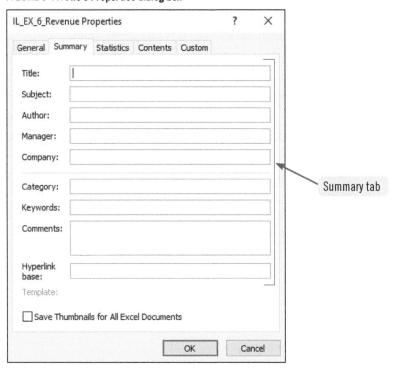

Summary tab

Adding a worksheet background

You can make your Excel data more attractive on the screen by adding a picture to the worksheet background. To add a worksheet background, click the Page Layout tab on the ribbon, click the Background button in the Page Setup group, choose From a file, Bing Image Search, or a OneDrive account in the Insert Pictures dialog box, click the image file in the next dialog boxes, then click Insert. The image appears tiled, repeating as necessary to fill the background behind the worksheet data on the screen. A worksheet background will not print with the worksheet.

Insert Hyperlinks

Learning
Outcomes
• Add a hyperlink in
a worksheet
• Add ScreenTips to
a hyperlink

As you manage the content and appearance of your workbooks, you might want the workbook user to view related information that exists in another location. A **hyperlink** is a specially formatted word, phrase, or graphic which, when clicked or tapped, displays a webpage on the Internet, another file, an email, or another location within the same file. The document, webpage, or place to which the hyperlink connects is called the **target**. You can also specify a ScreenTip that users see when they point to a hyperlink in your workbook. **CASE** ▶ *Ellie wants the office managers who view the Revenue workbook to also be able to view the division totals for their offices. She asks you to create a hyperlink to a file with this information for the London manager.*

STEPS

1. **Click cell A3 on the Worldwide worksheet**

2. **Click the Insert tab on the ribbon, then click the Link button in the Links group**

   The Insert Hyperlink dialog box opens. The icons under "Link to" on the left side of the dialog box let you specify the type of location to where you want the link to jump: an existing file or webpage, a place in the same document, a new document, or an email address.

3. **Click the Existing File or Web Page button if necessary, click the Look in list arrow, navigate to where you store your Data Files if necessary, then click Support_EX_6-2.xlsx**

   The filename you selected and its path appear in the Address text box, as shown in **FIGURE 6-12**. Your path to the Support_EX_6-2.xlsx file may be different depending on how you set up your files on your computer. This is the file users will see when they click the hyperlink.

4. **Click ScreenTip, type Division revenue, click OK, then click OK again**

   Cell A3 now contains underlined blue text, indicating that it is a hyperlink. The default color of a hyperlink depends on the current theme colors.

5. **Point to the London text until the pointer changes to 🖑, view the ScreenTip, then click once; if a dialog box opens asking you to confirm the file is from a trustworthy source, click OK**

   After you click, the Support_EX_6-2.xlsx workbook opens, displaying the London revenue data, as shown in **FIGURE 6-13**.

6. **Close the Support_EX_6-2.xlsx workbook, click Don't Save if necessary, then save your changes to the IL_EX_6_Revenue workbook**

FIGURE 6-12: Insert Hyperlink dialog box

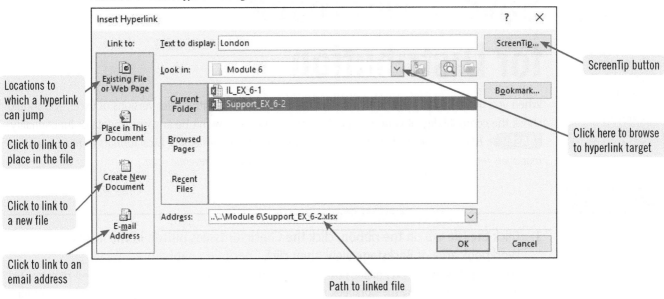

Locations to which a hyperlink can jump

Click to link to a place in the file

Click to link to a new file

Click to link to an email address

ScreenTip button

Click here to browse to hyperlink target

Path to linked file

FIGURE 6-13: Target document

	A	B	C	D	E	F	G	H	I	J	K	L	M	N	O	P	Q	R	S
1						London Revenue													
2		Jan	Feb	Mar	Apr	May	Jun	Jul	Aug	Sep	Oct	Nov	Dec						
3	Finance & Accounting	5947	1545	2930	5320	3570	3410	5297	2897	3362	2971	4964	3481						
4	Technical	4346	1892	3308	3674	2838	2826	3969	2745	4990	5829	4278	5938						
5	Creative	5202	4530	5467	2943	1628	2219	5647	3806	4598	4092	1673	2508						
6	Office Support	2567	1539	3804	3154	2683	3235	4977	2586	2882	5412	5019	4405						
7	Total	$18,062	$9,506	$15,509	$15,091	$10,719	$11,690	$19,890	$12,034	$15,832	$18,304	$15,934	$16,332						
8																			
9																			

Save a Workbook for Distribution

**Learning
Outcomes**
• Check workbook
  compatibility
• Check
  compatibility
  for different
  Excel versions

When you need to distribute your Excel files to people working with earlier versions of Excel, you should check the compatibility of your workbook to make sure there won't be any loss of data or functionality. **CASE** ▶ *Ellie asks you to check the workbook's compatibility with earlier Excel formats to make sure that managers running an earlier version of Excel can accurately view the revenue data.*

STEPS

1. **Click the** File tab **on the ribbon, click the** Check for Issues button **in the Inspect Workbook area of Backstage view, then click** Check Compatibility

    The Compatibility Checker dialog box opens, alerting you to the features that will be lost or converted when saving or opening the workbook in earlier versions of Excel. The Summary box displays a warning titled "Minor loss of fidelity," indicating that some of the worksheet's formatting might either not be available, or it appears differently in earlier versions of Excel. Minor loss of fidelity warnings won't result in lost data or worksheet functionality.

2. **Click the** Select versions to show arrow, **then click** Excel 97-2003 **to deselect it**

    The warning in the Summary box is no longer displayed, as shown in FIGURE 6-14, because it applies only to 97-2003 versions of Excel.

3. **Click the** Select versions to show arrow, **click** Excel 97-2003 **to select it, then click** OK

4. **Click the** Home tab **on the ribbon, click the** Find & Select button **in the Editing group, click** Go To, **type** LL1 **in the Reference box, click** OK, **type** 1 **in cell LL1, then press** ENTER

5. **Click the** File tab **on the ribbon, click the** Check for Issues button **in the Inspect Workbook area of Backstage view, then click** Check Compatibility

    The Compatibility Checker now displays a "Significant loss of functionality warning," as shown in FIGURE 6-15. This type of warning indicates a loss of data or functionality when a workbook is opened in an earlier Excel version. The data that was entered in cell LL1 could be lost because column LL is outside the limit of 256 columns in the 97-2003 versions of Excel.

6. **Click** OK **to close the Compatibility Checker, click cell LL1, press** DEL **to remove the data from the cell, then press** CTRL+HOME

7. **Click the** File tab, **click the** Check for Issues button **in the Inspect Workbook area of Backstage, click** Check Compatibility, **verify there is no longer a significant loss of functionality, then click** OK

8. **Save the workbook**

FIGURE 6-14: Compatibility Checker dialog box

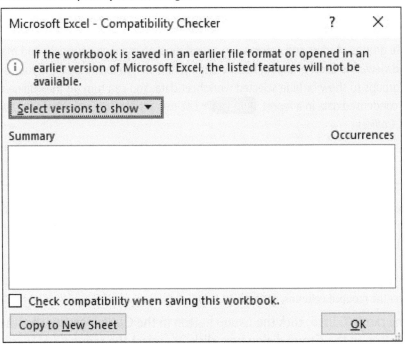

FIGURE 6-15: Significant loss of functionality warning

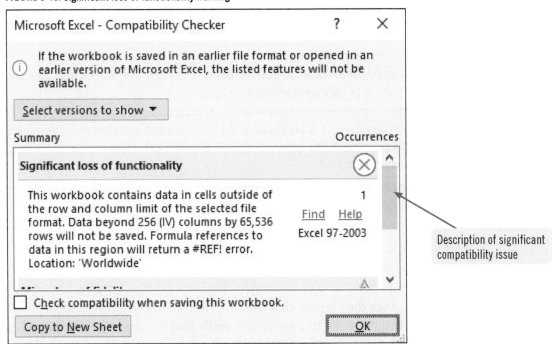

Description of significant compatibility issue

Exporting a workbook to other file types

You can export Excel workbooks to many other different formats. Clicking File, then clicking Export opens the Export pane, where you can either Create a PDF/XPS Document or Change File Type. PDFs and XPS files have the advantage of preserving formatting, fonts, and images, and making it difficult to change the file. These files can be opened and viewed in free viewers available online. To select this option, click Create PDF/XPS in the Create PDF/XPS Document section, choose the file type in the Save as type box, then click Publish. If you click Change File Type in the Export pane you can choose from several file types, including Macro Enabled Workbook, Excel 97-2003 workbook, Template, OpenDocument Spreadsheet (which can be used with OpenOffice), Text, special types of text file such as CSV and Formatted Text, or a Binary workbook that is optimized for fast loading and saving. Click the format you want, click Save As, then click Save in the Save As dialog box.

Excel

Work with Grouped Data

Learning
Outcomes
• Group worksheet
  data
• Apply symbols to
  view outlined data

You can create groups of rows and columns on a worksheet to manage your data and make it easier to work with and view. The Excel grouping feature displays outline symbols that allow you to easily expand and collapse groups to show or hide selected worksheet data. You can turn off the outline symbols if you are using the condensed data in a report. **CASE** ▶ *Ellie asks you for a report showing the quarterly revenue totals for all JCL offices.*

STEPS

1. **Click the** International sheet, **select the range** C3:E16, **click the** Data tab **on the ribbon, click the** Group button **in the Outline group, click the** Columns option button **in the Group dialog box, then click** OK

   The first-quarter data details are grouped. The quarter summary data isn't contained in the group to allow for that summary information to be displayed. The **outline symbols** that let you hide and display details appear over the grouped columns, as shown in FIGURE 6-16.

2. **Select the range** G3:I16, **click the** Group button **in the Outline group, click the** Columns option button **in the Group dialog box, click** OK, **select the range** K3:M16, **click the** Group button **in the Outline group, click the** Columns option button **in the Group dialog box, click** OK, **select the range** O3:Q16, **click the** Group button **in the Outline group, click the** Columns option button **in the Group dialog box, click** OK, **then click cell** A1

   All four quarters are grouped.

3. **Click the** Collapse Outline button ⊟ **above the** column F label, **then click the** Expand Outline button ⊞ **above the** column F label

   Clicking the (−) symbol temporarily hides the Q1 detail columns, and the (−) symbol changes to a (+) symbol. Clicking the (+) symbol expands the Q1 details and redisplays the hidden columns. The numbered Outline symbols in the upper-left corner of the worksheet are used to display and hide levels of detail across the entire worksheet.

4. **Click the** level 1 Outline Symbol button ☐1

   All the group details, considered Level 2, collapse, and only the quarter totals, considered Level 1, are displayed.

5. **Click the** level 2 Outline Symbol button ☐2

   You see the quarter details again. Ellie asks you to hide the quarter details and the outline symbols for the summary report.

6. **Click** ☐1, **click the** File tab, **click** Options, **click** Advanced **in the category list, scroll down to** Display options for this worksheet, **verify that** International **is displayed as the worksheet name, click the** Show outline symbols if an outline is applied check box **to deselect it, then click** OK

   The worksheet displays quarter totals without outline symbols, as shown in FIGURE 6-17.

7. **Save the workbook**

FIGURE 6-16: First-quarter data grouped

Outline symbols

Column-level buttons

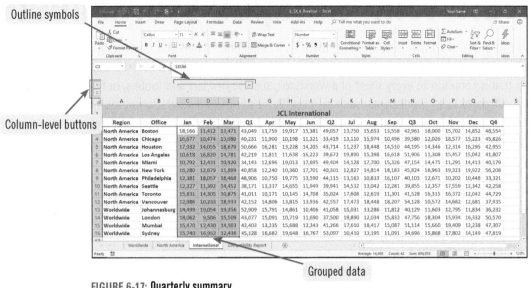

Grouped data

FIGURE 6-17: Quarterly summary

Breaks in column
letter sequence
indicate data is
grouped

	Region	Office	Q1	Q2	Q3	Q4
		JCL International				
3	North America	Boston	43,049	49,057	42,961	48,554
4	North America	Chicago	40,231	33,419	39,580	45,826
5	North America	Houston	50,666	43,714	44,195	42,955
6	North America	Los Angeles	42,219	39,672	51,906	41,807
7	North America	Miami	34,143	49,404	47,154	40,179
8	North America	New York	40,858	40,301	45,824	56,208
9	North America	Philadelphia	48,906	44,115	40,103	33,321
10	North America	Seattle	38,171	39,941	39,855	42,258
11	North America	Toronto	41,011	35,024	41,528	44,729
12	North America	Vancouver	42,152	42,557	54,128	37,935
13	Worldwide	Johannesburg	52,909	41,058	40,129	36,232
14	Worldwide	London	43,077	37,500	47,756	50,570
15	Worldwide	Mumbai	42,403	41,266	51,114	47,307
16	Worldwide	Sydney	45,128	53,097	34,696	47,819

Creating Subtotals

The Excel Subtotals feature provides a quick, easy way to group and summarize a range of data. It lets you create not only subtotals using the SUM function, but other statistics as well, including COUNT, AVERAGE, MAX, and MIN. In order to get meaningful statistics, data must be sorted on the field on which you will group. To create subtotals, first select the range of data you want to subtotal, click the Data tab on the ribbon, click the Subtotal button in the Outline group, click the At each change in arrow in the Subtotal dialog box, select the field by which you want to group the data, such as region, click the Use function arrow, click the function you want to use, select the fields that you want to subtotal in the "Add subtotal to" list, then click OK. **FIGURE 6-18** shows data grouped by region and summed on each quarter.

FIGURE 6-18: Worksheet subtotals and grand total

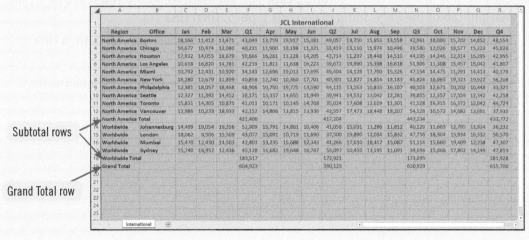

Subtotal rows

Grand Total row

Excel

Work with Grouped Worksheets

You can group worksheets to work on them as a collection. When you enter data into one grouped worksheet, that data is also automatically entered into all the worksheets in the group. This is useful for data that is common to every sheet of a workbook, such as headers and footers, or for column headings that will apply to all worksheets, such as monthly headings in a yearly summary. You can also group worksheets to print them all at one time. **CASE** *Ellie asks you to add text in a new, second row of the Worldwide, North America, and International worksheets. You also need to adjust the margin at the top of these worksheets.*

STEPS

1. **Select the** Worldwide sheet tab, **press and hold** SHIFT, **click the** International sheet tab, **then release** SHIFT

   The Worldwide, North America, and International sheets are selected, and the title bar now displays "IL_EX_6_Revenue.xlsx - Group" to indicate that the worksheets are grouped together and this is the first group in the workbook. Now, any changes you make to the Worldwide sheet will also be made to the other sheets.

2. **Select row** 2, **click the** Home tab **on the ribbon, click the** Insert button **in the Cells group, click cell** A2, **enter** Revenue, **click the** Enter button ☑ **on the Formula bar, select the range** A2:M2, **then click the** Merge & Center button **in the Alignment group**

   FIGURE 6-19 shows the Worldwide worksheet with the new Revenue row.

3. **Right-click the** Worldwide sheet tab, **click** Ungroup Sheets **on the shortcut menu, then verify the revenue label appears on the North America and International sheets**

4. **Select the** Worldwide sheet tab, **press and hold** SHIFT, **click the** International sheet, **release** SHIFT, **click the** Insert tab **on the ribbon, click the** Header & Footer button **in the Text group, enter your name in the** center header section, **click any cell on the worksheet, click the** Normal button ▦ **on the status bar, then press** CTRL+HOME

5. **With the worksheets still grouped, click the** File tab, **click** Print, **click** No Scaling under **Settings, click** Fit All Columns on One Page, **preview the first page, then click the** Next Page button ▶ **to preview the other three pages**

   Because the worksheets are grouped, all worksheets are ready to print and all pages contain the header with your name.

6. **Click** Normal Margins under **Settings, click** Custom Margins, **in the Top text box on the Margins tab of the Page Setup dialog box type** .5, **then click** OK

7. **Return to the worksheet, right-click the** Worldwide worksheet sheet tab, **then click** Ungroup Sheets

8. **sam⬆ Save and close the workbook, close** Excel, **then submit the workbook to your instructor**

   The completed worksheets are shown in FIGURE 6-20.

FIGURE 6-19: **Worldwide worksheet with Revenue label**

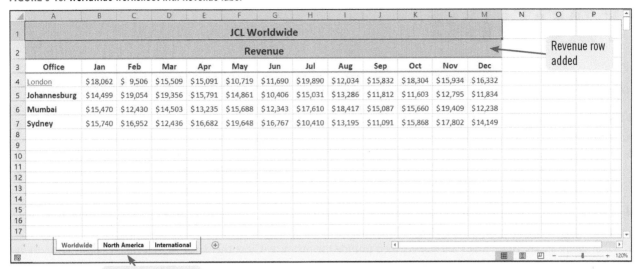

FIGURE 6-20: **Completed worksheets**

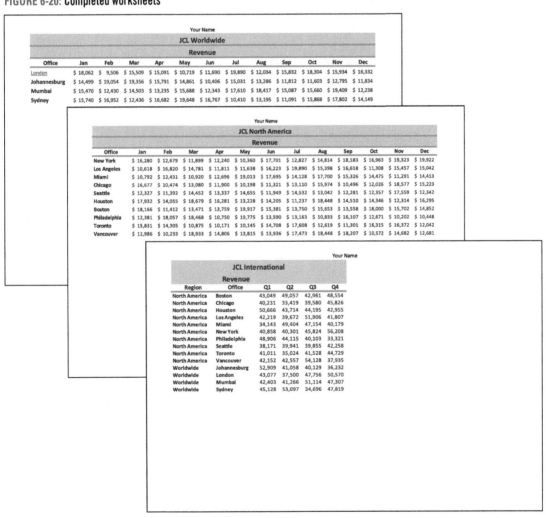

Practice

Skills Review

1. **View and arrange worksheets.**
   a. Start Excel, open IL_EX_6-3.xlsx from the location where you store your Data Files, then save it as **IL_EX_6_Travel**.
   b. Open a new window that contains another instance of the workbook.
   c. Verify the Business sheet is active in the IL_EX_6_Travel.xlsx - 1 instance of the workbook. Activate the Personal sheet in the IL_EX_6_Travel.xlsx - 2 instance.
   d. Use the Arrange Windows dialog box to view the IL_EX_6_Travel.xlsx - 1 and IL_EX_6_Travel.xlsx - 2 workbook windows tiled horizontally, then compare the workbooks in a vertical arrangement.
   e. Hide the IL_EX_6_Travel.xlsx - 2 instance, then unhide the instance. Close the IL_EX_6_Travel.xlsx - 2 instance, then maximize the IL_EX_6_Travel.xlsx workbook.

2. **Protect worksheets and workbooks.**
   a. On the Business sheet, unlock the expense data in the range B12:F19.
   b. Protect the sheet without using a password, accepting the default settings in the Protect Sheet dialog box.
   c. To make sure the other cells are locked, attempt to make an entry in cell D4 and verify that you receive an error message.
   d. Change the first-quarter real estate expense in cell B12 to **15,000**.
   e. Protect the workbook's structure without applying a password.
   f. Right-click the Business and Personal sheet tabs to verify that you cannot insert, delete, rename, move, copy, hide or unhide the sheets, or change their tab color.
   g. Unprotect the workbook. Unprotect the Business worksheet.
   h. Save the workbook.

3. **Save custom views of a worksheet.**
   a. With the Business sheet active, create a custom view of the entire worksheet called **Entire Business Budget**.
   b. Hide rows 10 through 23, then create a new custom view called **Business Income** that shows only the current data.
   c. Use the Custom Views dialog box to display the Entire Business Budget view of the Business worksheet.
   d. Use the Custom Views dialog box to display only the Business Income view of the Business worksheet.
   e. Return to the Entire Business Budget view.
   f. Save the workbook.

4. **Prepare a workbook for distribution.**
   a. Use the Info pane in Backstage view to check for issues in the workbook, then use the Document Inspector to remove all document properties and personal data.
   b. Use the Summary tab of the file's Properties dialog box to add a title of **Quarterly Budget** and the keyword **travel**.
   c. Mark the workbook as final, then verify that "Read-Only" appears in the title bar.
   d. Remove the final status using the Edit Anyway button, then save the workbook.

5. **Insert hyperlinks.**
   a. On the Business worksheet, make cell I1 a hyperlink to cell A22 on the worksheet. (*Hint:* In the Insert Hyperlink dialog box, use the Place in This Document button and enter the target cell reference in the Type the cell reference box.)
   b. Test the link.
   c. Edit the hyperlink in cell I1 to add a ScreenTip that reads **Cash Flow by Quarter**, then verify that the ScreenTip opens.
   d. Remove the hyperlink in cell I1, then delete the text in the cell.
   e. Save the workbook.

Skills Review (continued)

6. **Save a workbook for distribution.**
   a. Check the compatibility of the IL_EX_6_Travel.xlsx with all previous versions of Excel.
   b. Review the Minor loss of fidelity issue in the Compatibility Checker.
   c. Deselect the Excel 97-2003 version in the Select versions to show list, then verify that the Minor loss of fidelity warning no longer appears.
   d. Select the Excel 97-2003 version in the Select versions to show list.
   e. Save the workbook.

7. **Work with grouped data.**
   a. Activate the Business sheet, then group the income information in the range A5:G9 as rows.
   b. Group the expenses information in the range A11:G20 as rows.
   c. Collapse the income details in rows 5 through 9.
   d. Collapse the expenses details in rows 11 through 20.
   e. Expand the income and expenses details.
   f. Save the workbook.

8. **Work with grouped worksheets.**
   a. Group the Business and Personal worksheets.
   b. Add your name to the center footer section of the grouped worksheets.
   c. Add a 1.25" custom margin to the top and bottom of the grouped worksheets.
   d. Preview the sheets, then ungroup the sheets.
   e. Save the workbook, then compare your Business worksheet to FIGURE 6-21.
   f. Submit IL_EX_6_Travel.xlsx file to your instructor, close all open files, then close Excel.

FIGURE 6-21

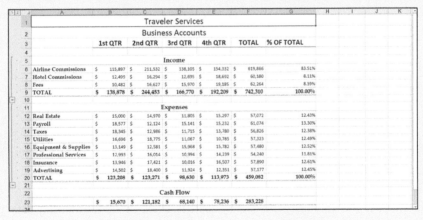

Independent Challenge 1

As the assistant to the CFO at Riverwalk Medical Clinic, you have been asked to analyze the annual insurance reimbursement data for the departments. After you complete your analysis, you will distribute the workbook to the clinic's vice presidents.

   a. Start Excel, open IL_EX_6-4.xlsx from the location where you store your Data Files, then save it as **IL_EX_6_RiverwalkReimbursements**.
   b. Display each worksheet in its own window, arrange the two sheets horizontally, then compare the data in the two windows.

Independent Challenge 1 (continued)

c. Hide the window displaying the Acute sheet. Unhide the Acute sheet window, then close this window.

d. Maximize the Elective window. Unlock the data in cells B5:D8.

e. Protect the worksheet without using a password. Verify the protection by trying to edit a locked cell, such as F5. Verify that you can edit the data in an unlocked cell, such as B5, but do not change the data.

f. Unprotect the Elective worksheet.

g. Protect the workbook without using a password.

h. Verify the protection by trying to change the Elective sheet name.

i. Unprotect the workbook.

j. On the Elective sheet, create a custom view called **Annual Reimbursements** that displays all the worksheet data. Hide columns F through Q. Create a custom view displaying the data in A1:E8, named **First Quarter Reimbursements**. Display all the data using a custom view. Display only the first-quarter reimbursement data using a custom view. Use a custom view to view all the reimbursement data for the year.

k. Insert a hyperlink in cell A5 on the Elective worksheet to the file Support_EX_6-5.xlsx. (*Hint:* If necessary, navigate to the location where you store your Data Files to locate and select the target file.) Add a ScreenTip that reads **Reimbursement by Procedure**, then test the hyperlink. Compare your screen to FIGURE 6-22.

FIGURE 6-22

	A	B
1	Ophthalmology	
2	Elective Procedures	
3	Procedure	Reimbursements
4	CK	$898,812
5	Lasik	$1,463,456
6	PRK	$797,425
7	LTK	$1,023,456
8	Intacs	$1,005,187

l. Close the Support_EX_6_5 file. Change the font of cell A5 to Calibri, to match the worksheet data.

m. Inspect the workbook for issues, then remove all document properties and personal data. Add a title property of **RMC Reimbursements** and keywords "**acute**" and "**elective**". Do not type the quotes. Mark the workbook as final, then remove the final status.

n. Check the compatibility of the workbook with previous Excel versions.

o. On the Elective worksheet, group the reimbursement data by quarters. (*Hint:* Group the monthly data by columns; do not include the quarter totals.) Use the outline buttons to collapse the monthly details and display only the quarter totals.

p. Group the three worksheets, add your name to the center footer section of the worksheets, then add 1.25" custom margins to the top of the worksheets.

q. Preview the worksheets, ungroup the worksheets, then save the workbook.

r. Submit the IL_EX_6_Riverwalk Reimbursements file to your instructor, close the workbook, then close Excel.

Managing Workbook Data

Independent Challenge 2

As the Director of Finances at LPR Business Services, you need to review the US monthly billings for the regions and industries the company serves. With two months of data in a workbook, you will create formatted monthly worksheets with subtotals for each region. The reports will be distributed to the regional managers.

a. Start Excel, open IL_EX_6-6.xlsx from the location where you store your Data Files, then save it as **IL_EX_6_BusinessServices**.

b. Group the US January and US February worksheets.

c. With the worksheets grouped, add a row at the top of the worksheet with the title **LPR Business Services** merged and centered across columns A through G.

d. Format the title in row 1 using the Title cell style. Format the column headings in row 2 using the Heading 3 cell style. Format the worksheet data in the range A3:G35 in the Calibri font with the font color Blue, Accent 1, Darker 50% (the fifth color from the left in the last row of theme colors).

e. Ungroup the worksheets. Arrange the worksheets as necessary to verify that both have the same title row and worksheet formatting. When you are finished, hide any unnecessary instances of the workbook.

f. On the US January worksheet, sort the data in A to Z order on the region field.

g. On this sheet, create subtotals for the billed amount and balance for each region. (*Hint:* In the Subtotals dialog box, select Region in the At each change in list and add subtotals to both the Billed Amount and Balance fields.) Widen column G to fully display the balance totals.

h. Remove the page break from the US January worksheet. (*Hint:* Use Page Break Preview to drag the blue page break line to the bottom of the worksheet data.)

i. Inspect the workbook and remove all document properties and personal information. Add the keywords, or tags, **business** and **consulting** to the workbook's summary properties.

j. Freeze the first two rows of the US January worksheet. Scroll down to row 40 to verify the first two rows appear at the top of the screen. Unfreeze the rows.

k. Check the compatibility of the workbook with earlier versions of Excel.

l. Group all three worksheets. With the worksheets grouped, change the custom top margin to .5".

m. With the worksheets grouped, add a header that includes your name in the left section and the sheet name in the center section. (*Hint:* To add a field that displays the current sheet name, click the Sheet Name button in the Header and Footer Elements group of the Header & Footer Tools Design tab.)

n. Ungroup the worksheets, then prepare the workbook for distribution by marking as final. Save the workbook, close the workbook, reopen the workbook, and enable editing.

o. Use the outline symbols on the US January worksheet to display only the regional totals and the grand total. Compare your US January worksheet to FIGURE 6-23.

p. Save the workbook, submit the workbook to your instructor, then close Excel.

FIGURE 6-23

	A	B	C	D	E	F	G	H	I	J	K	L	M	N
1				LPR Business Services										
2	Invoice #	Date	Region	Industry	Billed Amount	Submitted	Balance							
11			East Total		$ 48,275		$25,071							
21			North Total		$ 53,879		$26,686							
31			South Total		$ 40,730		$14,514							
39			West Total		$ 32,816		$13,081							
40			Grand Total		$ 175,700		$79,352							
41														
42														
43														
44														
45														
46														
47														
48														
49														
50														

Excel

Visual Workshop

Open IL_EX_6-7.xlsx from the location where you store your Data Files, then save it as
IL_EX_6_BusinessCommunications. Use the skills you learned in this module to complete
the worksheet so it looks like the one shown in FIGURE 6-24. The text in cell A6 is a hyperlink to the
Support_EX_6-8.xlsx workbook, in the location where you store your Data Files. (*Hint:* You will first need to
add columns and formulas to calculate each quarter's total; you can then group the worksheets and use the
outline symbols to display only the necessary information.) Resize columns as necessary, and adjust merged
and centered data to include any new columns. Enter your name in the center footer section, save the workbook,
submit your work to your instructor as directed, close the workbook, then close Excel.

FIGURE 6-24

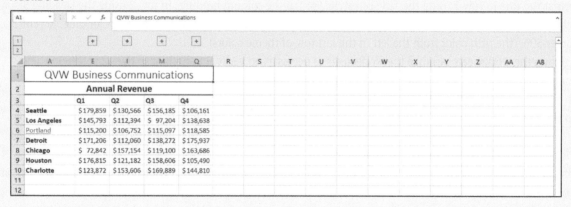

Managing Workbook Data

Working with Images and Integrating with Other Programs

CASE Ellie Schwartz, the vice president of finance, is researching the possible purchase of Tech Career Services (TCS), a small company specializing in technology career placements. Ellie needs to review the organization's files and develop a presentation on the feasibility of acquisition. To create the necessary documents, she asks you to create data exchanges between Excel and other programs.

Module Objectives

After completing this module, you will be able to:

- Plan a data exchange
- Import a text file
- Import data from another workbook
- Import a database table

- Link worksheet data to a Word document
- Link an Excel chart to a PowerPoint slide
- Import Excel data into Access
- Insert a graphic file in a worksheet

Files You Will Need

Support_EX_7-1.txt	Support_EX_7-8.txt	Support_EX_7-15.xlsx
Support_EX_7-2.xlsx	Support_EX_7-9.xlsx	Support_EX_7-16.txt
Support_EX_7-3.accdb	Support_EX_7-10.accdb	Support_EX_7-17.accdb
IL_EX_7-4.docx	IL_EX_7-11.docx	Support_EX_7-18.jpg
IL_EX_7-5.pptx	IL_EX_7-12.pptx	Support_EX_7-19.txt
Support_EX_7-6.xlsx	Support_EX_7-13.xlsx	IL_EX_7-20.xlsx
Support_EX_7-7.jpg	Support_EX_7-14.jpg	IL_EX_7-21.pptx

Plan a Data Exchange

Learning
Outcomes
• Plan a data
exchange between
Office programs
• Develop an
understanding of
data exchange
vocabulary

Because the tools available in Microsoft Office apps are designed to be compatible, exchanging data between Excel and other Office programs is easy. The first step in each data exchange involves planning what you want to accomplish. **CASE** ▶ *Ellie asks you to use the following guidelines to plan data exchanges between Excel and other apps to support her business analysis of Tech Career Services.*

DETAILS

To plan an exchange of data:

- **Identify the data you want to exchange, its file type, and, if possible, the app used to create it**

  Whether the data you want to exchange is a graphics file, database file, worksheet, or simply a text file, it is important to identify its **source program** (the program used to create the data you are linking or embedding) and file type. Once you identify the source program, you can determine options for exchanging the data with Excel. Ellie needs to analyze a text file containing the TCS revenue data. A file that contains data but no formatting is sometimes called an **ASCII file** or a **text file**.

- **Determine the app with which you want to exchange data**

  Besides knowing which program created the data you want to exchange, you must also identify the program that will receive the data, called the **destination program**. This determines the procedure you use to perform the exchange. Ellie received a database table created with the Access database app. You decide to import the database file into Excel so Ellie can analyze it using Excel tools.

- **Determine the method of your data exchange**

  In this module, you use queries to import data into an Excel workbook. A **query** is a request for information from a data source. You can use Excel's Get & Transform tools to import data from other sources. Get & Transform creates a dynamic connection between an Excel workbook and a data source. After connecting to a data source, you can use the **Power Query** tool, which is a BI, or Business Intelligence, tool to query almost any kind of data source in order to transform the data into a more desirable format. For example, you can remove a column, remove a row, split a column, or change a data type in the Query Editor before you manipulate the data in the worksheet window. FIGURE 7-1 shows data to be imported in the Power Query Editor. You may have multiple queries in a workbook.

  Windows supports a technology called **object linking and embedding (OLE)**, which lets you share information among the Office programs, copying from a source file and pasting, embedding, or linking into a destination file. The data to be exchanged, called an **object**, may consist of text, a worksheet, or any other type of data. You can copy Excel data and paste it in other applications using OLE. The copied data can be linked or embedded in the destination file. When you **embed**, you simply insert a copy of the original object into the destination document; you can later, if necessary, edit this embedded data separately from the source document. You **link** when you want the information you insert to be updated automatically if the data in the source document changes. FIGURE 7-2 shows an Excel chart that is linked to a Power-Point slide. You will use object linking when pasting Excel data in other applications so any changes in the Excel data will be updated in the destination files.

FIGURE 7-1: Data to be imported in the Power Query Editor

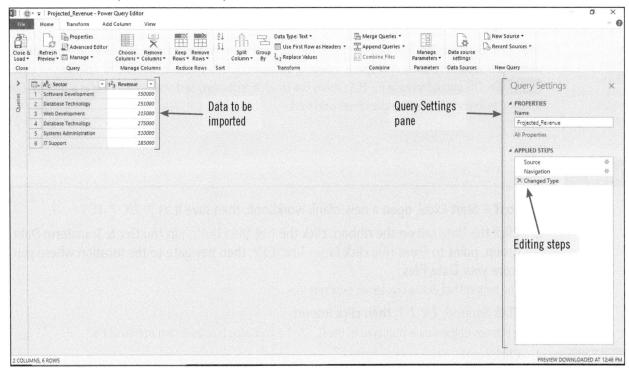

FIGURE 7-2: Excel chart linked to a PowerPoint slide

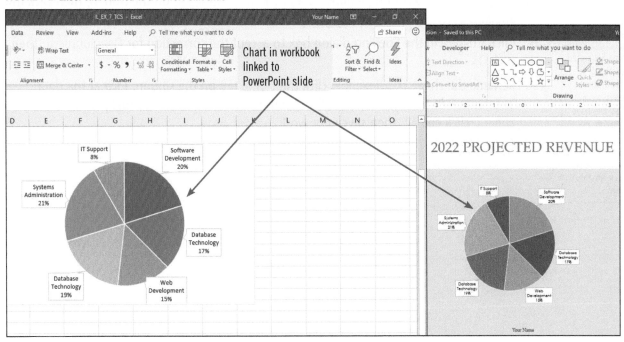

Excel

Import a Text File

Learning Outcomes
- Import a text file into an Excel workbook
- Format imported data

You can import text data into Excel and save the imported data in Excel format. Text files use a **delimiter**, which is a separator, such as a space, comma, or semicolon between elements, or columns of data.

CASE ▸ *The annual revenue for TCS broken out by each technology sector was submitted in a text file. Ellie asks you to import that data into an Excel workbook.*

STEPS

1. **sam** ⬇ Start Excel, open a new blank workbook, then save it as IL_EX_7_TCS

2. **Click the** Data tab **on the ribbon, click the** Get Data button **in the Get & Transform Data group, point to** From File, **click** From Text/CSV, **then navigate to the location where you store your Data Files**

   The Import Data dialog box shows only text files.

3. **Click** Support_EX_7-1, **then click** Import

   A preview of the data is displayed in the IL_EX_7-1.txt dialog box, as shown in **FIGURE 7-3**.

4. **Click** Load

   The data appears in table format on a new sheet in the workbook. The Queries & Connections pane opens on the right with the Queries tab showing the file name and the number of rows loaded into the worksheet. Because text editors do not have spell-checking functionality, text files are more likely to contain spelling errors.

5. **Close the Queries & Connections pane, click the** Review tab **on the ribbon, then click the** Spelling button **in the Proofing group**

6. **Click** Change **in the Spelling dialog box to accept the correction for** Development, **then click** OK

7. **Rename the sheet** TCS Revenue, **click the** Home tab **on the ribbon, format the data in column B in the Accounting style with the $ symbol and no decimal places, delete** Sheet1, **click cell A1, then save your work**

   FIGURE 7-4 shows the worksheet with the data you imported into Excel.

FIGURE 7-3: Preview of data from text file

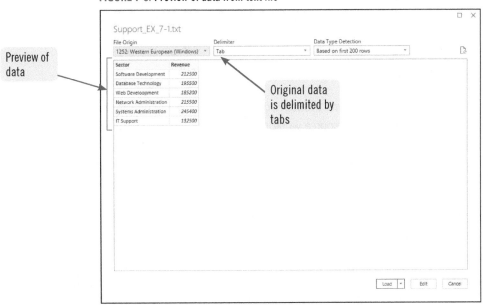

Preview of data

Original data is delimited by tabs

FIGURE 7-4: Worksheet with imported and formatted text file data

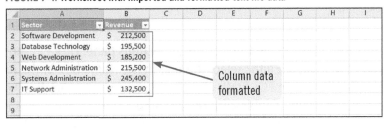

Column data formatted

Importing text files using the Text Import Wizard

Another way to import a text file into Excel is to use the Text Import Wizard. Click the File tab, click Open, then navigate to the location where you store your Data Files. By default, the Open dialog box displays only Excel files. To import a text file, you need to change your view so you see the file you want to open. To do this, click All Excel Files, click Text Files, click the name of the desired text file, then click Open. The Text Import Wizard opens, where you can complete the import by completing each step of the Wizard.

Learning
Outcomes
• Import data from
  another Excel
  workbook
• Format imported
  data

Import Data from Another Workbook

You can import worksheet data from another workbook into Excel. If you use the Get & Transform tool, any changes you later make in the source workbook are updated when you refresh the destination workbook. **CASE** *The human resources office at TCS has provided an Excel file listing the employees and their positions. You will import that information into the workbook containing the revenue information.*

STEPS

1. **Open the workbook** Support_EX_7-2 **from the location where you store your Data Files, then save it as** IL_EX_7_Staff

2. **Activate the** IL_EX_7_TCS **workbook, click the** Data tab **on the ribbon, click the** Get Data button **in the Get & Transform Data group, point to** From File, **click** From Workbook, **then navigate to the location where you store your Data Files**

3. **Click** IL_EX_7_Staff, **then click** Import
    The Navigator dialog box opens.

4. **Click** Sheet1 **in the Navigator dialog box**
    The data in Sheet1 is displayed in the preview area on the right side of the dialog box, as shown in **FIGURE 7-5**.

5. **Click** Load
    The Queries & Connections pane shows that 10 rows were loaded into a new sheet, called Sheet1.

It is best to keep linked workbooks in the same folder to ensure that linked data updates in the destination document. Linked, structured references in Excel table formulas require the linked workbook to remain open for formulas to work.

6. **Right-click** Sheet1 **in the Queries & Connections pane, click** Edit **on the shortcut menu, in the Power Query Editor select the text in the Name box in the** Properties box **under Query Settings, type** TCS Staff, **click the** Transform tab, **click the** Rename button **in the Any Column group, double-click the heading** Column1, **type** Position, **replace the** Column2 **heading with** Employee, **click the** Home tab, **then click the** Close & Load button **in the Close group**

7. **Close the Queries & Connections pane, then rename the sheet** TCS Staff

8. **Activate the** IL_EX_7_Staff workbook, **change Ashley McFadden's name in cell B5 to** Ashley Elwell, **then save and close the IL_EX_7_Staff workbook**

9. **In the** IL_EX_7_TCS workbook **click the** Data tab, **click the** Refresh All button **in the Queries & Connections group, then save your work**
    FIGURE 7-6 shows the worksheet with the updated staff data.

FIGURE 7-5: Preview of worksheet data in dialog box

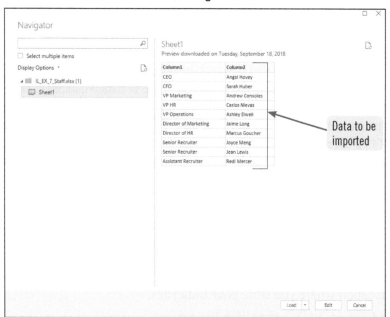

Data to be imported

FIGURE 7-6: Refreshed and updated worksheet data

Updated data

Name is updated

Converting text to columns

You can convert text into columns if, for example, you want to split a column of first and last names into two separate columns. To do so, select the range containing the names, click the Data tab on the ribbon, click the Text to Columns button in the Data Tools group, click the Space check box as the delimiter in the second step of the Convert Text to Columns Wizard dialog box, then click Finish.

Import a Database Table

Learning
Outcomes
• Import Access
  data into an Excel
  workbook
• Format imported
  data

You can import data from database tables into Excel. A **database table** is a set of data organized using columns and rows, which is created in a database program. A **database program** is an application, such as Microsoft Access, that lets you manage large amounts of data organized in tables. To import data from an Access table into Excel you will use the Get & Transform tool, so that any changes in the Access database can be seen when the workbook is refreshed. **CASE** *Ellie received a database table in Access containing TCS's projected revenue for the year ahead. She asks you to import this table into the Excel workbook containing the TCS revenue and staff data. The data has a column that needs to be removed and Ellie would like you to transform the data before it is imported.*

STEPS

1. **Click the** Data tab **on the ribbon, click the** Get Data button **in the Get & Transform Data group, point to** From Database, **click** From Microsoft Access Database, **then navigate to the location where you store your Data Files**

2. **Click** Support_EX_7-3, **then click** Import
   The Navigator dialog box opens, showing the Access file and the Projected Revenue table on the left and a preview window on the right.

QUICK TIP
You can delete rows in the data by clicking the Remove Rows button in the Reduce Rows group.

3. **Click** Projected Revenue **in the Navigator dialog box**
   The data in the Projected Revenue table is displayed in the preview area, as shown in **FIGURE 7-7**.

4. **Click** Transform Data, **then in the Power Query Editor with the ID column selected click the** Remove Columns button **in the Manage Columns group on the Home tab**
   The Power Query Editor allows you to edit data before importing it into Excel. In the Power Query Editor's Query Settings pane on the right, the editing steps are listed in the Applied Steps area.

QUICK TIP
To update changes made to a linked Access database in a workbook, click the Data tab, then click the Refresh All button in the Queries & Connections group.

5. **Click the** Close & Load button **in the Close group**
   The Access data is imported into the worksheet as a table, and the Queries & Connections pane confirms that six rows were loaded using the Projected Revenue query.

6. **Format the data in column** B **in the Accounting format and no decimal places**
   Your formatted worksheet should match **FIGURE 7-8**.

7. **Change the sheet name to** TCS Projected Revenue

QUICK TIP
You can also open the Power Query Editor by clicking inside the imported data, clicking the Query Tools Query tab on the ribbon, then clicking Edit in the Edit group.

8. **Click the** TCS Revenue worksheet, **hold** SHIFT, **click the** TCS Projected Revenue **worksheet, release** SHIFT, **click the** Insert tab **on the ribbon, click the** Text button, **click the** Header & Footer button, **enter your name in the** center header section, **click any cell on the worksheet, click the** Normal button ⊞ **in the status bar, press** CTRL+HOME, **right-click** any worksheet, **then click** Ungroup Sheets

9. **Save your work**

FIGURE 7-7: Preview of Access data

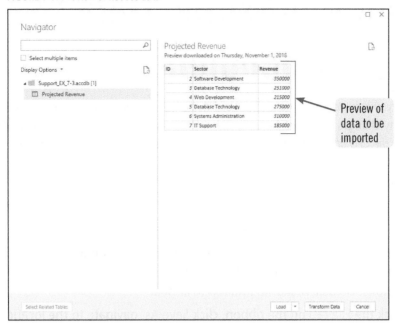

Preview of data to be imported

FIGURE 7-8: Formatted worksheet containing imported data

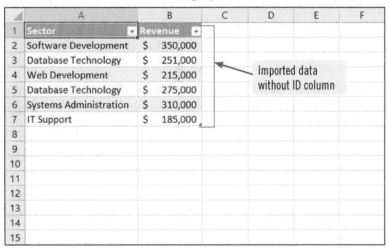

Imported data without ID column

Excel

Link Worksheet Data to a Word Document

**Learning
Outcomes**
• Link data from an
  Excel worksheet to
  a Word document
• Update links in a
  Word document

When you link worksheet data to a Word document, the link contains a connection to the workbook so that any changes you make to the workbook are reflected in the linked object. **CASE** ▶ *Ellie wants to update the CEO of JCL on the project status. She asks you to prepare a Word memo that includes the projected revenue workbook data. To ensure that any workbook changes will be reflected in the memo, you decide to link the workbook data.*

STEPS

TROUBLE
If a dialog box
opens, asking "How
do you want to
open this file?," click
Microsoft Word,
then click OK.

1. **Open a File Explorer window, navigate to the location where you store your Data Files, then double-click the Word document** IL_EX_7-4

   Microsoft Word starts, and the memo opens in Word.

2. **Click the** File tab **on the ribbon, click** Save As, **navigate to the location where you store your Data Files, replace the text in the File name text box with** IL_EX_7_TCSMemo, **then click** Save

3. **Activate the** IL_EX_7_TCS workbook, **then copy the data in the range A1:B7 on the** TCS Projected Revenue **sheet**

   The workbook data is copied to the Clipboard.

4. **Activate the** Word memo, **then press** CTRL+END

   The insertion point moves to the end of the memo.

5. **Click the** Home tab **on the ribbon if necessary, click the** Paste arrow **in the Clipboard group, then click the** Link & Use Destination Styles button 🖻 **under Paste Options**

6. **If the revenue data and $ sign wrap to two lines, point to the** right edge of the table **until the** column resize pointer ↔ appears, **then drag the** right edge **to the right, so your screen matches** FIGURE 7-9

7. **Activate the** IL_EX_7_TCS workbook, **on the TCS Projected Revenue worksheet click cell B2, type 300,000, then click the** Enter button ✓ **on the Formula Bar**

8. **Activate the** IL_EX_7_TCSMemo document, **select the** table, right-click the table, **then click** Update Link

   The table data is updated to reflect the change in the linked Excel workbook, as shown in **FIGURE 7-10**.

9. **Click the** Insert tab **on the ribbon, click the** Header button **in the Header & Footer group, click** Edit Header, **type your name in the Header area, click the** Close Header and Footer button **in the Close group, save the Word file, close the Word document, then close Word**

FIGURE 7-9: Memo with linked worksheet data

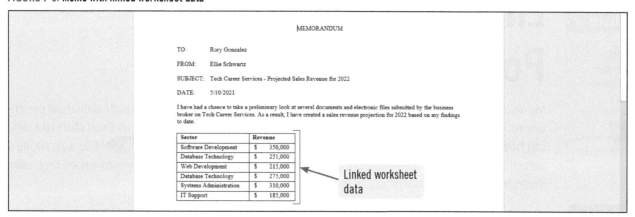

FIGURE 7-10: Memo with updated table data

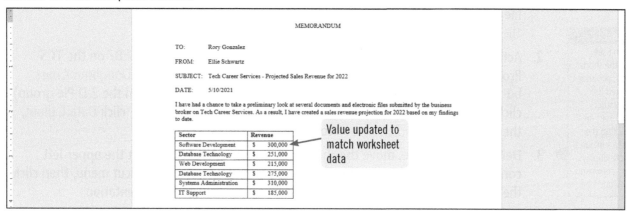

Managing and breaking links

When you open a Word document containing linked data, you are asked if you want to update the linked data. You can manage the updating of links by clicking the File tab on the ribbon, then clicking Edit Links to Files in the right pane. The Links dialog box opens, allowing you to change a link's update method from the default setting of automatic to manual. The Links dialog box also allows you to change the link source, permanently break a link, open the source file, or manually update a link. If you send your linked files to another user, the links will be broken because the linked file path references the local computer where you inserted the links. Because the file path will not be valid on the recipient user's device, the links will no longer be updated when the user opens the destination document. To correct this, recipients who have both the destination and source documents can use the Links dialog box to change the link's source in the destination document to their own device. Then the links will be automatically updated when they open the destination document in the future. If you are managing links in an Excel workbook you can click the Data tab, then click the Edit Links button in the Queries & Connections group to open the Edit Links dialog box.

Link an Excel Chart to a PowerPoint Slide

Learning
Outcomes
• Insert a linked
  chart in a
  PowerPoint slide
• Configure
  automatic links in
  a PowerPoint file

Microsoft PowerPoint is a **presentation graphics** program that you can use to create slide show presentations. PowerPoint slides can include a mix of text, data, and graphics. Adding an Excel chart to a slide can help to illustrate data and give your presentation more visual appeal. **CASE** ▶ *Ellie is preparing a presentation for JCL management about the potential acquisition of TCS. She asks you to link an Excel chart illustrating the 2022 revenue projection for TCS to one of her PowerPoint slides.*

STEPS

1. Click the Start button on the Windows taskbar, begin typing PowerPoint in the Search box, click PowerPoint in the list that opens, click Open on the left side of the Open pane, navigate to where you store your Data Files, double-click IL_EX_7-5, then save the file as IL_EX_7_ManagementPresentation

   The presentation appears in Normal view, as shown in FIGURE 7-11.

2. Activate the IL_EX_7_TCS workbook, select the data in the range A2:B7 on the TCS Projected Revenue sheet, click the Insert tab, click the Insert Pie or Doughnut Chart button 🟤 in the Charts group, click the Pie chart (the first chart in the 2-D Pie group), click the Chart Elements button ⊞, click the Data Labels arrow ▶, click Data Callout, then click the Legend check box to deselect it

3. Delete the chart title, move the chart until its upper-left corner is at the upper-left corner of cell D1, right-click the Chart Area, click Copy on the shortcut menu, then click the PowerPoint program button on the taskbar to display the presentation

4. Click Slide 2 in the Thumbnails pane, right-click Slide 2 in the Slide pane, then click the Use Destination Theme & Link Data button 📋 in the Paste Options group

   A pie chart illustrating the projected revenue appears in the slide. The chart matches the colors and fonts in the presentation that is the destination document.

5. Click the File tab on the ribbon, click Info, click Edit Links to Files at the bottom of the right pane, in the Links dialog box click the Automatic Update check box to add a checkmark, click Close in the dialog box, click the Back button ⬅ at the top of the pane, then in the presentation click the Save button 🖫 on the Quick Access Toolbar

   The default setting for updating links in a PowerPoint file is Manual, but you have changed it so that the links will be automatically updated if the Excel file changes.

6. Switch to Excel, switch to the TCS Projected Revenue sheet, type 125,000 in cell B7, click the Enter button ✓ on the Formula bar, then click the PowerPoint program button on the taskbar to display the presentation

   The IT Support percentage decreases from 12% to 8%, reflecting the change in the Excel data.

7. Click the Slide Show button 🖳 on the status bar

   Slide Show view shows the slide full screen, the way the audience will see it, as shown in FIGURE 7-12.

8. Press ESC to return to Normal view, with Slide 2 selected click the Insert tab on the ribbon, click the Header & Footer button in the Text group, add a checkmark in the Footer check box, type your name in the Footer text box, click Apply to All, save and close the presentation, then close PowerPoint

FIGURE 7-11: Presentation in Normal view

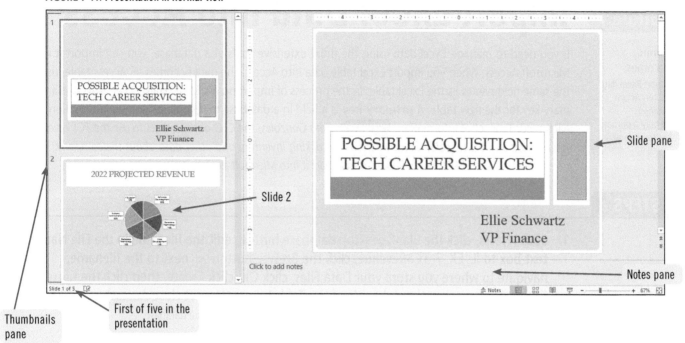

FIGURE 7-12: Completed slide

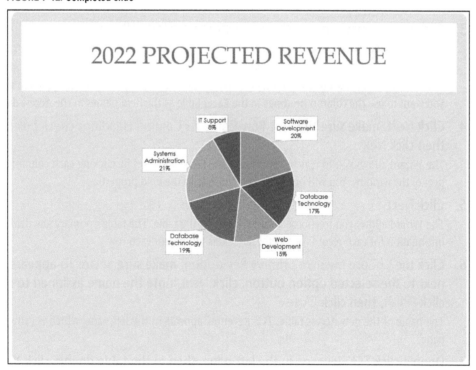

Import Excel Data into Access

Learning
Outcomes
• Import Excel data
  into an Access
  database
• Identify a primary
  key for a database

If you need to manage Excel data using the more extensive tools of a database, you can import it into Microsoft Access. When you import Excel table data into Access, the data becomes an Access table, using the same field names as the Excel table. In the process of importing an Excel table, Access specifies a primary key for the new table. A **primary key** is a field in a database that contains unique information for each record, or set of information. **CASE** *Rory Gonzales, the CEO of JCL, wants to use the TCS revenue information in an Access database, where he is tracking inventory and other data about the company. This revenue data is in an Excel file, so you need to import it into Microsoft Access.*

STEPS

1. **Start Access, click the** Blank desktop database button, **edit the filename in the File Name text box to** IL_EX_7_TCSRevenue, **click the** Browse button next to the filename, **navigate to where you store your Data Files, click** OK, **click** Create, **then click the** Close Table1 button ⊠ **on the right side of the Table1 pane (Do not close Access)**

   The IL_EX_7_Revenue database is created, and Table1 is removed from the database.

2. **Click the** External Data tab **on the ribbon, click the** New Data Source button **in the** Import & Link group, **click** From File, **then click** Excel

   The Get External Data - Excel Spreadsheet dialog box opens, as shown in **FIGURE 7-13**. This dialog box allows you to specify how you want the data to be stored in Access.

3. **Click** Browse, **navigate to where you store your Data Files, click** Support_EX_7-6, **click** Open, **if necessary click the** Import the source data into a new table in the current database. option button, **then click** OK

   The first Import Spreadsheet Wizard dialog box opens, with a sample of the sheet data in the lower section. You want to use the column headings in the Excel table as the field names in the Access database.

4. **Click** Next, **make sure the** First Row Contains Column Headings check box **is selected, then click** Next

   The Wizard allows you to review and change the field properties by clicking each column in the lower section of the window. You will not make any changes to the field properties.

5. **Click** Next

   The Wizard allows you to choose a primary key for the table. The table's primary key field contains unique information for each record; the Sector ID field is unique for each row.

QUICK TIP
Specifying a primary
key allows you to
retrieve data more
quickly in the future.

6. **Click the** Choose my own primary key option, **make sure** Sector ID **appears in the box next to the selected option button, click** Next, **note the name assigned to the new table, click** Finish, **then click** Close

   The name of the new Access table, TCS Revenue, appears in the left pane, which is called the Navigation pane.

7. **Double-click** TCS Revenue **in the left pane, then in the table double-click the** border **between the** Sector **and the** Revenue **column headings**

   The Sector column widens. The Access table is shown in **FIGURE 7-14**.

8. **Click in the last** row **of the table, in the Sector ID column type** 9999, **press TAB, then type your name in the Sector column**

9. **Click the** Save button **on the Quick Access Toolbar, close the file, then close Access**

FIGURE 7-13: Get External Data - Excel Spreadsheet dialog box

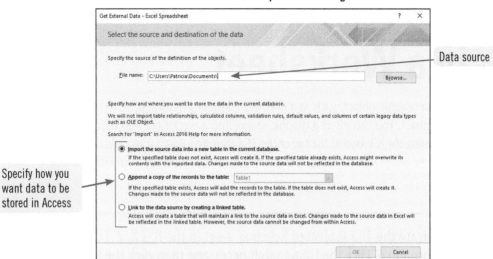

Data source

Specify how you want data to be stored in Access

FIGURE 7-14: Completed Access table with data imported from Excel

Sector ID	Sector	Revenue	Click to Add
1425	Software Development	$212,500	
2654	Database Technology	$195,500	
3125	Web Develoopment	$185,200	
4365	Network Administration	$215,500	
5654	Systems Administration	$245,400	
6335	IT Support	$132,500	

TCS Revenue

Access table

Primary key

Adding SmartArt graphics

SmartArt graphics provide another way to visually communicate information on a worksheet. Each SmartArt type communicates a kind of information or relationship, such as a list, process, or hierarchy. Each type has various layouts you can choose. To insert a SmartArt graphic into a worksheet, click the Insert tab, then click the Insert a SmartArt Graphic button 🔲 in the Illustrations group. In the Choose a SmartArt Graphic dialog box, choose from eight SmartArt types: List, Process, Cycle, Hierarchy, Relationship, Matrix, Pyramid, and Picture. There is also a link for SmartArt available on Office.com. The dialog box describes the type of information that is appropriate for each selected layout. After you choose a layout and click OK, a SmartArt object appears on your worksheet. **FIGURE 7-15** shows examples of SmartArt graphics. You can enter text directly in the placeholders or use the SmartArt text pane. If this pane is in your way, you can close it by clicking the Close button in the upper-right corner of the pane. As you enter text, the font automatically resizes to fit the graphic. You can change the layout by selecting the SmartArt, then clicking a different layout in the Layouts group on the SmartArt Tools Design tab.

FIGURE 7-15: Examples of SmartArt graphics

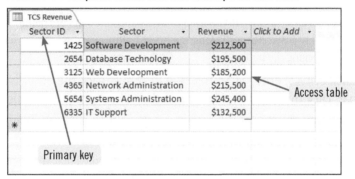

Hierarchy layout

Cycle layout

Pyramid layout

Excel

Insert a Graphic File in a Worksheet

Learning Outcomes
• Insert an image into an Excel worksheet
• Add a style to an image

Adding a graphic object, such as a drawing, logo, or photograph, can greatly enhance your worksheet's visual impact. You can insert a graphic image into a worksheet and then format it. **CASE** ▶ *Ellie wants you to insert the JCL logo at the top of the TCS Projected Revenue worksheet. The company's graphic designer created the image and saved it in JPG (commonly pronounced "jay-peg") format.*

STEPS

1. **Activate the** TCS Projected Revenue sheet **in the** IL_EX_7_TCS **workbook, select rows 1 through 6, click the** Home tab **if necessary, then click the** Insert button **in the Cells group**

   Six blank rows appear at the top of the worksheet, leaving space to insert column headings for the workbook data and the logo. If you need to insert multiple rows or columns, it saves time to select the number you need to insert before clicking the Insert button. Six rows were inserted because you selected six rows before clicking the button.

2. **Click cell** A6, **enter** TCS Projected Revenue, **click the** Enter button ✓ **on the Formula bar, click the** Cell Styles button **in the Styles group, then click** Title

3. **Click cell** A1, **click the** Insert tab **on the ribbon, click the** Illustrations button, **then click the** Pictures button **in the Illustrations group**

   The Insert Picture dialog box opens. Because you specified that you want to insert a picture, the dialog box displays only files that contain graphics file extensions, such as .jpg.

4. **Navigate to where you store your Data Files if necessary, click** Support_EX_7-7, **then click** Insert

   Excel inserts the image and displays the Picture Tools Format tab. The small circles around the picture's edge are sizing handles. Sizing handles appear when a picture is selected; you use them to change the size of a picture.

5. **Position the** pointer **over the** sizing handle **in the logo's lower-right corner until the pointer becomes** ⬊, **then drag the** sizing handle **up and to the left so that the logo's outline fits within rows 1 through 5**

   Compare your screen to **FIGURE 7-16**.

6. **With the image selected, click the** More button ▼ **in the Picture Styles group, point to several styles and observe the effect on the graphic, click the** Bevel Rectangle style **(the last in the third row), click the** Picture Border button **in the Picture Styles group, then click** Green, Accent 6 **in the Theme Colors group**

7. **Click the** Picture Effects button **in the Picture Styles group, click** Glow, **click** More Glow Colors, **click** Green, Accent 6 **in the Theme Colors group, resize the logo again to fit it in rows 1 through 5, then drag it to center it over the data in columns** A **and** B

   Compare your worksheet to **FIGURE 7-17**.

8. **sam↟ Save the workbook, change the worksheet orientation to landscape, preview the worksheet, close the workbook, close Excel, then submit the workbook to your instructor**

FIGURE 7-16: **Resized logo**

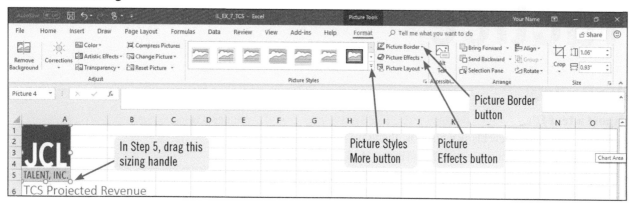

FIGURE 7-17: **Worksheet with formatted picture**

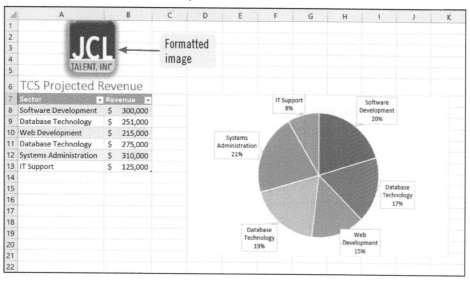

Working with SmartArt graphics

You can add shapes to a SmartArt graphic by selecting the position where the shape will appear, clicking the Add Shape arrow in the Create Graphic group of the SmartArt Tools Design tab, then selecting the desired position. Also in the Create Graphic group are the Promote and Demote buttons, which you can use to increase or decrease the level of a selected shape. The SmartArt Tools Design tab lets you choose color schemes and styles for your SmartArt. You can add shape styles, fills, outlines, and other shape effects to SmartArt graphics using choices on the SmartArt Tools Format tab. Clicking the Shape Fill button in the Shape Styles group of this tab, then clicking Picture inserts a picture in a shape.

You can also add fills, outlines, and other effects to text using this tab. You can change the size of a SmartArt shape by selecting the shape, then clicking the Larger button or the Smaller button in the Shapes group on the SmartArt Tools Format tab. You can resize an entire SmartArt graphic by clicking it and dragging a resizing handle. To resize a graphic proportionally, drag any corner sizing handle. If you drag an edge sizing handle instead, the graphic will be resized non-proportionally. You can align multiple SmartArt graphics at once by selecting them, clicking Align in the Arrange group on the Drawing Tools Format tab, then selecting the alignment option. (This also aligns other objects on a worksheet.)

Practice

Skills Review

1. Import a text file.

a. Start Excel, create a new blank workbook, then save the workbook in the location where you store your Data Files as **IL_EX_7_OLP**.

b. Use the Get & Transform tool to import the text file Support_EX_7-8 from the location where you store your Data Files. The data is delimited using tabs.

c. Format the data in column B using the Accounting style and no decimal places.

d. Rename the sheet tab **May**, then delete Sheet1.

e. Add a table total row to show the total expenses, as shown in **FIGURE 7-18**.

f. Save the workbook.

FIGURE 7-18

	A	B	C
1	Category	Expenses	
2	Compensation	$ 323,060	
3	Facility	$ 317,638	
4	Supplies	$ 251,461	
5	Equipment	$ 271,334	
6	Total	$ 1,163,493	
7			
8			

2. Import data from another workbook.

a. Use the Get & Transform tool to import the data on the April Expenses sheet in the Excel file Support_EX_7-9 from the location where you store your Data Files.

b. After loading the data, open the Power Query Editor using the Queries & Connections pane. In the Power Query Editor, change the column labels in row 1 to **Category** and **Expenses**. Close and load the edits.

c. Rename the sheet with the imported data **April**.

d. Format the expense data using the Accounting style and no decimal places.

e. Add a total row to the table to display the sum of the expense amounts.

f. Save the workbook.

3. Import a database table.

a. Use the Get & Transform tool to import the data on the Expenses table in the Access Data File Support_EX_7-10 from the location where you store your Data Files.

b. Rename the sheet with the imported data **May Details**.

c. Format the amount data in column D using the Accounting style and no decimal places.

d. Add a total row to the table to display the sum of the expense amounts. Autofit column D if necessary to display all the data.

e. Scroll down to see the entire table, save the workbook, then compare your screen to **FIGURE 7-19**.

FIGURE 7-19

	A	B	C	D	E
1	Category	Item	Month	Amount	
2	Compensation	Benefits	May	$ 50,000	
3	Compensation	Bonuses	May	$ 40,000	
4	Compensation	Commissions	May	$ 35,000	
5	Compensation	Conferences	May	$ 42,000	
6	Compensation	Promotions	May	$ 65,048	
7	Compensation	Payroll Taxes	May	$ 18,954	
8	Compensation	Salaries	May	$ 63,514	
9	Compensation	Training	May	$ 8,544	
10	Facility	Lease	May	$ 42,184	
11	Facility	Maintenance	May	$ 63,214	
12	Facility	Other	May	$ 11,478	
13	Facility	Rent	May	$ 80,214	
14	Facility	Telephone	May	$ 62,584	
15	Facility	Utilities	May	$ 57,964	
16	Supplies	Food	May	$ 61,775	
17	Supplies	Computer	May	$ 43,217	
18	Supplies	General Office	May	$ 47,854	
19	Supplies	Other	May	$ 56,741	
20	Supplies	Outside Services	May	$ 41,874	
21	Equipment	Computer	May	$ 49,874	
22	Equipment	Other	May	$ 43,547	
23	Equipment	Cash Registers	May	$ 55,987	
24	Equipment	Software	May	$ 63,147	
25	Equipment	Telecommunications	May	$ 58,779	
26	Total			$1,163,493	

Skills Review (continued)

4. Link worksheet data to a Word document.

a. With the May Details sheet active, copy the range A1:D26.

b. Open a File Explorer window, then double-click the Word file IL_EX_7-11 from the location where you store your Data Files. When the file opens in Word, save it as **IL_EX_7_OLPMemo**.

c. At the end of the memo body, use the Paste menu to paste the copied worksheet data by linking it and using the destination styles. Widen the Amount column if necessary to display the values on one line.

d. Note that the first compensation value in the memo is currently $50,000. Switch to Excel, activate the May Details worksheet in the IL_EX_7_OLP workbook, press ESC to deactivate the copied range, then change the value in cell D2 to **$35,000**.

e. Activate the IL_EX_7_OLPMemo document in Word, update the linked data, then verify that the first compensation value has changed to $35,000, as shown in **FIGURE 7-20**. (*Hint:* To update the link, right-click the table in the memo, then click Update Link.)

f. Use a tool on the Insert tab of the ribbon to edit the header, enter your name in the header, save your changes to the IL_EX_7_OLPMemo document, preview the memo, close the document, then close Word.

FIGURE 7-20

Category	Item	Month	Amount
Compensation	Benefits	May	$ 35,000
Compensation	Bonuses	May	$ 40,000
Compensation	Commissions	May	$ 35,000
Compensation	Conferences	May	$ 42,000
Compensation	Promotions	May	$ 65,048
Compensation	Payroll Taxes	May	$ 18,954
Compensation	Salaries	May	$ 63,514
Compensation	Training	May	$ 8,544
Facility	Lease	May	$ 42,184
Facility	Maintenance	May	$ 63,214
Facility	Other	May	$ 11,478
Facility	Rent	May	$ 80,214
Facility	Telephone	May	$ 62,584
Facility	Utilities	May	$ 57,964
Supplies	Food	May	$ 61,775
Supplies	Computer	May	$ 43,217
Supplies	General Office	May	$ 47,854
Supplies	Other	May	$ 56,741
Supplies	Outside Services	May	$ 41,874
Equipment	Computer	May	$ 49,874
Equipment	Other	May	$ 43,547
Equipment	Cash Registers	May	$ 55,987
Equipment	Software	May	$ 63,147
Equipment	Telecommunications	May	$ 58,779
Total			$ 1,148,493

5. Link an Excel chart to a PowerPoint slide.

a. Start PowerPoint, open the presentation IL_EX_7-12 from the location where you store your Data Files, then save it as **IL_EX_7_OLPPresentation**.

b. Switch to Excel, activate the May worksheet in the IL_EX_7_OLP workbook, then using the data in the range A2:B5, create a 2-D pie chart. Delete the chart title, add data callouts, then delete the chart legend. Move the chart so its upper-left corner is at the upper-left corner of cell D1.

c. Copy the chart, activate the PowerPoint file, then display Slide 6, May Expenses. (*Hint:* Click slide 6 in the Thumbnails pane.)

d. Link the copied chart to Slide 6, using the theme of the destination file. Notice that Compensation is currently 28% of total expenses.

Skills Review (continued)

e. Open the Info pane on the File tab, then edit the file's links to automatically update. Return to the presentation.

f. Switch to Excel, then change the compensation amount in cell B2 of the May worksheet to **$500,000**. Notice in the pie chart that Compensation is now 37% of total expenses.

g. Activate the IL_EX_7_OLPPresentation file, then verify the Compensation percentage in the chart on Slide 6 changed to 37%.

h. Enlarge the chart and re-center it if necessary under the title, so it matches FIGURE 7-21.

i. Use a tool on the Insert tab to add a footer containing your name to all of the slides.

j. Save the presentation, close the presentation, then close PowerPoint.

FIGURE 7-21

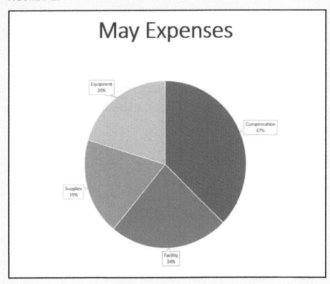

6. **Import Excel data into Access.**

a. Start Access, then create a blank desktop database named **IL_EX_7_RevisedMay** in the location where you store your Data Files. Close Table1.

b. Use the External Data tab to import the Excel table in the Support_EX_7-13 file from the location where you store your Data Files. In the Get External Data dialog box, choose the first option to import the source data into a new Access table. Step through the Import Spreadsheet Wizard, making sure the First Row Contains Column Headings check box is selected, and accepting the default assignment of field names. Identify a primary key by letting Access add one. Accept the default table name, and do not save the import steps.

c. Open the Revised May Expenses table in Access, then compare your screen to FIGURE 7-22.

d. Enter your name in the Category column of row 5 in the table, save the database file, then close Access.

FIGURE 7-22

ID	Category	Expenses	Click to Add
1	Compensation	$312,500	
2	Facility	$307,851	
3	Supplies	$235,487	
4	Equipment	$251,487	
* (New)			

Skills Review (continued)

7. Insert a graphic file in a worksheet.

   a. Activate the April worksheet in the IL-EX_7_OLP file. Select rows 1 through 4, then use a tool on the Home tab of the ribbon to insert four blank rows above row 1 to create space for an image.

   b. In rows 1 through 4, insert the picture file Support_EX_7-14.jpg from the location where you store your Data Files.

   c. Resize and reposition the logo as necessary to make it fit in rows 1 through 4.

   d. Apply the Beveled Matte, White Picture Style, then change the picture border color to Green, Accent 6 in the Theme colors.

   e. Resize the picture to fit the image and the border in the first four rows. Move the picture to center it between columns A and B. Compare your worksheet to FIGURE 7-23.

   f. Group the worksheets, change the orientation of the worksheets to landscape, add your name to the center section of the footer, preview the workbook, save and close the workbook, then submit the workbook to your instructor.

FIGURE 7-23

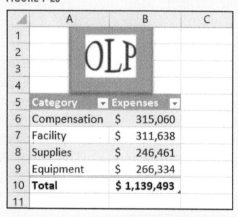

Excel

Independent Challenge 1

You have started a new position managing the respiratory therapy clinic at Riverwalk Medical Center. The previous manager left important data for the first quarter of the year in various text, workbook, and database files. You need to bring the data from all these sources into an Excel workbook, so you can analyze it together.

a. Start Excel, create a new workbook, then save it as **IL_EX_7_RiverwalkQ1** in the location where you store your Data Files.

b. Use the Get & Transform tool to import the data from Sheet1 of the Excel workbook file Support_EX_7-15. Rename the worksheet **Jan**, then delete Sheet1.

c. Format the billing data in column B using the Accounting number format and no decimal places.

d. Use the Get & Transform tool to import the data from the tab delimited text file Support_EX_7-16. Rename the worksheet **Feb**.

e. Format the billing data in column B using the Accounting number format and no decimal places.

f. Use the Get & Transform tool to import the data from the March Billings table in the Access file Support_EX_7-17. Rename the worksheet **Mar**.

g. Delete column A in the Mar worksheet, then format the Billings data in column B as Accounting with no decimal places.

h. Activate the Jan worksheet. Insert four blank rows at the top of the worksheet.

i. Insert the Support_EX_7-18 image file and resize it to fit in rows 1 through 4.

j. Apply the Center Shadow Rectangle Picture Style (second row, second from the right), then change the picture border color to Green, Accent 6, Darker 50% in the Theme colors. Resize the picture to fit the image and the border in the first four rows. Move the picture so it appears centered above the range A1:C1.

k. Compare your Jan worksheet to FIGURE 7-24.

l. Group the worksheets, add the sheet name to the center header section, add your name to the center section of the footer, preview the workbook, ungroup the worksheets, save and close the workbook, then submit the workbook to your instructor.

FIGURE 7-24

	A	B	C	D
1				
2				
3				
4				
5	Provider	Billings	Month	
6	R. Juan	$ 3,022	January	
7	M. Lyons	$ 4,463	January	
8	P. Volez	$ 4,287	January	
9	J.Jerry	$ 4,198	January	
10	H.Tran	$ 2,479	January	
11	W. Kitter	$ 3,589	January	
12	J. Walsh	$ 4,978	January	
13				

Independent Challenge 2

You are the executive assistant for the CEO of a national credit institution. The CEO has asked for an organizational chart of the company's upper management. The employee data is stored in a text file that you will import into Excel.

a. Start Excel, create a new workbook, then save it as **IL_EX_7_OrgChart** in the location where you store your Data Files.

b. Use the Get & Transform tool to import the data from the Support_EX_7-19 text file.

Independent Challenge 2 (continued)

c. Delete Sheet1, then rename the sheet with the imported data **Hierarchy**.

d. Open the Power Query Editor and rename the first column header **Employee** and the second column header **Position**. (*Hint:* To change a column header, select the column header label in the Power Query Editor, click the Transform tab, click Rename in the Any Column group, then enter the new name.)

e. Click any cell outside the data, then insert a SmartArt graphic, choosing the first Organization Chart in the Hierarchy category. (*Hint:* Click the Insert tab on the ribbon, then click the SmartArt button in the Illustrations group.)

f. Close the Queries & Connections pane, then move the SmartArt graphic to line up the upper-left corner with the upper-left corner of cell C1.

g. Referring to the imported data, enter the employee name, **Seth Werthen**, and the position, **CEO**, in the top shape of the SmartArt graphic, with the name appearing in the first line and the position in the second line. (*Hint:* Press ENTER to move to the next line in a shape.)

h. In the shape on the second level, enter Julie Hadley's information using the same format of name on the first line and position on the second line.

i. In the leftmost box on the third level, enter the information for Justin Phillips using the same format used for the previous shapes.

j. In the middle box on the third level, enter the information for Katelyn Wolff using the same format used for the previous shapes.

k. In the box farthest to the right on the third level, enter the information for Connor Ogah using the same format used for the previous shapes.

l. Add a shape below Justin Phillips, then enter Lucille Fischer's information in the new shape. (*Hint:* You can add a shape below a selected shape by clicking the Add Shape arrow and clicking Add Shape Below.)

m. Add a shape below Katelyn Wolff, then enter Christine Hassan's information in the new shape. Add a shape below Connor Ogah, then enter Huiwei Phillip's information in the new shape.

n. Change the SmartArt style to Subtle Effect.

o. Change the SmartArt colors to Gradient Loop – Accent 6. (*Hint:* Use the Change Colors tool on the SmartArt Tools Design tab.)

p. Resize the SmartArt graphic proportionally to line up the lower-right corner with the lower-right corner of cell J16, then compare your worksheet to FIGURE 7-25.

q. Enter your name in the worksheet footer, change the orientation to landscape, preview the workbook, save and close the workbook, then submit the workbook to your instructor.

FIGURE 7-25

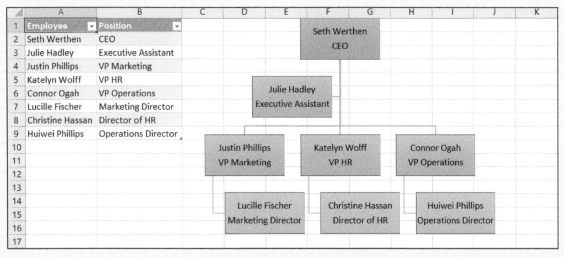

Visual Workshop

Open IL_EX_7-20.xlsx from the location where your Data Files are stored, then save it as **IL_EX_7_Systems**. Start PowerPoint, open the presentation IL_EX_7-21.pptx from the location where your Data Files are stored, then save it as **IL_EX_7_Northern**. Edit the Annual Revenue slide to match **FIGURE 7-26** by creating the pie chart in the IL_EX_7_Systems file, showing data labels with the category names and percentages on the outside end of the data series and linking the chart on slide 2 of the IL_EX_7_Northern file. (*Hint:* The chart links to the Excel file and uses the destination theme.) Add a footer of your name to all the slides, save the worksheet and presentation, close the presentation and workbook, then close PowerPoint and Excel. Submit the PowerPoint file to your instructor.

FIGURE 7-26

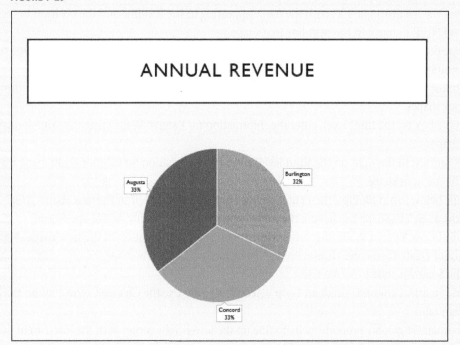

Analyzing Data with PivotTables

CASE JCL uses PivotTables to analyze revenue data. Ellie Schwartz is preparing for the annual directors' meeting and asks you to analyze revenue in JCL's Northeast offices over the past year. You will create a PivotTable to summarize last year's revenue data by quarter, position, office, and division. You will also illustrate the information using a PivotChart.

Module Objectives

After completing this module, you will be able to:

- Plan and design a PivotTable report
- Create a PivotTable report
- Change a PivotTable's summary function and design
- Filter PivotTable data

- Explore PivotTable Data Relationships
- Create a PivotChart report
- Update a PivotTable report
- Use the GETPIVOTDATA function

Files You Will Need

IL_EX_8-1.xlsx   IL_EX_8-4.xlsx
IL_EX_8-2.xlsx   IL_EX_8-5.xlsx
IL_EX_8-3.xlsx

Excel
Module 8

Learning
Outcomes
• Develop guidelines
  for a PivotTable
• Develop an under-
  standing of Pivot-
  Table vocabulary

Plan and Design a PivotTable Report

The PivotTable Report feature lets you summarize large amounts of worksheet data in a compact table format. Then you can freely rearrange, or "pivot," PivotTable rows and columns to explore the relationships within your data. Before you begin creating a PivotTable report (often called a PivotTable), you need to review the data and consider how a PivotTable can best summarize it. **CASE** ▶ *Ellie asks you to design a PivotTable to display JCL's revenue information for its offices in the Northeast. You begin by reviewing guidelines for creating PivotTables.*

DETAILS

Before you create a PivotTable, think about the following guidelines:

- **Review the source data**

  Before you can effectively summarize data in a PivotTable, you need to understand the source data's scope and structure. The source data does not have to be defined as a table, but it should be in a table-like format; that is, it should have column headings and the same type of data in each column, and it should not have any blank rows or columns. To create a meaningful PivotTable, make sure that at least one of the fields has repeated information so that the PivotTable can effectively group it. Also, be sure to include numeric data that the PivotTable can total for each group. The data columns represent categories of data, which are called fields, just as in a table. You are working with revenue information that Ellie received from JCL's Northeastern office managers, shown in **FIGURE 8-1**. Information is repeated in the Position ID, Division, Office, and Quarter Columns, and numeric information is displayed in the revenue column, so you will be able to summarize this data effectively in a PivotTable.

- **Determine the purpose of the PivotTable**

  The purpose of your PivotTable is to summarize revenue information by quarter across various offices.

- **Identify the fields you want to include**

  You want your PivotTable to summarize the data in the Position ID, Division, Office, Quarter, and Revenue columns, so you need to include those fields in your PivotTable.

- **Determine which field contains the data you want to summarize and which summary function you want to use**

  The JCL offices are organized into divisions, such as Technical, Finance & Accounting, Creative, and Office Support. You want to summarize revenue information by summing that field for each division in an office by quarter. You'll do this by using the Sum function.

- **Decide how you want to arrange the data**

  The PivotTable layout you choose determines the information you want to communicate. Position ID values will appear in the PivotTable columns, office and quarter numbers will appear in rows, and the PivotTable will summarize revenue figures, as shown in **FIGURE 8-2**.

- **Determine the location of the PivotTable**

  You can place a PivotTable in any worksheet of any workbook. Placing a PivotTable on a separate worksheet makes it easier to locate and prevents you from accidentally overwriting parts of an existing sheet. You decide to create the PivotTable as a new worksheet in the current workbook.

FIGURE 8-1: Revenue data

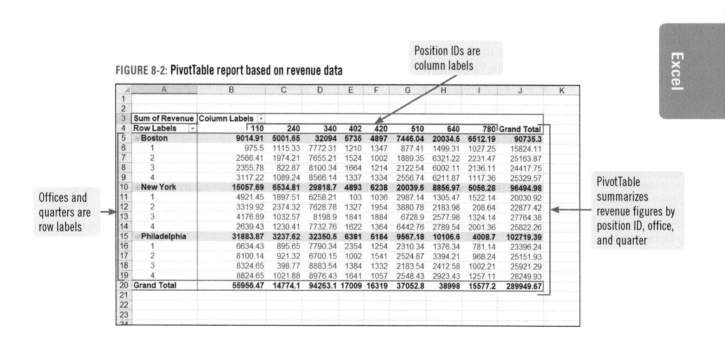

	A	B	C	D	E
1		JCL Revenue			
2	Position ID	Division	Office	Quarter	Revenue
3	240	Finance & Accounting	Boston	1	$ 1,115.33
4	240	Finance & Accounting	Boston	2	$ 1,974.21
5	240	Finance & Accounting	Boston	3	$ 822.87
6	240	Finance & Accounting	Boston	4	$ 1,089.24
7	110	Technical	Boston	1	$ 975.50
8	110	Technical	Boston	2	$ 2,566.41
9	110	Technical	Boston	3	$ 2,355.78
10	110	Technical	Boston	4	$ 3,117.22
11	340	Creative	Boston	1	$ 7,772.31
12	340	Creative	Boston	2	$ 7,655.21
13	340	Creative	Boston	3	$ 8,100.34
14	340	Creative	Boston	4	$ 8,566.14
15	402	Office Support	Boston	1	$ 1,210.00
16	402	Office Support	Boston	2	$ 1,524.00
17	402	Office Support	Boston	3	$ 1,664.00
18	402	Office Support	Boston	4	$ 1,337.00
19	780	Finance & Accounting	Boston	1	$ 1,027.25
20	780	Finance & Accounting	Boston	2	$ 2,231.47
21	780	Finance & Accounting	Boston	3	$ 2,136.11
22	780	Finance & Accounting	Boston	4	$ 1,117.36
23	640	Technical	Boston	1	$ 1,499.31

Northeast

Ready

Data with repeated information

Numeric data

FIGURE 8-2: PivotTable report based on revenue data

Position IDs are column labels

	A	B	C	D	E	F	G	H	I	J	K
1											
2											
3	Sum of Revenue	Column Labels									
4	Row Labels	110	240	340	402	420	510	640	780	Grand Total	
5	Boston	9014.91	5001.65	32094	5735	4897	7446.04	20034.5	6512.19	90735.3	
6	1	975.5	1115.33	7772.31	1210	1347	877.41	1499.31	1027.25	15824.11	
7	2	2566.41	1974.21	7655.21	1524	1002	1889.35	6321.22	2231.47	25163.87	
8	3	2355.78	822.87	8100.34	1664	1214	2122.54	6002.11	2136.11	24417.75	
9	4	3117.22	1089.24	8566.14	1337	1334	2556.74	6211.87	1117.36	25329.57	
10	New York	15057.69	6534.81	29818.7	4893	6238	20039.6	8856.97	5056.28	96494.98	
11	1	4921.45	1897.51	6258.21	103	1036	2987.14	1305.47	1522.14	20030.92	
12	2	3319.92	2374.32	7628.78	1327	1954	3880.78	2183.98	208.64	22877.42	
13	3	4176.89	1032.57	8198.9	1841	1884	6728.9	2577.98	1324.14	27764.38	
14	4	2639.43	1230.41	7732.76	1622	1364	6442.76	2789.54	2001.36	25822.26	
15	Philadelphia	31883.87	3237.62	32350.5	6381	5184	9567.18	10106.6	4008.7	102719.39	
16	1	6634.43	895.65	7790.34	2354	1254	2310.34	1376.34	781.14	23396.24	
17	2	8100.14	921.32	6700.15	1002	1541	2524.87	3394.21	968.24	25151.93	
18	3	8324.65	398.77	8883.54	1384	1332	2183.54	2412.58	1002.21	25921.29	
19	4	8824.65	1021.88	8976.43	1641	1057	2548.43	2923.43	1257.11	28249.93	
20	Grand Total	55956.47	14774.1	94263.1	17009	16319	37052.8	38998	15577.2	289949.67	
21											
22											
23											

Offices and quarters are row labels

PivotTable summarizes revenue figures by position ID, office, and quarter

Excel

Create a PivotTable Report

Once you've planned and designed your PivotTable report, you are ready to create it. Then you can **populate** it by adding fields to areas in the PivotTable. A PivotTable has four areas: the Report Filter, which is the field by which you want to filter the PivotTable; the Row Labels, which contain the fields whose labels will describe the values in the rows; the Column Labels, which appear above the PivotTable values and describe the columns; and the Values, which summarize the numeric data. **CASE** ▸ *With the planning and design stage complete, you are ready to create a PivotTable that summarizes revenue information.*

STEPS

1. **sam** ↓ **Start Excel, open IL_EX_8-1.xlsx from the location where you store your Data Files, then save it as IL_EX_8-NERevenue**

2. **Click the Insert tab on the ribbon, click the Recommended PivotTables button in the Tables group, then click each layout in the dialog box, scrolling as necessary**
   The Recommended PivotTables dialog box displays recommended layouts, as shown in **FIGURE 8-3**.

3. **Click Blank PivotTable at the bottom of the dialog box**
   A new, blank PivotTable appears on the left side of the worksheet and the PivotTable Fields List appears in a pane on the right, as shown in **FIGURE 8-4**. To populate the PivotTable, you can click field check boxes in the PivotTable Fields List pane, often simply called the Field List. The diagram area at the bottom of the pane represents the main PivotTable areas and helps you track field locations as you populate the PivotTable. You can also drag fields among the diagram areas to change the PivotTable layout.

4. **Click the Office field check box in the Field List**
   Because the office field is a text, rather than a numeric, field, Excel adds the offices to the Rows area of the PivotTable and adds the Office field name to the Rows area in the PivotTable Fields pane.

5. **Click the Position ID check box in the Field List**
   The Position ID information is automatically added to the PivotTable, and "Sum of Position ID" appears in the Values area in the diagram area. Because the data type of the Position ID field is numeric, the field is added to the Values area of the PivotTable and the Position ID values are summed, which is not meaningful in this case. Instead, you want the Position IDs as column headers in the PivotTable.

6. **Click the Sum of Position ID arrow in the Values area at the bottom of the PivotTable Fields List pane, then click Move to Column Labels**
   The Position ID field becomes a column label, so the Position ID values appear as column headers.

7. **Drag the Quarter field from the PivotTable Fields List pane and drop it below the Office field in the Rows area, then click the Revenue field check box in the pane to add a checkmark**
   You have created a PivotTable that totals revenue, with the position IDs as column headers, and offices and quarters as row labels. Sum is the Excel default function for data fields containing numbers, so Excel automatically calculates the sum of the revenue. The PivotTable tells you that Philadelphia revenue of position #110 (Technical) was twice the New York revenue and more than three times the Boston revenue. Position #340 (Creative) had the highest overall revenue, as shown in the Grand Total row in **FIGURE 8-5**.

8. **Click the Collapse button ⊟ to the left of the Boston label, then click the Expand button ⊞**
   The quarterly total details for Boston are hidden, then redisplayed. When you have two levels of data in the rows or columns area, you can drill down and drill up in the data to expand or collapse the second-level field details below the top field.

FIGURE 8-3: Recommended PivotTables dialog box

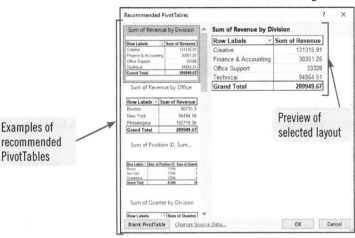

Examples of recommended PivotTables

Preview of selected layout

FIGURE 8-4: Empty PivotTable ready to receive field data

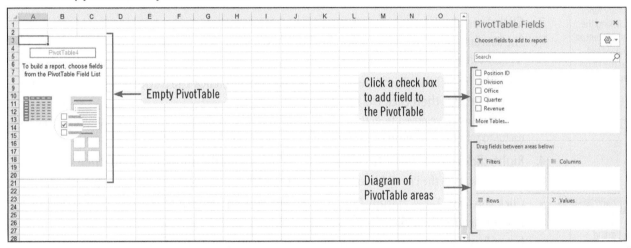

Empty PivotTable

Click a check box to add field to the PivotTable

Diagram of PivotTable areas

FIGURE 8-5: New PivotTable with fields in place

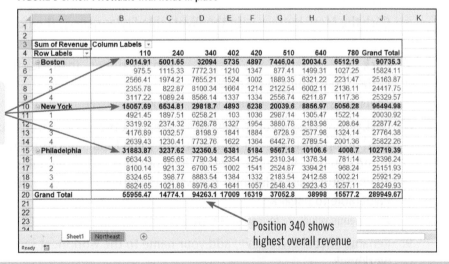

Philadelphia revenue for position 110 is twice as high as New York and three times Boston's revenue

Position 340 shows highest overall revenue

Changing a PivotTable layout

The default layout for PivotTables is the compact form; the row labels are displayed in a single column, and the second-level field items (such as the quarters in the JCL example) are indented for readability. You can change the layout of your PivotTable by clicking the PivotTable Tools Design tab, clicking the Report Layout button in the Layout group, then clicking either Show in Outline Form or Show in Tabular Form. The tabular form and the outline form show each row label in its own column. The tabular and outline layouts take up more space on a worksheet than the compact layout.

Change a PivotTable's Summary Function and Design

Learning
Outcomes
• Change a Pivot-
Table's summary
function
• Format a
PivotTable

A PivotTable's **summary function** determines what type of calculation Excel applies, or uses to summarize the table data. Unless you specify otherwise, Excel applies the Sum function to numeric data and the Count function to data fields containing text. However, you can easily change the default summary functions. **CASE** ▶ *Ellie wants you to explore using the average function to summarize the revenue for the Northeast offices. She would like you to improve the appearance of the PivotTable for her presentation.*

STEPS

QUICK TIP
You can also change
the summary func-
tion by clicking the
Field Settings button
in the Active Field
group on the Pivot-
Table Tools Analyze
tab.

1. **Right-click cell A3, then point to Summarize Values By in the shortcut menu**

   The shortcut menu shows that the Sum function is selected by default, as shown in FIGURE 8-6.

2. **Click Average**

   The data area of the PivotTable shows the average revenue for each position by office and quarter, and cell A3 now contains "Average of Revenue."

3. **Click the PivotTable Tools Design tab on the ribbon, click the Subtotals button in the Layout group, then click Do Not Show Subtotals**

   The subtotals are removed from the PivotTable. After reviewing the data, you decide that it would be more useful to sum the revenue information than to average it, and to see subtotals.

4. **Right-click cell A3, point to Summarize Values By on the shortcut menu, then click Sum**

   Excel recalculates the PivotTable, now summing the revenue data instead of averaging it.

QUICK TIP
You can control the
display of grand
totals by clicking
the PivotTable Tools
Design tab, then
clicking the Grand
Totals button in the
Layout group.

5. **Click the PivotTable Design Tools tab on the ribbon, click the Subtotals button in the Layout group, then click Show all Subtotals at Top of Group**

   Just as Excel tables have styles that let you quickly format them, PivotTables have a gallery of styles from which to choose.

6. **Click the More button ⤓ in the PivotTable Styles gallery, then click White, Pivot Style Light 3**

7. **Click the PivotTable Tools Analyze tab on the ribbon, then click the Field Headers button in the Show group to deselect it**

   The unnecessary headers "Column Labels" and "Row Labels" are removed.

8. **Click any revenue value in the PivotTable, click the Field Settings button in the Active Field group, click Number Format in the Value Field Settings dialog box, click Currency in the Category list, make sure Decimal places is 2 and Symbol is $, click OK, click OK again, AutoFit any columns if necessary to display all the data, then compare your PivotTable to FIGURE 8-7**

   The revenue values are formatted as currency.

9. **Rename Sheet1 PivotTable, add your name to the worksheet footer, then save the workbook**

FIGURE 8-6: Shortcut menu showing Sum function selected

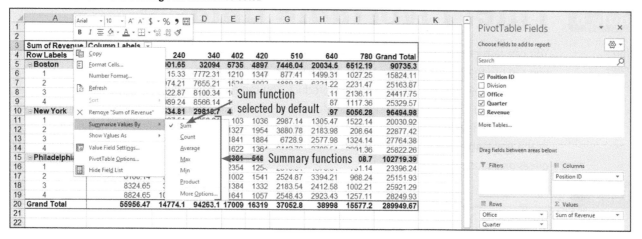

FIGURE 8-7: Formatted PivotTable

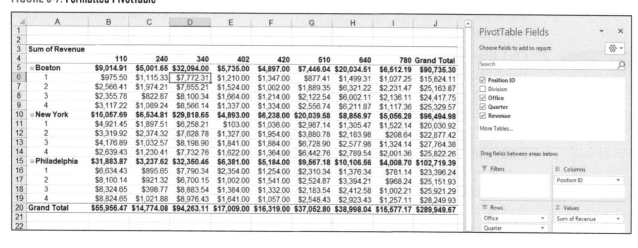

Using the Show buttons

To display and hide PivotTable elements, you can use the toggle buttons in the Show group on the PivotTable Tools Analyze tab. For example, clicking the Field List button hides or displays the PivotTable Fields List pane. Clicking the +/– button hides or displays the Expand and Collapse Outline buttons, and clicking the Field Headers button hides or displays the Row and Column Label headers on the PivotTable.

Filter PivotTable Data

Learning
Outcomes
• Filter a PivotTable
using a slicer
• Filter a PivotTable
using a report
filter

You can restrict the display of PivotTable data using slicers and report filters. A **slicer** is a graphic object you can use to filter data in a PivotTable, to show only the data you need. For example, you can use slicer buttons to show only data about a specific product. You can also filter a PivotTable using a **report filter**, which lets you filter the data to show data for one or more fields, using a list arrow. For example, if you add a month field to the Filters area, you can filter a PivotTable so that only January revenue data appears in the PivotTable. **CASE** ▶ *Ellie wants to compare revenue data about specific positions across specific offices and quarters.*

STEPS

1. **Click any cell in the PivotTable, click the PivotTable Tools Analyze tab on the ribbon if necessary, click the Insert Slicer button in the Filter group, in the Insert Slicers dialog box click the Position ID check box and the Office check box to add checkmarks to both fields, click OK, then drag both slicers to the right of the PivotTable**

   The slicers contain buttons representing the position ID numbers and office names. You can move and resize a slicer similarly to other graphic objects.

QUICK TIP
You can add a slicer
style, edit a slicer
caption, and change
the button order
using the buttons
and options on the
Slicer Tools Options
tab.

2. **Click the Office slicer, click the Slicer Tools Options tab on the ribbon, type 1.18 in the Height box in the Size group, type 2 in the Width box, click the Position ID slicer, type 2.6 in the Height box in the Size group, then type 2 in the Width box**

   The slicers are resized to display the buttons, as shown in **FIGURE 8-8**.

3. **Click the 110 button in the Position ID slicer, press CTRL, click the 510 button, release CTRL, click the New York button in the Office slicer, press CTRL, click the Philadelphia button in the Office slicer, then release CTRL**

   The PivotTable displays only the data for position IDs 110 and 510 in New York and Philadelphia, as shown in **FIGURE 8-9**. In the slicers, the Filter symbol changes, indicating the PivotTable is filtered to display the selected fields.

4. **Click the Clear Filter button 🔽 in the Position ID slicer, click 🔽 in the Office slicer, click the top of the Office slicer, press CTRL, click the top of the Position ID slicer, release CTRL, right-click the Position ID slicer, then click Remove Slicers on the shortcut menu**

   The filters are cleared and the slicers are removed.

TROUBLE
If the PivotTable
Fields List pane is
not visible, click the
PivotTable Tools Ana-
lyze tab, then click
the Field List button
in the Show group.

5. **In the PivotTable Fields List pane, click the Quarter field arrow in the Rows area, then click Move to Report Filter in the list that opens**

   The Quarter field moves to cell A1, and a list arrow and the word "(All)" appears in cell B1. The list arrow lets you filter the data in the PivotTable by Quarter. "(All)" indicates that the PivotTable currently shows data for all quarters.

6. **Click the cell B1 list arrow, click 4, click OK, then save your work**

   The PivotTable filters the revenue data to display the fourth quarter only, as shown in **FIGURE 8-10**. The Quarter field list arrow changes to a filter symbol. A filter symbol also appears to the right of the Quarter field in the PivotTable Fields List pane, indicating that the PivotTable is filtered and summarizes only a portion of the PivotTable data.

FIGURE 8-8: Slicers for Position ID and Office fields

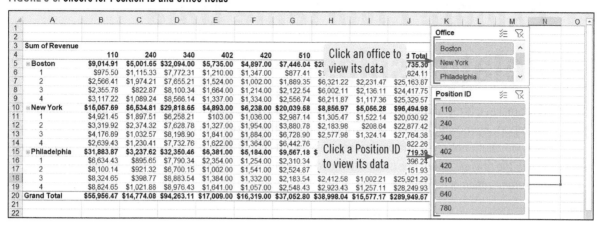

FIGURE 8-9: PivotTable filtered by Position ID and Office

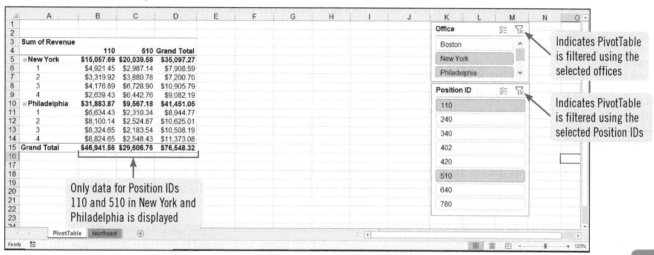

FIGURE 8-10: PivotTable filtered by fourth quarter

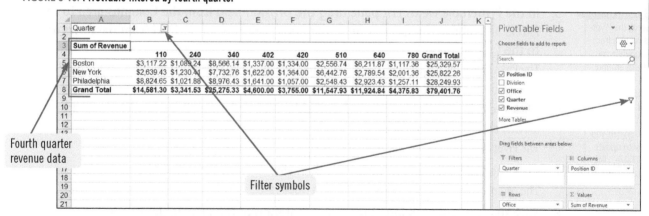

Filtering PivotTables using multiple values

Instead of using slicers to display multiple values when filtering a PivotTable report, you can use a report filter. After clicking a field's report filter list arrow in the top section of the PivotTable Fields List pane or in cell B1 on the PivotTable itself, click the Select Multiple Items check box at the bottom of the filter selections. You can then select multiple values for the filter. For example, selecting quarters 1 and 2 as the report filter in a PivotTable with quarters displays all the data for those quarters. You can also select multiple values for the row and column labels by clicking the PivotTable Tools Analyze tab, clicking the Field Headers button in the Show group, clicking the Row Labels list arrow or the Column Labels list arrow in cells A4 and B3 on the PivotTable, then selecting the data items that you want to display.

Explore PivotTable Data Relationships

Learning Outcomes
- Change a PivotTable's organization
- Add fields to a PivotTable

What makes a PivotTable such a powerful analysis tool is the ability to change the way data is organized in the report. By moving fields to different positions in the report, you can explore relationships and trends that you might not see in the original report structure. **CASE** *Ellie asks you to include division information in the revenue report. She is also interested in viewing the PivotTable in different arrangements to find the best organization of data for her presentation.*

STEPS

1. **Make sure that the PivotTable sheet is active, that the active cell is anywhere inside the PivotTable, and that the PivotTable Fields List pane is visible**

QUICK TIP

You can change the amount an inner row is indented by clicking the Options button in the PivotTable group on the PivotTable Tools Analyze tab, clicking the Layout & Format tab, then changing the number for the character(s) in the Layout section.

2. **Click the Division check box in the Field List**

   The Division data is added to the Rows area below the corresponding office data.

3. **In the Rows area of the PivotTable Fields List pane, drag the Division field up and drop it above the Office field**

   As you drag, a green bar shows where the field will be inserted. The division field is now the outer or upper field, and the office field is the inner or lower field. The PivotTable is restructured to display the revenue data first by division and then by office, as shown in **FIGURE 8-11**.

4. **In the PivotTable Fields List pane drag the Division field from the Rows area to anywhere in the Columns area, then drag the Position ID field from the Columns area to the Rows area below the Office field**

   The PivotTable now displays the revenue data with the division values in the columns and the position IDs grouped by offices in the rows. The Position ID values are indented below the offices because the Position ID field is the inner row label.

QUICK TIP

To prevent the Pivot-Table structure from updating while you move fields around, click the Defer Layout Update check box at the bottom of the PivotTable Fields List pane. When you are ready to update the PivotTable, click the Update button.

5. **In the PivotTable Fields List pane drag the Division field from the Columns area to the Filters area above the Quarter field, then drag the Position ID field from the Rows area to the Columns area**

   The PivotTable now has two report filters. The upper report filter, Division, summarizes data using the position IDs for all four divisions.

6. **Click the cell B1 list arrow of the PivotTable, click Creative, click OK, click the cell B2 list arrow, click (All), then click OK**

   The PivotTable displays revenue totals for the creative division for all quarters.

7. **Click the cell B1 list arrow, click (All), then click OK**

   The completed PivotTable appears, as shown in **FIGURE 8-12**.

8. **Save the workbook, change the page orientation of the PivotTable sheet to Landscape, then preview the PivotTable**

FIGURE 8-11: PivotTable structured by offices within divisions

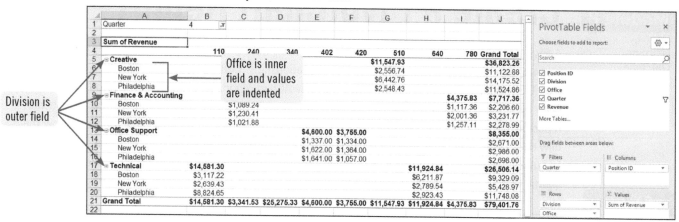

FIGURE 8-12: Completed PivotTable report

Grouping PivotTable data

You can group PivotTable data to analyze specific values in a field as a unit. For example, you may want to group revenue data for quarters 1 and 2 to analyze the first half of the year. To group PivotTable data, first select the Rows and Columns that you want to group, click the PivotTable Tools Analyze tab, then click the Group Selection button in the Group group. The default group name of Group1 can be edited by entering the new name in the cell with the default name. Once data is grouped, it can be expanded or collapsed to show the grouped details using the Collapse button ⊟ or the Expand button ⊞ next to the group name. **FIGURE 8-13** shows a PivotTable grouped by quarters with the first two quarters expanded and the last two quarters collapsed. To ungroup data, select the Group name in the PivotTable, then click the Ungroup button in the Group group.

FIGURE 8-13: Grouped PivotTable data

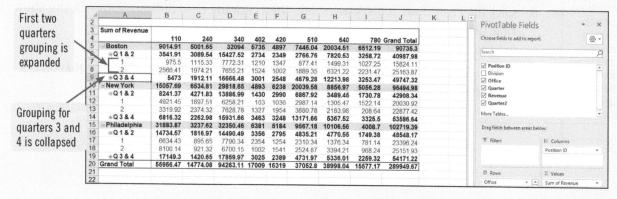

First two quarters grouping is expanded

Grouping for quarters 3 and 4 is collapsed

Excel

Create a PivotChart Report

A **PivotChart report** is a chart that you create from data or from a PivotTable report that lets you summarize and rearrange to explore new data relationships. TABLE 8-1 describes how the elements in a PivotTable report correspond to the elements in a PivotChart report. When you create a PivotChart directly from data, Excel automatically creates a corresponding PivotTable report. If you change a PivotChart report by filtering the charted elements, Excel updates the corresponding PivotTable report to show the new data values. You can move the fields of a PivotChart using the PivotChart Fields List window; the new layout will be reflected in the PivotTable. **CASE** ▶ *For her presentation, Ellie wants you to chart the fourth quarter creative revenue for all offices and the Boston office's yearly creative revenue.*

STEPS

1. **Click the cell B1 list arrow, click Creative, click OK, click the Quarter list arrow, click 4, then click OK**

   The fourth quarter creative revenue information appears in the PivotTable. You want to create the PivotChart from the PivotTable information you have displayed.

2. **Click any cell in the PivotTable, click the PivotTable Tools Analyze tab on the ribbon, then click the PivotChart button in the Tools group**

   The Insert Chart dialog box opens and shows a gallery of chart types.

> **QUICK TIP**
> You can change a PivotChart's type by clicking the Change Chart Type button in the Type group on the PivotChart Tools Design tab.

3. **Click the Clustered Column chart if necessary, then click OK**

   The PivotChart appears on the worksheet, as shown in FIGURE 8-14. The chart has field buttons that let you filter a PivotChart in the same way you do a PivotTable. You can also add a slicer to filter a PivotChart.

4. **Click the PivotChart Tools Analyze tab on the ribbon, click the Insert Slicer button in the Filter group, click the Office check box, click OK, move the slicer to the right of the chart, then click Boston in the slicer**

   Only the Boston revenue data is shown in the chart.

> **QUICK TIP**
> You can add a chart style to a PivotChart by clicking a style in the Chart Styles group on the PivotChart Tools Design tab.

5. **Click the PivotChart to select it, click the PivotChart Tools Design tab on the ribbon, click the Move Chart button in the Location group, click the New sheet option button, type PivotChart in the text box, then click OK**

6. **Click the Quarter field button at the top of the PivotChart, click All, then click OK**

   The chart now represents the Boston office's creative revenue for the year, as shown in FIGURE 8-15.

> **QUICK TIP**
> If you have more than one field in the Axis area, you can drill up or down in a PivotChart using the Collapse button ⊟ to hide the details of the second field and the Expand button ⊞ to display the second field details. If the buttons are not visible, click the Field Buttons button in the Show/Hide group on the PivotChart Analyze tab.

7. **Click the PivotChart Tools Design tab, click the Quick Layout button in the Chart Layouts group, click Layout 3, click the Chart Title element to select it, type Annual Creative Revenue, then press ENTER**

   You are finished filtering the chart data.

8. **Click the PivotChart Tools Analyze tab, then click the Field Buttons button in the Show/Hide group**

   Removing the field buttons improves the chart's appearance.

9. **Enter your name in the center section of the PivotChart sheet footer, save the workbook, then preview the PivotChart report**

   The final PivotChart report displaying Boston's creative revenue for the year is shown in FIGURE 8-16.

FIGURE 8-14: PivotChart with fourth quarter creative revenue

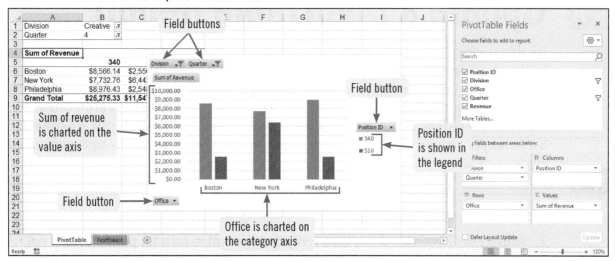

FIGURE 8-15: PivotChart displaying Boston's creative revenue for the year

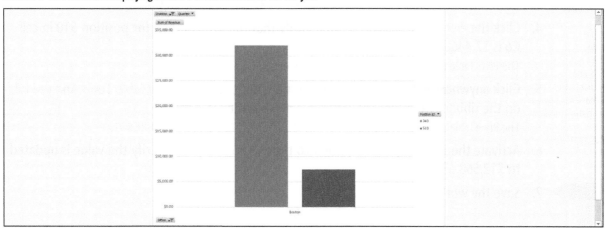

FIGURE 8-16: Completed PivotChart report

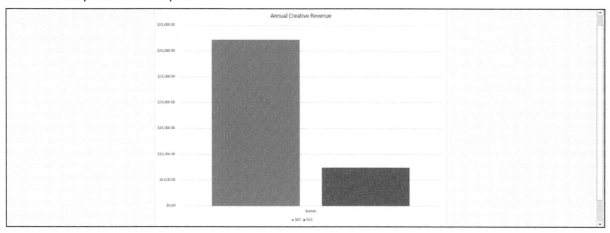

TABLE 8-1: PivotTable and PivotChart elements

PivotTable items	PivotChart items
Row labels	Axis fields
Column labels	Legend fields
Report Filters	Report Filters

Update a PivotTable Report

- Edit data in a PivotTable data source
- Refresh a PivotTable

The data in a PivotTable report looks like typical worksheet data. However, because the PivotTable data is linked to a **data source** (the data you used to create the PivotTable), the results it displays are read-only. That means you cannot move or modify a part of a PivotTable by inserting or deleting rows, editing results, or moving cells. To change PivotTable data, you must edit the items directly in the data source, then update, or **refresh**, the PivotTable so it reflects the changes to the underlying data. **CASE** *Ellie just learned that there was an error in the Boston office's creative revenue information for the first quarter. She asks you to fix this error.*

STEPS

1. **On the PivotChart sheet point to the** 510 column, **then verify the value is** $7,446.04

2. **Activate the** PivotTable sheet, **then verify that the Boston total for position 510 in cell C6 is $7,446.04**

3. **Click the** Northeast sheet tab, **click cell** E27, **enter** 6000, **then press** ENTER

4. **Click the** PivotTable sheet tab, **then verify that the Boston total for position 510 in cell C6 is $7,446.04**

   The PivotTable does not yet reflect the changed data.

5. **Click anywhere within the PivotTable if necessary, click the** PivotTable Tools Analyze tab **on the ribbon, then click the** Refresh button **in the Data group**

   The PivotTable now shows Boston's 510 total as $12,568.63, as shown in FIGURE 8-17.

6. **Activate the** PivotChart sheet, **point to the** 510 column, **then verify the value is updated to $12,568.63**

7. **Save the workbook**

FIGURE 8-17: Updated PivotTable report

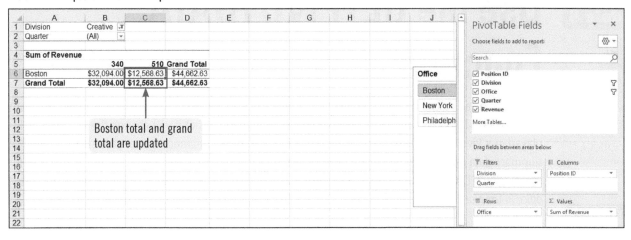

Adding a calculated field to a PivotTable and a PivotChart

You can use formulas to analyze PivotTable and PivotChart data in a field by adding a calculated field. A calculated field appears in the PivotTable's or PivotChart's Field List and can be manipulated like other PivotTable fields. To add a calculated field, click any cell in the PivotTable, click the PivotTable Tools Analyze tab, click the Fields, Items, & Sets button in the Calculations group, then click Calculated Field. The Insert Calculated Field dialog box opens. Enter the field name in the Name text box, click in the Formula text box, click a field name in the Field list that you want to use in the formula, and click Insert Field. Use standard arithmetic operators to enter the formula you want to use. For example, you can enter a formula such as [PRODUCTION FORMAT IN MONOSPACE FONT TO INDICATE INPUT TEXT]= **Revenue*1.2**[PRODUCTION END SPECIAL FORMATTING], to increase the revenue data by 20 percent. After entering the formula in the Insert Calculated Field dialog box, click Add, then click OK. The new field with the formula results appears in the PivotTable and the PivotChart, and the field is added to the PivotTable and PivotChart Fields List pane. FIGURE 8-18 shows a calculated field added to a PivotTable.

FIGURE 8-18: PivotTable with calculated field

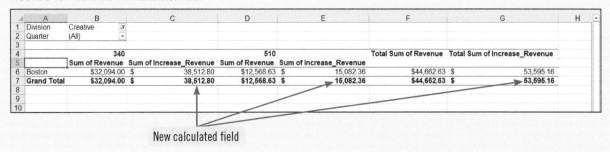

Use the GETPIVOTDATA Function

Learning
Outcomes
• Analyze the
  GETPIVOTDATA
  function
• Retrieve infor-
  mation using the
  GETPIVOTDATA
  function

Because you can rearrange a PivotTable so easily, you can't use an ordinary cell reference when you want to reference a PivotTable cell in another worksheet. The reason is that if you change the way data is displayed in a PivotTable, the data moves, making an ordinary cell reference incorrect. Instead, to retrieve summary data from a PivotTable, you need to use the Excel GETPIVOTDATA function. See FIGURE 8-19 for the GETPIVOTDATA function format. **CASE** *Ellie wants to include the yearly revenue total for the Boston office in the Northeast sheet. You use the GETPIVOTDATA function to retrieve this information.*

STEPS

1. **Activate the** PivotTable **sheet**

   The revenue figures in the PivotTable are filtered to show only the creative positions.

2. **Click the** Division filter arrow **in cell B1, click (All), then click** OK

   The PivotChart report displays revenue information for all Boston positions.

3. **Activate the** Northeast sheet, **click cell** G1, **type** Total Boston Revenue, **click the** Enter **button** ✓ **on the formula bar, click the** Home tab **on the ribbon, click the** Align Right **button** ≣ **in the Alignment group, click the** Bold button **B** **in the Font group, then adjust the width of column** G **to display the new label**

4. **Click cell** G2, **type** =, **click the** PivotTable **sheet tab, click cell** J6 **on the PivotTable, then click** ✓

   Cell J6 on the PivotTable contains the data you want to display on the Northeast sheet. The GETPIVOT-DATA function, along with its arguments, is inserted into cell G2 of the Northeast sheet. You want to format the revenue total.

5. **Click the** Accounting Number Format button **$** **in the Number group**

   The current revenue total for the Boston office is $95,857.89 as shown in FIGURE 8-20. This is the same value displayed in cell J6 of the PivotTable.

6. **Add your name to the Northeast sheet custom footer, save the workbook, then preview the Northeast worksheet**

7. **sam ✦ Close the file, close Excel, then submit the workbook to your instructor**

   The Northeast worksheet is shown in FIGURE 8-21.

FIGURE 8-19: Format of GETPIVOTDATA function

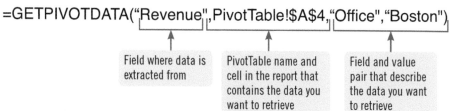

=GETPIVOTDATA("Revenue",PivotTable!$A$4,"Office","Boston")

Field where data is extracted from

PivotTable name and cell in the report that contains the data you want to retrieve

Field and value pair that describe the data you want to retrieve

FIGURE 8-20: GETPIVOTDATA function in the Northeast sheet

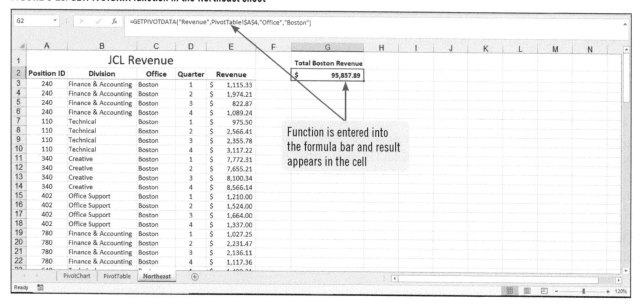

FIGURE 8-21: Completed Northeast worksheet showing total Boston revenue

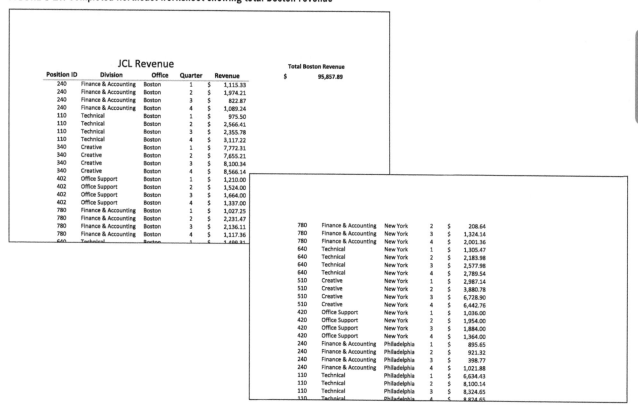

Excel

Practice

Skills Review

1. **Plan and design a PivotTable report.**
   a. Start Excel, open IL_EX_8-2.xlsx from the location where you store your Data Files, then save it as **IL_EX_8_Pharma**.
   b. Review the fields and values in the worksheet.
   c. Verify that the worksheet contains repeated values in one or more fields.
   d. Verify that there are not any blank rows or columns in the range A1:E25.
   e. Verify that the worksheet contains a field that can be summed in a PivotTable.

2. **Create a PivotTable report.**
   a. Create a blank PivotTable report on a new worksheet using the January Expenses worksheet data in the range A1:E25.
   b. Add the Division field in the PivotTable Fields List pane to the Columns area.
   c. Add the Expenses field in the PivotTable Fields List pane to the Values area.
   d. Add the Location field in the PivotTable Fields List pane to the Rows area.
   e. Add the Manager field in the PivotTable Fields List pane to the Rows area below the Location field.

3. **Change a PivotTable's summary function and design.**
   a. Change the PivotTable summary function to Average.
   b. Rename the new sheet **Jan Expenses PT**.
   c. Change the PivotTable Style to Light Orange, Pivot Style Light 14. Format the expense values in the PivotTable as currency with a $ symbol and no decimal places.
   d. Enter your name in the center section of the PivotTable report footer, then save the workbook.
   e. Change the summary function back to Sum. Use a tool on the PivotTable Tools Analyze tab to hide the field headers.

4. **Filter PivotTable data.**
   a. Use slicers to filter the PivotTable to display expenses for the production division only in the Basel and Pittsburgh locations.
   b. Clear the filters and delete the slicer.
   c. Add the Product area field to the Filters area in the PivotTable Fields List pane. Use the filter list arrow to display expenses for only the Consumer Health product area.
   d. Display expenses for all product areas.
   e. Save the workbook.

5. **Explore PivotTable Data Relationships.**
   a. In the PivotTable Fields List pane, drag the Division field from the Columns area to the Rows area below the Manager field. Drag the Manager field from the Rows area to the Columns area.
   b. Drag the Location field from the Rows area to the Filters area below the Product Area field. Drag the Division field back to the Columns area.
   c. Drag the Location field back to the Rows area.
   d. Remove the Manager field from the PivotTable.
   e. Compare your completed PivotTable to **FIGURE 8-22**, then save the workbook.

FIGURE 8-22

	A	B	C	D	E	F
1						
2	Product Area	(All)				
3						
4	**Sum of Expenses**					
5		**Production**	**R & D**	**Support**	**Grand Total**	
6	Basel	$60,986	$57,453	$41,629	$160,068	
7	Pittsburgh	$51,709	$60,550	$29,597	$141,856	
8	Seattle	$53,466	$58,527	$38,355	$150,348	
9	Singapore	$35,170	$54,153	$30,461	$119,784	
10	**Grand Total**	**$201,331**	**$230,683**	**$140,042**	**$572,056**	
11						
12						

Analyzing Data with PivotTables

Skills Review (continued)

6. Create a PivotChart report.

   a. Use the existing PivotTable data to create a Clustered Column PivotChart report.

   b. Move the PivotChart to a new worksheet, then name the sheet **PivotChart**.

   c. Apply the Quick Layout, Layout 1, to the PivotChart. Add the title **January Expenses** to the chart.

   d. Filter the chart to display only expense data for the Crop Science product area. Display the expense data for all product areas. Hide the field buttons.

   e. Add your name to the center section of the PivotChart custom sheet footer. Compare your PivotChart with FIGURE 8-23, then save the workbook.

FIGURE 8-23

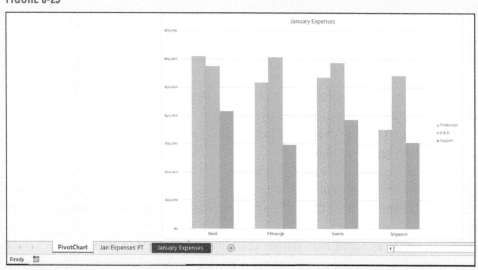

7. Update a PivotTable report.

   a. Activate the Jan Expenses PT sheet, then note the Seattle total for production.

   b. Activate the January Expenses sheet and change the Expenses value in cell D14 to **$30,000**.

   c. Refresh the PivotTable so it reflects the new value.

   d. Verify that the Seattle total for production increased to $60,287 on both the PivotTable and the PivotChart.

   e. Save the workbook.

8. Use the GETPIVOTDATA function.

   a. In cell D27 of the January Expenses sheet type =, click the Jan Expenses PT sheet, click the cell that contains the grand total for Pittsburgh, then press ENTER.

   b. Review the GETPIVOTDATA function that was entered in cell D27, then format the value in cell D27 in Accounting Number format and no decimal places.

   c. Enter your name in the January Expenses sheet footer, compare your January Expenses sheet to FIGURE 8-24, save the workbook, then preview the January Expenses worksheet.

   d. Close the workbook, then close Excel.

   e. Submit the workbook to your instructor.

FIGURE 8-24

	A	B	C	D	E	F
1	Division	Product Area	Location	Expenses	Manager	
2	Production	Consumer Health	Basel	$ 29,518	C. Berwick	
3	R & D	Consumer Health	Basel	$ 30,234	C. Berwick	
4	Support	Consumer Health	Basel	$ 23,971	C. Berwick	
5	Production	Crop Science	Basel	$ 31,468	J. Allen	
6	R & D	Crop Science	Basel	$ 27,219	J. Allen	
7	Support	Crop Science	Basel	$ 17,658	J. Allen	
8	Production	Consumer Health	Pittsburgh	$ 22,075	D. Macey	
9	R & D	Consumer Health	Pittsburgh	$ 31,355	D. Macey	
10	Support	Consumer Health	Pittsburgh	$ 15,940	D. Macey	
11	Production	Crop Science	Pittsburgh	$ 29,634	T. Holland	
12	R & D	Crop Science	Pittsburgh	$ 29,195	T. Holland	
13	Support	Crop Science	Pittsburgh	$ 13,657	T. Holland	
14	Production	Consumer Health	Seattle	$ 30,000	L. Bartlet	
15	R & D	Consumer Health	Seattle	$ 32,443	L. Bartlet	
16	Support	Consumer Health	Seattle	$ 26,603	L. Bartlet	
17	Production	Crop Science	Seattle	$ 30,287	S. Simpson	
18	R & D	Crop Science	Seattle	$ 26,084	S. Simpson	
19	Support	Crop Science	Seattle	$ 11,752	S. Simpson	
20	Production	Consumer Health	Singapore	$ 13,056	P. Lee	
21	R & D	Consumer Health	Singapore	$ 24,883	P. Lee	
22	Support	Consumer Health	Singapore	$ 16,957	P. Lee	
23	Production	Crop Science	Singapore	$ 22,114	L. Williams	
24	R & D	Crop Science	Singapore	$ 29,270	L. Williams	
25	Support	Crop Science	Singapore	$ 13,504	L. Williams	
26						
27		Pittsburgh Expenses for January:		$ 141,856		
28						

Independent Challenge 1

As the office manager for the occupational therapy clinic at the Riverwalk Medical Clinic, you have been asked to review the billings for the month of February. The CFO of the clinic has asked you to analyze the hours being spent on the various categories of occupational therapy and how the services are paid.

FIGURE 8-25

a. Start Excel, open IL_EX_8-3.xlsx from the location where you store your Data Files, then save it as **IL_EX_8_RiverwalkOT**.

b. Create a blank PivotTable on a separate worksheet that sums hours by Provider and Division, using FIGURE 8-25 as a guide.

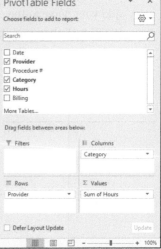

c. Name the new sheet **PivotTable**, and apply the White, Pivot Style Light 5 PivotTable style.

d. Change the summary function of the PivotTable to average.

e. Add slicers to the PivotTable for the category and provider data. Display only data for Jolan's and Ryan's level 1 and 2 procedures. Remove the filters and remove the slicers.

f. Add the Procedure # field to the Columns area under the Category field. Move the Procedure # field to the Rows area under the Provider field.

g. Add the Billing field to the Filters area of the PivotTable. Display only the PivotTable data for insurance procedures.

h. Change the summary function of the PivotTable to sum.

i. Hide the field headers in the PivotTable.

j. Create a clustered column PivotChart that shows the insurance hours. Move the PivotChart to a new sheet named **PivotChart**.

k. Apply Quick Layout 3 to the PivotChart. Edit the chart title to **Insurance Hours**.

l. Activate the February OT sheet and change the hours in cell E4 to 2. Update the PivotTable to reflect this change.

m. Activate the February OT sheet, then use the GETPIVOTDATA function to display the total number of insurance hours in cell A29.

n. Add your name to the center section of the three worksheet footers, then save the workbook. Preview the three worksheets, comparing them to FIGURE 8-26.

o. Close the workbook, then close Excel. Submit the workbook to your instructor.

FIGURE 8-26

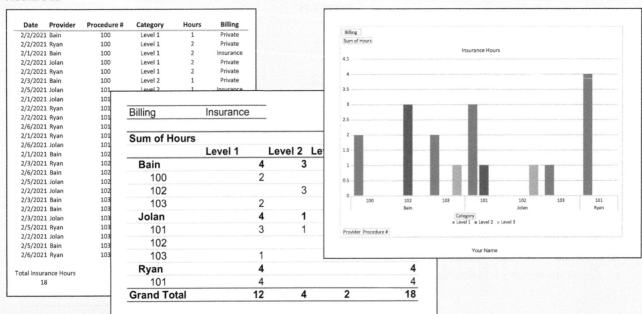

Independent Challenge 2

You are the assistant to the CFO of an international hotel group with properties in North America, Europe, and Asia. The properties in your collection cater to both business and leisure travelers. You want to create a PivotTable to analyze and graph the revenue in each quarter by purpose and region.

a. Start Excel, open IL_EX_8-4.xlsx from the location where you store your Data Files, then save it as **IL_EX_8_Accommodations**.

FIGURE 8-27

b. Create a PivotTable on a new worksheet named **PivotTable** that sums the revenue amount for each region across the rows and each purpose down the columns. Add the quarter field as an inner row label. Use **FIGURE 8-27** as a guide.

c. Widen column C of the PivotTable if necessary to fully display the grand total value for that column.

d. Group the first two quarters (*Hint:* Select the first two quarter cells in any region, then click the Group Selection button in the Group group on the PivotTable Analyze tab.)

e. Rename the Group1 label **First Half**. (*Hint:* Enter the new name in any cell with the Group1 label.)

f. Group the third and fourth quarters, then name this new group **Last Half**.

g. Collapse both the First Half and Last Half groups.

h. Turn off the grand totals for the Columns. (*Hint:* Click the Grand Totals button in the Layout group on the PivotTable Tools Design tab, then click On for Rows Only.)

i. Format the revenue values using the Currency format with the $ symbol and no decimal places.

j. On the Revenue worksheet, change the North America Quarter 1 Business Revenue value in cell D2 to **$50,000,000**. Update the PivotTable to reflect this increase in revenue.

k. Create a stacked column PivotChart report for the revenue data for all three regions. (*Hint:* Choose the first Stacked Column Chart type in the dialog box.)

l. Move the PivotChart to a new sheet, and name the chart sheet **PivotChart**.

m. Apply a quick layout of Layout 4 to the PivotChart.

n. Use the Region field button at the bottom of the PivotChart to filter the chart to display only Europe and North America properties.

o. Add a Quarter 2 slicer to the PivotTable. Use the slicer to display the revenue for the first half of the year only.

p. Check the PivotChart to be sure it displays only the filtered data.

q. On the PivotTable sheet, resize the slicer to display the button in two columns that are each 0.5" height and 1" width. (*Hint:* Use the Buttons group on the Slicer Tools Options tab.)

r. Change the slicer caption to **Grouped Quarters**. (*Hint:* Use the Slicer group on the Slicer Tools Options tab.)

FIGURE 8-28

s. Change the slicer size to 1" height and 2.5" width. (*Hint:* Use the Size group on the Slicer Tools Options tab.)

t. Add a slicer style of Light Blue, Slicer Style Dark 1, then move the slicer below the PivotTable.

u. Add your name to the center section of the three worksheet footers, save the workbook, compare your PivotTable worksheet to **FIGURE 8-28**, then preview the PivotTable and the PivotChart. Close the workbook and close Excel. Submit the workbook to your instructor.

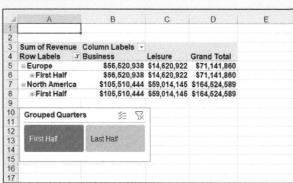

Visual Workshop

Open IL_EX_8-5.xlsx from the location where you store your Data Files, then save it as **IL_EX_8_Insurance**. Using the data on the First Quarter worksheet, create the PivotTable and slicer shown in FIGURE 8-29 on a new worksheet named **PivotTable**. Format the table, slicer, and data as necessary to match the figure. (*Hint:* The PivotTable has been formatted using the Ice Blue, Pivot Style Medium 9 Pivot Style.) Add your name to the PivotTable footer, then preview the PivotTable. Save the workbook, close the workbook, close Excel, then submit the workbook to your instructor.

FIGURE 8-29

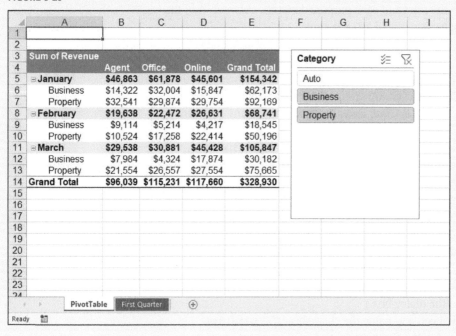

Analyzing Data with PivotTables

Automating Worksheet Tasks

CASE ▸ Cheri McNeil, manager of the Boston office at JCL, is in the process of reviewing the annual revenue generated by each recruiter in the office. She created a worksheet with test data that will act as a form for the collection of data for each recruiter. Cheri asks you to create macros to calculate the annual revenue total and evaluate whether quotas for bonus payments are met.

Module Objectives

After completing this module, you will be able to:

- Plan a macro
- Enable a macro
- Record a macro
- Run a macro
- Edit a macro
- Assign a macro to a button
- Assign a macro to a command button
- Assign a macro to a form control

Files You Will Need

IL_EX_9-1.xlsx	IL_EX_9-4.xlsx
IL_EX_9-2.xlsx	IL_EX_9-5.xlsx
IL_EX_9-3.xlsx	

Plan a Macro

Learning Outcomes
- Plan a macro
- Determine the storage location for a macro

A **macro** is a named set of instructions, written in the Visual Basic programming language, that perform tasks automatically in a specified order. You can create macros to automate Excel tasks that you perform frequently. You don't need to know the Visual Basic programming language to create a macro, because instead of writing code you can simply record a series of actions using the macro recorder built into Excel. When recording a macro, the sequence of actions in a macro is important, so you need to plan the macro carefully before you begin recording. **CASE** ► *You need to create a macro to calculate the total revenue for the Boston office. You work with Cheri to plan the macro.*

DETAILS

To plan a macro, use the following guidelines:

- **Assign the macro a descriptive name**

  The first character of a macro name must be a letter; the remaining characters can be letters, numbers, or underscores. Letters can be uppercase or lowercase. Spaces are not allowed in macro names; use underscores instead. You can press SHIFT+HYPHEN (-) to enter an underscore character. You decide to name the macro AddTotal. See **TABLE 9-1** for a list of macros that could be created to automate other common tasks in JCL spreadsheets.

- **Write out the steps the macro will perform**

  This planning helps eliminate careless errors. After a discussion with Cheri, you write down a description of the new AddTotal macro, as shown in **FIGURE 9-1**.

- **Decide how you will perform the actions you want to record**

  You can use the mouse, the keyboard, or a combination of the two. For the new AddTotal macro, you want to use both the mouse and the keyboard.

- **Practice the steps you want Excel to record, and write them down**

  During your meeting with Cheri, you write down the sequence of actions to include in the macro.

- **Decide where to store the description of the macro and the macro itself**

  Macros can be stored in an active workbook, in a new workbook, or in the **Personal Macro Workbook**, a special workbook that can contain macros that are available to any open workbook; it opens whenever you start Excel to make macros available at any time but is hidden by default. You decide to store the macro in the active workbook.

FIGURE 9-1: Handwritten description of planned macro

Macro to calculate the annual revenue total

Name: AddTotal

Description: Calculates the annual revenue

Steps: 1. Select cell A9
                2. Enter Total
                3. Click the Enter button
                4. Select cell B9
                5. Click the AutoSum button
                6. Click the Enter button

TABLE 9-1: Possible macros and their descriptive names

description of macro	descriptive name
Enter a frequently used division, such as Technology	TechDiv
Enter a frequently used company name, such as JCL	Company_Name
Print the active worksheet on a single page, in landscape orientation	FitToLand
Add a footer to a worksheet	FooterStamp
Add a total to a worksheet	AddTotal

Excel

Enable a Macro

Because a macro may contain a virus, a destructive type of computer program that can damage your computer files, the default security setting in Excel disables macros from running. Although a workbook containing a macro will open, if macros are disabled they will not function. You can manually change the Excel security setting to allow macros to run if you know a macro came from a trusted source. When saving a workbook with a macro, you need to save it as a macro-enabled workbook with the extension .xlsm.

CASE ▶ *Cheri asks you to change the security level to enable all macros. For your security, as well as that of others who are sharing your computer, you will change the security level back to the default setting after you create and run your macros.*

STEPS

1. **sam↓** **Start Excel, open IL_EX_9-1xlsx from the location where you store your Data Files, click the** File tab, **click** Save As, **navigate to where you store your Data Files, in the Save As dialog box click the** Save as type list arrow, **click** Excel Macro-Enabled Workbook (*.xlsm), **in the File name text box type** IL_EX_9_Bonus, **then click** Save

   The security settings that enable macros are available on the Developer tab on the ribbon. The Developer tab does not appear by default.

2. **Click the** File tab **on the ribbon, click** Options, **then click** Customize Ribbon **in the category list**

   The Customize the Ribbon options open in the Excel Options dialog box, as shown in **FIGURE 9-2**.

3. **Click the** Developer checkbox **in the Main Tabs area on the right side of the screen to add a checkmark if necessary, then click** OK

   The Developer tab appears on the Ribbon. You are ready to change the security settings.

4. **Click the** Developer tab **on the ribbon, then click the** Macro Security button **in the Code group**

   The Trust Center dialog box opens.

5. **Click** Macro Settings **in the category list if necessary, click the** Enable all macros (not recommended; potentially dangerous code can run) option button **to select it, as shown in FIGURE 9-3, then click** OK

   The dialog box closes. Macros will remain enabled until you disable them by deselecting the Enable all macros option. As you work with Excel, you should disable macros when you are not working with them.

Adding security to your macro projects

To add security to your projects, you can add a digital signature to the project. A **digital signature** is an electronic attachment not visible in the file that verifies the authenticity of the author or the version of the file by comparing the digital signature to a digital certificate. In Excel, it guarantees your project hasn't been altered since it was signed. Sign macros only after you have tested them and are ready to distribute them. If the code in a digitally signed macro project is changed in any way, its digital signature is removed. To add a digital signature to a Visual Basic project, select the project that you want to sign in the Visual Basic Project Explorer window, click the Tools menu in the Visual Basic Editor, click Digital Signature, click Choose, select the certificate, then click OK twice. If there aren't any certificates available, you will be directed to contact your administrator or insert a smart card. Digital certificates and smart cards, which store digital certificates, can be issued by your administrator. There are also third-party certification authorities that issue certificates that are trusted by Microsoft. When you add a digital signature to a project, the macro project is automatically re-signed whenever it is saved on your computer.

FIGURE 9-2: Excel Options dialog box

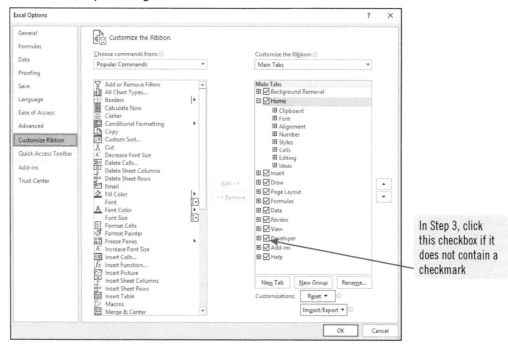

In Step 3, click this checkbox if it does not contain a checkmark

FIGURE 9-3: Trust Center dialog box

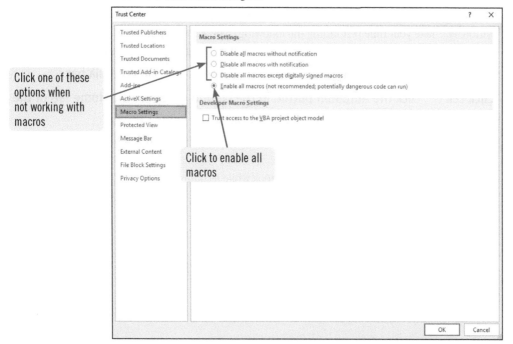

Click one of these options when not working with macros

Click to enable all macros

Disabling macros

To prevent viruses from running on your computer, you should disable all macros when you are not working with them. To disable macros, click the Developer tab, then click the Macro Security button in the Code group. Clicking any of the first three options disables macros. The first option disables all macros without notifying you. The second option notifies you when macros are disabled, and the third option allows only digitally signed macros to run.

Record a Macro

Learning
Outcomes
• Choose a macro
  storage location
• Create a macro by
  recording steps

The easiest way to create a macro is to record it using the Excel Macro Recorder. You turn the Macro Recorder on, name the macro, enter the keystrokes and select the commands you want the macro to perform, then stop the recorder. As you record the macro, Excel automatically translates each action into program code that you can later view and modify. **CASE** ▶ *You are ready to create a macro that totals the revenue values in column B of the active worksheet. You create this macro by recording your actions.*

STEPS

1. **Click the** Start Recording button 📇 **on the left side of the status bar**

    The Record Macro dialog box opens, as shown in **FIGURE 9-4**. The default name Macro1 is selected. You can either assign this name or enter a new name. This dialog box also lets you assign a shortcut key for running the macro and assign a storage location for the macro.

2. **Type** AddTotal **in the Macro name text box**

    It is important to check where the macro will be stored because the default choice is the last location that was selected.

3. **If the Store macro in box does not display "This Workbook," click the** Store macro in list arrow, **then click** This Workbook

4. **Type your name in the Description text box, then click** OK

    The dialog box closes, and the Start Recording button on the status bar is replaced with a Stop Recording button ▣. Take your time performing the following steps. Excel records every keystroke, menu selection, and mouse action that you make, not the amount of time you take to record them.

5. **Click cell A9, type** Total, **then click the** Enter button ✓ **on the formula bar**

6. **Click cell B9, click the** AutoSum button **in the Editing group on the Home tab of the ribbon, then click** ✓ **on the formula bar**

7. **Click the** Stop Recording button ▣ **on the left side of the status bar, then save the workbook**

    FIGURE 9-5 shows the result of the actions you took while recording the macro.

FIGURE 9-4: Record Macro dialog box

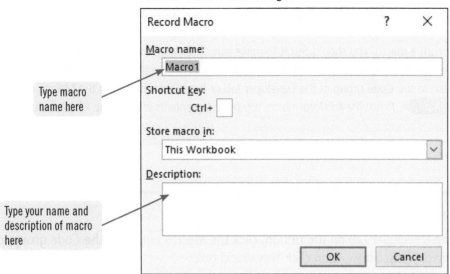

Type macro name here

Type your name and description of macro here

FIGURE 9-5: Worksheet with new data and formula

	A	B	C	D	E	F	G	H	I	J
1		JCL	Recruiter #							
2	**Annual Bonus Report**		Bonus Status:							
3	Quota:		Quota Status:							
4	**Quarter**	**Revenue**								
5	Q1	$1,000.00								
6	Q2	$2,000.00								
7	Q3	$3,000.00								
8	Q4	$4,000.00								
9	Total	$10,000.00								
10										
11										

Run a Macro

Once you record a macro, you should test it to make sure that the actions it performs are correct. To test a macro, you **run** (play) it, which performs the actions the macro contains. You can run a macro using the Macros button in the Code group of the Developer tab or the Macros button in the Macros group of the View tab. **CASE** *To test the AddTotal macro, you clear the contents of the range A9:B9 and add test data.*

STEPS

1. **Select the range A9:B9, press DEL, then select cell A1**

2. **Click the Developer tab on the ribbon, click the Macros button in the Code group, click the Macros in list arrow, then click This Workbook**

   The Macro dialog box, shown in **FIGURE 9-6**, displays all the macros contained in the current workbook.

3. **Click AddTotal in the Macro name list if necessary, then click Run**

   The macro quickly plays back the steps you recorded in the previous lesson. When the macro is finished, your screen should look like **FIGURE 9-7**.

4. **Select the range A9:B9, press DEL, then select cell A1**

   The total label and the total value are deleted to test the macro again.

5. **Click the View tab on the ribbon, then click the Macros button in the Macros group**

6. **Verify that This Workbook appears in the Macros in box, click AddTotal in the Macro name list if necessary, click Run, then save your work**

Running a macro automatically

You can create a macro that automatically performs certain tasks when the workbook in which it is saved opens. This is useful for actions you want to do every time you open a workbook. For example, you may always import data from an external data source into a workbook or format the worksheet data in a certain way. To create a macro that automatically runs when you open the workbook, you need to name the macro Auto_Open and save it in that workbook.

FIGURE 9-6: **Macro dialog box**

Lists macros stored in the workbook

FIGURE 9-7: **Result of running AddTotal macro**

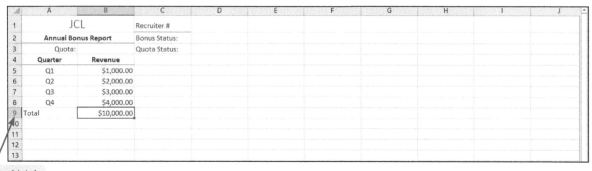

Total label and total revenue in row 9

Creating a main procedure

A sequence of VBA statements is called a procedure. For this reason, macros are often referred to as procedures. When you routinely need to run several macros one after another, you can save time by executing them in one procedure. This type of procedure, which contains multiple procedures that run sequentially, is referred to as the **main procedure**. To create a main procedure,

you type a **Call statement**, a Visual Basic statement that retrieves a procedure, using the format Call *procedurename*, where *procedurename* is the name of the procedure, or macro, you want to run. For example, Call AddTotal in a main procedure would run the AddTotal macro.

Edit a Macro

When you use the Macro Recorder to create a macro, the macro instructions, called **program code**, are written in the **Visual Basic for Applications (VBA)** programming language, and the macro is stored as a **module**, or program code container, attached to the workbook. After you record a macro, you might need to change it. You can edit the macro code, also called a procedure, directly using the **Visual Basic Editor**, a full-screen editor that lets you display and edit lines of code. **CASE** *Cheri wants the AddTotal macro to display the total label aligned right in the cell. This is a small change you can easily make by editing the macro code.*

STEPS

1. **Click the** Developer tab **on the ribbon, click the** Macros button **in the Code group, make sure** AddTotal **is selected, click** Edit, **then maximize the Code window, if necessary**

   The Visual Basic Editor starts, displaying three windows: the Project Explorer window, the Properties window, and the Code window.

2. **Drag the** left edge of the Project Explorer window **to expand it if necessary, click** Module 1 **in the VBAProject (IL_EX_9_Bonus.xlsm) within the Project Explorer window if it's not already selected, then examine the steps in the macro**

   Compare your screen to **FIGURE 9-8**. Excel has translated your keystrokes and commands into macro code. For example, the line Range("A9").Select was generated when you selected cell A9. In the first line of the macro code, the keyword Sub indicates that this is a Sub procedure, a series of Visual Basic statements that perform an action. The code lines in green, beginning with an apostrophe, are comments that help explain the procedure. Items that appear in blue are keywords, which are words Excel recognizes as part of the VBA programming language. Notice that twice in the procedure, a line of code (or statement) selects a range, and then subsequent lines act on that selection. The lines that begin with ActiveCell.Formula insert the information enclosed in quotation marks into the active, selected, cell. The last line, End Sub, indicates the end of the Sub procedure.

3. **Click at the end of the line** Range("A9").Select, **press** ENTER, **then type** With Selection

   You have entered the first line of code in a With Selection/End With block, which allows you to change all properties within the block at once.

4. **Click at the end of the line** ActiveCell.FormulaR1C1 = "Total", **press** ENTER, **type** .HorizontalAlignment = xlRight, **press** ENTER, **type** End With, **then compare your work with the code shown in** FIGURE 9-9

   You have added a With Selection/End With block to the procedure, so that you only need to refer to the selection once, rather than multiple times.

5. **Click** File **on the menu bar, then click** Close and Return to Microsoft Excel

   You want to rerun the AddTotal macro to make sure the macro reflects the change you made using the Visual Basic Editor.

6. **Select the range** A9:B9, **press** DEL, **then activate cell** A1

7. **Click the** Macros button **in the Code group on the Developer tab, make sure** AddTotal **is selected, then click** Run

   The Total label is right-aligned in the cell, as shown in **FIGURE 9-10**.

8. **Save the workbook**

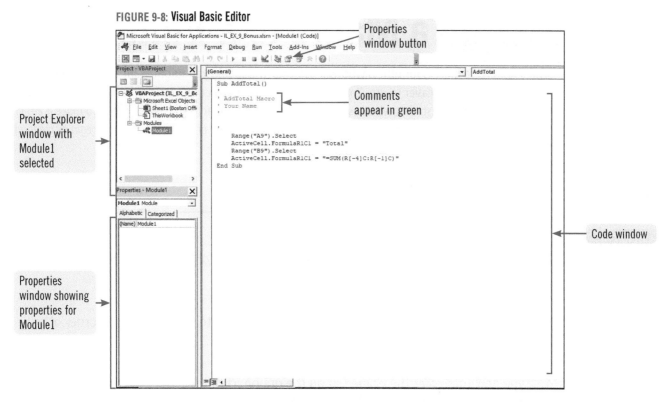

FIGURE 9-8: Visual Basic Editor

Properties window button

Project Explorer window with Module1 selected

Comments appear in green

Code window

Properties window showing properties for Module1

```
Sub AddTotal()
'
' AddTotal Macro
' Your Name
'
'
    Range("A9").Select
    ActiveCell.FormulaR1C1 = "Total"
    Range("B9").Select
    ActiveCell.FormulaR1C1 = "=SUM(R[-4]C:R[-1]C)"
End Sub
```

FIGURE 9-9: Edited Visual Basic code

```
Sub AddTotal()
'
' AddTotal Macro
' Your Name
'
'
    Range("A9").Select
    With Selection
    ActiveCell.FormulaR1C1 = "Total"
    .HorizontalAlignment = xlRight
    End With
    Range("B9").Select
    ActiveCell.FormulaR1C1 = "=SUM(R[-4]C:R[-1]C)"
End Sub
```

FIGURE 9-10: Result of running the edited AddTotal macro

▲	A	B	C	D	E	F	G	H	I	J
1	JCL		Recruiter #							
2	**Annual Bonus Report**		Bonus Status:							
3	Quota:		Quota Status:							
4	**Quarter**	**Revenue**								
5	Q1	$1,000.00								
6	Q2	$2,000.00								
7	Q3	$3,000.00								
8	Q4	$4,000.00								
9	Total	$10,000.00								
10										
11										

Total label is aligned right

Using relative referencing when creating a macro

By default, Excel records absolute cell references in macros, but you can record a macro's actions based on the relative position of the active cell by clicking the Use Relative References button in the Code group prior to recording the action. For example, when you create a macro using the default setting of absolute referencing, bolding the range A1:A3 will always bold that range when the macro is run. However, if you click the Use Relative References button when recording the macro before bolding the range, then running the macro will not necessarily result in bolding the range A1:A3. The range that is bolded will depend on the location of the active cell when the macro is run. If the active cell is F1, then the range F1:F3 will be bolded. Selecting the Use Relative References button highlights the button name, indicating it is active, and it remains active until you click it again to deselect it.

Assign a Macro to a Button

Learning
Outcomes
• Create a button
  shape in a
  worksheet
• Assign a macro to
  a button

When you create macros for others who will use your workbook, you might want to make the macros more visible so they're easier to use. You can create a button object on your worksheet and then assign the button to a macro, so that when users click the button the macro runs. **CASE** ▸ *To make it easier for Cheri to run the AddTotal macro, you decide to assign it to a button on the workbook. You begin by creating the button.*

STEPS

QUICK TIP
To format a macro
button using 3-D
effects, clip art,
photographs, fills,
and shadows, right-
click it, select Format
Shape from the
shortcut menu, then
select the desired
options in the
Format Shape pane.

1. **Select the range** A9:B9, **then press** DEL

2. **Click the** Insert tab **on the ribbon, click the** Shapes button **in the Illustrations group, then click the** first rectangle shape **under Rectangles**
   The mouse pointer changes to a ╋ symbol.

3. **Click at the** upper-left corner of cell A10, **then drag** ╋ **to the** lower-right corner of cell A11
   Compare your screen to **FIGURE 9-11**.

4. **Type** Add Total, **click the** Home tab **on the ribbon, click the** Center button ☰ **in the Alignment group, then click the** Middle Align button ☰ **in the Alignment group**
   Now that you have created the button and added a text label, you are ready to assign the macro to it.

QUICK TIP
You can move a
shape button by
placing the cursor
on the shape and
dragging it to a
new location on the
worksheet.

5. **Right-click the** new button, **then on the shortcut menu click** Assign Macro
   The Assign Macro dialog box opens.

6. **Click** AddTotal **under Macro name, then click** OK
   You have assigned the AddTotal macro to the button.

7. **Click any cell to deselect the button, then click the** button
   The AddTotal macro runs, and the total label and value appear in the range A9:B9, as shown in **FIGURE 9-12**.

8. **Save the workbook**

FIGURE 9-11: Button shape

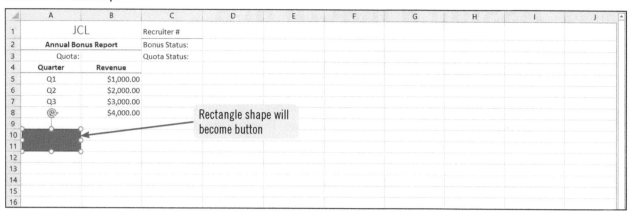

Rectangle shape will become button

FIGURE 9-12: Result of clicking the macro button

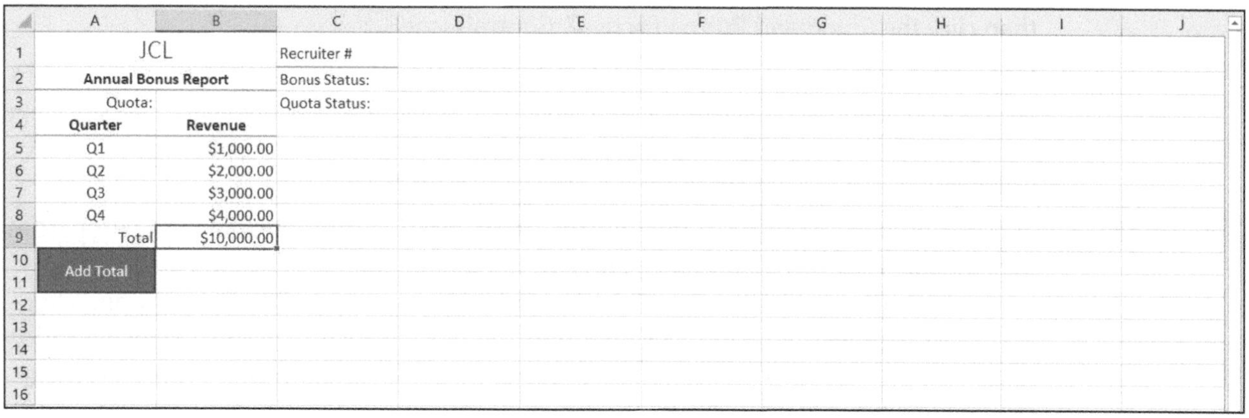

Copying a macro to another workbook

If you would like to use a macro in another macro-enabled workbook, you can copy the module to that workbook using the Visual Basic Editor. To do so, open both the source workbook (the one containing the macro) and destination workbook (the one where you want to use the macro). Open the Visual Basic Editor by clicking the Visual Basic button in the Code group on the Developer tab, then verify that macros are enabled in each workbook. In Project Explorer, drag the module that will be copied from the source workbook to the destination workbook.

Assign a macro to a command button

You can use Excel controls to run macros. Controls help users enter data in a worksheet, and include buttons, check boxes, option buttons, and text boxes. There are two different types of Excel controls: form controls and ActiveX controls. In addition to collecting data, form controls can have macros assigned to them, similarly to shape buttons. An ActiveX command button contains the VBA code rather than having existing code assigned to it. When you use an ActiveX command button, the procedure code is entered using the VBA Editor. **CASE** ▸ *Recruiters in the Boston office receive bonuses when they meet annual revenue quotas. Cheri asks you to add a button that can be used to determine if a recruiter's annual quota is met.*

STEPS

1. **Click the** Developer tab **on the ribbon, click the** Insert button **in the Controls group, then click the** Command Button (ActiveX Control) **icon** ▣

2. **Click at the** upper-left corner of cell A13, **then drag** ╋ **to the** lower-right corner of cell A14
   An ActiveX control named CommandButton1 is displayed on the worksheet. The button name isn't fully displayed because the button isn't large enough. The Design Mode button in the Controls group is selected, indicating you are working in Design Mode, where properties can be changed.

3. **Click the** Properties button **in the Control group, on the Alphabetic tab in the Properties pane double-click the** (Name) **box, enter** QuotaButton, **double-click the** Caption **box, enter** Check Quota, **click the** BackColor **box, click the** arrow, **scroll if necessary and click** Active Title Bar **on the System tab, click the** Font **box, click the** ... **button, scroll to and click** Times New Roman **in the Font dialog box, click** OK, **compare your Properties pane to** FIGURE 9-13, **then close the Properties pane**
   The name of the command button is used internally to reference it. The caption name is displayed as a label for the button.

4. **Click the** View Code button **in the Controls group**
   The Visual Basic Editor opens. You will enter the code for the button in the Code window. This button will compare the revenue total in cell B9 with the quota in cell B3. If the total revenue is less than the quota, the text "Missed Quota" will be entered in cell D3; otherwise "Met Quota" will be entered. To specify an action based on certain conditions, you will use an If...Then...Else conditional statement.

5. **Click the** General arrow **at the top of the Code window, click** QuotaButton, **then type the procedure code between the Private Sub and End Sub lines exactly as shown in** FIGURE 9-14, **making sure not to duplicate the Private Sub and End Sub lines**

6. **Click** File **on the menu bar, click** Close and Return to Microsoft Excel, **then click the** Design Mode button **in the Controls group**
   Design Mode is turned off. This mode allows you to change the properties and enter Visual Basic Code for a command button, but for a button to function, it needs to be off.

7. **Click cell B3, type** 11000, **press ENTER, then click the** Check Quota button
   You need to enter a quota value to test the macro. The text *Missed Quota* is entered in cell D3.

8. **Click cell B3, enter** 8000, **click the** Check Quota button, **then save the workbook**
   The new test quota data checks the message entered when the quota is met. The text *Met Quota* is entered in cell D3.

FIGURE 9-13: Properties pane

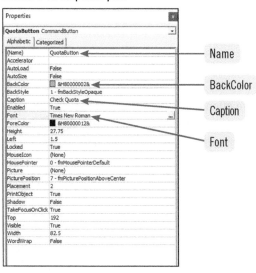

FIGURE 9-14: Code for ActiveX command button

```
Private Sub QuotaButton_Click()

'If the total revenue is less than B3 then
    'insert "Missed Quota" in cell D3

    If Range("B9") <= Range("B3") Then

        Range("D3").Select
        ActiveCell.Formula = "Missed Quota"

    'otherwise, insert "Met Quota" in cell D3

    Else
        Range("D3").Select
        ActiveCell.Formula = "Met Quota"

    End If

    Range("A1").Select

End Sub
```

Working with ActiveX text boxes

To add an ActiveX text box into a worksheet, click the Developer tab on the ribbon, click the Insert button in the Controls group, then click the Text Box (ActiveX Control) button [abl] under ActiveX Controls. Click the upper-left corner of the cell where you want to locate the text box, then drag ┼ to draw the desired shape. To edit the text box's properties, switch to Design Mode if necessary, then click the Properties button in the Controls group. In the LinkedCell box, enter the cell where you want the text box data to be displayed. The Shadow property provides the options True for a shadow and False for no shadow. FIGURE 9-15 shows the properties for a text box with the name Notes in the range A1:D2. Because the LinkedCell in the properties is Quarter1!A9, text entered in the text box will appear on the Quarter1 worksheet in cell A9.

FIGURE 9-15: ActiveX text box properties

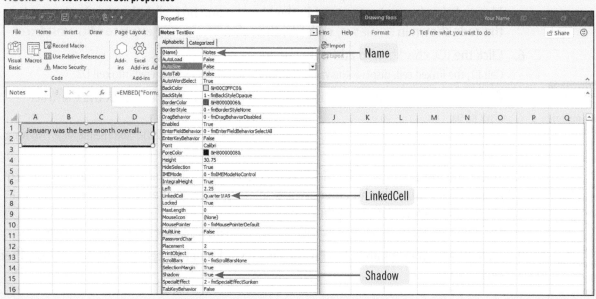

Excel

Assign a Macro to a Form Control

Learning
Outcomes
• Create a Check
Box form control
• Assign a cell link
to a Check Box
control

Form controls such as checkboxes and option buttons are often used on a worksheet to help with data entry. To perform an action based on entered data, you assign a macro to a form control. **CASE** *JCL recruiters who meet their revenue quotas receive bonuses. Although revenue and quota data are tracked for contract workers as a consideration for future contracts, contract workers are not eligible for bonuses. To make it easier for Cheri to determine if a recruiter should receive a bonus, you will add checkboxes to the worksheet form and enter macros for each checkbox.*

STEPS

QUICK TIP

In addition to changing a checkbox caption, you can change the internal name of the checkbox object by right-clicking the checkbox object, then entering the object name in the Name Box.

1. **Click the** Developer tab **on the ribbon if necessary, click the** Insert button **in the Controls group, click the** Check Box (Form Control) button shape ☑ **in the first row, click the upper-left corner of cell A16, drag** ╋ **to the** lower-right corner of that cell, **select the** text label **for the control, then type** JCL

2. **Click the** Properties button **in the Controls group, in the Format Control dialog box click the** Control tab **if necessary, enter** E1 **in the Cell link box, then click** OK
   The cell entered in the Cell link box will display TRUE if the checkbox contains a checkmark.

3. **Right-click the** checkbox object, **click** Assign Macro **on the shortcut menu, in the Assign Macro dialog box type** JCL **in the Macro name box, click** New, **enter the code shown in** FIGURE 9-16, **click** File, **then click** Close and Return to Microsoft Excel

4. **Click any cell outside the checkbox object to deselect it, click the** Insert button **in the Controls group, click the** Check Box (Form Control) button ☑ **in the first row, click at the** upper-left corner of cell B16, **drag** ╋ **to the lower-right corner of the cell, select the** text label **for the object, enter** Contract, **click the** Properties button **in the Controls group, in the Format Control dialog box enter** E2 **in the Cell link box, then click** OK

5. **Right-click the** checkbox object, **click** Assign Macro **on the shortcut menu, in the Assign Macro dialog box enter** Contract **in the Macro name box, click the** New button, **enter the code shown in** FIGURE 9-17, **click** File, **then click** Close and Return to Microsoft Excel

6. **Click the** JCL checkbox **to add a checkmark**
   Cell E1, the linked cell, displays the value TRUE and Annual Bonus is entered into cell D2.

QUICK TIP

When you finish working with macros you should disable all macros by clicking the Developer tab, clicking the Macro Security button in the Code group, clicking Macro Settings if necessary, clicking the Disable all macros with notification option button to select it, then clicking OK.

7. **Click cell D2 if necessary, press** DEL, **click cell E1, press** DEL, **then click the** Contract checkbox
   Cell E2, the linked cell for the Contract checkbox, displays the value "TRUE" and the message "No Annual Bonus" is entered into cell D2.

8. **Select the range** E1:E2, **right-click the selected range, click** Format Cells **on the shortcut menu, click** Custom **in the Category list, select** General **in the Type: box, enter** ;;;, **click** OK, **then compare your worksheet to** FIGURE 9-18
   The custom number format ;;; improves the appearance of the worksheet by hiding the values in cells.

9. **sam**✦ **Enter your name in the Boston Office worksheet footer, save the workbook, then close Excel**

FIGURE 9-16: Code for JCL checkbox

```
Sub JCL()

If Range("E1") = True And Range("D3") = "Met Quota" Then

        Range("D2").Select
        ActiveCell.Formula = "Annual Bonus"

    Else

    If Range("E1") = True And Range("D3") = "Missed Quota" Then

        Range("D2").Select
        ActiveCell.Formula = "No Annual Bonus"

    End If
    End If

End Sub
```

FIGURE 9-17: Code for Contract check box control

```
Sub Contract()

If Range("E2") = True Then

        Range("D2").Select
        ActiveCell.Formula = "No Annual Bonus"

End If

End Sub
```

FIGURE 9-18: Worksheet with checkboxes

	A	B	C	D	E	F	G	H	I	J
1		JCL		Recruiter #						
2	Annual Bonus Report		Bonus Status:	No Annual Bonus						
3	Quota:	$8,000.00	Quota Status:	Met Quota						
4	Quarter	Revenue								
5	Q1	$1,000.00								
6	Q2	$2,000.00								
7	Q3	$3,000.00								
8	Q4	$4,000.00								
9	Total	$10,000.00								
10	Add Total									
11										
12										
13	Check Quota									
14										
15										
16	☐ JCL	☑ Contract								
17										
18										

Working with option buttons

You can add option button form controls to a worksheet to allow users to select from a list of available options. To add an option button to a worksheet, click the Developer tab, click the Insert button in the Controls group, then click the Option Button Form Control ⊙ in the first row and drag ╋ to draw the option button. After adding the desired option buttons, right-click an option button, click Format Control on the shortcut menu, then enter the desired linked cell in the Cell link box in the Format Control dialog box. The clicked option button position will be entered in the linked cell. For example, if you click the second option button, the number *2* will be entered in the linked cell.

You can use an index list (a range to which an Index function refers) with this type of form control to facilitate data entry using option buttons. The index list range consists of all the options, in the order they appear on the worksheet, as option buttons. Then, an Index formula is added to the worksheet with the syntax *Index(range, row)* where *range* equals the list of options corresponding to the option buttons and *row* is the linked cell that holds the number of the clicked option. The result of this Index function is that the range value, at the given row position, is placed in the cell with the Index function. For example, **FIGURE 9-19** shows option buttons for the four divisions at JCL. The cell link for the option buttons is B1 and the Index formula in cell D1 references the range named Divisions, which is F1:F4 on the worksheet. The named range can be located on a different worksheet. Clicking the Technical option button places the number *2* (the second option button) in cell B1 (the linked cell), and the index function returns the second entry in the range list.

FIGURE 9-19: Worksheet with option buttons

	A	B	C	D	E	F
1	JCL Divisions		2	Division:	Technical		Finance & Acco
2	Select Division:					Technical
3	○ Finance & Accounting					Creative
4						Office Support
5	◉ Technical					
6						
7	○ Creative					
8						
9	○ Office Support					
10						
11						

Excel

Practice

Skills Review

1. Plan and enable a macro.
a. You need to plan a macro that enters a Total label in cell D17 and a formula in cell E17 that totals the managed assets in the range E3:E16.
b. Write out the steps the macro will perform, and plan to store the macro in the workbook where you will use it.
c. Start Excel, open IL_EX_9-2.xlsx from the location where you store your Data Files, then save it as a macro-enabled workbook named **IL_EX_9_Assets**. (*Hint*: The file will have the file extension .xlsm.)
d. Use the Excel Options feature to display the Developer tab if it does not appear on the Ribbon.
e. Using the Trust Center dialog box, enable all macros.

2. Record a macro.
a. Open the Record Macro dialog box.
b. Name the new macro **Total**, store it in the current workbook, and enter your name in the Description text box.
c. Record the macro, entering the label **Total** in cell D17.
d. Right-align the label in cell D17.
e. Add bold formatting to the label in cell D17.
f. Use AutoSum to enter a function in cell E17 that totals the range E3:E16.
g. Stop the recorder, then save the workbook.

3. Run a macro.
a. Delete the contents of the range D17:E17.
b. Run the Total macro.
c. Confirm that the total text is right-aligned and bolded in cell D17.
d. Confirm that the total assets appear in cell E17.
e. Clear the cell entries generated by running the Total macro.
f. Save the workbook.

4. Edit a macro.
a. Open the Macros dialog box, then open the Total macro for editing.
b. In the Visual Basic window, change the line of code Selection.Font.Bold = True to **Selection.Font.Bold = False**.
c. Use the Close and Return to Microsoft Excel command on the File menu to return to Excel.
d. Test the Total macro, verifying that the Total label is not bold.
e. Save the workbook.

5. Assign a macro to a button.
a. Clear the cell entries generated by running the Total macro.
b. Using the first rectangle shape under Rectangles on the Shapes palette, draw a rectangle in cell A17.
c. Label the button with the text **Total Assets**, then center and middle align the text.
d. Assign the Total macro to the button, then test the button.
e. Verify that the Total label and the total assets are entered in the range D17:E17.

Skills Review (continued)

6. Assign a macro to a command button.

FIGURE 9-20

a. Add an ActiveX command button control in the range A18:B19.

b. Add a caption to the button with the text **Target** and change the BackColor property to System Active Title Bar.

c. Enter the macro code shown in FIGURE 9-20 in the Visual Basic code window. (*Hint*: Remember to use the list arrow at the upper left of the VBA Editor to select the command object.)

d. Save the macro code and test the Target button. (*Hint*: Remember to deselect the Design Mode button before testing the button.)

e. Verify that "Met Target" is displayed in cell F2.

```
Private Sub CommandButton1_Click()

If Range("E17") <= Range("G1") Then

        Range("F2").Select
        ActiveCell.Formula = "Missed Target"

    Else
        Range("F2").Select
        ActiveCell.Formula = "Met Target"

    End If

    Range("A1").Select

End Sub
```

7. Assign a macro to a form control.

a. Add a form control check box in the range A21:B21.

b. Change the name of the check box to **Jill Hurley**.

c. Format the check box to enter the cell link of J1.

d. Assign a new macro to the check box by opening the Visual Basic code window for the object and entering the code shown in FIGURE 9-21.

FIGURE 9-21

```
Sub CheckBox2_Click()

If Range("J1") = True Then

        Range("I1").Select
        ActiveCell.Formula = "Boston Office Manager"


End If

End Sub
```

e. Save the macro code, close the VBA window, deselect the check box, then select it.

f. Widen column I to fully display the text in cell I1 and verify that the text "Boston Office Manager" is displayed in that cell. Verify that "True" is displayed in cell J1.

g. Format the text in cell J1 to hide the value. (*Hint*: Switch to Design Mode to make this change.)

h. Add your name to the Texas Office footer, then save the workbook.

i. Disable all macros with notification if you are finished working with macros.

j. Close the workbook, then close Excel.

Independent Challenge 1

As the office manager of Riverwalk Medical Clinic, you want to develop macros to help work more efficiently with the weekly time sheets. You will modify a worksheet that can be used as a form to collect time sheet data for therapists from the OT and PT departments. You will enter sample data in the form, add macros within the workbook to format the worksheet, calculate the total weekly hours, and determine whether there are overtime hours for the week.

a. Start Excel, open IL_EX_9-3.xlsx from where you store your Data Files, then save it as a macro-enabled workbook called **IL_EX_9_Timesheet**.

b. Check your macro security setting on the Developer tab to be sure that all macros are enabled.

c. Enter the data shown in FIGURE 9-22.

FIGURE 9-22

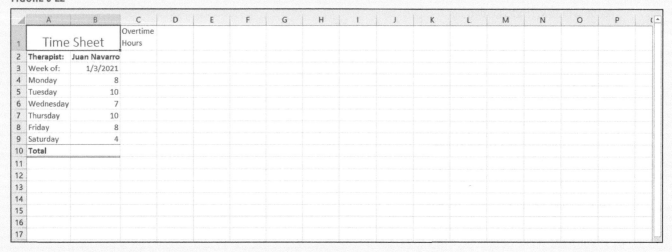

d. Create a macro named **Format_Total**, enter your name in the macro description, then save it in the current workbook. Record the macro using the following instructions:
   - Add a row to the top of the worksheet.
   - Add the text **Riverwalk Medical Clinic** to the inserted top row and format the text using the Title cell style.
   - Merge and Center the Riverwalk Medical Clinic text over the range A1:D1.
   - In cell B11 enter a function to total the range B5:B10. (*Hint*: Ignore the formula warning that the date isn't included in the summed cells.)
   - End the macro recording.

e. Create a button using the first Rectangle shape tool in the range A12:B13. Label the button **Format & Total**. Center and middle align the button label.

f. Assign the Format_Total macro to the new button.

g. Delete the first row of the worksheet and the total in cell B10, then test the Format_Total macro using the Format & Total button.

h. Insert an ActiveX command button in the range A15:B16. Using the properties panel, change the caption of the button to **Check Overtime**.

i. Enter the ActiveX command button code shown in FIGURE 9-23. (*Hint*: Don't forget to select the Command button in the VBA window by clicking the list arrow at the top of the code window.)

Independent Challenge 1 (continued)

FIGURE 9-23

```
Private Sub CommandButton1_Click()


  If Range("B11") <= "40" Then


        Range("D2").Select
        ActiveCell.Formula = "No Overtime"



    Else
        Range("D2").Select
        ActiveCell.Formula = Range("B11") - "40"


    End If


End Sub
```

j. Click the Check Overtime button to display overtime hours. (*Hint*: Don't forget to deselect Design Mode before using the button.)

k. In cells A18 and B18, create two form control check boxes, the first named **PT** and the second named **OT**. Assign cell E1 as the cell link for the first check box and cell E2 as the cell link for the second check box.

l. Enter the check box code shown in FIGURE 9-24 for the first check box.

m. Enter the check box code for the second check box by copying the code for the first check box and pasting it in the code window for the second check box.

n. Make sure both check boxes aren't checked, exit Design Mode, then check the PT check box. Verify that "PT" is shown in the worksheet header. Delete True from cell E1, then click the OT check box. Verify that "OT" is shown in the worksheet header.

o. Format the range E1:E2 to hide the values.

p. Enter your name in the worksheet footer. Save the file, disable all macros with notification if you are finished working with macros, close the workbook, then close Excel.

FIGURE 9-24

```
Sub CheckBox2_Click()

If Range("E1") = "True" Then

  ActiveWindow.View = xlPageLayoutView
    With ActiveSheet.PageSetup
     .CenterHeader = "PT"
    End With
    Range("A1").Select
    Application.Wait (Now + TimeValue("0:00:02"))
    ActiveWindow.View = xlNormalView

Else

If Range("E2") = "True" Then
ActiveWindow.View = xlPageLayoutView
    With ActiveSheet.PageSetup
     .CenterHeader = "OT"
    End With
    Range("A1").Select
    Application.Wait (Now + TimeValue("0:00:02"))
    ActiveWindow.View = xlNormalView

End If
End If
End Sub
```

Independent Challenge 2

You are an assistant to the CFO at a national real estate firm. As part of your work, you analyze royalty payments for different offices of the company. The company is planning to expand and offer multiple offices in regions of the country and will begin noting the office's region as documentation on each worksheet. You will create option button form controls to look up the region for an office. You will also create a macro to total royalty payments. (*Note:* Remember to disable all macros when you are finished working with them.)

a. Check your macro security settings to confirm that macros are enabled.

b. Start Excel, open IL_EX_9-4.xlsx from the location where you store your Data Files, then save it as a macro-enabled workbook called **IL_EX_9_Region**.

c. With the Payments sheet active, record a macro with the name **Totals**. Store the macro in this workbook, add your name to the description, and assign the macro a shortcut key combination of CTRL+SHIFT+F (or a different combination if necessary) and store it in the current workbook. (*Hint:* Use the Shortcut key combination in the Record Macro dialog box.)

The macro should do the following:
- Total the residential, commercial, and rental payments in column F.
- Total the Q1, Q2, Q3, Q4, and Total columns in row 6.
- Change the page orientation to landscape.

d. After you finish recording the macro, change the page orientation to Portrait, then delete the totals in the ranges B6:F6 and F3:F5. Test the macro using the shortcut key combination you set in Step B. Verify the macro results are correct.

e. Edit the Format macro to insert an instruction that formats the totals as bold. To do this, add the following code lines before the End Sub line:

Range("F3:F6").Select
Selection.Font.Bold = True
Range("B6:E6").Select
Selection.Font.Bold = True

f. Change the page orientation to Portrait, delete the totals in the range B6:F6 and F3:F5. Test the macro to verify that it runs correctly and that the totals appear in bold format.

g. Create four option button form controls in the range A9:D9. (*Hint:* To insert each button, click the Insert button in the Controls group, then click the Option Button [Form Control].)

h. Label the first button **Boston**, the second button **Chicago**, the third button **Miami**, and the fourth button **Los Angeles**.

i. Align the tops of the buttons. (*Hints:* Right-click one of the buttons, hold CTRL, then right-click each remaining button. With the buttons selected, click the Align button in the Arrange group on the Drawing Tools Format tab, then click Align Top.)

j. Format one of the buttons to enter the cell link of cell I1. (*Hint:* Right-click a button, click Format Control, then enter I1 in the Cell link box in the Format Control dialog box. The cell link is the same for all option buttons, so you only need to enter it for one button.)

k. Test the cell link by clicking each option button. The first option button should enter 1 in cell I1, the second should enter 2, and the third and fourth should enter 3 and 4, respectively.

l. Activate the Regions sheet, then select the range A1:A4 and verify the range name in the Name box is Region.

Independent Challenge 2 (continued)

m. Activate the Payments sheet, then enter an Index function in cell H2 that looks up the Region range on the Regions sheet using the value in cell I1 for its position. (*Hint*: The Index formula =INDEX(Region,I1) should be entered in cell H2.)

n. Test each option button to verify the correct region appears in cell H2 for each office.

o. Apply a custom format so the value in cell I1 is hidden, click the Boston button, then compare your worksheet to **FIGURE 9-25**.

FIGURE 9-25

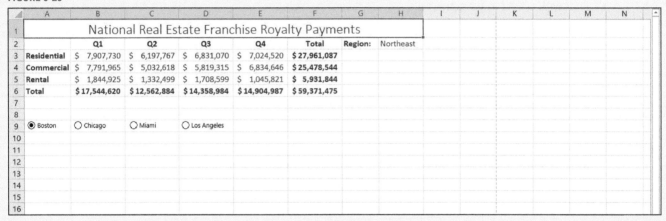

p. Enter your name in the worksheet footer, save the workbook, close the workbook, close Excel, then submit the workbook to your instructor.

Visual Workshop

Start Excel, open IL_EX_9-5.xlsx from the location where you store your Data Files, then save it as a macro-enabled workbook named **IL_EX_9_Services**. Modify and format the worksheet to match FIGURE 9-26. The button named Format & Total runs a macro named Format_Total stored in the workbook that does the following:

- Adds a row at the top of the worksheet
- Inserts a label of MES Commercial Engineering in cell A1, formatted with the Title cell style and merged and centered across columns A through H
- Adds totals in row 9 and column H
- Applies the Accounting format with zero decimal places to the range B3:H9
- Autofits the widths of columns A through H
- Ends with cell A1 as the active cell

Save the workbook, close the workbook, submit the workbook to your instructor, then close Excel. (*Note:* Remember to enable all macros before beginning this visual workshop, and to disable them when you are finished.)

FIGURE 9-26

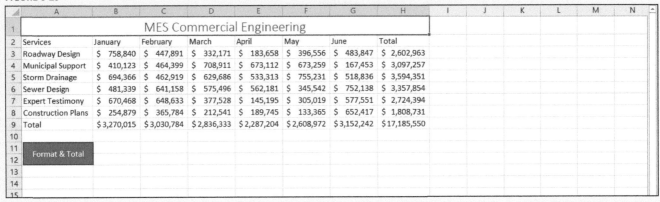

	A	B	C	D	E	F	G	H
1				MES Commercial Engineering				
2	Services	January	February	March	April	May	June	Total
3	Roadway Design	$ 758,840	$ 447,891	$ 332,171	$ 183,658	$ 396,556	$ 483,847	$ 2,602,963
4	Municipal Support	$ 410,123	$ 464,399	$ 708,911	$ 673,112	$ 673,259	$ 167,453	$ 3,097,257
5	Storm Drainage	$ 694,366	$ 462,919	$ 629,686	$ 533,313	$ 755,231	$ 518,836	$ 3,594,351
6	Sewer Design	$ 481,339	$ 641,158	$ 575,496	$ 562,181	$ 345,542	$ 752,138	$ 3,357,854
7	Expert Testimony	$ 670,468	$ 648,633	$ 377,528	$ 145,195	$ 305,019	$ 577,551	$ 2,724,394
8	Construction Plans	$ 254,879	$ 365,784	$ 212,541	$ 189,745	$ 133,365	$ 652,417	$ 1,808,731
9	Total	$ 3,270,015	$ 3,030,784	$ 2,836,333	$ 2,287,204	$ 2,608,972	$ 3,152,242	$ 17,185,550

Advanced Worksheet Management

> **CASE** ▶ Ellie Schwartz, JCL's vice president of Finance, wants to facilitate future tracking of expenses at JCL Talent's U.S. offices. She asks you to use Excel tools and options to help her staff work quickly and efficiently in a customized environment.

Module Objectives

After completing this module, you will be able to:

- Create and apply a template
- Import HTML data
- Create a custom AutoFill list
- Work with themes

- Work with cell comments
- Customize an Excel workbook
- Encrypt a workbook with a password
- Work with Ideas

Files You Will Need

IL_EX_10-1.xlsx	Support_EX_10-6.htm
Support_EX_10-2.htm	IL_EX_10-7.xlsx
IL_EX_10-3.xlsx	Support_EX_10-8.htm
Support_EX_10-4.htm	IL_EX_10-9.xlsx
IL_EX_10-5.xlsx	Support_EX_10-10.htm

Create and Apply a Template

Learning Outcomes
• Create a template
• Apply a template

A template is a workbook with an .xltx file extension that contains text, formulas, and formatting that you use repeatedly. When you save a workbook as a template, you can then use it to a create new workbook without having to reenter the repetitive data and formatting. To use a template, you apply it, which means you create a workbook *based on* the template. A workbook based on a template contains the same content, formulas, and formatting contained in the template, but is saved in the .xlsx format. The template file itself remains unchanged. **CASE** *Ellie has a workbook that contains formulas, styles, and labels for tracking this year's expenses at JCL. She asks you to use the workbook to create a template that will allow her to quickly create new workbooks for tracking expenses in future years.*

STEPS

1. **sam** ⬇ **Start Excel, then open IL_EX_10-1.xlsx from the location where you store your Data Files**

   The U.S. worksheet contains formulas that analyze this year's expenses for the U.S. offices and is formatted to be easy to read. You can reuse some of this formatting and content in workbooks you create to track future expenses.

2. **Click the File tab on the ribbon, click Save As, click the Save as type list arrow, click Excel Template (*.xltx), click Browse in Backstage view, navigate to where you store your Data Files, type IL_EX_10_Expenses in the File name box, then click Save**

   Excel saves the file as a template, with the .xltx extension.

3. **Select the range C5:F12, press DEL, then click cell A1**

   The data specific to this worksheet is not needed for future worksheets. The reusable information and formatting remain to serve as the basis for future yearly worksheets, as shown in **FIGURE 10-1**.

4. **Save the template, then close the template**

   The completed template IL_EX_10_Expenses is now available to use in creating new workbooks.

5. **Open File Explorer, navigate to the location where you store your Data Files, then double-click IL_EX_10_Expenses.xltx**

   A new workbook is created and has the default name IL_EX_10_Expenses1, as shown in **FIGURE 10-2**. The "1" at the end of the name identifies it as a new workbook based on the IL_EX_10_Expenses template, just as "1" at the end of "Book1" identifies a new workbook based on the blank Excel template.

6. **Click cell C5, enter 200, click cell C6, enter 300, select the range C5:C6, then use the fill handle to fill the range C7:C12 with this series**

   You are entering test data to make sure the template contains accurate formulas.

7. **Copy the range C5:C12, paste it into the range D5:F12, then compare your workbook to FIGURE 10-3**

   The totals and percentages appear to be correct.

8. **Close the workbook without saving it**

   Because you created this workbook only to test the template's formulas and formatting, you don't need to save it for future use.

FIGURE 10-1: **Completed template**

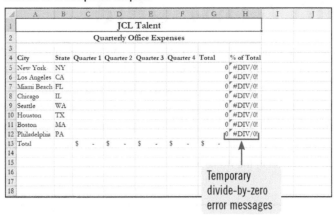

Temporary
divide-by-zero
error messages

FIGURE 10-2: **New workbook based on Expenses template**

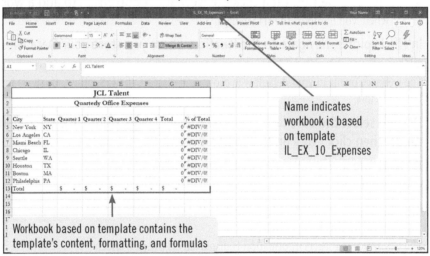

Name indicates
workbook is based
on template
IL_EX_10_Expenses

Workbook based on template contains the
template's content, formatting, and formulas

FIGURE 10-3: **Test data entered in new workbook**

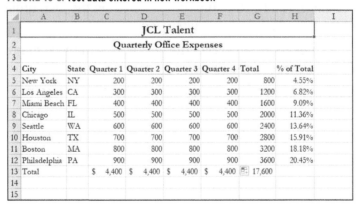

Creating a new workbook using a template

In addition to creating your own templates, you can use one of the many templates Excel offers for common documents such as balance sheets, budgets, or time cards. To create a workbook using an Excel template, click the File tab on the ribbon, then click New on the navigation bar. The New place in Backstage view displays thumbnails of some of the many templates available. The Blank workbook template is selected by default; when you create a new, blank workbook with no content or special formatting, this is the template the workbook is based on. To select a different template, click one of the selections in the New place, view the preview, then click Create.

Import HTML Data

When you need data available on a webpage, you can import the data into Excel in a few ways. You can open an HTML file directly in Excel if it's stored on an accessible drive, but often the information is published on the web and is not available as a file. In this situation, you can import the HTML data by copying the data on the webpage and pasting it into an Excel worksheet. This allows you to import only the information you need. Once the HTML data is in your worksheet, you can analyze it using Excel features. **CASE** ▶ *A list of the U.S. office managers is published on JCL's website. Ellie asks you to import this data into a new worksheet in the workbook.*

STEPS

1. **Open** IL_EX_10-1.xlsx **from the location where you store your Data Files, save it as** IL_EX_10_USExpenses, **then** click the New Sheet button ⊕ **to add a worksheet**
   This is where you'll import the HTML data.

2. **In File Explorer, navigate to the location where you store your Data Files, then double-click** Support_EX_10-2.htm
   The webpage opens in your default web browser. It displays the U.S. office managers information, as shown in **FIGURE 10-4**.

3. **Drag to select the** nine table rows **on the webpage, right-click** any cell **in the selected range, then click** Copy **on the shortcut menu**

4. **Activate the** IL_EX_10_USExpenses **workbook**
   The new worksheet is active and ready for you to import the data.

5. **Right-click cell** A1 **on the new worksheet, then click the** Match Destination Formatting button 📋 **in the Paste Options list**
   The U.S. office managers information is displayed on the new sheet.

6. **Double-click the** Sheet1 **sheet tab, type** Managers, **then press ENTER**

7. **Select columns** A **and** B, **click the** Format button **in the Cells group on the Home tab of the ribbon, then click** AutoFit Column Width

8. **Select the range** A1:B1, **then click the** Bold button **in the Font group**
   Compare your worksheet to **FIGURE 10-5**.

9. **Close your web browser, then save the workbook**

Importing XML data

Excel allows you to import and export XML data, a format often used for storing and exchanging data. To import XML data, click the Developer tab on the ribbon, click the Import button in the XML group, in the Import XML dialog box navigate to the xml file, click Import, then click OK twice. If you wish to specify a schema, or a map that describes the incoming data, before importing it, click the Source button in the XML group, in the XML Source pane click XML Maps, click Add in the XML Maps dialog box, navigate to a schema file in the Select XML source dialog box, click Open, then click OK.

FIGURE 10-4: Webpage listing JCL U.S. office managers

U.S. Managers

Office	Manager
New York	Nyack Afolayan
Los Angeles	Shavonn Rudd
Miami	Rosella Leigh
Chicago	Gary Jaeger
Seattle	Sophie Tan
Houston	Max Gallardo
Boston	Cheri McNeil
Philadelphia	Chris Wang

Data displayed in a browser ←

FIGURE 10-5: Imported and formatted HTML data

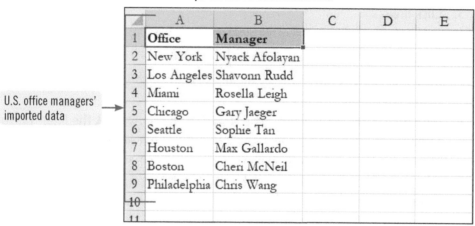

U.S. office managers' imported data →

	A	B	C	D	E
1	Office	Manager			
2	New York	Nyack Afolayan			
3	Los Angeles	Shavonn Rudd			
4	Miami	Rosella Leigh			
5	Chicago	Gary Jaeger			
6	Seattle	Sophie Tan			
7	Houston	Max Gallardo			
8	Boston	Cheri McNeil			
9	Philadelphia	Chris Wang			
10					
11					

Importing HTML files directly into Excel

If you have an Internet connection, you can import data from a webpage online into an Excel worksheet by clicking the Data tab, clicking the From Web button in the Get & Transform group, verifying the Basic option is selected, entering the web address in the URL box of the From Web dialog box, clicking OK, selecting the items you wish to import in the Display Options section of the Navigator dialog box, selecting the Web View or Table view tab, then clicking Load. If you wish to use this method to import html data from a file stored locally on your computer, enter the path to the webpage file in the URL box rather than a web address. If you receive an Unable to Connect error regarding the file path, click Edit, click Browse, navigate to the file, click Import in the Import Data dialog box, click OK, select the data you wish to import and either Web or Table view in the Navigator dialog box, then click Load.

You can also import a locally stored HTML file directly into an Excel workbook by clicking the File tab, clicking Open, clicking Browse, selecting All Files in the Open dialog box, browsing to the HTML file, then clicking Open.

Create a Custom AutoFill List

Learning
Outcomes
• Create a custom
list
• Use a custom list

Whenever you need to type a list of words regularly, you can save time by creating a custom list. Then you can simply enter the first value in a blank cell and drag the fill handle. Excel AutoFills the range, entering the rest of the information for you. FIGURE 10-6 shows examples of custom lists that are built into Excel. **CASE** *JCL's offices are identified by the city where they are located. Ellie often has to enter a list of JCL's U.S. offices in her worksheets. She asks you to create a custom list to save having to manually enter the information each time she needs it.*

STEPS

1. **Click the** U.S. sheet, **then select the range** A5:A12

2. **Click the** File tab **on the ribbon, click** Options, **click the** Advanced **category, scroll down to the** General section, **then click** Edit Custom Lists

   The Custom Lists dialog box displays all existing custom lists, including those already built into Excel, as shown in FIGURE 10-7. The Import list from cells text box contains the range you selected before opening the dialog box.

3. **Click** Import

   The list of offices is highlighted in the Custom lists box and appears in the List entries box.

4. **Click** OK **to confirm the list, then click** OK **again**

5. **Click the** New Sheet button ⊕, **double-click the** Sheet2 **worksheet tab, type** Offices, **then press** ENTER

6. **With the Offices sheet active, type** New York **in cell A1, click the** Enter button ☑ **on the formula bar, then drag the** fill handle **to AutoFill the range** A2:A8

   The highlighted range now contains the custom list of offices you created, as shown in FIGURE 10-8.

7. **Click cell A1, click the** File tab **on the ribbon, click** Options, **click** Advanced **in the Excel Options list, scroll down to the** General section, **click** Edit Custom Lists, **click the list beginning with New York in the Custom lists box, click** Delete, **click** OK **to confirm the deletion, then click** OK **two more times**

   If you share a computer with others, it is best to delete any custom lists you create after you are finished using them.

8. **Save the workbook**

Advanced Worksheet Management

FIGURE 10-6: **Examples of custom lists**

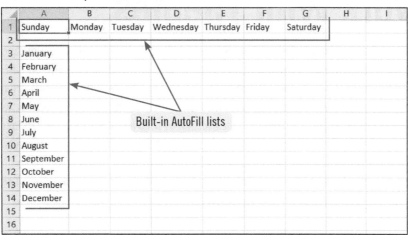

FIGURE 10-7: **Custom Lists dialog box**

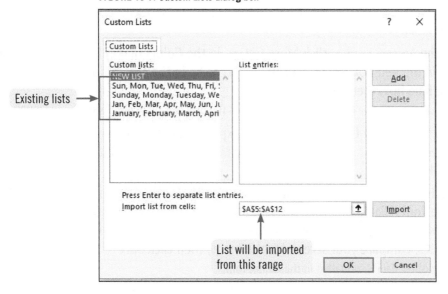

FIGURE 10-8: **Custom list of offices**

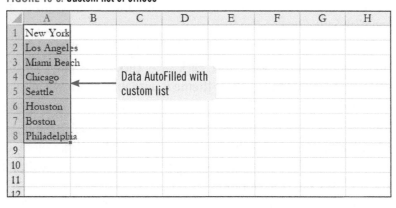

Work with Themes

You have used workbook themes to apply a predefined set of formats to a workbook. Formatting choices included in a theme are colors, fonts, cell styles, and line and fill effects. You can create custom theme fonts and color sets, which you can then use in any theme, and you can create custom themes to reflect current formatting settings under a new name, so that the original theme remains unchanged.

CASE ▸ *Ellie asks you to create a theme that will be used for all JCL future workbooks. The preselected colors and fonts of the workbook's current theme, Organic, are displayed in galleries when you select colors and fonts for worksheet data. You will explore changes to these theme fonts and colors to create a custom theme that will provide a consistent look across all JCL workbooks. (To preserve the settings on shared computers, these changes will be removed at the end of the lesson.)*

STEPS

1. **Click the** U.S. **sheet tab, click cell** A1, **click the** Page Layout tab **on the ribbon, click the** Colors button **in the Themes group, then click** Customize Colors

   The Create New Theme Colors dialog box opens, where you can see the current colors in this theme and change them.

2. **Click the** Accent 1 color, **click** More Colors, **in the Colors dialog box double-click the value in the** Red **box, enter** 0, **press** TAB, **type** 84 **in the Green box, press** TAB, **type** 166 **in the Blue box, then click** OK

   The Create New Theme Colors dialog box displays the new Accent 1 color, as shown in **FIGURE 10-9**.

3. **Select** Custom 1 **in the Name box, type** Expenses, **then click** Save

   You have created a new set of theme colors called Expenses. The worksheet colors change to reflect the new Accent 1 color.

4. **Click the** Fonts button **in the Themes group, click** Customize Fonts, **in the Create New Theme Fonts dialog box click the** Heading **font arrow, scroll up to and click** Calibri, **click the** Body **font arrow, scroll to and click** Calibri, **select** Custom 1 **in the Name box, type** Expenses, **compare your screen to** FIGURE 10-10, **then click** Save

   The worksheet data is formatted in the Calibri font.

5. **Select** column G, **click the** Home tab **on the ribbon, click the** Format button **in the Cells group, click** AutoFit Column Width, **then click cell** A1

   The column fully displays the data in the Calibri font.

6. **Click the** Page Layout tab **on the ribbon, click the** Themes button **in the Themes group, then click** Save Current Theme

   The Document Themes folder opens. This is the location where themes are stored for Office files.

7. **Enter** Expenses **in the Name box, click** Save, **click the** Themes button **in the Themes group, then verify the Expenses theme is available, as shown in** FIGURE 10-11

   User-created themes are listed in the Custom themes section, above Office themes.

8. **Right-click the** Expenses **theme, click** Delete, **click** Yes, **click the** Colors button **in the Themes group, right-click the** Expenses **custom color, click** Delete, **click** Yes, **click the** Fonts button **in the Themes group, right-click the** Expenses **custom font, click** Delete, **click** Yes, **then save the workbook**

   It is best to remove custom fonts, colors, and themes from Office if you are sharing a computer with other people.

FIGURE 10-9: **Create New Theme Colors dialog box**

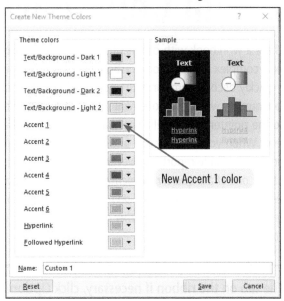

New Accent 1 color

FIGURE 10-10: **Create New Theme Fonts dialog box**

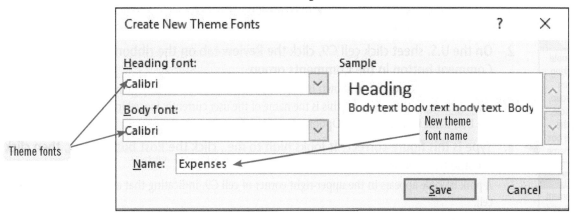

Theme fonts

New theme font name

FIGURE 10-11: **Workbook themes**

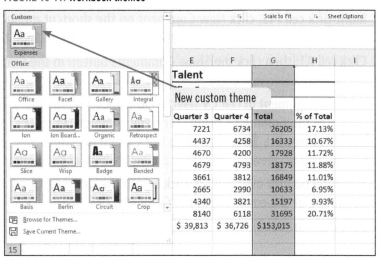

New custom theme

Customize an Excel Workbook

The Excel default settings for editing and viewing a worksheet are designed to meet the needs of most Excel users. You may find, however, that you want to change some of these settings. You have already used the Advanced category in the Excel Options dialog box to create custom lists and the Formulas category to switch to manual calculation. The most commonly used categories of the Excel Options are explained in more detail in TABLE 10-1. **CASE** *Ellie is interested in working more efficiently. She asks you to customize the workbook and check on other workbook settings to increase efficiency in Excel.*

STEPS

1. **Click the** File tab **on the ribbon, then click** Options

   The General category of the Excel Options list displays default options that Excel uses in new workbooks, as shown in FIGURE 10-14.

2. **In the Personalize your copy of Microsoft Office section, verify that the correct name is displayed in the** User name box, **then scroll down to view the other settings for the workbook**

3. **Click** Language **in the Excel Options list**

   The Set the Office Language Preferences category of the Excel Options dialog box displays default options that Excel uses in workbooks, as shown in FIGURE 10-15.

4. **Verify your preferred language is listed in the Choose Editing Languages section, click the** [Add additional editing languages] arrow, **scroll to view the available languages, then click the arrow again to close the list without making changes**

5. **In the Choose Display Language section, verify the first listing under Display Language is** Match Microsoft Windows <default> **and the second listing is your preferred language, then verify the first listing under the Help Language setting is** Match Display Language <default> **and the second listing is your preferred language**

6. **Click** Proofing **in the Excel Options list, then verify the Dictionary language shows your preferred language**

7. **Click** Quick Access Toolbar **in the Excel Options list, in the Customize the Quick Access Toolbar section select** Email **under Popular Commands, click** Add, **then click** OK

   The Email icon is added to the Quick Access Toolbar.

8. **Click** File, **click** Options, **click** Quick Access Toolbar **in the Excel Options list, click** Reset, **click** Reset only Quick Access Toolbar, **click** Yes, **then click** OK

   If you are working on a shared computer, you should restore the original settings to remove customizations.

Tracking changes in a workbook

You can track modifications to a workbook when you want to show what changes are being made to it from the present point onward. To use this feature, you can add the Track Changes button to the ribbon. To do so, right-click the ribbon, click Customize the Ribbon, right-click Review, click Add New Group, click the Choose Commands from arrow, click Commands Not in the Ribbon, click Track changes (Legacy) in the list of commands, click Add, then click OK. You can use the Highlight Changes command to specify what types of changes to track. Note that this legacy feature is not compatible with newer features in Excel, such as uploading to OneDrive.

FIGURE 10-14: General category of Excel options

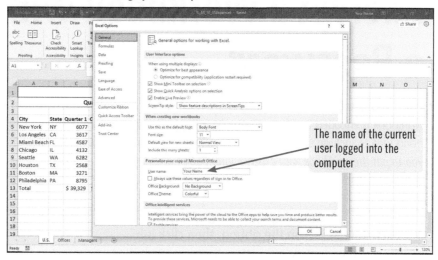

FIGURE 10-15: Language category of Excel Options dialog box

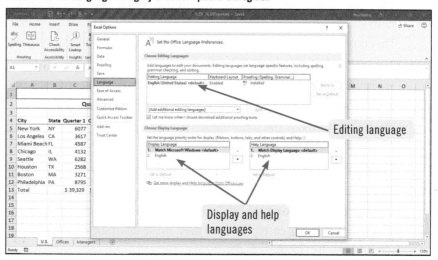

TABLE 10-1: Categories of Excel options you can change

category	allows you to
General	Change the username, customize default settings of new workbooks, enable LinkedIn features, and customize the user interface
Formulas	Control how the worksheet is calculated, how formulas appear, and error-checking settings and rules
Data	Control how data is analyzed and imported
Proofing	Control AutoCorrect and spell-checking options
Save	Select a default format and location for saving files, and customize AutoRecover settings
Language	Control the languages displayed and add additional languages and proofing tools
Ease of Access	Specify options to make Excel more accessible, such as changing the document display font size
Advanced	Set options for pen settings, create custom lists, and customize editing and display options
Customize Ribbon	Add commands, tabs, and groups to the Ribbon
Quick Access Toolbar	Add commands to the Quick Access Toolbar
Add-Ins	Install Excel Add-in programs such as Solver and Analysis ToolPak
Trust Center	Change Trust Center settings to protect your Excel files and your computer

Encrypt a Workbook with a Password

Learning
Outcomes
• Use a password
  to encrypt a
  workbook
• Delete a password
  on an encrypted
  workbook

When you distribute a workbook you may want to encrypt it with a password to protect it. An encrypted workbook is encoded in a form that only authorized people with a password can read. For security, it is a good idea to include uppercase and lowercase letters and numbers in a password. **CASE** *Ellie wants you to put the workbook with expense information on one of JCL's servers. You decide to encrypt the workbook with a password so only authorized JCL users can open it.*

STEPS

1. **Click the File tab on the ribbon, then click Info**

   The Info pane displays information about your file. It also includes tools you can use to check for security issues.

2. **Click the Protect Workbook button in the Protect Workbook area, then click Encrypt with Password**

   The Encrypt Document dialog box opens and displays a Password box, as shown in **FIGURE 10-16**.

3. **Type JcLQe2021%, then click OK**

   When you enter passwords, the characters you type are masked with bullets (• • •) for security purposes.

4. **In the Confirm password box type JcLQe2021%, then click OK**

   The Protect Workbook area is highlighted in yellow and the message "A password is required to open this workbook" is displayed.

5. **Click the Back button ⬅ in the Info pane, save the workbook, then close the workbook**

6. **Open IL_EX_10_USExpenses from the location where you store your Data Files, in the Password dialog box type JcLQe2021% in the Password box, then click OK**

   To remove workbook encryption, you must first enter the encryption password, to verify that you are qualified to make changes.

7. **Click the File tab on the ribbon, click Info, click the Protect Workbook button in the Protect Workbook area, then click Encrypt with Password**

   The Encrypt Document dialog is displayed with the masked password, as shown in **FIGURE 10-17**.

8. **In the Password box select the masked password, press DEL, then click OK**

   The password is removed from the Workbook, and encryption is turned off.

9. **Click ⬅, then save the workbook**

FIGURE 10-16: Encrypt Document dialog box

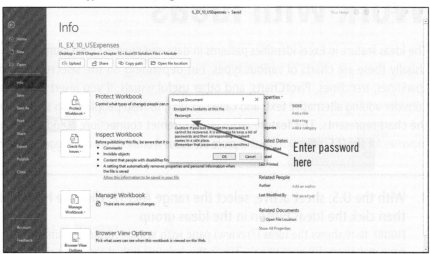

FIGURE 10-17: Masked password

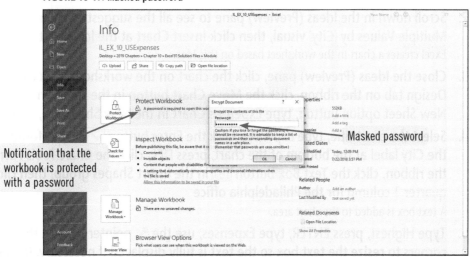

Working with a previous version of an Excel workbook

When you save your Excel files on OneDrive, AutoSave is automatically turned on to save versions of your workbook while you make changes. The older saved versions can be restored if you make errors in newer versions using Version history by clicking the File tab on the ribbon, clicking View and restore previous versions in the Version History area, then clicking the desired version in the Version History pane. FIGURE 10-18 shows two version of a workbook. After your desired version opens, you can click the Restore button above the formula bar to save the file.

FIGURE 10-18: Version History pane

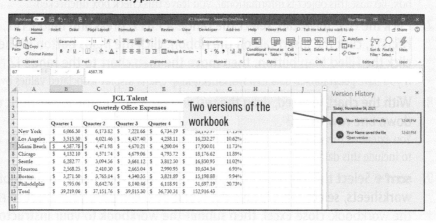

Practice

Skills Review

1. **Create and apply a template.**
   a. Start Excel, then open IL_EX_10-3.xlsx from the location where you store your Data Files.
   b. Save the workbook as a template in the location where you store your Data Files with the name **IL_EX_10_FirstQuarter.xltx**.
   c. Delete the values in ranges B3:D6 and F3:F6. Leave the worksheet formulas intact.
   d. Close the template, then open a new workbook based on the template.
   e. In the new IL_EX_10_FirstQuarter1 workbook, test the template by entering the data in ranges B3:D6 and F3:F6, shown in FIGURE 10-22.

FIGURE 10-22

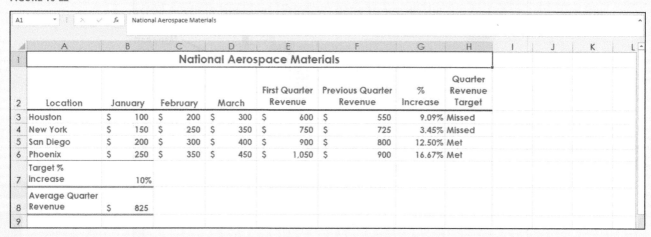

   f. After verifying that the formulas and formatting in the workbook appear to work correctly, close the workbook without saving it.

2. **Import HTML data.**
   a. Re-open IL_EX_10-3.xlsx from the location where you store your Data Files, then save the workbook as **IL_EX_10_Aerospace**.
   b. Open File Explorer, navigate to the location where you store your Data Files, then open the webpage Support_EX_10-4.htm in your web browser. Copy the data in the five rows of the webpage table, including the column headings.
   c. Activate the IL_EX_10_Aerospace workbook, then create a new worksheet. Rename the new sheet **Quality Ratings**.
   d. Paste the copied webpage data into the worksheet starting at cell A1, using Paste Options to match the destination formatting.
   e. Autofit columns A and B to fully display the Location data and narrow the Ratings column.
   f. Activate your web browser, close the Support_EX_10-4.htm file, then in Excel save the workbook.

Skills Review (continued)

3. **Create a custom AutoFill list.**

   a. Activate the First Quarter sheet, then select the range A3:A6.

   b. Open the Custom Lists dialog box, then import the selected data.

   c. Close the dialog box.

   d. Add a worksheet to the workbook. Rename the new worksheet **Locations** and move it so it is the last worksheet in the workbook. On the Locations worksheet, enter **Houston** in cell A1.

   e. Use the fill handle to enter the custom list through cell A4, then widen column A to fully display the locations.

   f. Open the Custom Lists dialog box again, delete the custom list you just created, then save the workbook.

4. **Work with themes.**

   a. Activate the First Quarter sheet and use the Create New Theme Colors dialog box to change the Accent 1 color to a custom color with the RGB values Red: **0**, Green: **138**, and Blue: **135**.

   b. Name the new theme color palette **FQ** and save it.

   c. Use the Create New Theme Fonts dialog box to change both the heading and body fonts to Calibri. Save the new theme font set as **FQ**.

   d. Save the current theme as **FQ**, then compare your worksheet to FIGURE 10-23.

   FIGURE 10-23

   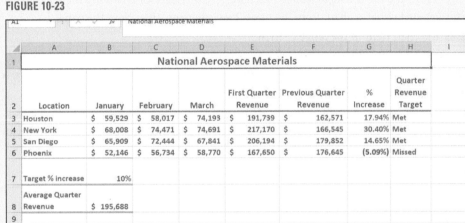

   e. Verify that the custom FQ color palette is listed in the Theme Colors list, the FQ font set is listed in the Theme Fonts list, and theme is listed the Themes list, then delete each custom setting.

   f. Save the workbook.

5. **Work with cell comments.**

   a. Insert a comment in cell E2 that reads **Are these final values?**. (*Hint:* Don't type the period.)

   b. Click anywhere outside the Comment box to close it.

   c. Insert a comment in cell G4 that reads **Nice Increase!**.

   d. Edit the comment in cell E2 to read **Are these final revenue values?**.

   e. Add a reply to the comment in cell G4 that reads **Thanks.**.

   f. Display all worksheet comments. Hide all worksheet comments.

   g. Delete the comment in cell E2.

   h. Save the workbook.

Skills Review (continued)

6. Customize an Excel workbook.

   a. Use the General category of the Excel Options dialog box to verify the correct username appears.

   b. Use the Language category of the Excel Options dialog box to verify the editing, display, and help languages are set correctly for your Excel workbook.

   c. Use the Proofing category of the Excel Options dialog box to verify the dictionary language setting is correct for your Excel workbook.

   d. Use the Quick Access Toolbar category of the Excel Options dialog box to add the Open button to the Quick Access Toolbar.

   e. Reset all customizations of the workbook to the defaults.

7. Encrypt a workbook with a password.

   a. Encrypt the workbook with the password **FjfmQpin8!**.

   b. Save and close the workbook.

   c. Open the workbook using the password.

   d. Delete the password.

   e. Save the workbook.

8. Work with Ideas.

   a. Select the range A2:D6 and use the Ideas feature to see suggested visuals for analyzing the selected data.

   b. Insert the first suggested visual, a chart, from the Ideas (Preview) pane, then close the pane.

   c. Move and resize the chart to fit in the range C7:H18.

   d. Edit the chart title to **Q1 Revenue**.

   e. Add the alternative text: **January, February, and March revenue for Houston, New York, San Diego, and Phoenix**.

   f. Close the Alt Text pane.

   g. Compare your First Quarter worksheet to FIGURE 10-24. Note that your chart may not match the one in FIGURE 10-24 if your Ideas pane displayed a different first visual.

FIGURE 10-24

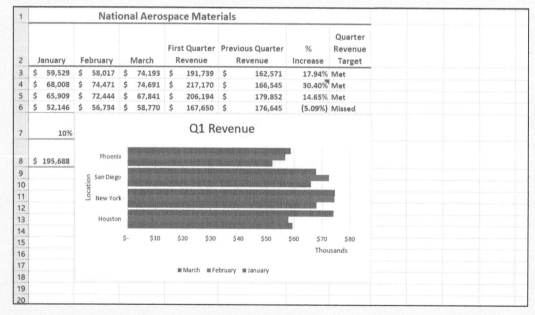

   h. Group the worksheets, add your name to the center footer section of the sheets, save the workbook, close the workbook, then submit the workbook to your instructor.

   i. Close Excel.

Independent Challenge 1

The manager at Riverwalk Medical Clinic has hired you to increase efficiency at an affiliated local imaging facility. You decide to create a template to speed up the facility's monthly billing process, and to use Excel features to make the billing easier to manage each month.

a. Open IL_EX_10-5.xlsx from the location where you store your Data Files.

b. Delete the billing and insurance data in columns B and C, leaving the total formulas. Save the workbook as a template with the name **IL_EX_10_MonthlyBilling.xltx** in the location where you store your Data Files, then close the template.

c. Open a new workbook based on the IL_EX_10_MonthlyBilling template. Enter test data of your choosing for billing and insurance, then check the results to verify the template is calculating the balance correctly. Close the IL_EX_10_MonthlyBilling1 workbook without saving it.

d. Re-open IL_EX_10-5.xlsx from the location where you store your Data Files, then save it as **IL_EX_10_Billing**. Create a new worksheet in the workbook named **NH Locations**. Open the webpage Support_EX_10-6.htm in your web browser from the location where you store your Data Files. Copy the data in the four rows of the webpage table, excluding the column heading. Paste the copied data to the range A1:A4 in the NH Locations worksheet. Match the destination formatting and Autofit column A to fully display the locations. Close the webpage file Support_EX_10-6.htm, then save the workbook.

e. Activate the Jan sheet, then create a custom list based on the locations in the range A3:A9. Test the custom AutoFill list on a new worksheet in the workbook named **Locations**. Position the Locations sheet between the Jan and NH Locations sheets. Use the Custom Lists dialog box to delete the custom list from your computer. Do not delete the list of locations on the Locations sheet.

f. In the Jan sheet, add a comment to cell D5 that reads: **High Balance**.

g. Add a comment to cell A9 that reads: **Is this facility merging with Beverly?**.

h. Use the Next and Previous buttons in the Comments group of the Review tab to move between comments on the worksheet.

i. Edit the comment in cell D5 so it reads **High Balance – any ideas why?**. Show the worksheet comments and compare your Jan worksheet to FIGURE 10-25. Delete the comment in cell A9, then hide the worksheet comments.

FIGURE 10-25

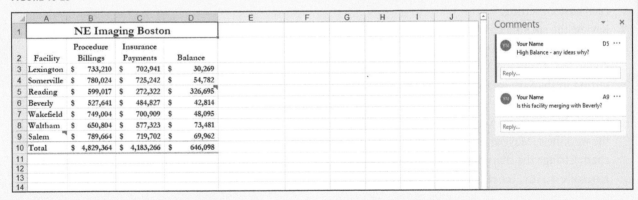

j. Use the Excel Options dialog box to review the user name as well as languages for editing, display, help, and the dictionary.

k. Add the Spelling command to the Quick Access Toolbar. Test the new button, then reset all customizations of the workbook to the defaults.

Independent Challenge 1 (continued)

l. Encrypt the workbook with the password **BilLne367$**. Test the password by saving the workbook, closing the workbook, and then opening the workbook. Remove encryption from the workbook.

m. Add your name to the center section of all the worksheet footers, then save the workbook.

n. Close the workbook, exit Excel, then submit the workbook to your instructor.

Independent Challenge 2

As the senior loan officer at South Shore Bank, one of your responsibilities is reviewing the quarterly loan portfolios for the four branches. This analysis is completed every quarter, so creating a template will simplify this process. You will also use Excel features to help with this quarterly analysis.

a. Start Excel, then open IL_EX_10-7.xlsx from the location where you store your Data Files.

b. Delete the values in the ranges B4:D7 and F4:F7. Change the label in cell F3 to **Previous Quarter Total**, change the label in cell E3 to **Total for Quarter**, change the label in cell G3 to **Quarter % Increase**, change the label in cell A10 to **Quarter Average**, then change the sheet tab name to **Quarter Report**. Save the workbook as a template with the name **IL_EX_10_QuarterAnalysis** in the location where you store your Data Files, then close the template.

c. Open a new workbook based on the template, verify the template is calculating the formulas correctly by entering test data, then close the IL_EX_10_QuarterAnalysis1 workbook without saving it.

d. Reopen IL_EX_10-7.xlsx from the location where you store your Data Files, then save it as **IL_EX_10_SecondQuarter**. Open the webpage Support_EX_10-8.htm in your browser from the location where you store your Data Files. Copy the data in the four rows of the webpage table, excluding the column heading. Activate the workbook, paste the copied data starting in cell H4 of the worksheet, matching the destination formatting. Delete column H. Enter the label **Survey Positive Rating** in cell H3. Format the new data font in the range H4:H7 as 11 point and bold so that it matches the other worksheet values.

e. Create a new set of theme colors with a custom Accent 1 color with the RGB settings of Red: **128**, Green: **157**, and Blue: **209**. Save the new theme custom colors with the name **QBlue**. Create a new set of theme fonts with both the heading and body fonts of Arial. Save the new theme font set as **QFont**. Widen the worksheet columns as necessary to display all worksheet data in the new font. Save the custom colors and fonts in a custom theme named **QTheme**. Verify the custom color palette, font set, and theme are available, then delete each custom setting.

f. Review the spelling correction settings in the Proofing category of the Excel Options dialog box. Click the AutoCorrect Options button, then review the entries in the Replace and With columns in the AutoCorrect dialog box. Close the AutoCorrect dialog box without making any changes. Review the AutoRecover save time setting in the Save category of the Excel Options then enter the save time in the left section of the worksheet footer.

g. Use the Ideas feature to see visuals that chart data in the range A3:D7. Insert the first suggested column chart into the worksheet. Move and resize the chart to fit in the range C10:G26. Delete the Branch label at the bottom of the chart. Change the chart title to **Second Quarter**. Add the alternative text **Second quarter personal, home equity, and business loans for branches**.

Independent Challenge 2 (continued)

h. Compare your worksheet to FIGURE 10-26. Your chart may not match the one in FIGURE 10-26 if your Ideas pane displayed a different first column chart.

FIGURE 10-26

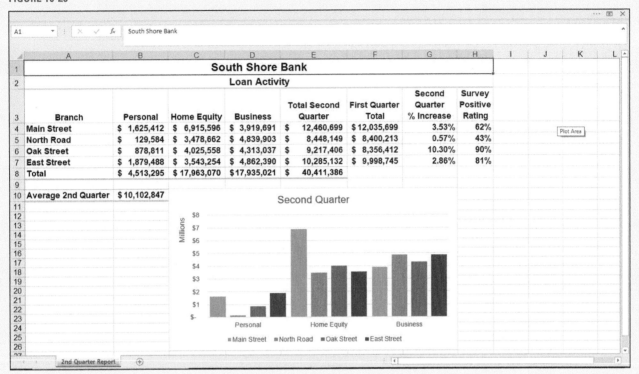

i. Add your name to the center section of the worksheet footer, then save the workbook.

j. Close the workbook, close Excel, then submit your workbook to your instructor.

Visual Workshop

Open IL_EX_10-9.xlsx from the location where you store your Data Files, then save it as **IL_EX_10_Hotels**. Import and add content as necessary so your screen matches **FIGURE 10-27**. (*Hint:* The file Support_EX_10-10.htm contains the data you need to import.) Add your name to the center section of the worksheet footer, then save the workbook. Close the workbook, close Excel, then submit the workbook to your instructor.

FIGURE 10-27

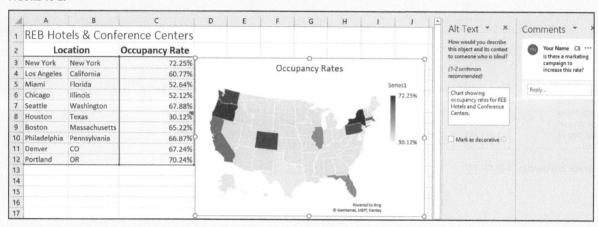

Advanced Formulas and Functions

CASE ▶ Ellie Schwartz, JCL's vice president of finance, uses Excel formulas and functions to analyze and consolidate data for the company's regions and divisions. Because management is considering adding a new regional office in the Northeast, Ellie asks you to format and summarize data from the current Northeast offices. You will compare commissions and placements in the Northeast offices and consolidate this data by division and office. Ellie also asks you to estimate the loan costs for the potential new office.

Module Objectives

After completing this module, you will be able to:

- Separate data using Flash Fill
- Format data using text functions
- Sum a data range based on conditions
- Find values based on conditions
- Construct formulas using named ranges

- Consolidate worksheet data
- Audit a worksheet
- Calculate payments with the PMT function

Files You Will Need

IL_EX_11-1.xlsx   IL_EX_11-4.xlsx
IL_EX_11-2.xlsx   IL_EX_11-5.xlsx
IL_EX_11-3.xlsx

Practice

Skills Review

1. **Separate data using Flash Fill.**
   a. Start Excel, open IL_EX_11-2.xlsx from the location where you store your Data Files, then save it as **IL_EX_11_LegalServices**.
   b. On the Managers worksheet, insert two new columns to the left of column B.
   c. Enter **Jay** in cell B1 and **Sears** in cell C1.
   d. Use Flash Fill to enter all first names in column B and all last names in column C.
   e. Save your work.

2. **Format data using text functions.**
   a. In cell E1, use a text function to convert the first letter of the department in cell D1 to uppercase, then copy the formula in cell E1 into the range E2:E8.
   b. In cell F1, use the CONCAT text function to display the first and last names together, with a space between them.
   c. Copy the formula in cell F1 into the range F2:F8, then widen column F to fully display the full names.
   d. In cell G1, use the TEXTJOIN text function to combine the department name in cell E1 with the text **Department**, using a space as a delimiter.
   e. Copy the formula in cell G1 into the range G2:G8, then widen column G to fully display the department names.
   f. Copy the range F1:G8, then paste the copied data as values starting in cell H1.
   g. Delete columns A through G, widen columns A and B to fully display the names and departments, then save your work. Compare your worksheet to FIGURE 11-25.

FIGURE 11-25

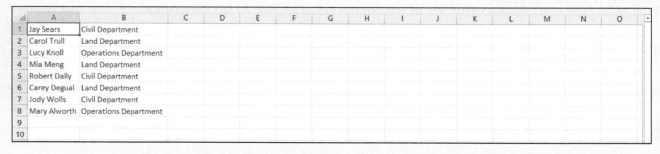

	A	B	C	D	E	F	G	H	I	J	K	L	M	N	O
1	Jay Sears	Civil Department													
2	Carol Trull	Land Department													
3	Lucy Knoll	Operations Department													
4	Mia Meng	Land Department													
5	Robert Dally	Civil Department													
6	Carey Degual	Land Department													
7	Jody Wolls	Civil Department													
8	Mary Alworth	Operations Department													
9															
10															

3. **Sum a data range based on conditions.**
   a. Activate the Partners worksheet.
   b. In cell B15, use the AVERAGEIF function to average the salaries and bonuses of those with a review of 5.
   c. In cell B16, use the SUMIF function to total the salaries of employees with a review of 5.
   d. Format cells B15 and B16 with the Accounting Number format using two decimals.
   e. Save your work.

4. **Find values based on conditions.**
   a. In cell B20, use the MAXIFS function to find the highest salary of employees with a rating of 5 and professional development hours of 10 or more. Use absolute cell references for the ranges in the formula.
   b. In cell B21, use the MINIFS function to find the lowest salary of employees with a rating of 5 and professional development hours of 10 or more. (*Hint:* You can copy the formula in cell B20 and edit it for MINIFS.)
   c. Format cells B20 and B21 with the Accounting Number format using two decimals.
   d. Save your work.

Skills Review (continued)

5. Construct formulas using named ranges.

a. On the Partners sheet, name the range C3:C11 **Review**, and limit the scope of the name to the Partners worksheet.

b. In cell B17, use the COUNTIF function to count the number of employees with a review of 5 using the named range.

c. Use the Name Manager to add a comment of **Scale of 1 to 5** to the review name. (*Hint:* In the Name Manager dialog box, click the Review name, then click Edit to enter the comment.)

d. Save your work.

e. Compare your worksheet to FIGURE 11-26.

FIGURE 11-26

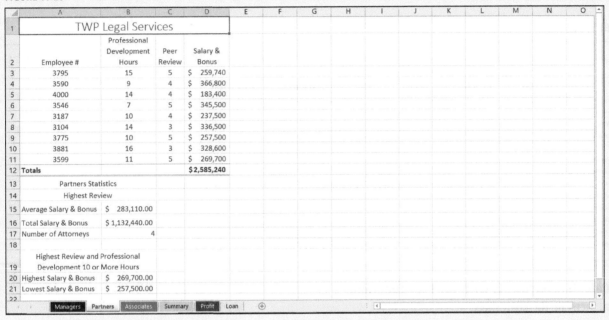

6. Consolidate data using a formula.

a. Activate the Summary sheet.

b. In cell B3, use the AutoSum function to total cell D12 on the Partners and Associates sheets.

c. Format cell B3 with the Accounting Number format with two decimal places.

d. In cell B4, use the Consolidate dialog box to total cell B16 on the Partners sheets and cell G5 on the Associates sheet, creating links to the source data.

e. Expand the outlined data, then enter **Associates** in cell A4 and **Partners** in cell A5.

f. Compare your worksheet to FIGURE 11-27.

FIGURE 11-27

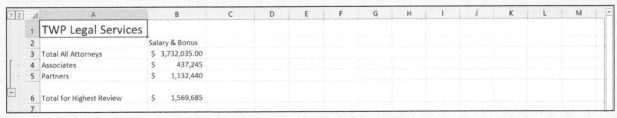

Independent Challenge 1 (continued)

q. Widen column F to fully display the monthly payment, then edit the formula in cell F4 to display the payment as a positive number.

r. In cell G4 enter a formula that calculates the total payments by multiplying the monthly payment by the number of months. In cell H4, enter a formula to calculate the total interest by subtracting the loan amount from the total payments, then widen column H to fully display the total interest.

s. Copy the formulas in the range F4:H4 into the range F5:H6, then compare your worksheet to FIGURE 11-30.

t. Group the worksheets, add your name to the center section of the grouped worksheet footers, ungroup the worksheets, save the workbook, then submit the workbook to your instructor.

u. Close the workbook, then close Excel.

FIGURE 11-30

	A	B	C	D	E	F	G	H	I	J
1				Riverwalk Clinic						
2				Imaging Center Loan Summary						
3	Lender	Loan Amount	Term (Years)	Interest Rate	Term (Months)	Monthly Payment	Total Payments	Total Interest		
4	Commercial Bank	$400,000	5	5.15%	60	$7,576.01	$454,560.78	$54,560.78		
5	Venture Capitalist	$400,000	3	5.05%	36	$11,997.34	$431,904.26	$31,904.26		
6	Investment Banker	$400,000	2	4.75%	24	$17,503.81	$420,091.34	$20,091.34		
7										
8										
9										
10										

Independent Challenge 2

As an accountant working in RSJ Advertising, you have been asked to analyze revenue in the Texas offices. The firm plans to open a new office in the state and you will examine the options for a loan to finance this expansion.

a. Start Excel, open IL_EX_11-4.xlsx from the location where you store your Data Files, then save it as **IL_EX_11_Revenue**.

b. Name the range containing the company's offices **Office** with a scope of the workbook, name the range containing the revenue data **Revenue** with a scope of the workbook, then name the range containing the type data **Type** with a scope of the workbook.

c. In cell G4, use the SUMIF function and named ranges to calculate the total revenue for print advertising. Use a relative reference to cell F4 for the criteria.

d. In cell H4, use the AVERAGEIF function and named ranges to calculate the average revenue for print advertising. Use a relative reference to cell F4 for the criteria.

e. In cell I4, use the COUNTIF function and a named range to calculate the total number of print ads. Use a relative reference to cell F4 for the criteria.

f. Copy the formulas in G4:I4 into the range G5:I7.

g. In cell G8, use the SUMIFS function and named ranges to calculate the total revenue for Houston broadcast media advertising.

h. In cell H8, use the AVERAGEIFS function and named ranges to calculate the average revenue for Houston broadcast media advertising.

i. In cell I8, use the COUNTIFS function and named ranges to calculate the total number of Houston broadcast media ads.

j. In cell G11, use the MINIFS function and named ranges to calculate the lowest revenue Houston broadcast media ad.

k. In cell G12, use the MAXIFS function and named ranges to calculate the highest revenue Houston broadcast media ad.

l. In cell C3 of the Loan sheet, use the NPER function to find the number of months required to pay off a $500,000 loan with monthly payments of $8000 at an interest rate of 5.15%. (*Hint:* The present value, pv, is in cell A3, the rate needs to be divided by 12 for a monthly rate, and a - needs to be typed before the pv value so the month is displayed as a positive value.)

m. Copy the loan amount in cell A3 into the range A4:A10, then copy the monthly payment in cell D3 into the range D4:D10.

n. Select cell B3, then use FIGURE 11-31 to enter interest rates in the range B4:B10 by increasing the rate by .25% until a rate of 7% is met. (*Hint:* To open the dialog box click the Home tab, click the Fill button in the Editing group, then click Series.)

o. Copy the formula in cell C3 into the range C4:C10.

p. Group the two worksheets, enter your name in the worksheet footer, ungroup the worksheets, save the workbook, then submit it to your instructor.

q. Close the workbook, then close Excel.

FIGURE 11-31

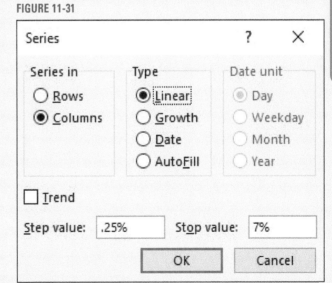

Visual Workshop

Open IL_EX_11-5.xlsx from the location where you store your Data Files, then save it as **IL_EX_11_Enrollment**. Use the data in the Fall, Spring, and Summer worksheets to create summary information on the Annual worksheet shown in FIGURE 11-32. The enrollment data are in the same location on all three worksheets. The number of graduates for each session appears in different locations on the three worksheets. Enter your name in the Annual worksheet footer, save the workbook, submit it to your instructor, then close Excel.

FIGURE 11-32

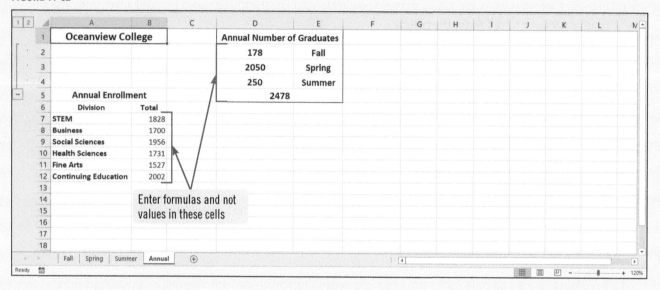

Advanced Formulas and Functions

Performing What-If Analysis

CASE ▶ Ellie Schwartz, JCL's vice president of finance, uses what-if analysis to analyze regional data and forecast possible outcomes. You will help Ellie using the data analysis tools and add-ins in Excel.

Module Objectives

After completing this module, you will be able to:

- Define what-if analysis
- Track what-if analysis with Scenario Manager
- Generate a scenario summary
- Project figures using a data table

- Use Goal Seek
- Find solutions using Solver
- Manage data using a data model
- Analyze data using Power Pivot

Files You Will Need

IL_EX_12-1.xlsx   IL_EX_12-5.xlsx
IL_EX_12-2.xlsx   IL_EX_12-6.xlsx
IL_EX_12-3.xlsx   IL_EX_12-7.xlsx
IL_EX_12-4.xlsx

Define What-If Analysis

Learning Outcomes
- Develop guidelines for performing what-if analysis
- Define what-if analysis terminology

By performing what-if analysis in a worksheet, you can get immediate answers to questions such as, "What happens to profits if we sell 25 percent more of a certain product?" or, "What happens to monthly payments if interest rates rise or fall?" A worksheet you use to perform what-if analysis is often called a **model** because it acts as the basis for multiple outcomes or sets of results. To perform what-if analysis in a worksheet, you change the value in one or more **input cells** (cells that contain data instead of formulas), then observe the effects on dependent cells. A **dependent cell** usually contains a formula whose resulting value changes depending on the values in the input cells. For more advanced data analysis, you can use Power Pivot, an Excel add-in, to create a Pivot Table from multiple tables to obtain answers to what-if questions. **CASE** *Ellie has received projected revenue, budget, and placement data from the Northeast office managers. She has created a worksheet model to perform an initial what-if analysis, as shown in* FIGURE 12-1. *She thinks the Boston revenue projections for the month of January should be higher. You first review the guidelines for performing what-if analysis.*

DETAILS

When performing what-if analysis, use the following guidelines:

- **Understand and state the purpose of the worksheet model**

  Identify what you want to accomplish with the model. What problem are you trying to solve? What questions do you want the model to answer for you? Ellie's worksheet model is designed to total JCL revenue projections for the four offices during the first half of the year and to calculate the percentage of total revenue for each office. It also calculates total revenues and percentages for each month within that period.

- **Determine the data input value(s) that, if changed, affect(s) dependent cell results**

  In what-if analysis, changes in the data input cells produce varying results in the output cells. You will use the model to work with one data input value: the January value for the Boston office, in cell B3.

- **Identify the dependent cell(s) that will contain results**

  The dependent cells usually contain formulas, and the formula results adjust as you enter different values in the input cells. The results of two dependent cell formulas appear in cells H3 (the Total for Boston) and I3 (the Percent of Total Revenue for Boston). Cell B6 (the Total for January) is also a dependent cell, as is cell B7 (the Percent of Total Revenue for January).

- **Formulate questions you want what-if analysis to answer and perform what-if analysis**

  It is important that you know the questions you want your model to answer before performing a what-if analysis. In the JCL model, one of the questions you want to answer is: What January Boston revenue target is required to bring the overall January revenue percentage to 18 percent?

- **Determine when to use advanced what-if analysis**

  If the answers to your what-if questions require data from multiple tables, you can use Power Pivot. Power Pivot enables you to create PivotTables using fields from multiple tables. FIGURE 12-2 shows a PivotTable created with fields from two tables.

FIGURE 12-1: Worksheet model for a what-if analysis

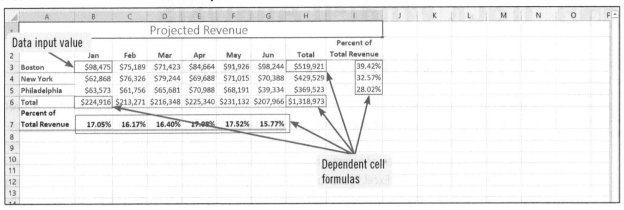

FIGURE 12-2: PivotTable using fields from two tables

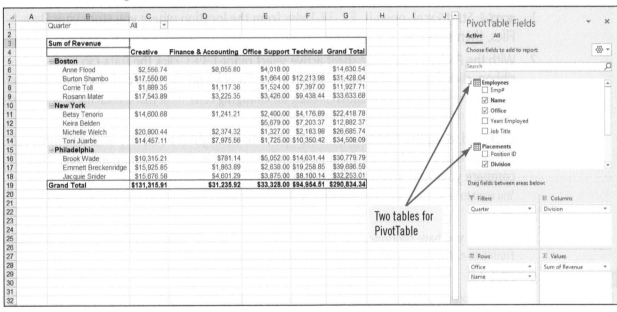

Excel

Generate a Scenario Summary

Learning
Outcomes
• Display scenarios
in a scenario
summary report
• Format a scenario
summary report

When comparing different scenario outcomes, it can be cumbersome to view each one separately. You might prefer to see a single report that summarizes the results of all the scenarios in a worksheet. A **scenario summary** is an Excel table that compiles data from various scenarios so that you can view the results next to each other, for easy comparison. For example, you can use a scenario summary to compare the best, worst, and most likely scenarios for a particular set of circumstances. Using cell naming makes the summary easier to read because the names, not the cell references, appear in the report.

CASE ▶ *Now that you have defined multiple scenarios, you want to generate a scenario summary report. You begin by creating selected cell names, which will make the report easier to read.*

STEPS

1. **Select the range B2:I3, click the** Formulas tab **on the ribbon, click the** Create from Selection button **in the Defined Names group, click the** Top row check box **to select it if necessary, then click** OK

   Excel creates the names for the selected data in row 3 based on the labels in row 2.

2. **Click the** Name Manager button **in the Defined Names group**

   Eight labels appear in the Name Manager dialog box, confirming that they were created, as shown in FIGURE 12-6.

3. **Click** Close **in the Name Manager dialog box, click the** Data tab **on the ribbon, click the** What-If Analysis button **in the Forecast group, click** Scenario Manager, **then click** Summary **in the Scenario Manager dialog box**

   Excel needs to know the location of the cells that contain the formula results you want to see in the report. You want to see the results for the Boston total and percentage of revenue, and for the total JCL revenue.

4. **With the contents of the Result cells box selected click cell** H3 **on the worksheet, type** ,, **click cell** I3, **type** ,, **click cell** H6, **compare your Scenario Summary dialog box to** FIGURE 12-7, **then click** OK

   A summary of the worksheet's scenarios appears on a new sheet named Scenario Summary. The report shows outline buttons to the left of and above the worksheet so that you can hide or show report details.

5. **Right-click the** column D heading, **then click** Delete **in the shortcut menu**

   The Current Values column isn't necessary because it shows the same values as the Original Revenue Figures column.

6. **Delete the contents of the range** B13:B15, **select cell** B2, **edit it to read** Scenario Summary for Boston Revenue, **click cell** C10, **then edit it to read** Total Boston Revenue

7. **Click cell** C11, **edit it to read** Percent Boston Revenue, **click cell** C12, **then edit it to read** Total JCL Revenue

8. **Right-click the** column A heading, **click** Delete **in the shortcut menu, right-click the** row 1 heading, **click** Delete **in the shortcut menu, change the page orientation to landscape, then save the workbook**

   The scenario summary is now easier to read and understand, as shown in FIGURE 12-8.

FIGURE 12-6: Name Manager dialog box displaying names

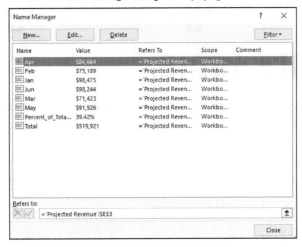

FIGURE 12-7: Scenario Summary dialog box

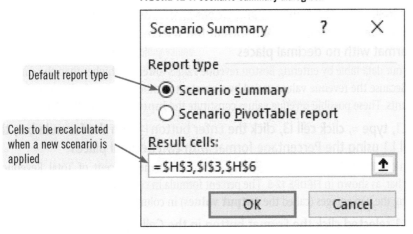

FIGURE 12-8: Completed Scenario Summary report

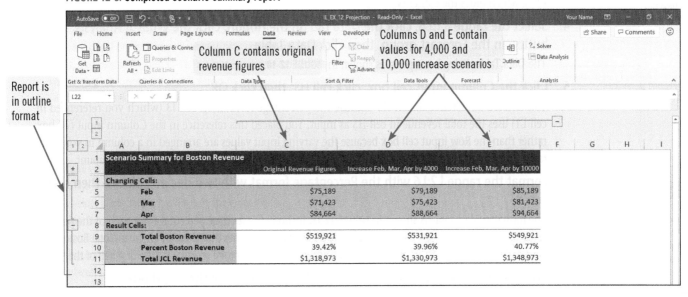

Find Solutions Using Solver

The Excel Solver is an **add-in**, software that adds features and commands to Excel or another Office app. It must be installed before you can use it. Solver finds the best solution to a problem that has several inputs. The cell containing the formula is called the **target cell**, or **objective**. Solver is helpful when you need to perform a complex what-if analysis involving multiple input values or when the input values must conform to specific limitations, called **constraints**. **CASE** ▶ *JCL's CEO directed Ellie to limit the budget total for JCL's Northeast offices to $2,000,000. Ellie is willing to adjust some budget items to meet this overall amount, but not others. You use Solver to help her find the best possible allocation.*

STEPS

1. **Click the Budget sheet tab**

   The budget constraints appear in the range A7:C11, as shown in **FIGURE 12-15**. The minimum office total budget, maximum salaries budget, minimum communication budget, and total budget requirements are shown in this range.

2. **Click the Data tab on the ribbon if necessary, then click the Solver button in the Analysis group**

   In the Solver Parameters dialog box, you indicate the target cell with its objective, the changing cells, and the constraints under which you want Solver to work.

3. **With the insertion point in the Set Objective box click cell I6 in the worksheet, click the Value Of option button if necessary, double-click the Value Of box, then type 2,000,000**

   You have specified an objective of $2,000,000 for the total budget.

4. **Click the By Changing Variable Cells box, select the range B3:B5, press and hold CTRL, then select the range E3:E5**

   You have told Excel which cells to vary to reach the goal of a $2,000,000 total budget.

5. **Click Add, with the insertion point in the Cell Reference box in the Add Constraint dialog box select the range I3:I5 in the worksheet, click the list arrow in the dialog box, click >=, then with the insertion point in the Constraint box click cell C8**

   These settings specify that the values in the range I3:I5, the total office budget amounts, should be greater than or equal to the value in cell C8, the minimum total office budget.

6. **Click Add, with the insertion point in the Cell Reference box select the range E3:E5, verify that <= is selected, click in the Constraint box, then click cell C9**

   You added the constraint that the budgeted salary amounts should be less than or equal to $400,000.

7. **Click Add, with the insertion point in the Cell Reference box select the range B3:B5, click the <= list arrow, click >=, with the insertion point in the Constraint box click cell C10, click OK, then click Solve**

   After you specified a constraint for all communications budgets to be a minimum of $65,000 and ran the Solver, Solver found a solution as indicated in the Solver Results dialog box.

8. **sam↟ With the Keep Solver Solution option selected, click OK, compare your results to FIGURE 12-16, change the worksheet orientation to landscape, group the worksheets, add your name to the footers of the grouped worksheets, ungroup the worksheets, save and close the workbook, then submit the workbook to your instructor as directed**

FIGURE 12-15: Worksheet with constraints

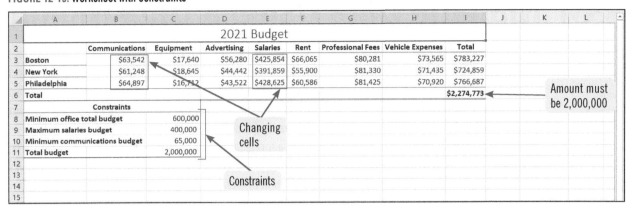

	Communications	Equipment	Advertising	Salaries	Rent	Professional Fees	Vehicle Expenses	Total
Boston	$63,542	$17,640	$56,280	$425,854	$66,065	$80,281	$73,565	$783,227
New York	$61,248	$18,645	$44,442	$391,859	$55,900	$81,330	$71,435	$724,859
Philadelphia	$64,897	$16,712	$43,522	$428,625	$60,586	$81,425	$70,920	$766,687
Total								$2,274,773

Amount must be 2,000,000

Constraints	
Minimum office total budget	600,000
Maximum salaries budget	400,000
Minimum communications budget	65,000
Total budget	2,000,000

Changing cells

Constraints

FIGURE 12-16: Solver Solution

2021 Budget

	Communications	Equipment	Advertising	Salaries	Rent	Professional Fees	Vehicle Expenses	Total
Boston	$65,000	$17,640	$56,280	$324,798	$66,065	$80,281	$73,565	$683,629
New York	$65,000	$18,645	$44,442	$316,657	$55,900	$81,330	$71,435	$653,409
Philadelphia	$65,000	$16,712	$43,522	$324,798	$60,586	$81,425	$70,920	$662,963
Total								$2,000,000

Constraints	
Minimum office total budget	600,000
Maximum salaries budget	400,000
Minimum communications budget	65,000
Total budget	2,000,000

Analyzing data using the Analysis ToolPak

The Analysis ToolPak is an Excel add-in that contains many statistical analysis tools. You can use one of these tools by clicking the Data tab, clicking the Data Analysis button in the Analysis group, selecting the desired analysis tool in the Data Analysis dialog box, clicking OK, entering the input range and other relevant specifications in the data tool's dialog box, then clicking OK. For example, clicking the Descriptive Statistics tool in the Data Analysis dialog box and selecting Summary statistics generates a statistical report including mean, median, mode, minimum, maximum, and sum for an input range you specify on your worksheet.

Creating an Answer Report

After solver finds a solution, you can generate an Answer Report summarizing the target cell information, the adjustable cells, and the constraints by selecting Answer from three types of reports in the Solver Results window, then clicking OK. The report appears as a separate worksheet named Answer Report 1 with three sections. The top section has the target cell information; it compares the original value of the target cell with the final value. The middle section of the report contains information about the adjustable cells. It lists the original and final values for all cells that were changed to reach the target value.

The last report section has information about the constraints. Each constraint you added into Solver is listed in the Formula column, along with the cell address and a description of the cell data. The Cell Value column contains the Solver solution values for the cells. The Status column contains information on whether the constraints were binding or not binding in reaching the solution. Binding constraints indicate all of the allocated resource was used or the constraint was pushed to its limit. Nonbinding constraints indicate there was extra resource available after the constraint was met.

Manage Data Using a Data Model

Learning Outcomes
- Add tables to the data model
- Create relationships between tables
- Update Power PivotTables

The **data model** is part of an Excel workbook that documents processes and events to capture and translate complex data into easy-to-understand information. It describes the structure of data tables and how they interact. You can use Power Pivot to add existing workbook data to a data model. Power Pivot is one of the Component Object Model (COM) add-ins that extend the functionality of Excel. It displays the workbook's data model and provides more advanced data analysis tools to work with data in different sources. Once data is included in the workbook data model, it can be used in PivotTables and PivotCharts.

CASE ▸ *Ellie has placement and employee data in separate tables in a workbook. She asks you to analyze the data in both workbooks. You will add the data from both tables to the data model to begin your analysis.*

STEPS

1. **Open IL_EX_12-2.xlsx from the location where you store your Data Files, save it as IL_EX_12_Placements, click the File tab on the ribbon, click Options in Backstage view, click Add-ins in the Excel Options dialog box menu, click the Manage arrow at the bottom of the dialog box, select COM Add-ins, click Go, in the COM Add-ins dialog box click the Microsoft Power Pivot for Excel check box to select it, then click OK**

2. **With the Placements sheet active click the Power Pivot tab on the ribbon, click the Add to Data Model button in the Tables group, then in the Create Table dialog box click OK**

   This method of adding data to a data model is referred to as adding a query. After you add the query, the Power Pivot window opens, as shown in **FIGURE 12-17**. The top pane in Power Pivot displays the table, and the bottom pane is the calculation area.

3. **Click the Switch to Workbook button 🔲 on the Quick Access Toolbar, click the Employees sheet tab, click cell A1, click the Power Pivot tab, click the Add to Data Model button in the Tables group, then click OK**

   The two tables are now part of the data model.

4. **Double-click the Table1 sheet tab in Power Pivot, type Placements, press ENTER, double-click the Table 2 sheet tab, type Employees, then press ENTER**

5. **Click the Design tab on the ribbon, then click the Create Relationship button in the Relationships group, in the Create Relationship dialog box click the first list arrow if necessary and click Employees, select the Emp# field if it is not already highlighted, click the second list arrow and click Placements, click the Recruiter ID field to highlight it, then click OK**

   Creating a relationship between tables allows you to access corresponding data from both tables.

6. **Click the Home tab, then click the Diagram View button in the View group**

   The two tables and their relationship are shown in **FIGURE 12-18**. This is a one-to-many relationship because each Emp# value can be associated with multiple RecruiterID rows in the Placements table.

7. **Click the Switch to Workbook button 🔲 on the Quick Access Toolbar, click the Employees sheet tab if necessary, click cell B2, edit the name Anne Chard to Anne Flood, click the Power Pivot tab, click the Manage button in the Data Model group, click the Data View button in the View group, then click the Refresh button**

   The Data Refresh dialog box shows that the data was successfully updated.

8. **Click Close in the Data Refresh dialog box, widen the Name column to fully display the Employees' names, verify that Anne's last name in row 1 is Flood, then save your work**

FIGURE 12-17: PowerPivot window

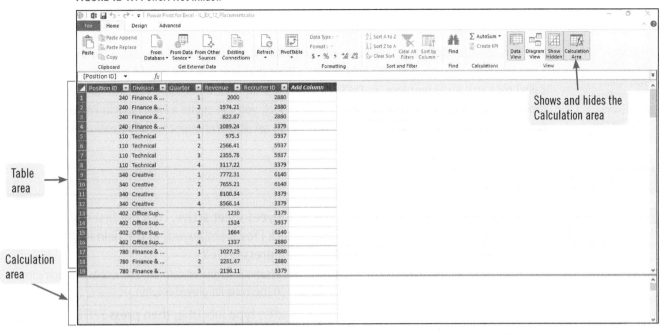

Table area →

Calculation area →

Shows and hides the Calculation area

FIGURE 12-18: Diagram of the relationship between tables

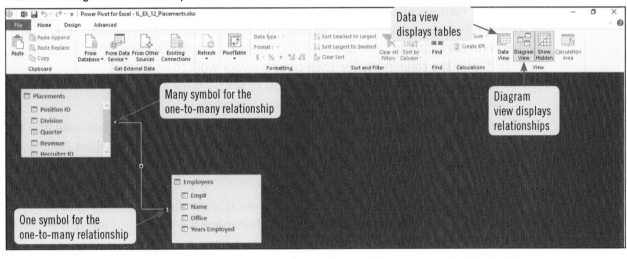

Data view displays tables

Diagram view displays relationships

Many symbol for the one-to-many relationship

One symbol for the one-to-many relationship

Analyze Data Using Power Pivot

Learning
Outcomes
• Add calcula-
tions to Power
PivotTables
• Create a PivotTa-
ble in Power Pivot

You can answer what-if questions in Power Pivot by creating calculated columns and measures. A **measure** is a calculated named field in Power Pivot that uses a special set of functions and commands called data analysis expressions, or DAX. Often answering what-if questions requires data from multiple tables. Once these tables are added to the data model, you can create a PivotTable in Power Pivot using fields from multiple tables. **CASE** *Ellie asks you to calculate a revenue total and create a PivotTable sum-marizing revenue by office and employee.*

STEPS

1. **In the Power Pivot window with the Employees sheet active, click the first cell under the Add Column header, type =IF([, double-click [Years Employed] in the field list, type >6, "Senior Recruiter","Junior Recruiter", then press ENTER**

   Entering a formula that uses a field from the table creates a calculated column. The results for each row are filled down the calculated column using the data in the Years Employed column.

2. **Double-click the Calculated Column 1 header, type Job Title, then press ENTER**

3. **Activate the Placements table in the PowerPivot window, click the first cell in the Calculation Area below the Revenue data, click the AutoSum button in the Calculations group, widen the Revenue column to fully display the Sum of Revenue, click the Apply Currency Format button $ in the Formatting group, click $ English (United States), click the Revenue column header to select the revenue data in that column, click $ in the Formatting group, $ click $ English (United States), widen the Recruiter ID field to fully display the column header, then compare your work to FIGURE 12-19**

   You inserted a measure in the calculation area that sums the revenue data. Where calculated columns summarize data in each row, a measure creates an overall summary.

4. **Click the PivotTable button on the Home tab, in the Create PivotTable dialog box make sure the New Worksheet option button is selected, click OK, then rename the new sheet PivotTable**

   The PivotTable Fields pane opens with both tables in the data model. When creating a PivotTable in Power Pivot, you can combine fields from multiple tables in a PivotTable.

5. **In the PivotTable Fields pane click the Employees table to display its fields, click the Name check box, click the Office check box, then move the Office field above the Name field in the Rows area**

   The data from the Name and Office fields are placed in the PivotTable rows.

6. **In the PivotTable Fields pane scroll down, click the Placements table to expand its fields, click the Division check box, move the Division field from the Rows area to the Columns area, click the Quarter check box, move the Quarter field to the Filters area, then click the Revenue check box**

   The PivotTable summarizes data from both tables and can answer questions about revenue from the Place-ments table related to the JCL offices in the Employee table.

7. **Click the PivotTable Analyze tab on the ribbon, click the Field Headers button in the Show group to deselect it, close the PivotTable Fields pane, change the worksheet orientation to landscape, then compare your PivotTable to FIGURE 12-20**

8. **sam'↑ Group the worksheets, add your name to the grouped footers, ungroup the sheets, save the workbook, close the workbook, close Excel, then submit the workbook to your instructor as directed**

FIGURE 12-19: Calculation Area with measure

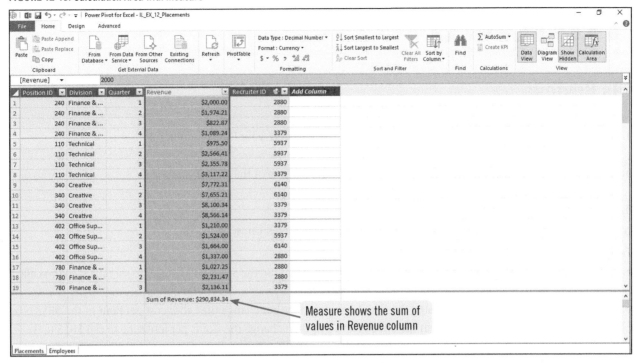

Sum of Revenue: $290,834.34 ← Measure shows the sum of values in Revenue column

FIGURE 12-20: PivotTable created in Power Pivot

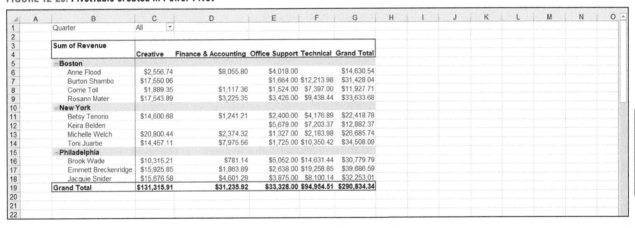

Using the Excel 3D Maps tool

Power Map, also called 3D Maps, is an Excel COM add-in that helps to visualize worksheet data in 3-D formats. To insert a Power Map into a worksheet, click the Insert tab, then click 3D Map in the Tours group. Data should be organized in a table for mapping. The 3D Maps window opens with its own ribbon containing a Home tab, a Tour pane on the left showing Tour 1, an automatically created Tour with a single scene, a Field List showing the fields available to map, and a Layer pane on the right with areas for map locations, height, category, and time. A tour is a list of maps in the 3D Map and each map is a scene. Most often 3D Maps contain several scenes that make up an animation offering different points of focus of the data. You can create a new scene by clicking the New Scene button in the Scene group, then dragging fields from the Field List to the desired areas on the Layer pane. Fields with location data can be dragged to the Location area, fields with values should be placed in the height area, the category area holds fields for different markers, and the time area shows the map changes over time. When you save your workbook, 3D Map tours and scenes are saved.

Practice

Skills Review

1. Define what-if analysis.

a. Start Excel, open IL_EX_12-3.xlsx from the location where you store your Data Files, then save it as **IL_EX_12_Freight**.

b. Examine the Equipment Repair worksheet to determine the purpose of the worksheet model.

c. Locate the data input cells.

d. Locate any dependent cells.

e. Examine the worksheet to determine problems the worksheet model can solve.

2. Track what-if analysis with Scenario Manager.

a. On the Equipment Repair worksheet, select the range B3:B5, then use the Scenario Manager to set up a scenario called **Most Likely** that includes the current data input values.

b. Add a scenario called **Best Case** using the same changing cells, but change the Labor cost per hour in the $B$3 box to **85**, change the Parts cost per job in the $B$4 box to **75**, then change the Hours per job value in cell $B$5 to **3**.

c. Add a scenario called **Worst Case**. For this scenario, change the Labor cost per hour in the $B$3 box to **95**, change the Parts cost per job in the $B$4 box to **85**, then change the Hours per job in the $B$5 box to **4**.

d. If necessary, drag the Scenario Manager dialog box to the right until columns A and B are visible.

e. Show the Worst Case scenario results, then observe the total job cost.

f. Show the Best Case scenario results, then observe the job cost. Finally, display the Most Likely scenario results.

g. Close the Scenario Manager dialog box.

h. Save the workbook.

3. Generate a scenario summary.

a. Create names for the input value cells and the dependent cell using the range selection A3:B7.

b. Verify that the names were created.

c. Create a scenario summary report, using the Cost to complete job value in cell B7 as the result cell.

d. Edit the title of the Summary report in cell B2 to **Scenario Summary for Equipment Repair**.

e. Delete the Current Values column.

f. Delete row 1, column A, and the notes beginning in cell B11. Compare your worksheet to FIGURE 12-21.

g. Add your name in the center section of the Scenario Summary sheet footer, then save the workbook.

FIGURE 12-21

	A	B	C	D	E
1	Scenario Summary for Equipment Repair				
2			Most Likely	Best Case	Worst Case
4	Changing Cells:				
5		Labor_cost_per_hour	$90.00	$85.00	$95.00
6		Parts_cost_per_job	$80.00	$75.00	$85.00
7		Hours_per_job	3.50	3.00	4.00
8	Result Cells:				
9		Cost_to_complete_job	$395.00	$330.00	$465.00
10					
11					
12					

Skills Review (continued)

4. Project figures using a data table.

    a. Activate the Equipment Repair sheet.

    b. Enter the label **Labor $** in cell D3.

    c. Format the label so that it is bold and right-aligned.

    d. In cell D4, enter **80**. Select the range D4:D8, then fill the range with values using a linear series in a column with a step value of 5.

    e. In cell E3, reference the job cost formula by entering **=B7**.

    f. Format the contents of cell E3 as hidden, entering the **;;;** Custom formatting type on the Number tab of the Format Cells dialog box.

    g. Generate the new job costs based on the varying labor costs. Select the range D3:E8 and create a data table. In the Data Table dialog box, make cell B3 (the labor cost) the column input cell.

    h. Format the range D4:E8 as currency with two decimal places.

    i. Enter your name in the center section of the worksheet footer, then save the workbook.

5. Use Goal Seek.

    a. Click cell B7, then open the Goal Seek dialog box.

    b. Assuming the labor rate and hours remain the same, determine what the parts cost per job would have to be so that the cost to complete the job is $350. (*Hint:* Enter a job cost of **350** as the To value, then enter **B4** as the By changing cell.) Write down the parts cost that Goal Seek finds.

    c. Click OK, then press CTRL+Z to reset the parts cost to its original value.

    d. Enter the parts cost that you found in Step 5b into cell A14, formatted as currency with no decimal places.

    e. Assuming the parts cost and hours remain the same, determine the labor cost per hour so that the cost to complete the job is $350. Press CTRL+Z to reset the labor cost to its original value. Enter the labor cost in cell A15.

    f. Save the workbook, then compare your worksheet to **FIGURE 12-22**.

FIGURE 12-22

	A	B	C	D	E	F	G	H	I	J	K	L	M
1	WTN Freight Transportation												
2													
3	Labor cost per hour	$90.00		Labor $									
4	Parts cost per job	$80.00		$80.00	$360.00								
5	Hours per job	3.50		$85.00	$377.50								
6				$90.00	$395.00								
7	Cost to complete job:	$395.00		$95.00	$412.50								
8				$100.00	$430.00								
9													
10													
11													
12													
13													
14	$35												
15	$77.14												
16													
17													
18													
19													
20													

Skills Review (continued)

6. Find solutions using Solver.

    a. Activate the Transportation Costs sheet, then open the Solver Parameters dialog box.

    b. Make B14 (the grand total cost) the objective cell, with a target value of 16,000.

    c. Use cells B6:D6 (the number of all scheduled trips) as the changing cells.

    d. Specify that cells B6:D6 must be integers. (*Hint:* Select int in the Add Constraint dialog box.)

    e. Specify that cells B6:D6 must be greater than or equal to 10.

    f. Use Solver to find a solution. Keep the Solver solution, then compare your worksheet to FIGURE 12-23.

FIGURE 12-23

	A	B	C	D	E	F	G	H	I	J	K	L	M
1	WTN Freight Transportation												
2													
3		Heavy	Standard	Small									
4	Labor Cost Per Trip	$110.00	$100.00	$95.00									
5	Parts Cost Per Trip	$150.00	$130.00	$100.00									
6	Trips Scheduled	23	33	13									
7													
8	Labor Cost Per Size	$2,483.89	$3,286.00	$1,252.63									
9	Parts Cost Per Size	$3,387.12	$4,271.79	$1,318.56									
10	Total Cost Per Size	$5,871.01	$7,557.79	$2,571.20									
11													
12	Total Labor Cost	$7,022.52											
13	Total Parts Cost	$8,977.48											
14	Grand Total Cost	$16,000.00											
15													
16													
17													
18													
19													
20													

    g. Enter your name in the center section of the worksheet footer, save the workbook, close the workbook, then submit the workbook to your instructor as directed.

7. Manage data using a data model.

    a. Open IL_EX_12-4.xlsx from the location where you store your Data Files, then save it as **IL_EX_12_Employee**.

    b. With the Employee sheet active, use Power Pivot to add the worksheet data to the data model.

    c. Switch to Worksheet view, activate the Routes sheet, then use Power Pivot to add the worksheet data to the data model.

    d. In Power Pivot, rename the Table1 sheet **Employee**, then name the Table2 sheet **Routes**.

    e. Create a relationship between the Employee # field in the Routes table and the Emp ID field in the Employee table.

    f. View the relationship between the tables in Diagram View and verify it is one to many.

g. Return to the workbook, activate the Employee sheet, then change the contents of cell B2 to **Concord** and cell D2 to **D. McKay**.

h. Return to the data model in Power Pivot, activate the Employee sheet, then refresh the worksheet data. (*Hint:* To return to the data model in Power Pivot, click the Manage button in the Data Model group.)

8. Analyze data using PowerPivot.

a. Activate the Routes sheet in the Power Pivot window, then add a measure in the calculation area to sum the Trip Cost data. (*Hint:* Click the first cell in the calculation area below the Trip Cost data, then use the AutoSum button in the Calculation group on the Home tab.)

b. Widen the Trip Cost column to fully display the Sum of Trip Cost, then format the value using the $ English (United States) Currency format and no decimal places.

c. Create a PivotTable on a new worksheet named **PivotTable** that adds the Location field from the Employee table to the Rows area, the Manager field from the Employee table to the Rows area, the Employee # field from the Routes table to the Rows area, the Trip Cost field from the Routes table to the Values area, and the Vehicle Size field from the Routes table to the Columns area.

d. Use a tool on the Power Pivot Analyze tab to hide the Field Headers, then compare your PivotTable to **FIGURE 12-24**.

FIGURE 12-24

	A	B	C	D	E	F	G	H	I	J	K	L	M	N	O	P	Q
1																	
2																	
3		Sum of Trip Cost															
4			Heavy	Small	Standard	Grand Total											
5		Concord															
6		D. McKay															
7		3471	32500			32500											
8		4545	6500	2925	16100	25525											
9		4814		5850	24150	30000											
10		Portland															
11		C. Burke															
12		4716			8050	8050											
13		Providence															
14		P. Lee															
15		2014	6500			6500											
16		4265		8775		8775											
17		Springfield															
18		L. Brine															
19		2179		2925	8050	10975											
20		2828	6500	2925	8050	17475											
21		Grand Total	52000	23400	64400	139800											
22																	
23																	
24																	
25																	
26																	
27																	
28																	
29																	

e. Close Power Pivot, group the worksheets, add your name to the footer of the worksheets, ungroup the worksheets, save and close the workbook, submit the workbook to your instructor, then close Excel.

Independent Challenge 1

You are assisting Tony Sanchez, the office manager at Riverwalk Medical Clinic, with a disaster recovery plan for the medical records at the clinic. As part of that plan you are looking at two options for storing backup medical records. The first option is to purchase a storage facility, and the second is to use a third-party backup storage company that offers off-site small, medium, and large storage areas. In both cases, you want to keep your monthly payments below $1700. You decide to use Goal Seek to look at various interest rates for purchasing a storage facility and to use Solver to help find the best possible combination of third-party storage areas.

a. Start Excel, open IL_EX_12-5.xlsx from the location where you store your Data Files, then save it as **IL_EX_12_Records**.

b. With the Purchase sheet active, use Goal Seek to find the interest rate that produces a monthly payment of $16,500, and write down the interest rate that Goal Seek finds. Reset the interest rate to its original value, record the interest rate in cell A7, then enter **Interest rate for $16,500 monthly payment** in cell B7.

c. Use Goal Seek to find the interest rate that produces a monthly payment of $16,000. Reset the interest rate to its original value, record the interest rate in cell A8, then enter **Interest rate for $16,000 monthly payment** in cell B8. Compare your worksheet to FIGURE 12-25.

FIGURE 12-25

	A	B	C	D	E
1		Riverwalk Clinic			
2	Annual Interest Rate	5.75%			
3	Term in Months	48			
4	Loan Amount	$ 725,000			
5	Monthly Payment	$16,943.67			
6					
7		4.40%	Interest rate for $16,500 monthly payment		
8		2.85%	Interest rate for $16,000 monthly payment		
9					
10					

d. Activate the Rental sheet. Open Solver, then use the Set Objective To option to maximize the storage amount in cell B12. (*Hint:* Select Max in the Set the Objective To area.)

e. In Solver, use the quantity, cells B6:D6, as the changing cells.

f. Add a constraint to Solver specifying the quantity in cells B6:D6 must be integers. (*Hint:* Choose int as the operator in the Add Constraint dialog box.)

g. Add a constraint specifying that the total monthly payment amount in cell B11 is less than or equal to 17000.

h. Generate a solution using Solver and accept Solver's solution. Compare your worksheet to FIGURE 12-26.

i. Group the worksheets, then enter your name in the center footer section of both worksheets. Preview both worksheets, then save the workbook.

j. Close the workbook, then submit the workbook to your instructor.

FIGURE 12-26

	A	B	C	D	
1		Riverwalk Clinic			
2					
3		Large	Medium	Small	
4	Rental Fee	$ 4,200	$ 3,000	$ 2,400	
5	Capacity (cubic feet)	210	150	100	
6	Quantity	3	2	0	
7					
8	Monthly Payment	$ 11,604	$ 5,396	$ -	
9	Storage Capacity	580	270	0	
10					
11	Total Monthly Payment	$ 17,000			
12	Total Storage Capacity	850			
13					

Independent Challenge 2

As a senior financial analyst at North Shore CPA Services, you are researching various options for financing a $250,000 loan for the purchase of a new estate-planning facility. You haven't decided whether to finance the project for three, four, or five years. Each loan term carries a different interest rate. To help with the comparison, you summarize these options using a scenario summary. You will also create a two-input data table to analyze additional interest rates and terms.

a. Start Excel, open IL_EX_12-6.xlsx from the location where you store your Data Files, then save it as **IL_EX_12_Loan**.

b. Create cell names for cells B4:B11 based on the labels in cells A4:A11, using the Create Names from Selection dialog box.

c. Use Scenario Manager to create scenarios that calculate the monthly payment on a $250,000 loan under the three sets of loan possibilities listed below. (*Hint:* Create three scenarios, using cells B5:B6 as the changing cells.)

Scenario Name	Interest Rate	Term
5% 5 Year	.05	60
4.5% 4 Year	.045	48
4% 3 Year	.04	36

d. View each scenario and confirm that it performs as intended, then display the 5% 5 Year scenario.

e. Generate a scenario summary titled **Finance Options**. Use cells B9:B11 as the Result cells.

f. Delete the Current Values column in the report and the notes at the bottom of the report, row 1, and column A. Rename the sheet **Estate Planning Project**.

g. Activate the Loan sheet. Using FIGURE 12-27 as a guide, enter the input values for a two-input data table with varying interest rates for 3-, 4-, and 5-year terms. Use a linear series to enter the interest rates.

h. Reference the monthly payment amount from cell B9 in cell A13, then format the contents of cell A13 so they are hidden.

i. Generate a data table, using cells A13:D22, that shows the effect of varying interest rates and loan terms on the monthly payments. (*Hint:* Use cell B6, Term in Months, as the Row input cell, and cell B5, the Annual Interest Rate, as the Column input cell.)

j. Format the range B14:D22 as currency with two decimal places.

k. Group the two worksheets, then enter your name in the center section of the grouped footer.

l. Save the workbook, close the workbook, submit the workbook to your instructor as directed, then close Excel.

FIGURE 12-27

	A	B	C	D	E
1	North Shore CPA Services				
2	Financing Options				
3					
4	Loan Amount	$250,000.00			
5	Annual Interest Rate	5.00%			
6	Term in Months	60			
7					
8					
9	Monthly Payment:	$4,717.81			
10	Total Payments:	$283,068.50			
11	Total Interest:	$33,068.50			
12					
13			36	48	60
14	3.00%				
15	3.25%				
16	3.50%				
17	3.75%				
18	4.00%				
19	4.25%				
20	4.50%				
21	4.75%				
22	5.00%				
23					

Excel

Visual Workshop

Open the file IL_EX_12-7.xlsx from the location where you store your Data Files, then save it as **IL_EX_12_Orders**. Using the two worksheets, create the data model shown in the Power Pivot window in **FIGURE 12-28**. (*Hint:* When entering the formula to calculate the balance, click each column header to enter the Total and Paid values.) Then, using the data model, create the PivotTable shown in **FIGURE 12-29**. (*Hint:* Create a one-to-many relationship between the ID field in the Customers table and the Cust_ID field in the Orders table, then create the PivotTable.) When you are finished, add your name to the center footer section of the PivotTable sheet, save the workbook, submit the workbook to your instructor as directed, then close Excel.

FIGURE 12-28

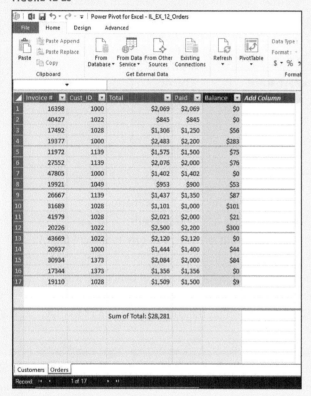

FIGURE 12-29

	A	B	C	D	E	F	G
3			Sum of Total	Sum of Balance			
4		Amy Folley					
5		212-555-0100					
6		16398	$2,069	$0			
7		19377	$2,483	$283			
8		20937	$1,444	$44			
9		47805	$1,402	$0			
10		Corey Olsen					
11		212-555-0115					
12		19921	$953	$53			
13		Gilbert Hahn					
14		813-555-0195					
15		17344	$1,356	$0			
16		30934	$2,084	$84			
17		Jack Watson					
18		305-555-0171					
19		20226	$2,500	$300			
20		40427	$845	$0			
21		43669	$2,120	$0			
22		Lisa Jones					
23		239-555-0174					
24		17492	$1,306	$56			
25		19110	$1,509	$9			
26		31689	$1,101	$101			
27		41979	$2,021	$21			
28		Sally Wilkins					
29		503-555-0134					
30		11972	$1,575	$75			
31		26667	$1,437	$87			
32		27552	$2,076	$76			
33		Grand Total	$28,281	$1,189			

Customers | Orders | PivotTable

Performing What-If Analysis

Index

K

keywords, EX 6-8

L

labels, EX 1-4
landscape orientation, EX 1-22
LEFT function, EX 11-5
legend, EX 4-2
LEN function, EX 11-5
(less than, <), EX 3-5
line chart, EX 4-3
line with markers chart, EX 4-3
link, EX 7-2
   data, EX 11-12
   Excel chart to PowerPoint slide, EX 7-3,
     EX 7-12–7-13
   managing and breaking, EX 7-11
Links dialog box, EX 7-11
Lock Cell option, EX 6-5
locking cells, **EX 6-4**. *See also* **cell(s)**
logical conditions, EX 5-10
logical formula
   with AND function, EX 3-6–3-7
   with IF function, EX 3-4–3-5
logical functions, EX 3-4
   IFS function, EX 11-9
   MAXIFS function, EX 11-9
   MINIFS function, EX 11-9
   SWITCH function, EX 11-9
   working with, EX 11-9
logical test, EX 3-4
look up values, in table, EX 5-12–5-13
LOWER function, EX 11-5

M

macro(s)
   assigning descriptive name, EX 9-2
   assigning to button, EX 9-12–9-13
   assignning to command button, EX 9-14–9-15
   assignning to form control, EX 9-16–9-17
   copying to another workbook, EX 9-13
   definition of, EX 9-2
   disabling, EX 9-5
   editing, EX 9-10–9-11
   enabling, EX 9-4–9-5
   handwritten description of planned, EX 9-3
   planning, EX 9-2–9-3
   recording, EX 9-6–9-7
   running, EX 9-8–9-9
   running automatically, EX 9-8
   using guidelines when planning, EX 9-2
   using relative referencing when creating, EX 9-11
macro-enabled workbook, EX 9-13
main procedure
   creating, EX 9-9
   definition of, EX 9-9

manual calculation, EX 3-16
map chart, EX 10-17
masked password, EX 10-15
MAXIFS function, EX 11-8
measure
   calculation area with, EX 12-17
   definition of, EX 12-16
memo
   with linked worksheet, EX 7-11
   with updated table data, EX 7-11
Merge Scenarios dialog box, EX 12-5
merging
   scenarios, EX 12-5
metadata, EX 6-8
Microsoft Excel 2019
   arithmetic operators, EX 1-11
   chart design, EX 4-8–4-9
   chart layout, EX 4-10–4-11
   colors, borders and documentation,
     EX 2-12–2-13
   column width, EX 2-8–2-9
   conditional formatting, EX 2-14–2-15
   control worksheet calculations, EX 3-16–3-17
   copy formulas with absolute cell references,
     EX 1-14–1-15
   copy formulas with relative cell references,
     EX 1-12–1-13
   copying and moving cell data, EX 1-8–1-9
   COUNTA function, EX 3-10–3-11
   creating chart, EX 4-4–4-5
   creating pie chart, EX 4-14–4-15
   data trends, EX 4-18–4-19
   Date function, EX 3-12–3-13
   editing data, EX 1-6–1-7
   entering data, EX 1-4–1-5
   entering formulas with multiple operators,
     EX 1-16–1-17
   font and font size, EX 2-4–2-5
   font styles and font alignment, EX 2-6–2-7
   formatting chart, EX 4-12–4-13
   format values, EX 2-2–2-3
   formulas and AutoSum, EX 1-10–1-11
   formula using Quick Analysis tool, EX 3-2–3-3
   inserting and deleting rows and columns,
     EX 2-10–2-11
   inserting function, EX 1-18–1-19
   logical formula with AND function, EX 3-6–3-7
   logical formula with IF function, EX 3-4–3-5
   moving and resizing chart, EX 4-6–4-7
   planning chart, EX 4-2–4-3
   pointers in, EX 1-7
   print options, EX 1-22–1-23
   renaming and moving worksheet,
     EX 2-16–2-17
   ROUND function, EX 3-8–3-9
   sparklines, EX 4-16–4-17
   spelling check, EX 2-18–2-19
   starting, EX 1-2–1-3
   switching worksheet views, EX 1-20–1-21
   working with equation tools, EX 3-14–3-15
MID function, EX 11-5
MINIFs function, EX 11-8–11-9

MINUTE function, EX 3-13
mixed reference, EX 1-15
mode indicator, EX 1-2
model, EX 12-2
module, EX 9-10
MONTH function, EX 3-13
Move pointer, EX 1-7
MROUND function, EX 3-9
multilevel sort, EX 5-6
multiplication operator (*), EX 11

N

Name box, EX 1-2
named ranges
   constructing formulas using, EX 11-10–11-11
Name Manager dialog box, EX 11-11, EX 12-7
names with Proper formatting, EX 11-5
nested IF function, EX 3-5
New Name dialog box, EX 11-10, EX 11-11
Normal pointer, EX 1-7
Normal view, EX 1-20
NOT logical function, EX 3-6
NOW function, EX 3-13
NPER function, EX 11-17
number format, EX 2-2

O

object, EX 4-6, EX 7-2
objective, EX 12-12
object linking and embedding (OLE), EX 7-2
OneDrive, EX 10-11, EX 10-15
one-input data table, EX 12-8
one-input data table structure, EX 12-9
Online Picture, EX 2-3
option buttons
   working with, EX 9-17
   worksheet with, EX 9-17
Or condition, EX 5-11
order of operations, EX 1-16
OR logical function, EX 3-6
output values, EX 12-8

P

Page Break Preview, EX 1-21, EX 6-7
page breaks, EX 6-7
Page Layout view, EX 1-20, EX 1-21
pane(s)
   definition of, EX 6-3, EX 6-5
   splitting worksheet into multiple, EX 6-3
password
   encrypting workbook with, EX 10-14–10-15
   masked, EX 10-15
Paste Options, EX 1-9
Paste Preview, EX 1-9